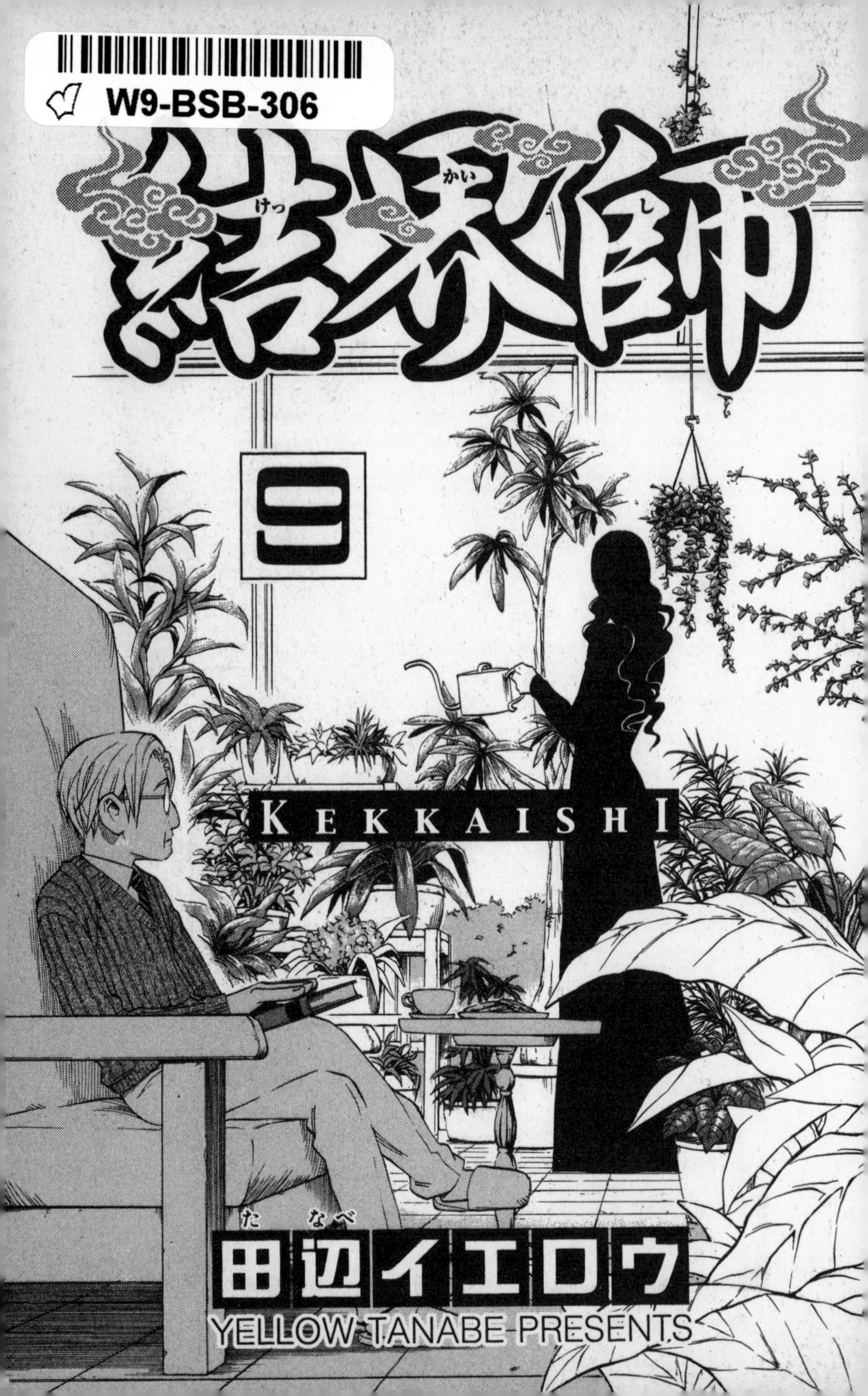
けっ かい し
結界師
9
KEKKAISHI
たなべ
田辺イエロウ
YELLOW TANABE PRESENTS

THe STOrY THUS Far

Yoshimori Sumimura and Tokine Yukimura have a special duty passed down through their families for generations—to protect Karasumori Forest from supernatural beings called *ayakashi*. People with their gift for terminating ayakashi are called *kekkaishi*, or "barrier masters."

The Night Troops, a group of outcasts within the Shadow Organization, send Gen Shishio, a half-ayakashi, to the Karasumori Site to assist Yoshimori and Tokine.

The Shadow Organization has forbidden Gen and his kind to transform completely into an ayakashi. But during a clash with assassins from the Kokuboro Clan, Gen loses his temper and nearly undergoes a total transformation!

Gen fears that the Shadow Organization will punish him for his transgression. The possibility that his tour of duty at the Karasumori Site might be terminated deeply distresses him.

But Yoshimori's big brother, Masamori, leader of the Night Troops, rallies behind Gen and permits him to continue fighting by Yoshimori and Tokine's side...

K E K K A I S H I VOL. 9
TABLE OF CONTENTS

Chapter 76: Caged Bird

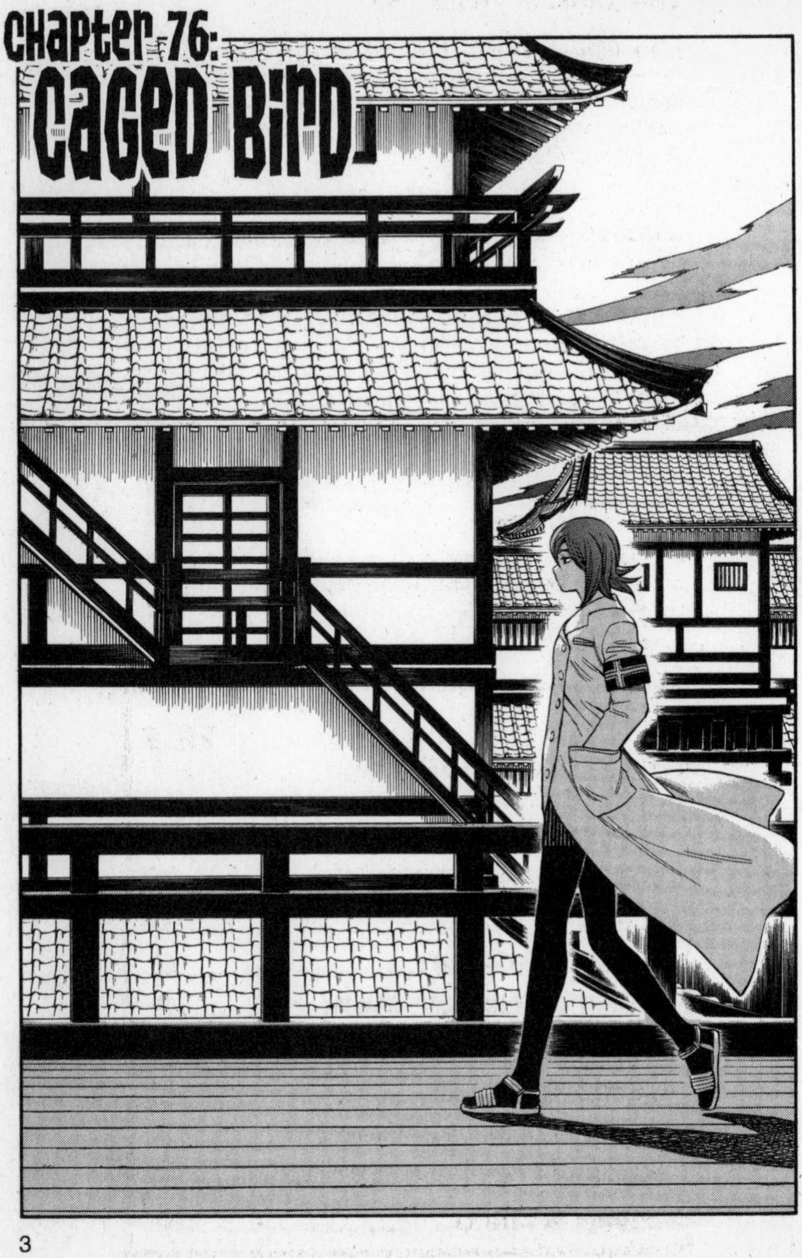

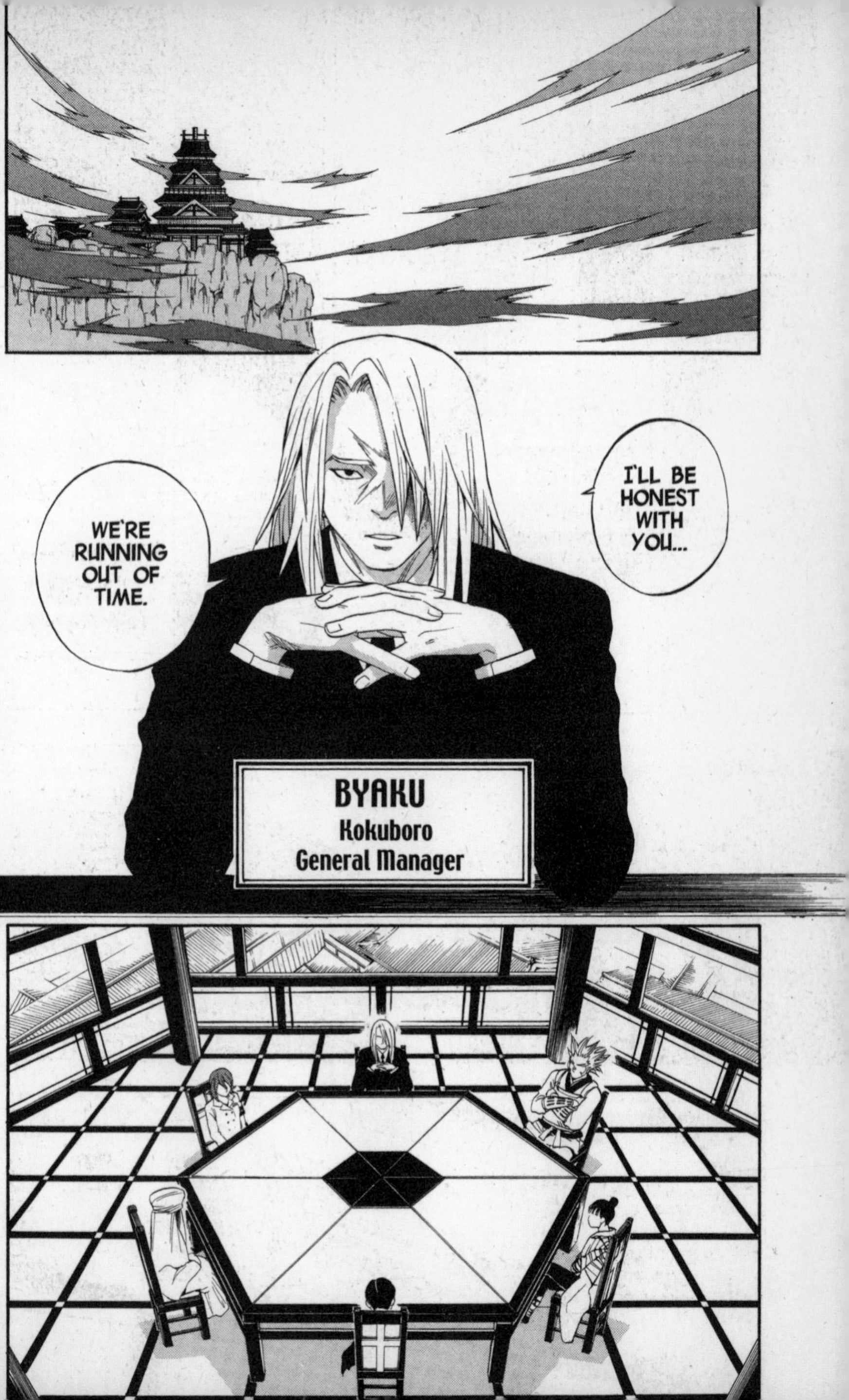
I'LL BE HONEST WITH YOU...
WE'RE RUNNING OUT OF TIME.
BYAKU
Kokuboro
General Manager

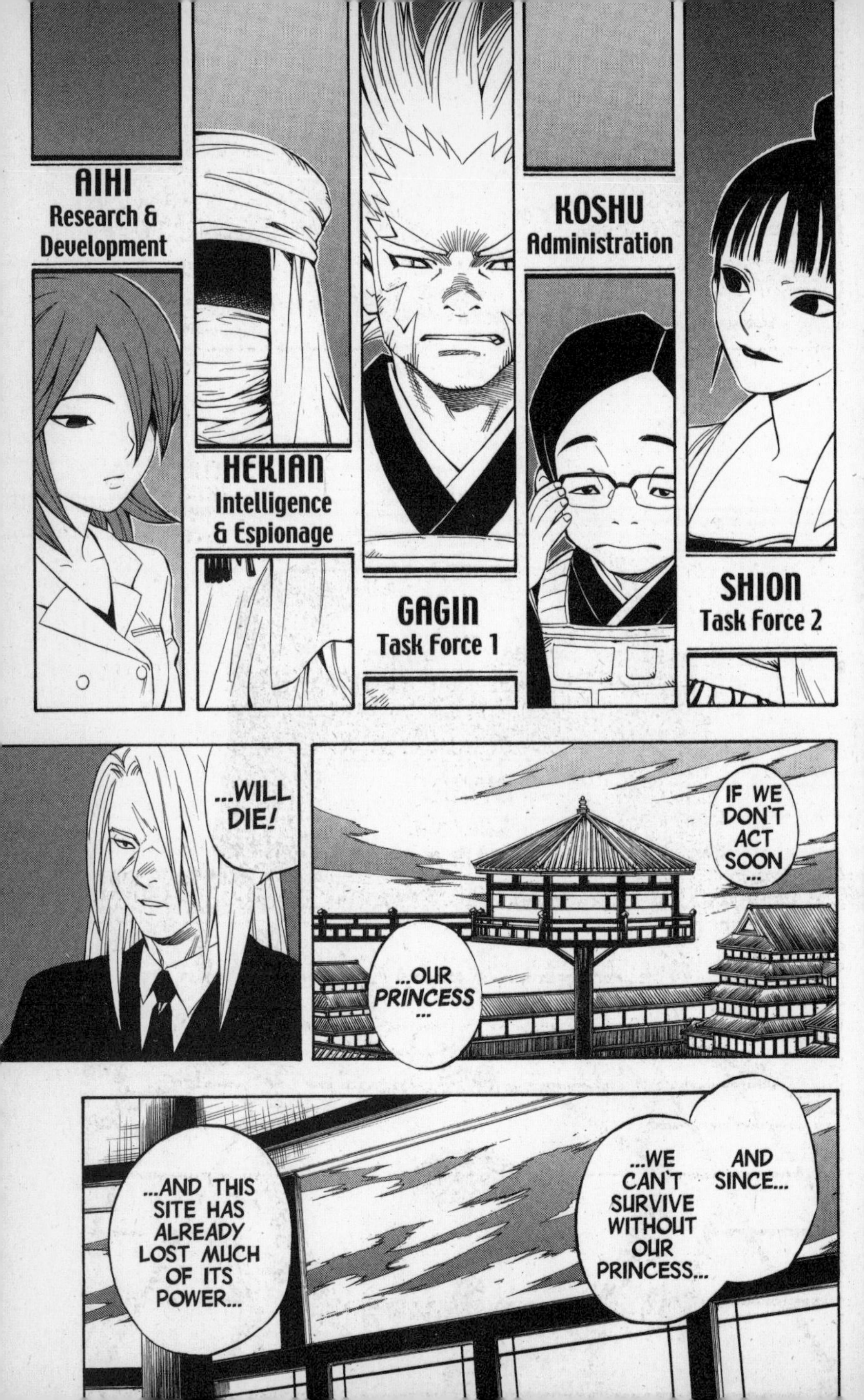
SHION
Task Force 2
KOSHU
Administration
GAGIN
Task Force 1
HEKIAN
Intelligence & Espionage
AIHI
Research & Development
IF WE DON'T ACT SOON ...
...OUR PRINCESS ...
...WILL DIE!
AND SINCE...
...WE CAN'T SURVIVE WITHOUT OUR PRINCESS...
...AND THIS SITE HAS ALREADY LOST MUCH OF ITS POWER...

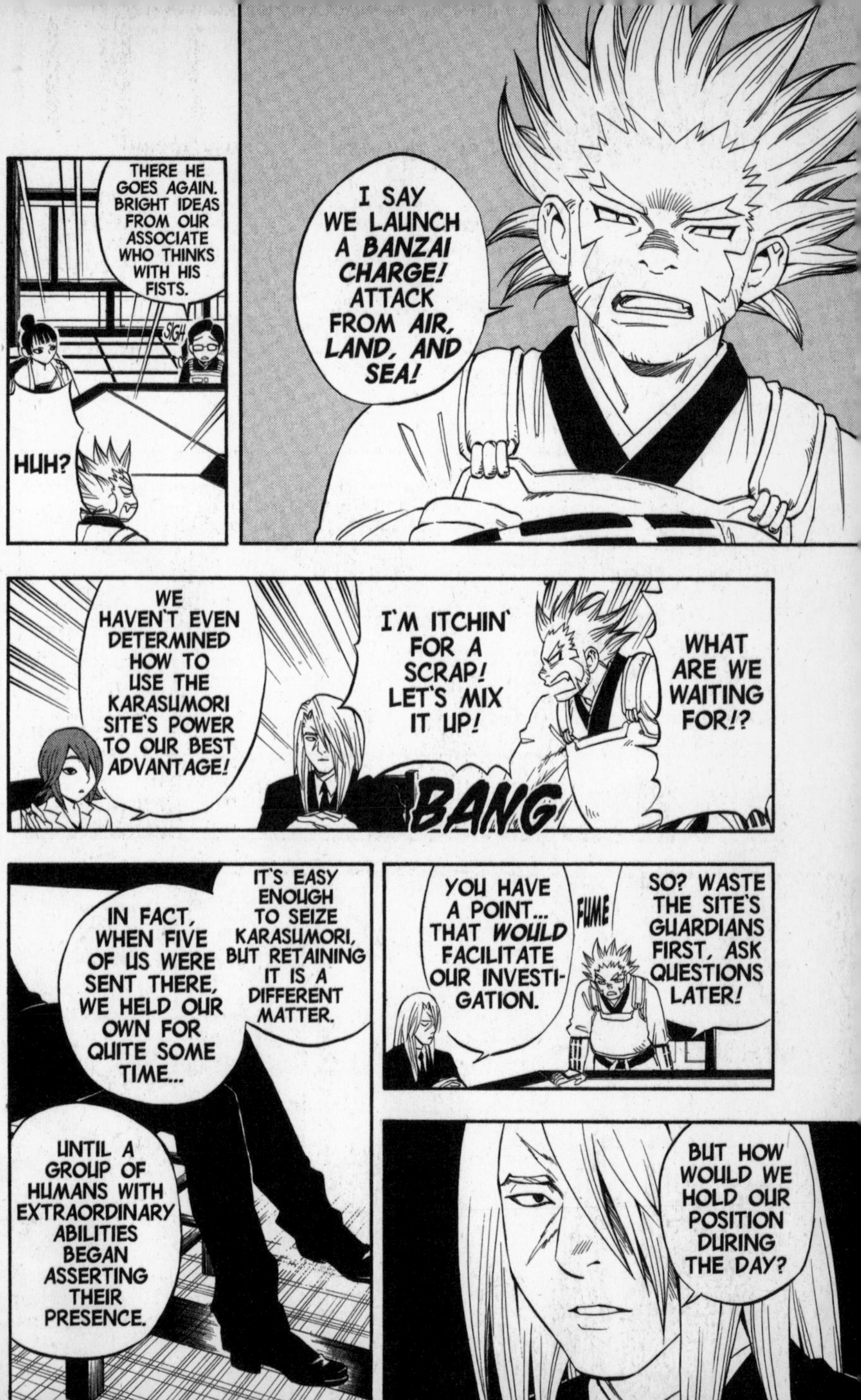
I SAY WE LAUNCH A BANZAI CHARGE! ATTACK FROM AIR, LAND, AND SEA!
THERE HE GOES AGAIN. BRIGHT IDEAS FROM OUR ASSOCIATE WHO THINKS WITH HIS FISTS.
SIGH
HUH?
WHAT ARE WE WAITING FOR!?
I'M ITCHIN' FOR A SCRAP! LET'S MIX IT UP!
BANG
WE HAVEN'T EVEN DETERMINED HOW TO USE THE KARASUMORI SITE'S POWER TO OUR BEST ADVANTAGE!
SO? WASTE THE SITE'S GUARDIANS FIRST, ASK QUESTIONS LATER!
FUME
YOU HAVE A POINT... THAT WOULD FACILITATE OUR INVESTIGATION.
BUT HOW WOULD WE HOLD OUR POSITION DURING THE DAY?
IT'S EASY ENOUGH TO SEIZE KARASUMORI, BUT RETAINING IT IS A DIFFERENT MATTER.
IN FACT, WHEN FIVE OF US WERE SENT THERE, WE HELD OUR OWN FOR QUITE SOME TIME...
UNTIL A GROUP OF HUMANS WITH EXTRAORDINARY ABILITIES BEGAN ASSERTING THEIR PRESENCE.

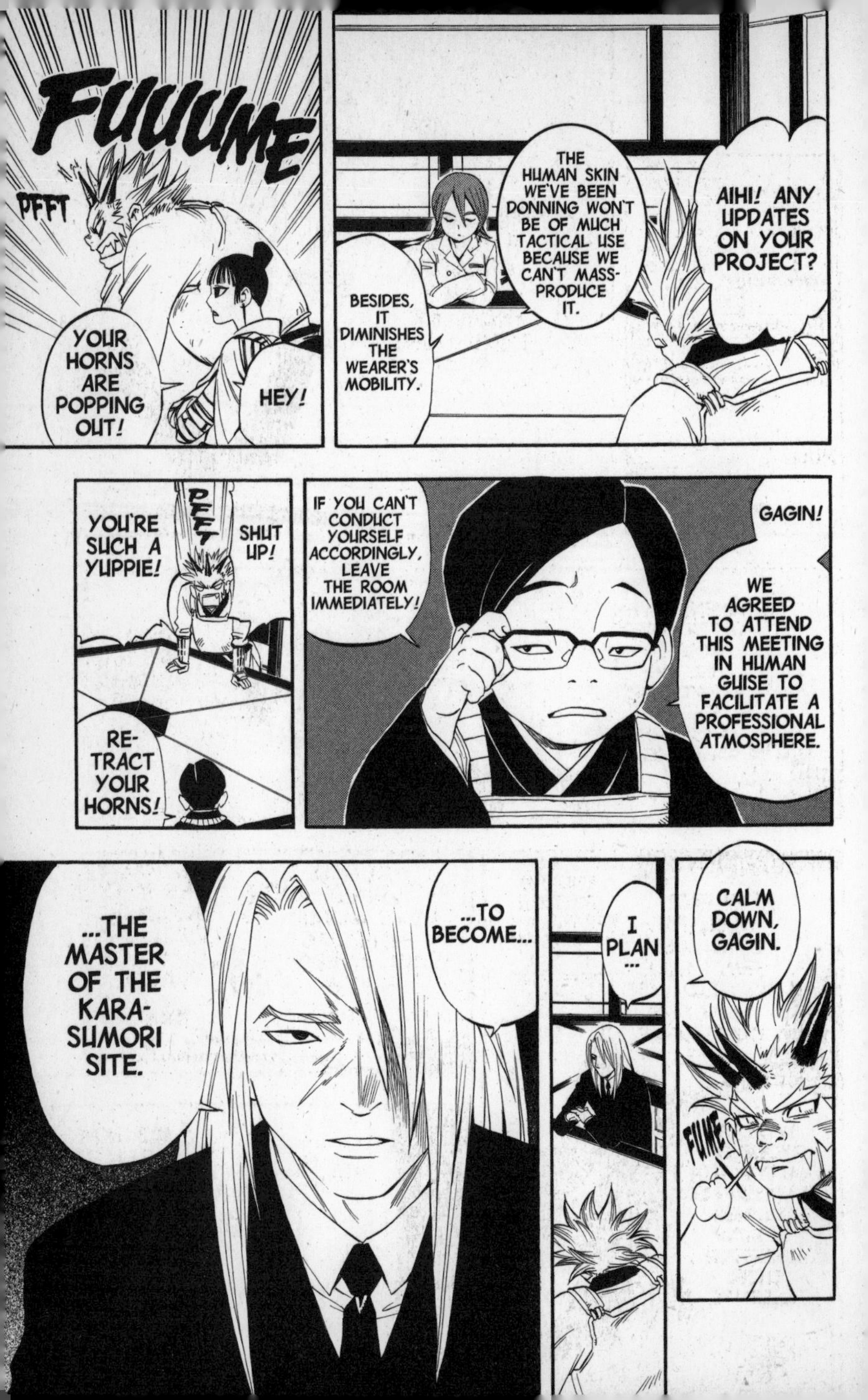
AIHI! ANY UPDATES ON YOUR PROJECT?
THE HUMAN SKIN WE'VE BEEN DONNING WON'T BE OF MUCH TACTICAL USE BECAUSE WE CAN'T MASS-PRODUCE IT.
BESIDES, IT DIMINISHES THE WEARER'S MOBILITY.
FUUUME
PFFT
HEY!
YOUR HORNS ARE POPPING OUT!
GAGIN!
WE AGREED TO ATTEND THIS MEETING IN HUMAN GUISE TO FACILITATE A PROFESSIONAL ATMOSPHERE.
IF YOU CAN'T CONDUCT YOURSELF ACCORDINGLY, LEAVE THE ROOM IMMEDIATELY!
SHUT UP!
PFFT
YOU'RE SUCH A YUPPIE!
RE-TRACT YOUR HORNS!
CALM DOWN, GAGIN.
FUME
I PLAN...
...TO BECOME...
...THE MASTER OF THE KARA-SUMORI SITE.

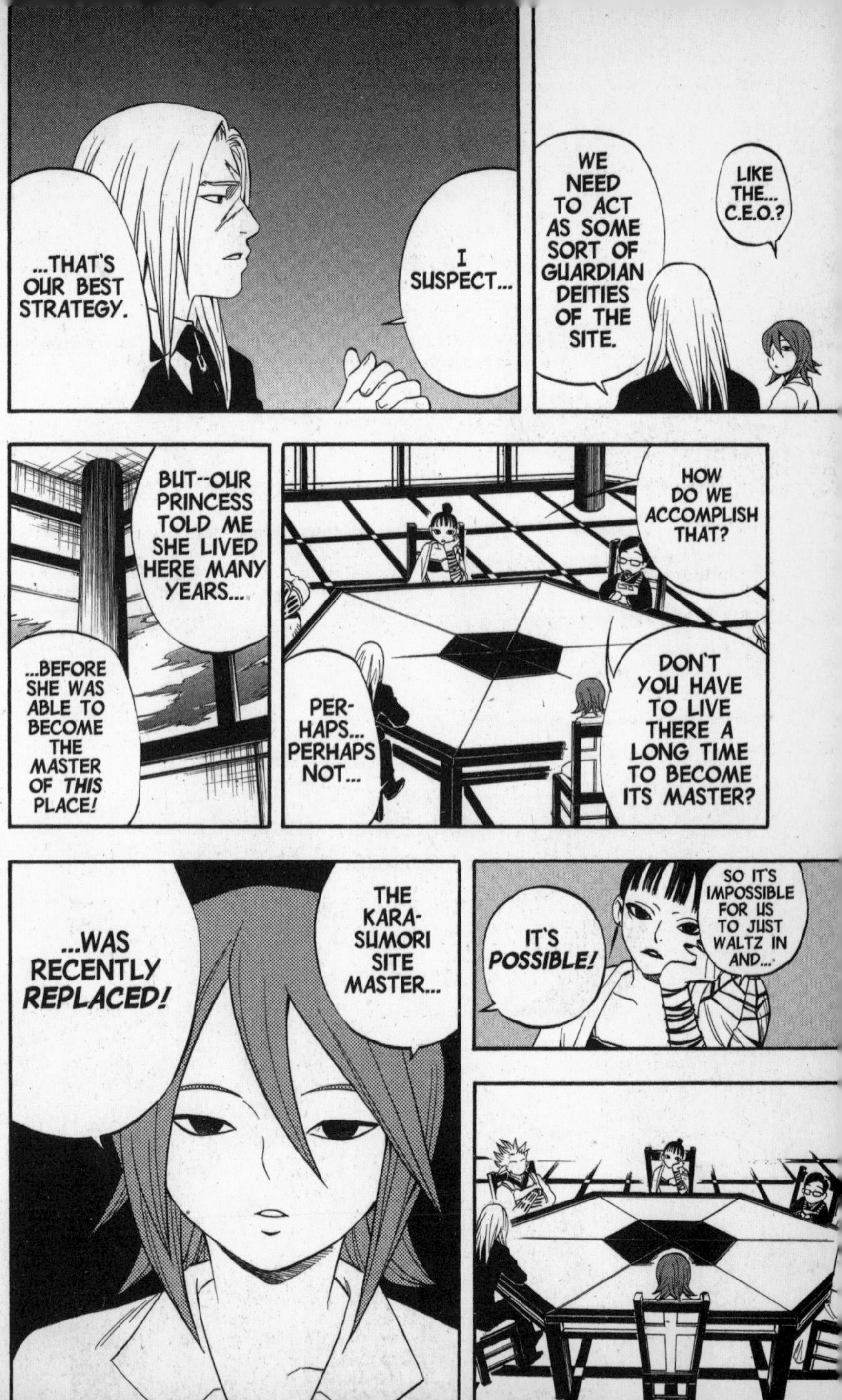
LIKE THE... C.E.O.?
WE NEED TO ACT AS SOME SORT OF GUARDIAN DEITIES OF THE SITE.
I SUSPECT...
...THAT'S OUR BEST STRATEGY.
HOW DO WE ACCOMPLISH THAT?
DON'T YOU HAVE TO LIVE THERE A LONG TIME TO BECOME ITS MASTER?
PER-HAPS... PERHAPS NOT...
BUT--OUR PRINCESS TOLD ME SHE LIVED HERE MANY YEARS...
...BEFORE SHE WAS ABLE TO BECOME THE MASTER OF *THIS* PLACE!
SO IT'S IMPOSSIBLE FOR US TO JUST WALTZ IN AND...
IT'S *POSSIBLE!*
THE KARA-SUMORI SITE MASTER...
...WAS RECENTLY *REPLACED!*

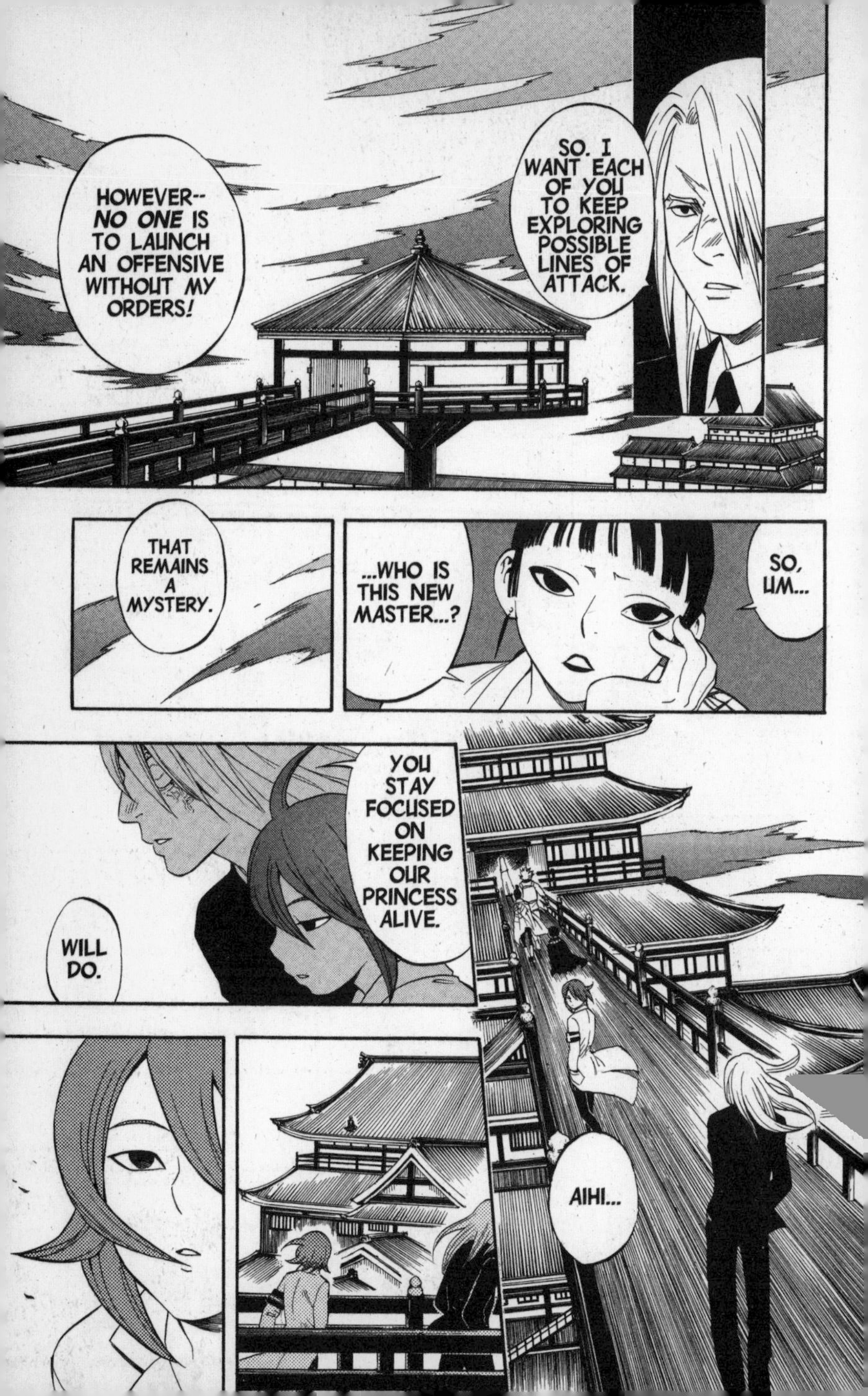
SO. I WANT EACH OF YOU TO KEEP EXPLORING POSSIBLE LINES OF ATTACK.
HOWEVER-- *NO ONE* IS TO LAUNCH AN OFFENSIVE WITHOUT MY ORDERS!
SO, UM...
...WHO IS THIS NEW MASTER...?
THAT REMAINS A MYSTERY.
YOU STAY FOCUSED ON KEEPING OUR PRINCESS ALIVE.
WILL DO.
AIHI...

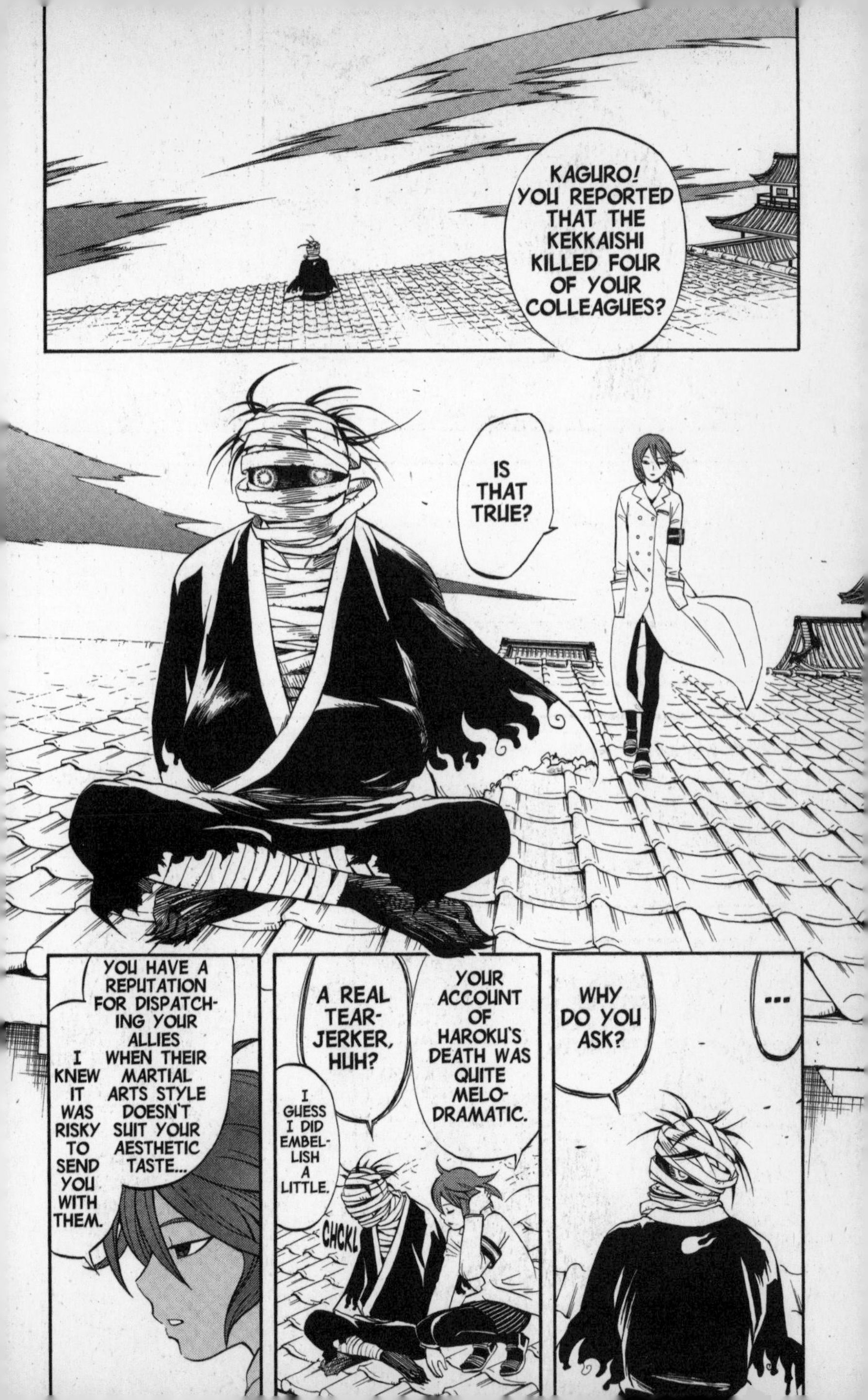
KAGURO! YOU REPORTED THAT THE KEKKAISHI KILLED FOUR OF YOUR COLLEAGUES?
IS THAT TRUE?
...
WHY DO YOU ASK?
YOUR ACCOUNT OF HAROKU'S DEATH WAS QUITE MELO-DRAMATIC.
A REAL TEAR-JERKER, HUH?
I GUESS I DID EMBEL-LISH A LITTLE.
CHCKL
YOU HAVE A REPUTATION FOR DISPATCH-ING YOUR ALLIES WHEN THEIR MARTIAL ARTS STYLE DOESN'T SUIT YOUR AESTHETIC TASTE...
I KNEW IT WAS RISKY TO SEND YOU WITH THEM.

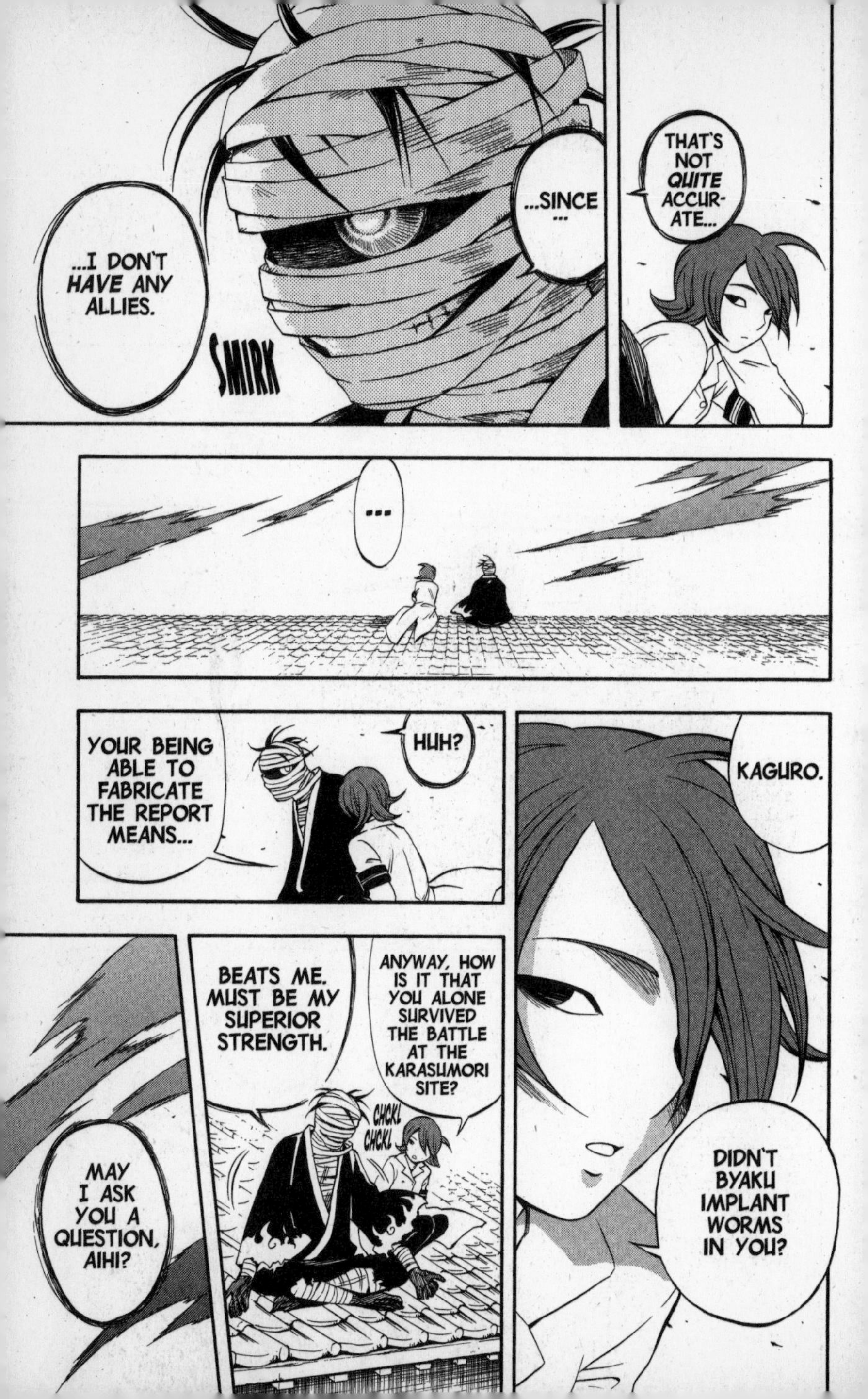

THAT'S NOT QUITE ACCURATE...
...SINCE ...
...I DON'T HAVE ANY ALLIES.
SMIRK
...
KAGURO.
DIDN'T BYAKU IMPLANT WORMS IN YOU?
HUH?
YOUR BEING ABLE TO FABRICATE THE REPORT MEANS...
ANYWAY, HOW IS IT THAT YOU ALONE SURVIVED THE BATTLE AT THE KARASUMORI SITE?
BEATS ME. MUST BE MY SUPERIOR STRENGTH.
CHCKL CHCKL
MAY I ASK YOU A QUESTION, AIHI?

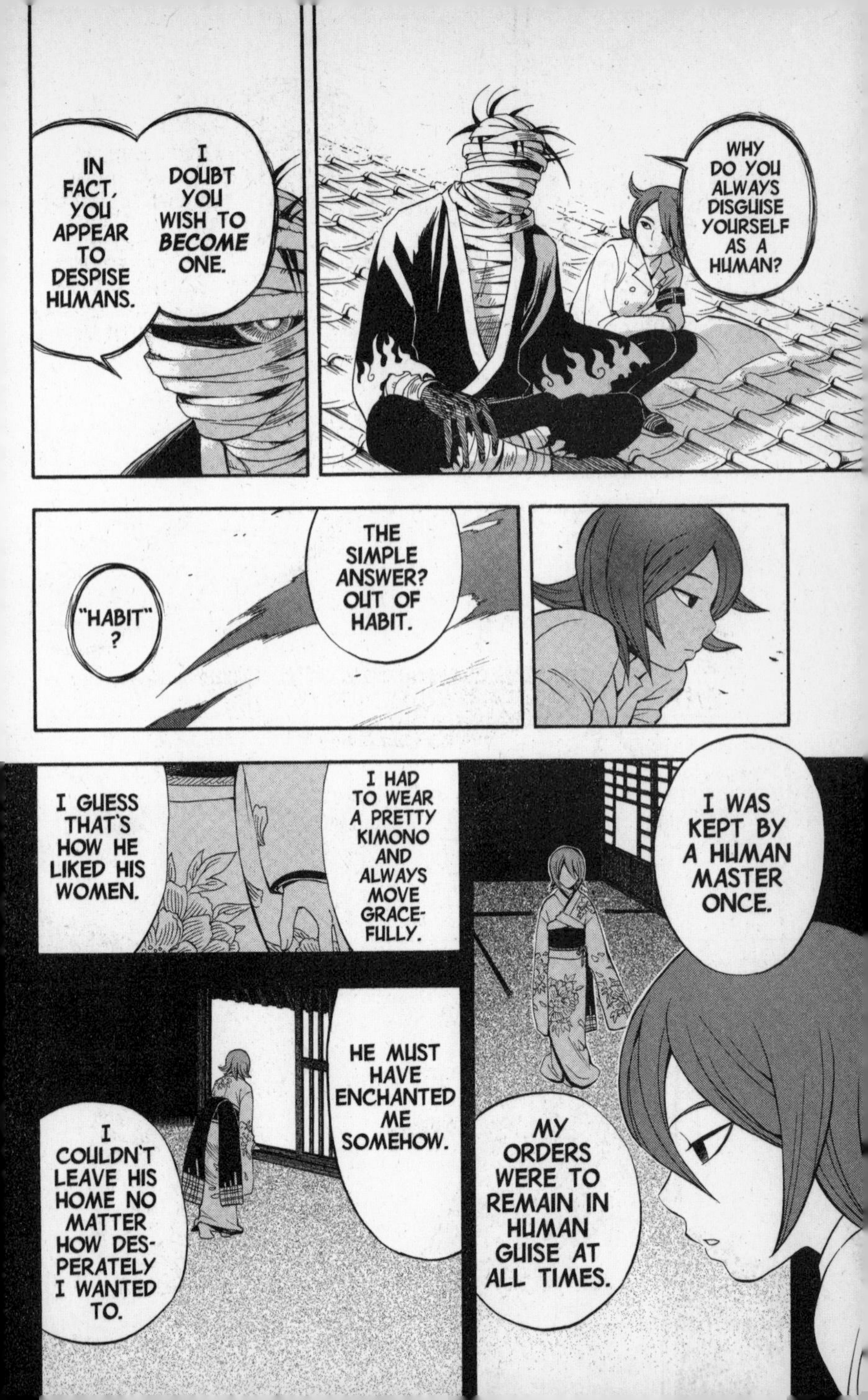
WHY DO YOU ALWAYS DISGUISE YOURSELF AS A HUMAN?
I DOUBT YOU WISH TO *BECOME* ONE.
IN FACT, YOU APPEAR TO DESPISE HUMANS.
THE SIMPLE ANSWER? OUT OF HABIT.
"HABIT"?
I WAS KEPT BY A HUMAN MASTER ONCE.
MY ORDERS WERE TO REMAIN IN HUMAN GUISE AT ALL TIMES.
I HAD TO WEAR A PRETTY KIMONO AND ALWAYS MOVE GRACE-FULLY.
I GUESS THAT'S HOW HE LIKED HIS WOMEN.
HE MUST HAVE ENCHANTED ME SOMEHOW.
I COULDN'T LEAVE HIS HOME NO MATTER HOW DES-PERATELY I WANTED TO.

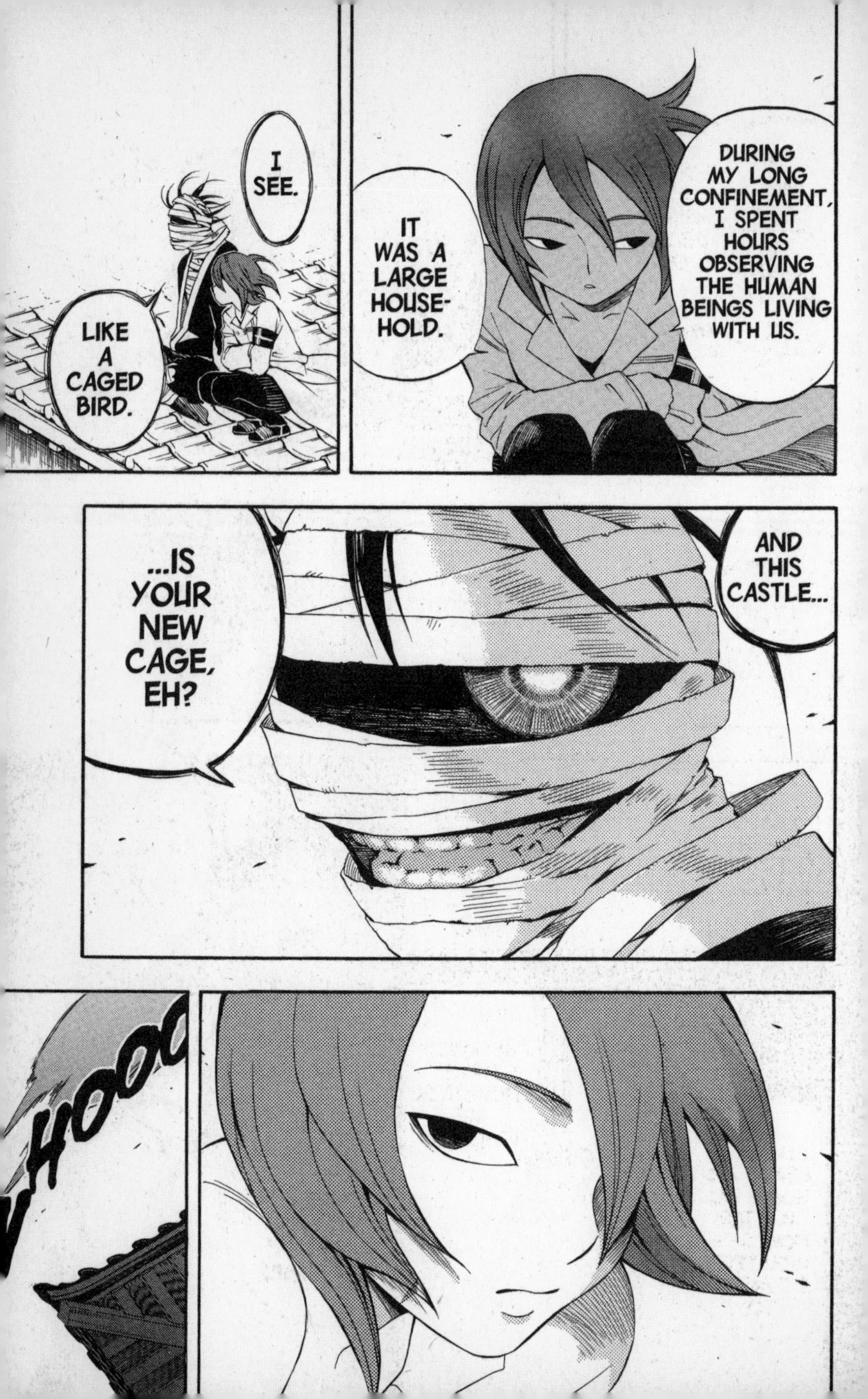
DURING MY LONG CONFINEMENT, I SPENT HOURS OBSERVING THE HUMAN BEINGS LIVING WITH US.
IT WAS A LARGE HOUSE-HOLD.
I SEE.
LIKE A CAGED BIRD.
AND THIS CASTLE...
...IS YOUR NEW CAGE, EH?

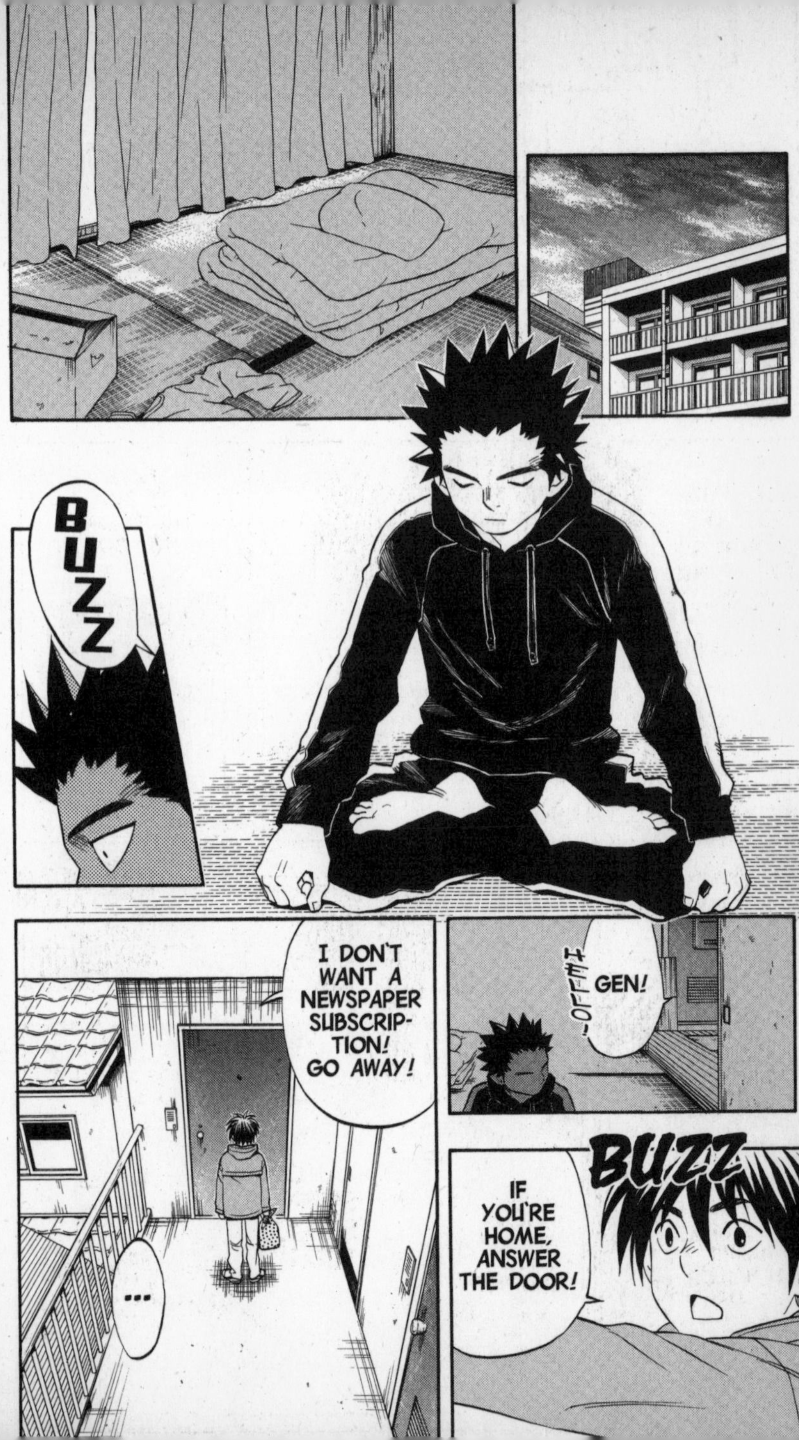
BUZZ
HELLO!
GEN!
BUZZ
IF YOU'RE HOME, ANSWER THE DOOR!
I DON'T WANT A NEWSPAPER SUBSCRIPTION! GO AWAY!
...

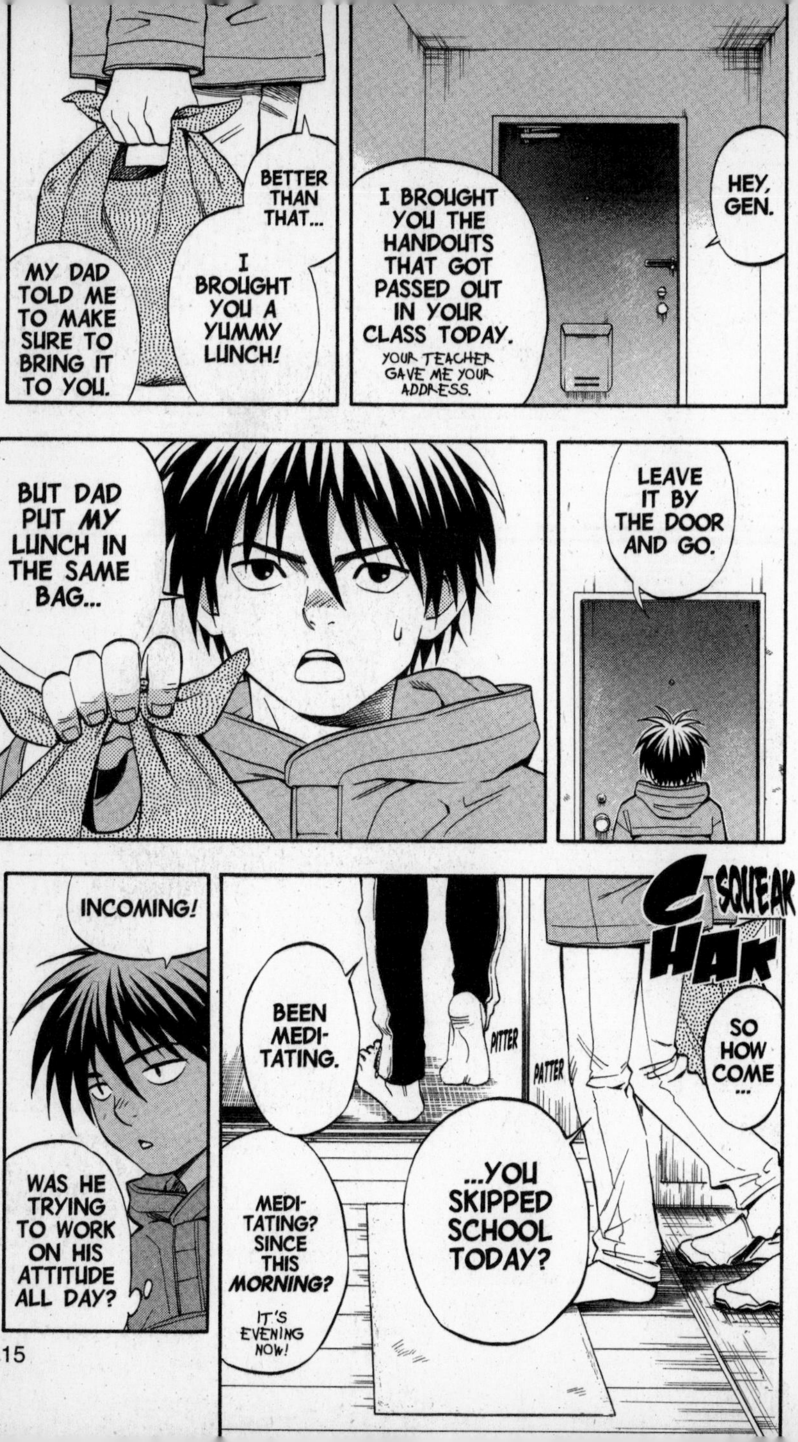

HEY, GEN.
I BROUGHT YOU THE HANDOUTS THAT GOT PASSED OUT IN YOUR CLASS TODAY.
YOUR TEACHER GAVE ME YOUR ADDRESS.
BETTER THAN THAT...
I BROUGHT YOU A YUMMY LUNCH!
MY DAD TOLD ME TO MAKE SURE TO BRING IT TO YOU.
LEAVE IT BY THE DOOR AND GO.
BUT DAD PUT *MY* LUNCH IN THE SAME BAG...
CHAK
SQUEAK
SO HOW COME ...
...YOU SKIPPED SCHOOL TODAY?
PITTER
PATTER
BEEN MEDI-TATING.
MEDI-TATING? SINCE THIS *MORNING?*
IT'S EVENING NOW!
INCOMING!
WAS HE TRYING TO WORK ON HIS ATTITUDE ALL DAY?

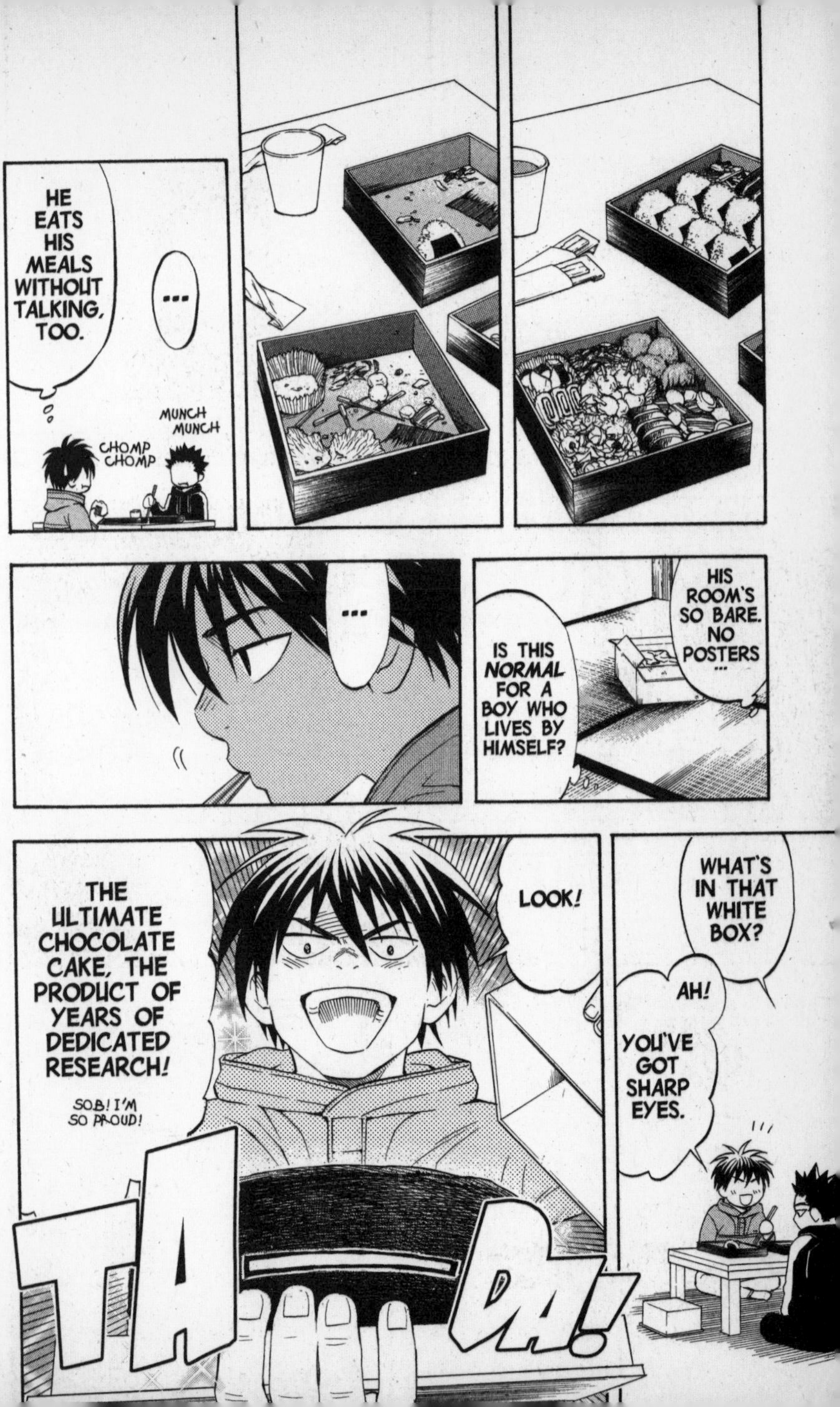
HE EATS HIS MEALS WITHOUT TALKING, TOO.
...
MUNCH MUNCH
CHOMP CHOMP
HIS ROOM'S SO BARE. NO POSTERS ...
IS THIS *NORMAL* FOR A BOY WHO LIVES BY HIMSELF?
...
WHAT'S IN THAT WHITE BOX?
AH!
YOU'VE GOT SHARP EYES.
LOOK!
THE ULTIMATE CHOCOLATE CAKE, THE PRODUCT OF YEARS OF DEDICATED RESEARCH!
SOB! I'M SO PROUD!
TA DA!

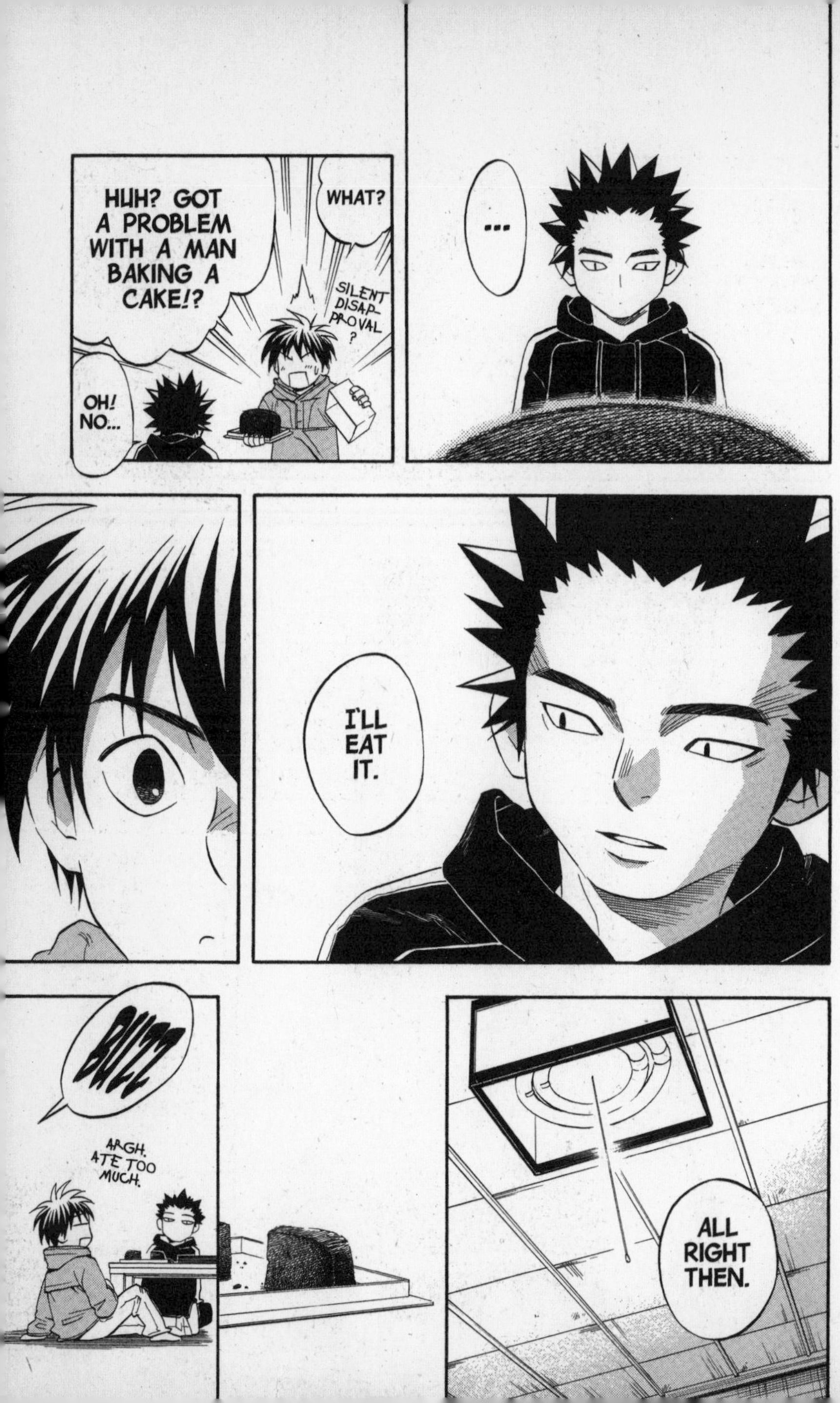
...
WHAT?
HUH? GOT A PROBLEM WITH A MAN BAKING A CAKE!?
SILENT DISAP-PROVAL ?
OH! NO...
I'LL EAT IT.
ALL RIGHT THEN.
BUZZ
ARGH. ATE TOO MUCH.

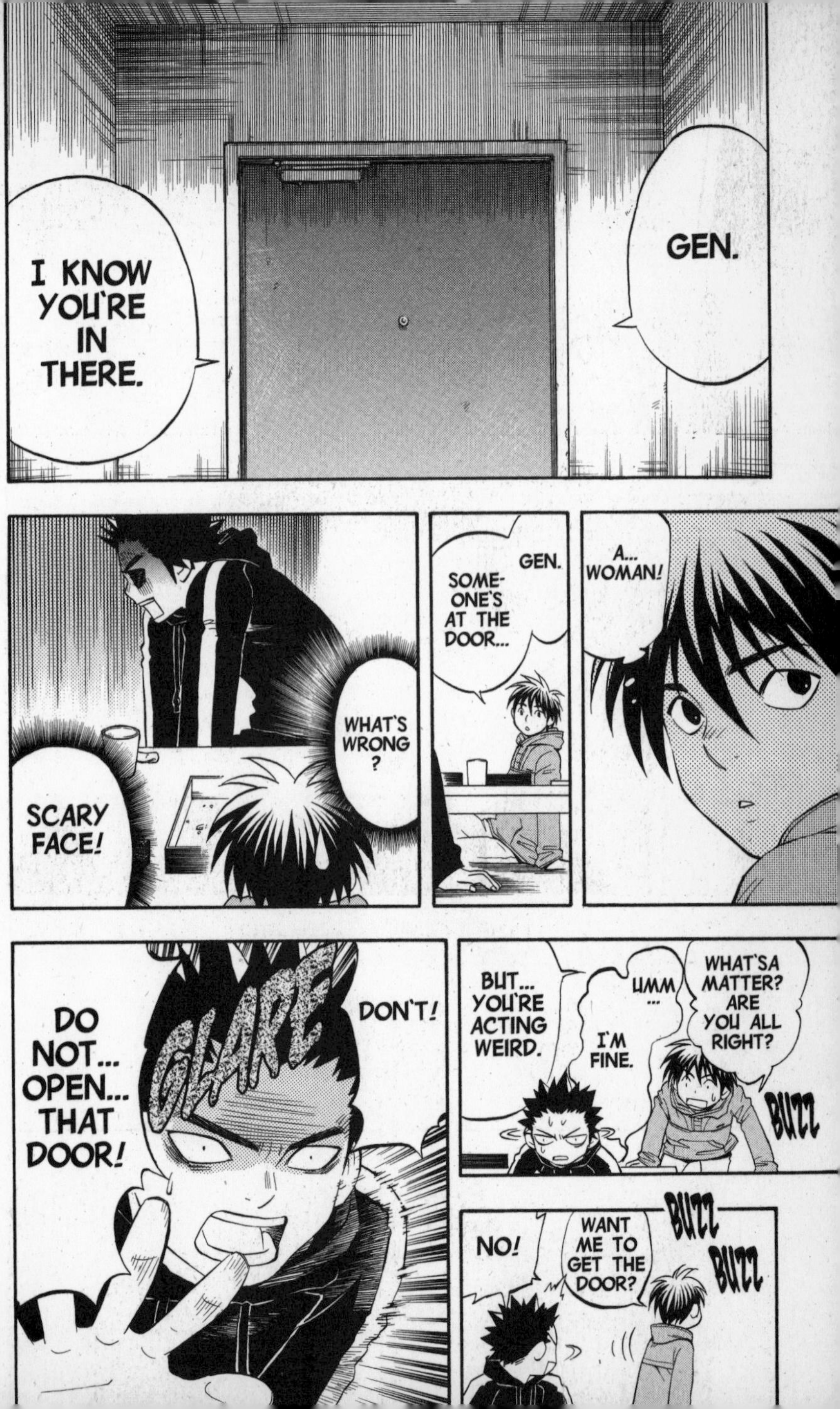
GEN.
I KNOW YOU'RE IN THERE.
A... WOMAN!
GEN.
SOME-ONE'S AT THE DOOR...
WHAT'S WRONG?
SCARY FACE!
WHAT'SA MATTER? ARE YOU ALL RIGHT?
BUZZ
UMM...
I'M FINE.
BUT... YOU'RE ACTING WEIRD.
BUZZ
BUZZ
WANT ME TO GET THE DOOR?
NO!
DON'T!
GLARE
DO NOT... OPEN... THAT DOOR!

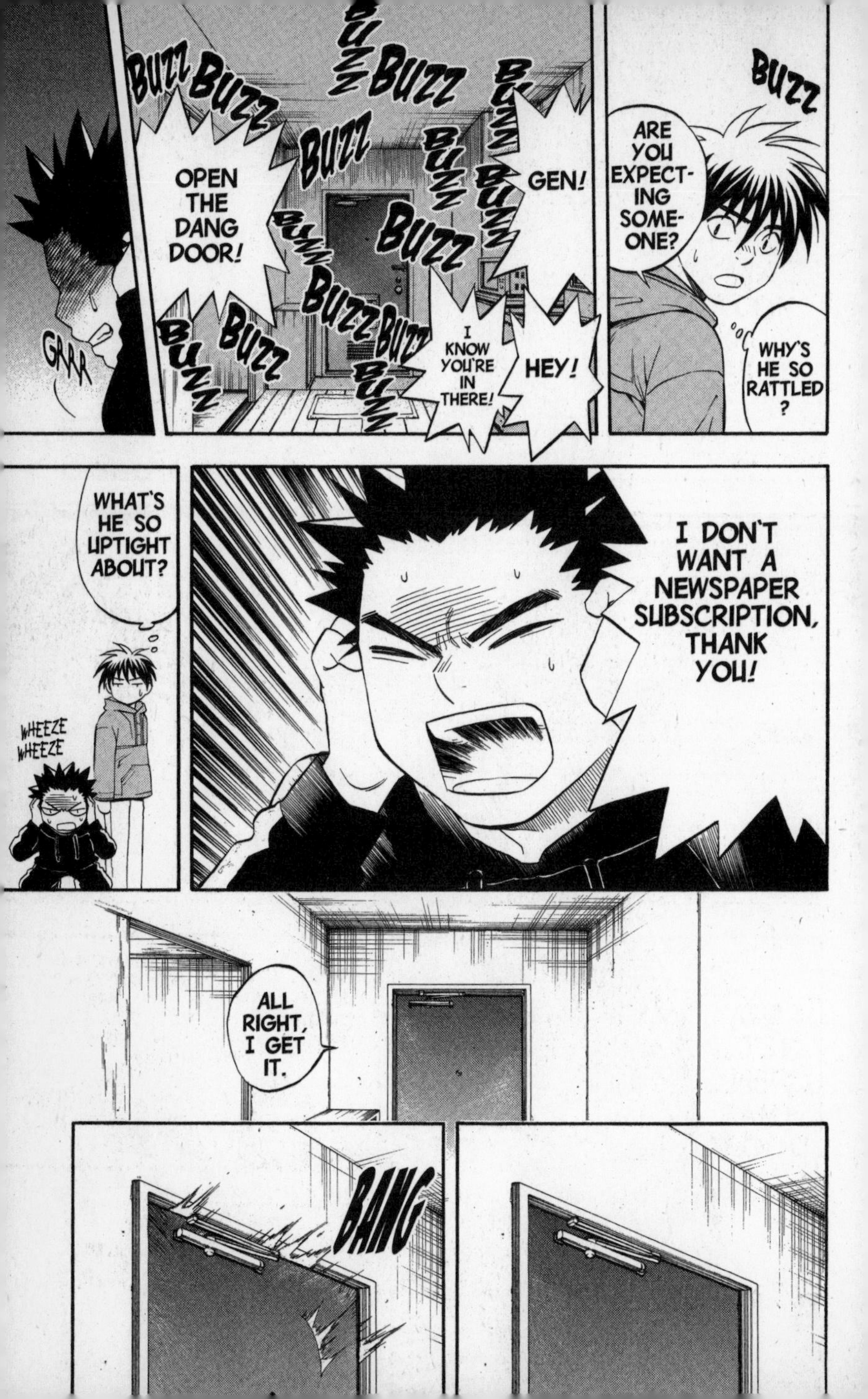
BUZZ
ARE YOU EXPECTING-ING SOME-ONE?
WHY'S HE SO RATTLED?
GEN!
HEY!
I KNOW YOU'RE IN THERE!
BUZZ BUZZ BUZZ BUZZ BUZZ BUZZ BUZZ BUZZ BUZZ BUZZ BUZZ BUZZ BUZZ BUZZ
OPEN THE DANG DOOR!
GRRR
I DON'T WANT A NEWSPAPER SUBSCRIPTION, THANK YOU!
WHAT'S HE SO UPTIGHT ABOUT?
WHEEZE WHEEZE
ALL RIGHT, I GET IT.
BANG

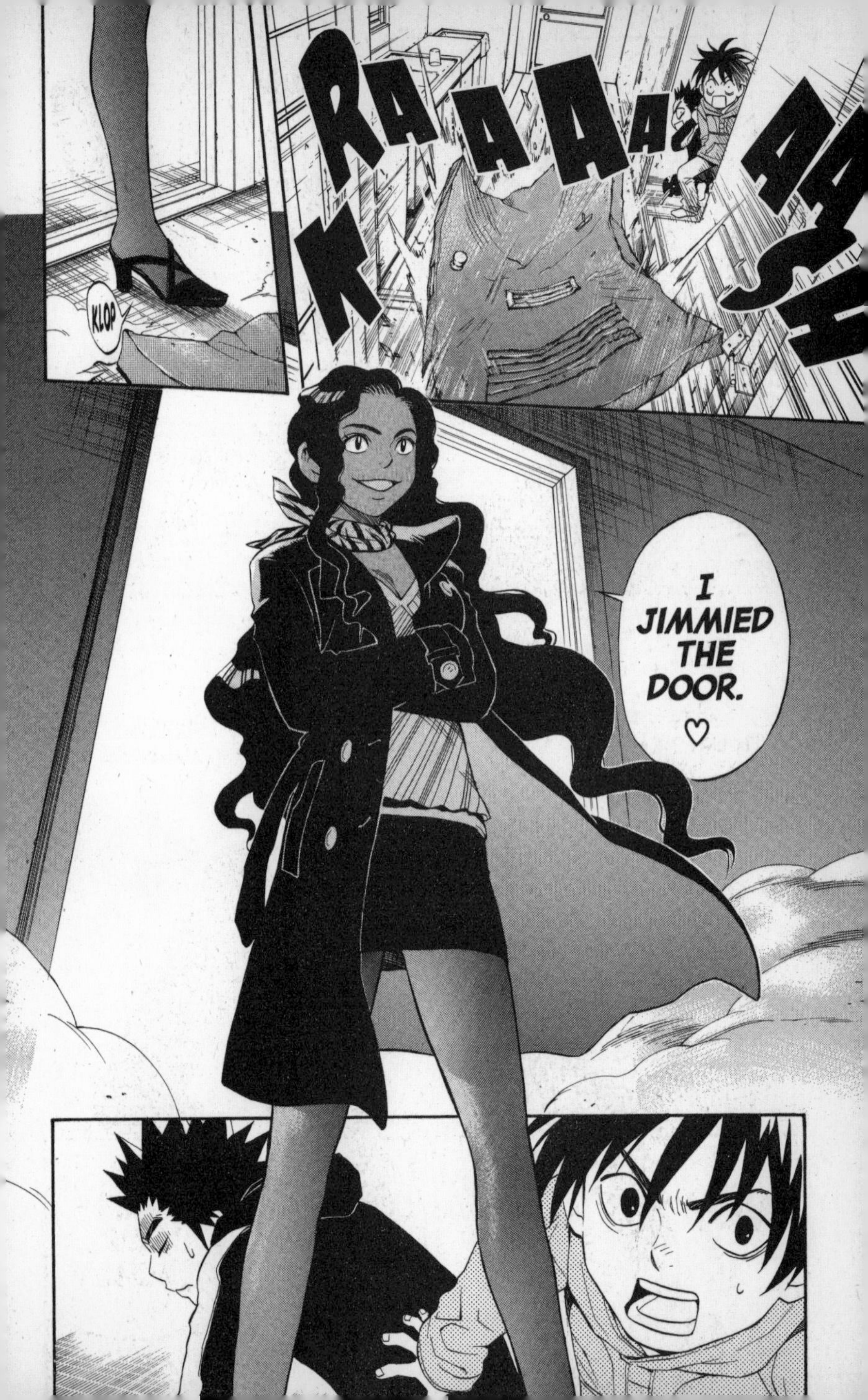
KRAAAAAASH
KLOP
I JIMMIED THE DOOR. ♡

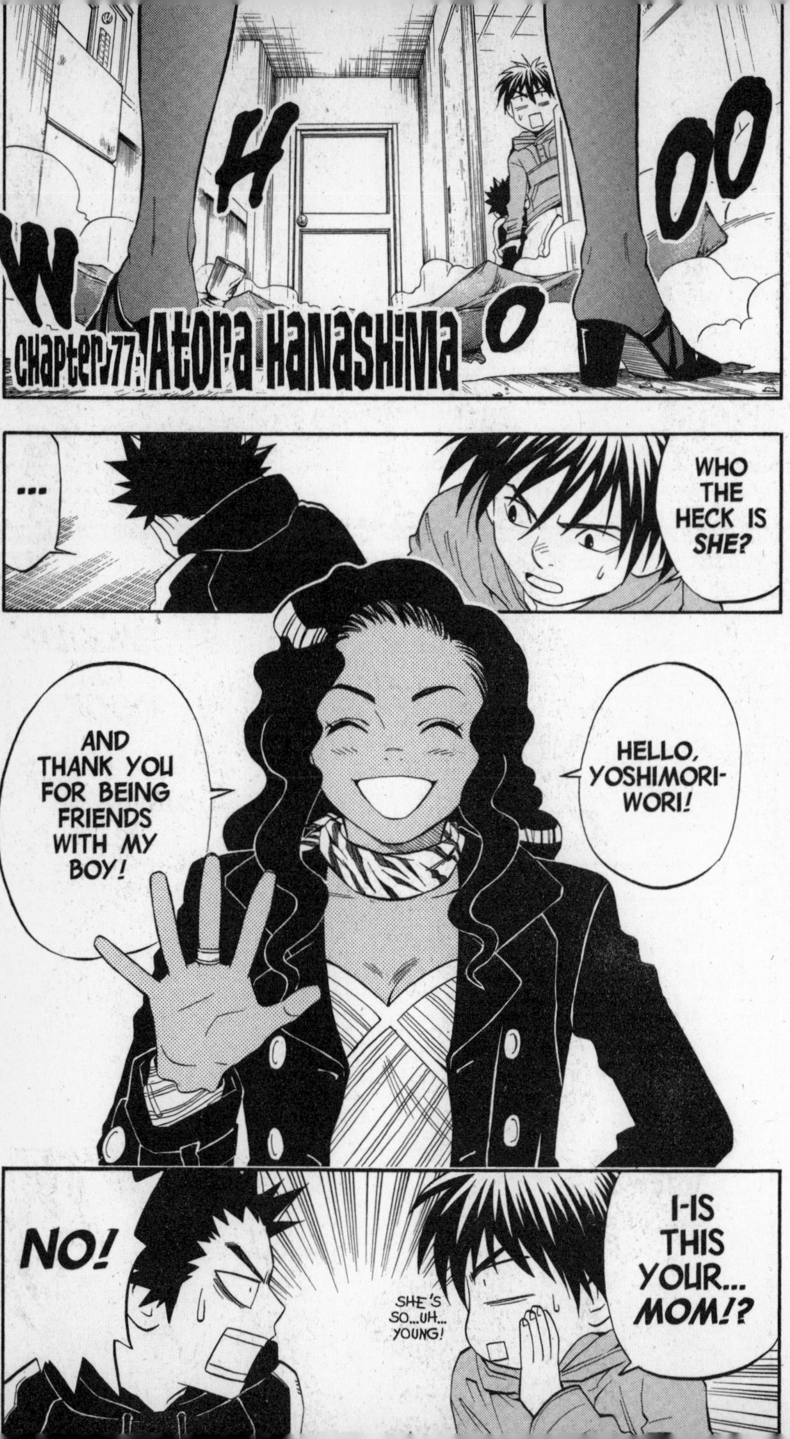
WHOOOOO
Chapter 77: Atora Hanashima
WHO THE HECK IS SHE?
...
HELLO, YOSHIMORI-WORI!
AND THANK YOU FOR BEING FRIENDS WITH MY BOY!
I-IS THIS YOUR... MOM!?
SHE'S SO...UH... YOUNG!
NO!

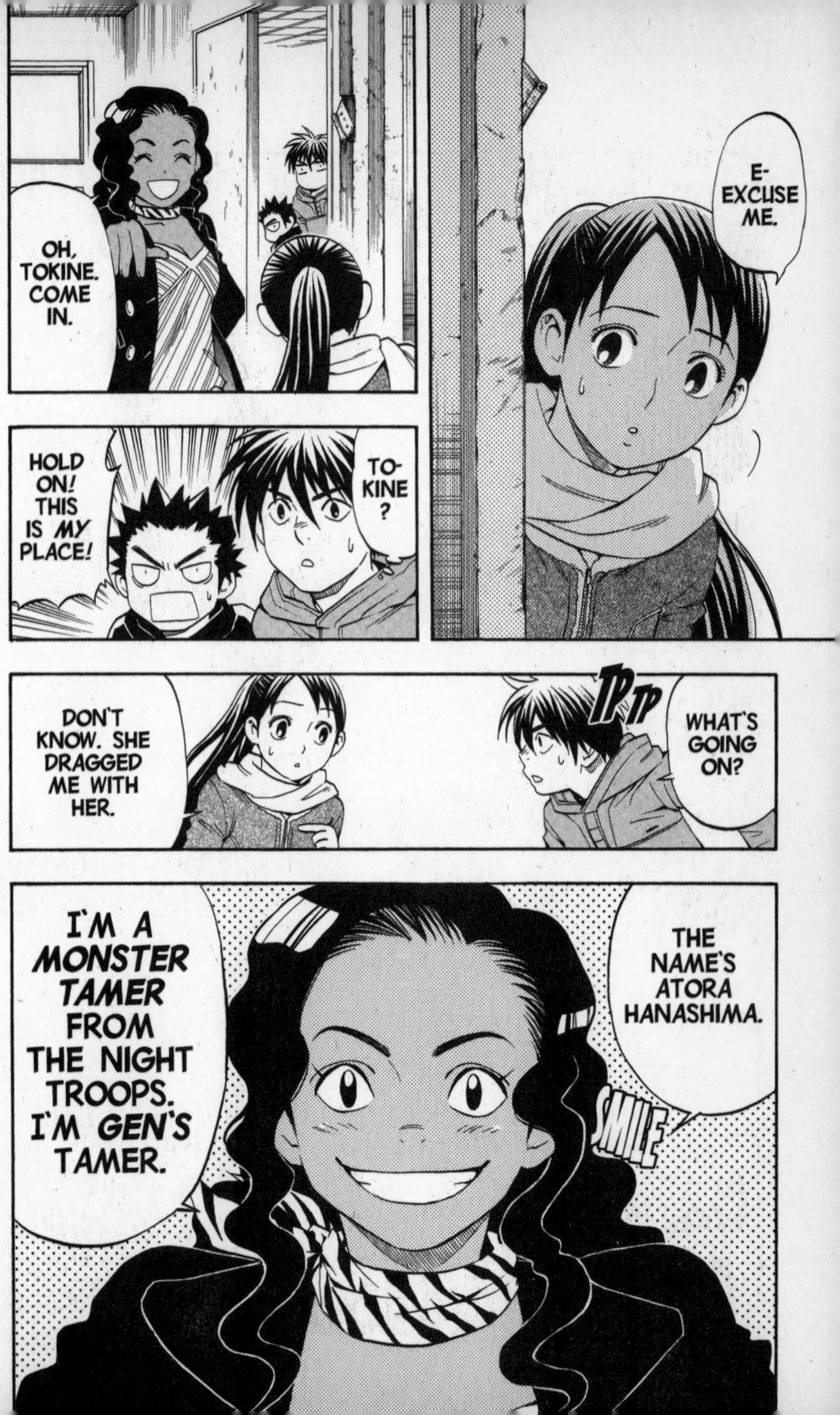
E-EXCUSE ME.
OH, TOKINE. COME IN.
TO-KINE?
HOLD ON! THIS IS *MY* PLACE!
TP TP
WHAT'S GOING ON?
DON'T KNOW. SHE DRAGGED ME WITH HER.
THE NAME'S ATORA HANASHIMA.
SMILE
I'M A *MONSTER TAMER* FROM THE NIGHT TROOPS. I'M *GEN'S* TAMER.

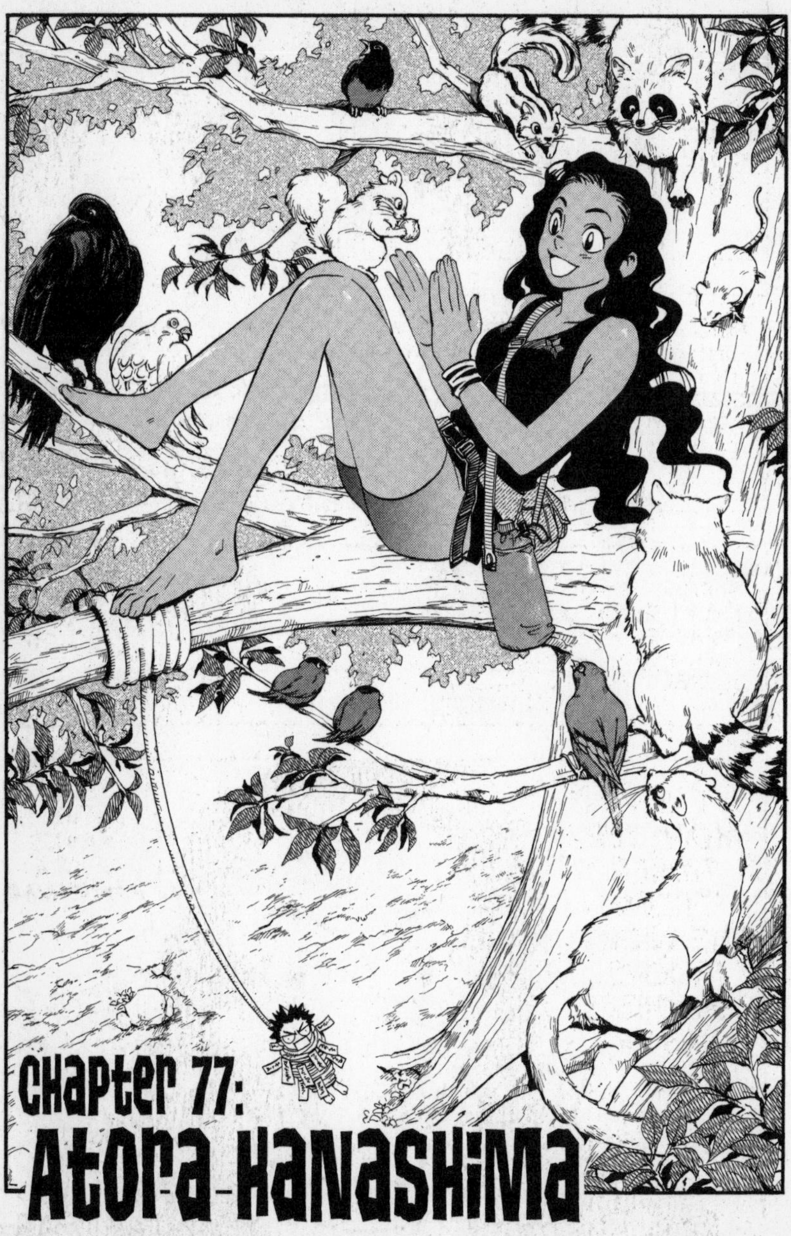

Chapter 77: Atora-Hanashima

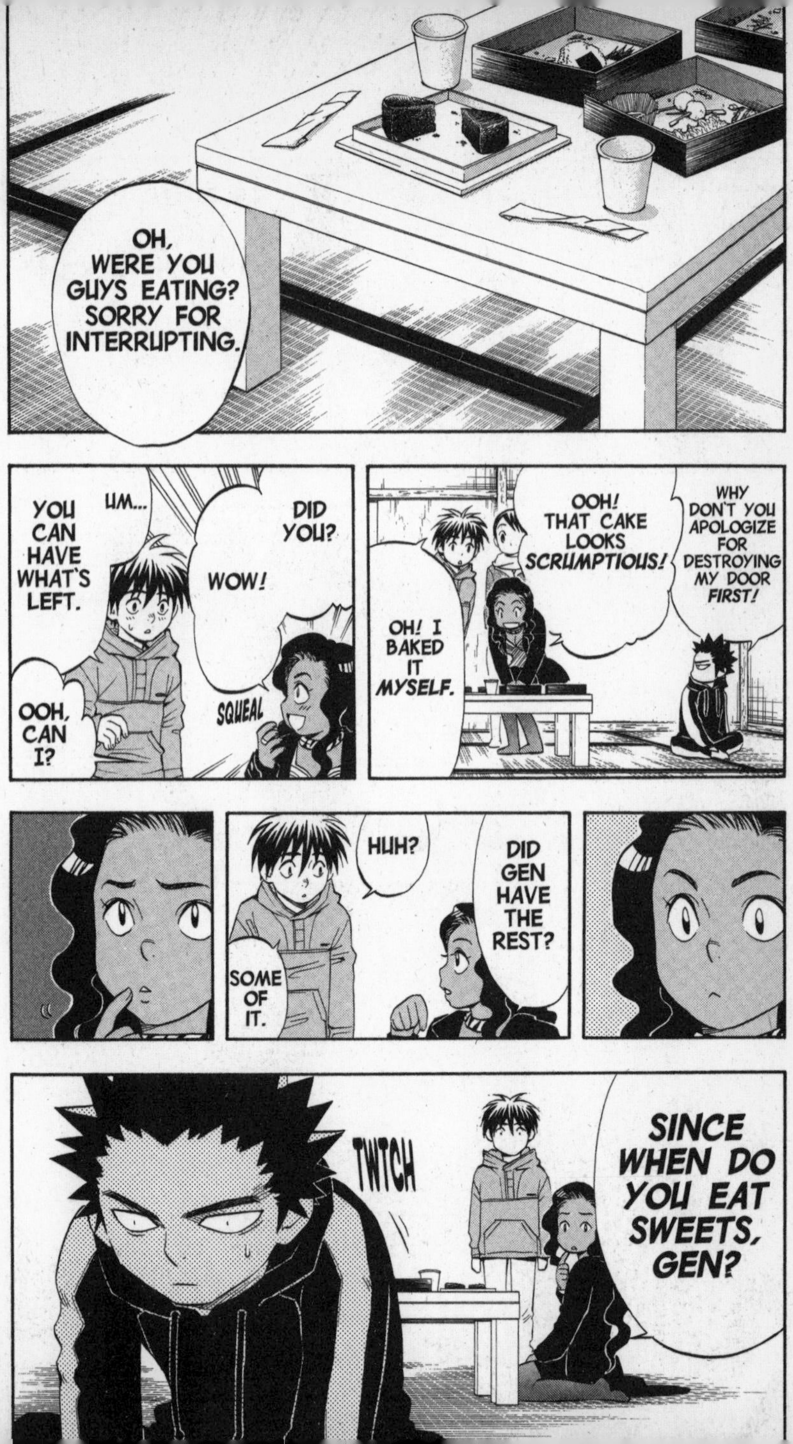
OH, WERE YOU GUYS EATING? SORRY FOR INTERRUPTING.
WHY DON'T YOU APOLOGIZE FOR DESTROYING MY DOOR FIRST!
OOH! THAT CAKE LOOKS SCRUMPTIOUS!
OH! I BAKED IT MYSELF.
DID YOU?
WOW!
SQUEAL
UM...
YOU CAN HAVE WHAT'S LEFT.
OOH, CAN I?
DID GEN HAVE THE REST?
HUH?
SOME OF IT.
SINCE WHEN DO YOU EAT SWEETS, GEN?
TWTCH

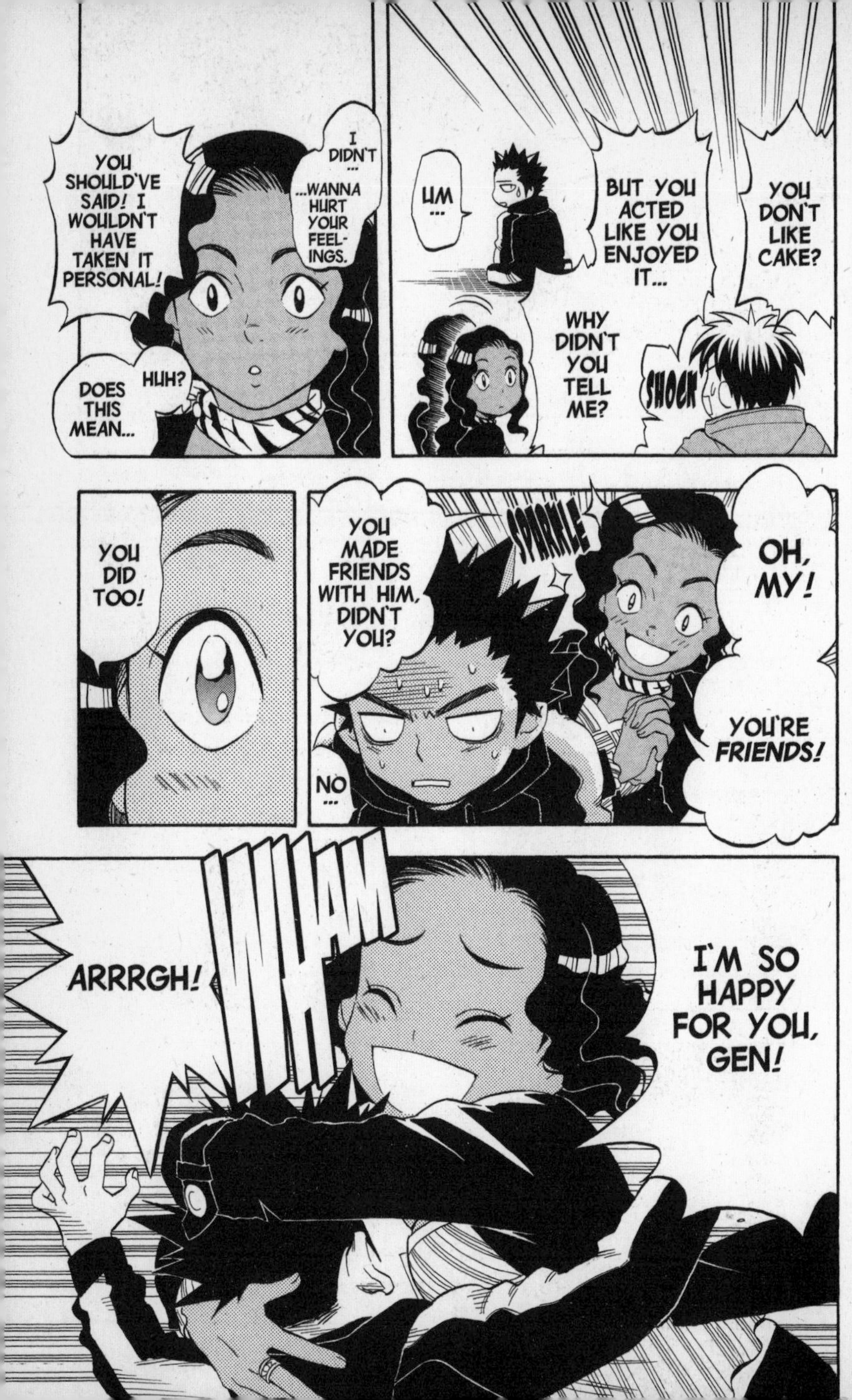
YOU DON'T LIKE CAKE?
BUT YOU ACTED LIKE YOU ENJOYED IT...
UM...
SHOCK
WHY DIDN'T YOU TELL ME?
I DIDN'T...
...WANNA HURT YOUR FEELINGS.
YOU SHOULD'VE SAID! I WOULDN'T HAVE TAKEN IT PERSONAL!
HUH?
DOES THIS MEAN...
OH, MY!
SPARKLE
YOU MADE FRIENDS WITH HIM, DIDN'T YOU?
YOU'RE FRIENDS!
NO...
YOU DID TOO!
I'M SO HAPPY FOR YOU, GEN!
WHAM
ARRRGH!

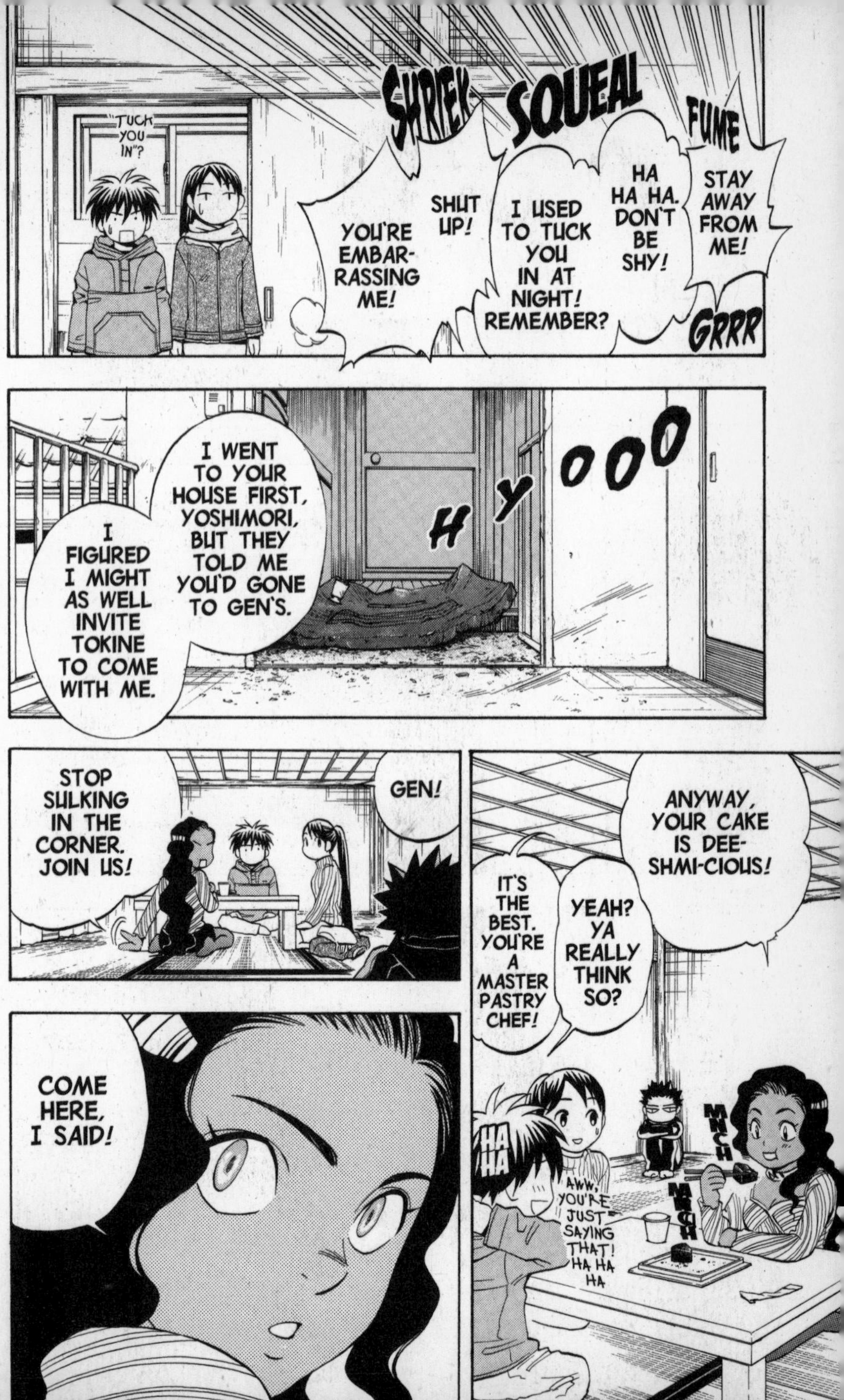
FUME
STAY AWAY FROM ME!
GRRR
HA HA HA. DON'T BE SHY!
I USED TO TUCK YOU IN AT NIGHT! REMEMBER?
SQUEAL
SHUT UP!
SHRIEK
YOU'RE EMBAR-RASSING ME!
"TUCK YOU IN"?
HYOOO
I WENT TO YOUR HOUSE FIRST, YOSHIMORI, BUT THEY TOLD ME YOU'D GONE TO GEN'S.
I FIGURED I MIGHT AS WELL INVITE TOKINE TO COME WITH ME.
ANYWAY, YOUR CAKE IS DEE-SHMI-CIOUS!
YEAH? YA REALLY THINK SO?
IT'S THE BEST. YOU'RE A MASTER PASTRY CHEF!
MNCH
MNCH
HA HA
AWW, YOU'RE JUST SAYING THAT! HA HA HA
GEN!
STOP SULKING IN THE CORNER. JOIN US!
COME HERE, I SAID!

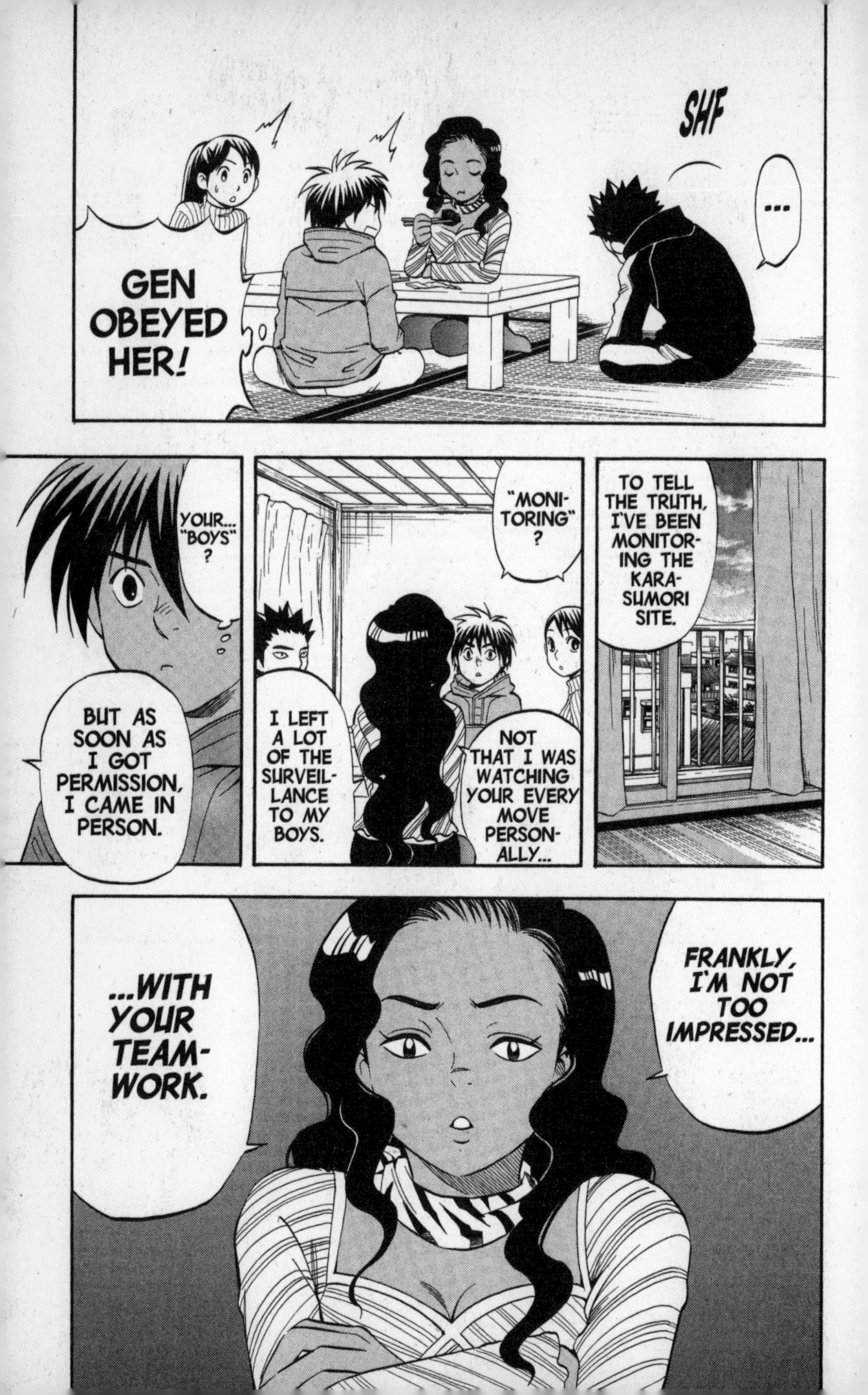
SHF
...
GEN OBEYED HER!
TO TELL THE TRUTH, I'VE BEEN MONITORING THE KARASUMORI SITE.
"MONITORING"?
NOT THAT I WAS WATCHING YOUR EVERY MOVE PERSONALLY...
I LEFT A LOT OF THE SURVEILLANCE TO MY BOYS.
YOUR... "BOYS"?
BUT AS SOON AS I GOT PERMISSION, I CAME IN PERSON.
FRANKLY, I'M NOT TOO IMPRESSED...
...WITH YOUR TEAMWORK.

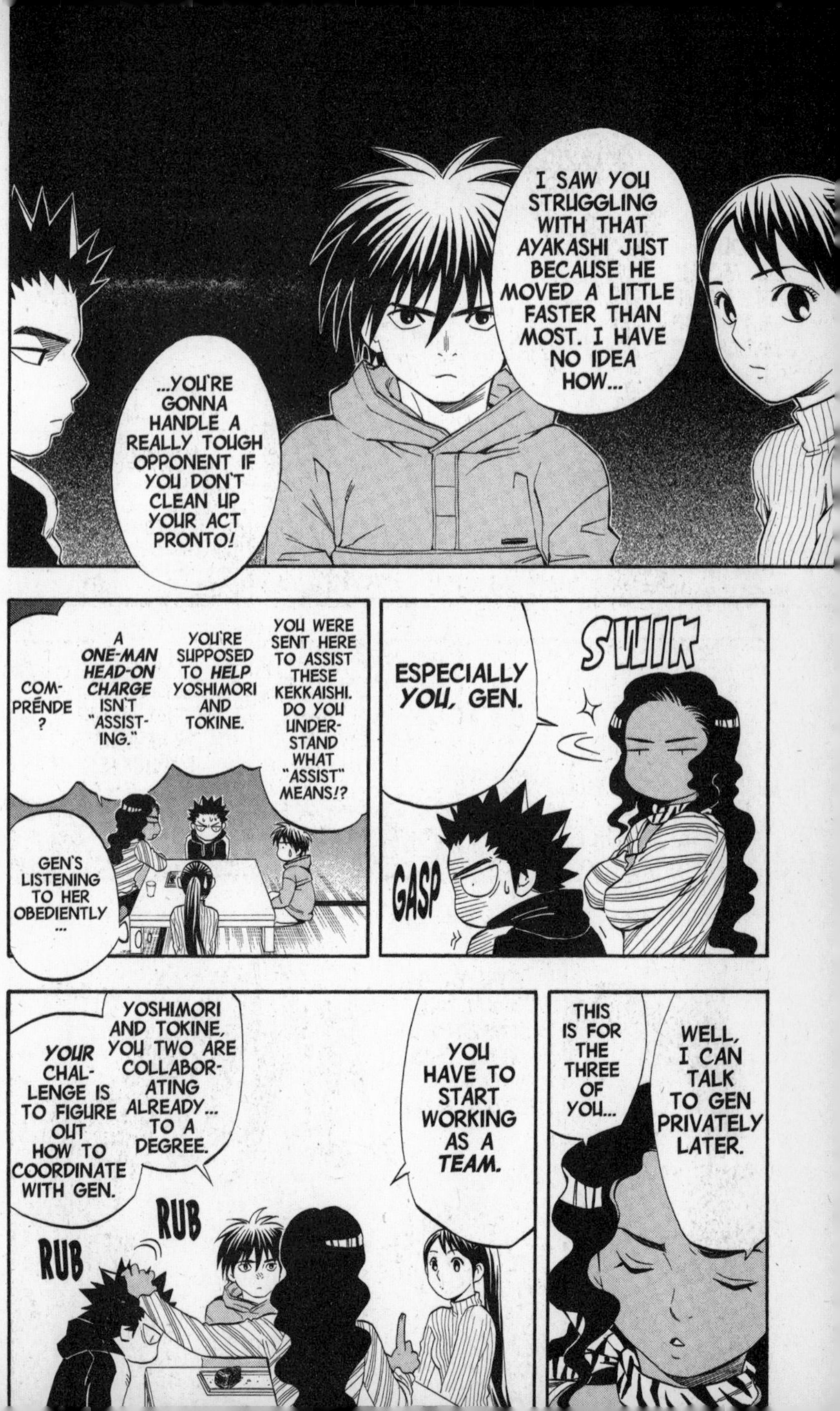
I SAW YOU STRUGGLING WITH THAT AYAKASHI JUST BECAUSE HE MOVED A LITTLE FASTER THAN MOST. I HAVE NO IDEA HOW...
...YOU'RE GONNA HANDLE A REALLY TOUGH OPPONENT IF YOU DON'T CLEAN UP YOUR ACT PRONTO!
SWIK
ESPECIALLY YOU, GEN.
GASP
YOU WERE SENT HERE TO ASSIST THESE KEKKAISHI. DO YOU UNDERSTAND WHAT "ASSIST" MEANS!?
YOU'RE SUPPOSED TO HELP YOSHIMORI AND TOKINE.
A ONE-MAN HEAD-ON CHARGE ISN'T "ASSISTING."
COMPRÉNDE?
GEN'S LISTENING TO HER OBEDIENTLY...
WELL, I CAN TALK TO GEN PRIVATELY LATER.
THIS IS FOR THE THREE OF YOU...
YOU HAVE TO START WORKING AS A TEAM.
YOSHIMORI AND TOKINE, YOU TWO ARE COLLABORATING ALREADY... TO A DEGREE.
YOUR CHALLENGE IS TO FIGURE OUT HOW TO COORDINATE WITH GEN.
RUB
RUB

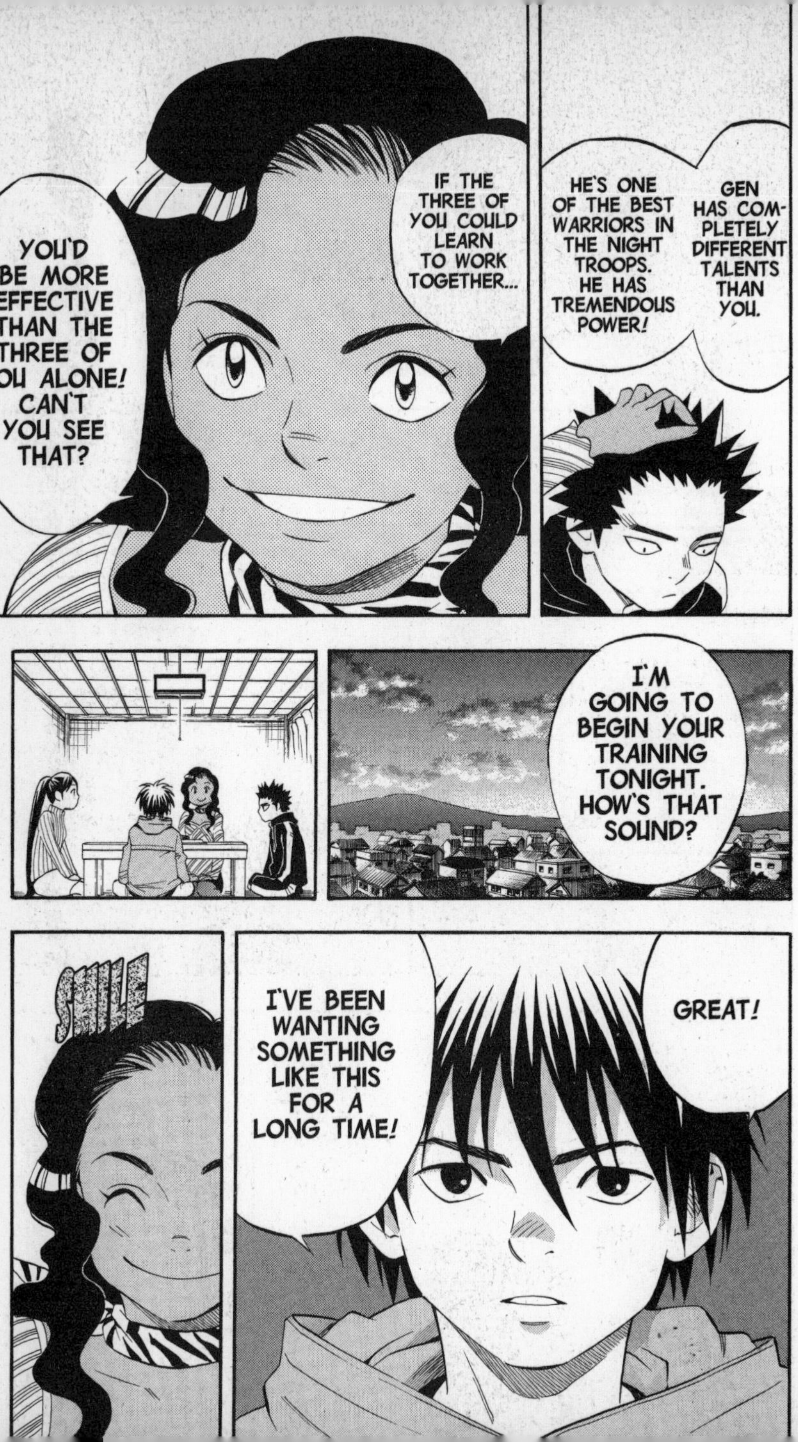
GEN HAS COMPLETELY DIFFERENT TALENTS THAN YOU.
HE'S ONE OF THE BEST WARRIORS IN THE NIGHT TROOPS. HE HAS TREMENDOUS POWER!
IF THE THREE OF YOU COULD LEARN TO WORK TOGETHER...
YOU'D BE MORE EFFECTIVE THAN THE THREE OF YOU ALONE! CAN'T YOU SEE THAT?
I'M GOING TO BEGIN YOUR TRAINING TONIGHT. HOW'S THAT SOUND?
GREAT!
I'VE BEEN WANTING SOMETHING LIKE THIS FOR A LONG TIME!
SMILE

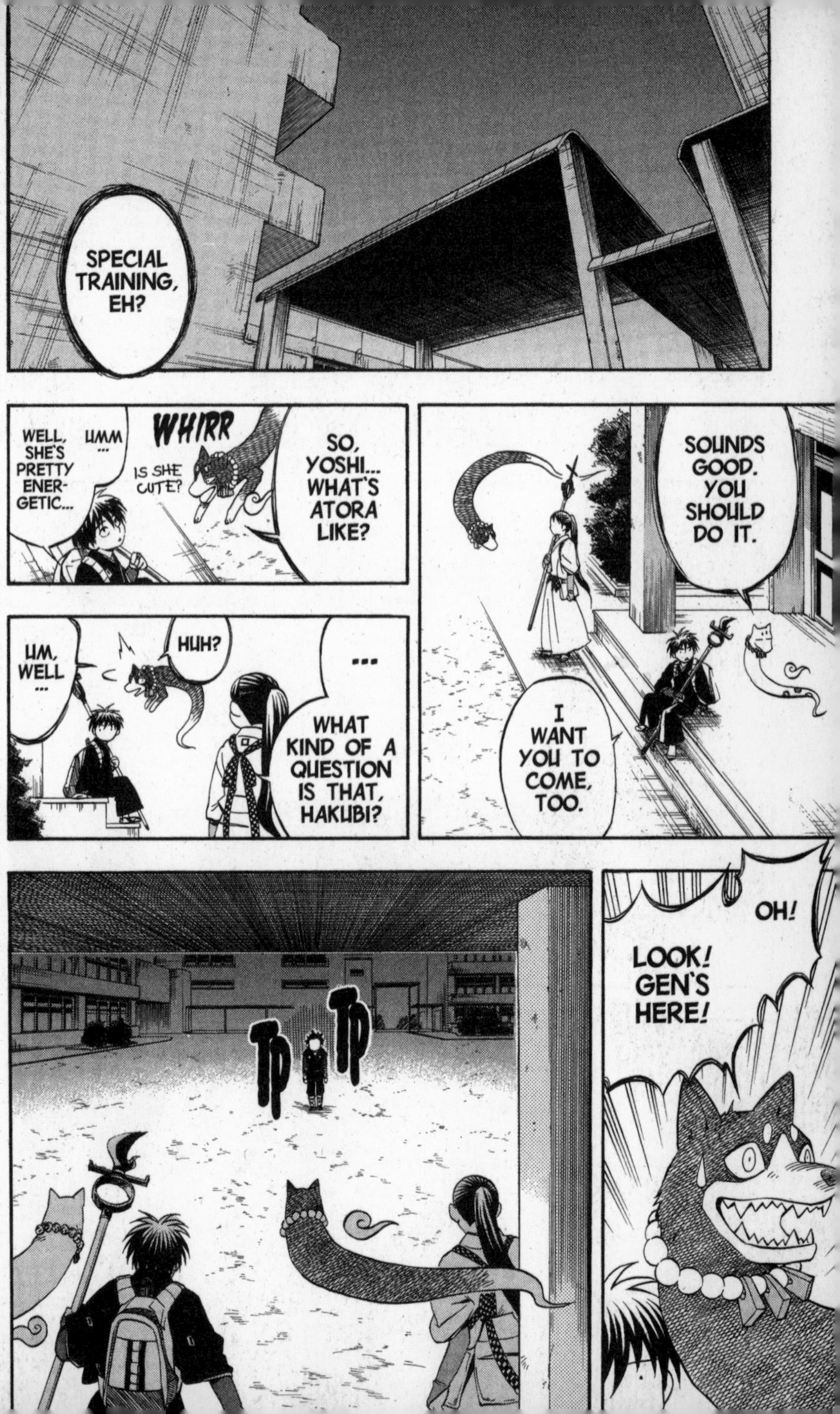
SPECIAL TRAINING, EH?
SOUNDS GOOD. YOU SHOULD DO IT.
I WANT YOU TO COME, TOO.
SO, YOSHI... WHAT'S ATORA LIKE?
WHIRR
IS SHE CUTE?
UMM ...
WELL, SHE'S PRETTY ENER-GETIC...
...
WHAT KIND OF A QUESTION IS THAT, HAKUBI?
HUH?
UM, WELL ...
OH!
LOOK! GEN'S HERE!
TP
TP

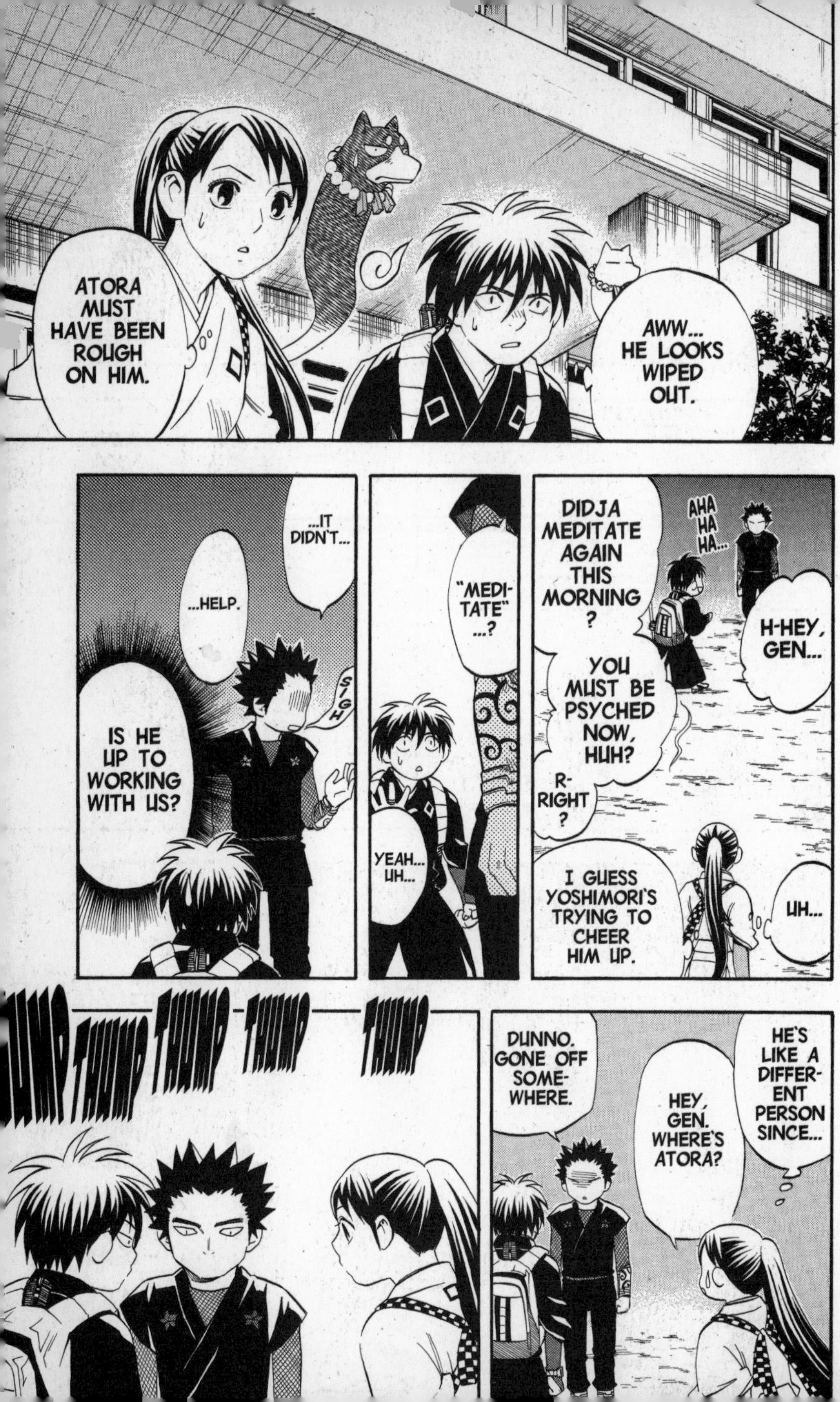
AWW... HE LOOKS WIPED OUT.
ATORA MUST HAVE BEEN ROUGH ON HIM.
AHA HA HA...
H-HEY, GEN...
DIDJA MEDITATE AGAIN THIS MORNING?
YOU MUST BE PSYCHED NOW, HUH?
R-RIGHT?
UH...
I GUESS YOSHIMORI'S TRYING TO CHEER HIM UP.
"MEDI-TATE"...?
YEAH... UH...
...IT DIDN'T...
...HELP.
SIGH
IS HE UP TO WORKING WITH US?
HE'S LIKE A DIFFER-ENT PERSON SINCE...
HEY, GEN. WHERE'S ATORA?
DUNNO. GONE OFF SOME-WHERE.
THUMP
THUMP
THUMP
THUMP
THUMP

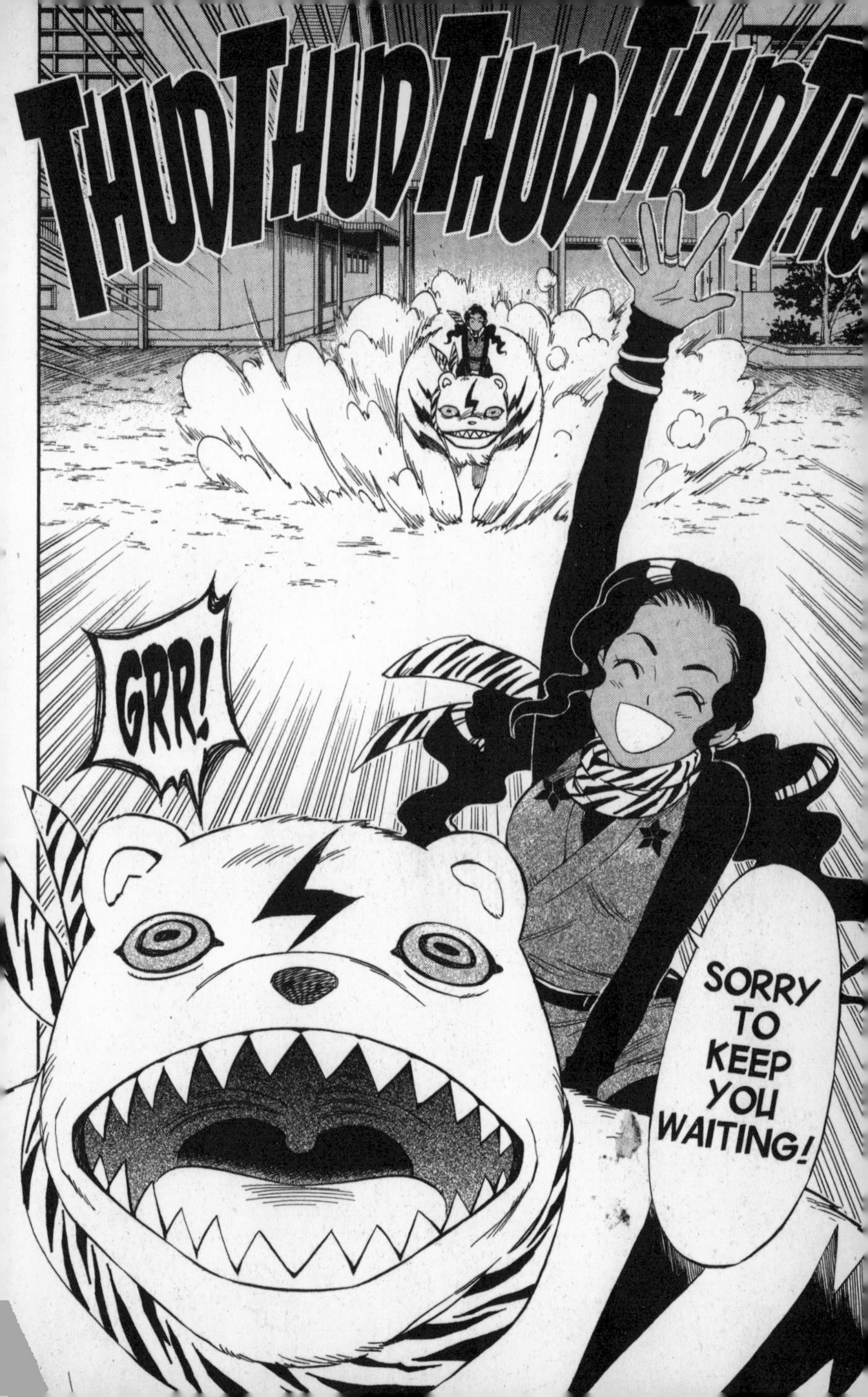
THUD THUD THUD THUD THU
GRR!
SORRY TO KEEP YOU WAITING!

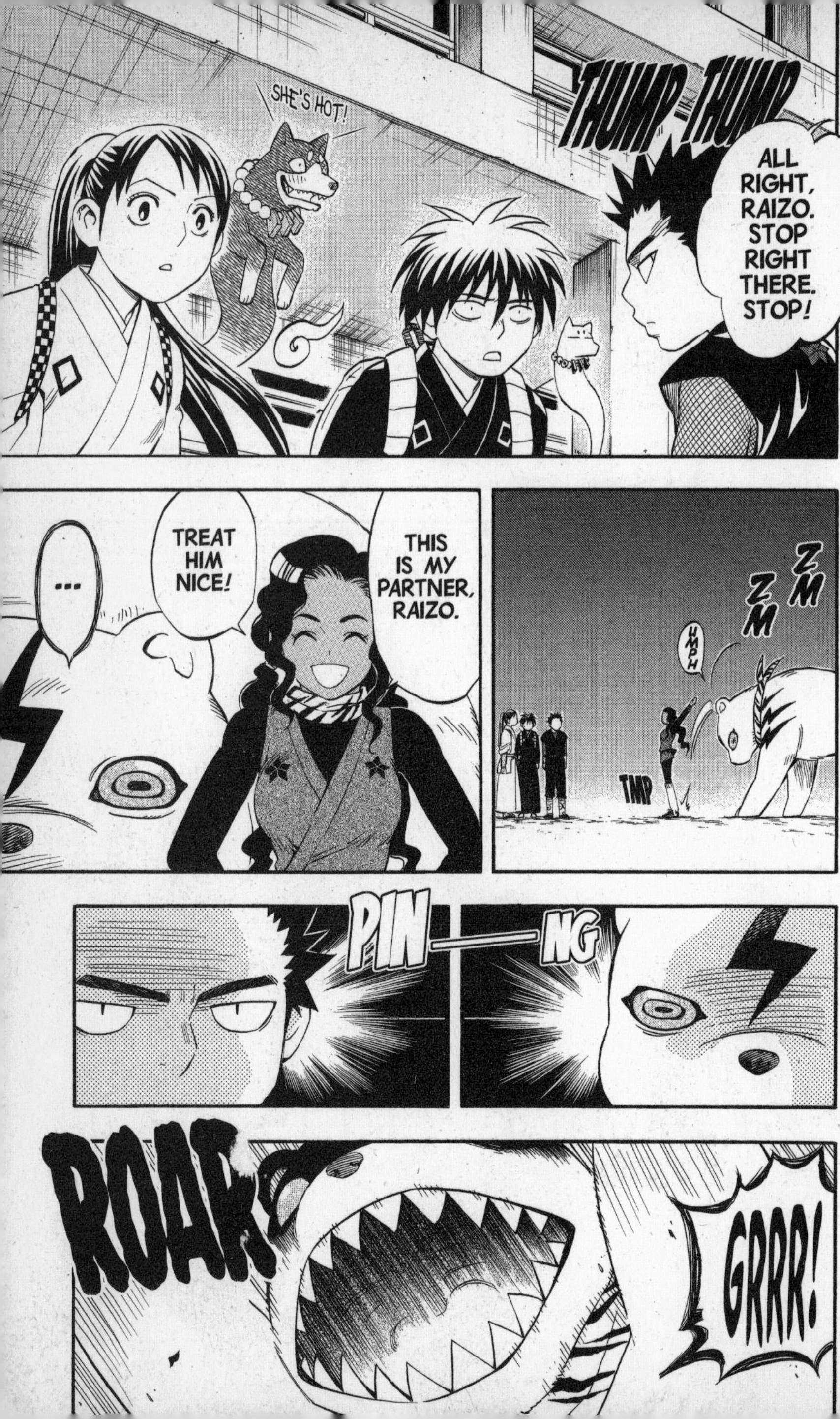
THUMP THUMP
ALL RIGHT, RAIZO. STOP RIGHT THERE. STOP!
SHE'S HOT!
ZM ZM
UMPH
TMP
THIS IS MY PARTNER, RAIZO.
TREAT HIM NICE!
...
PIN—NG
GRRR!
ROAR!

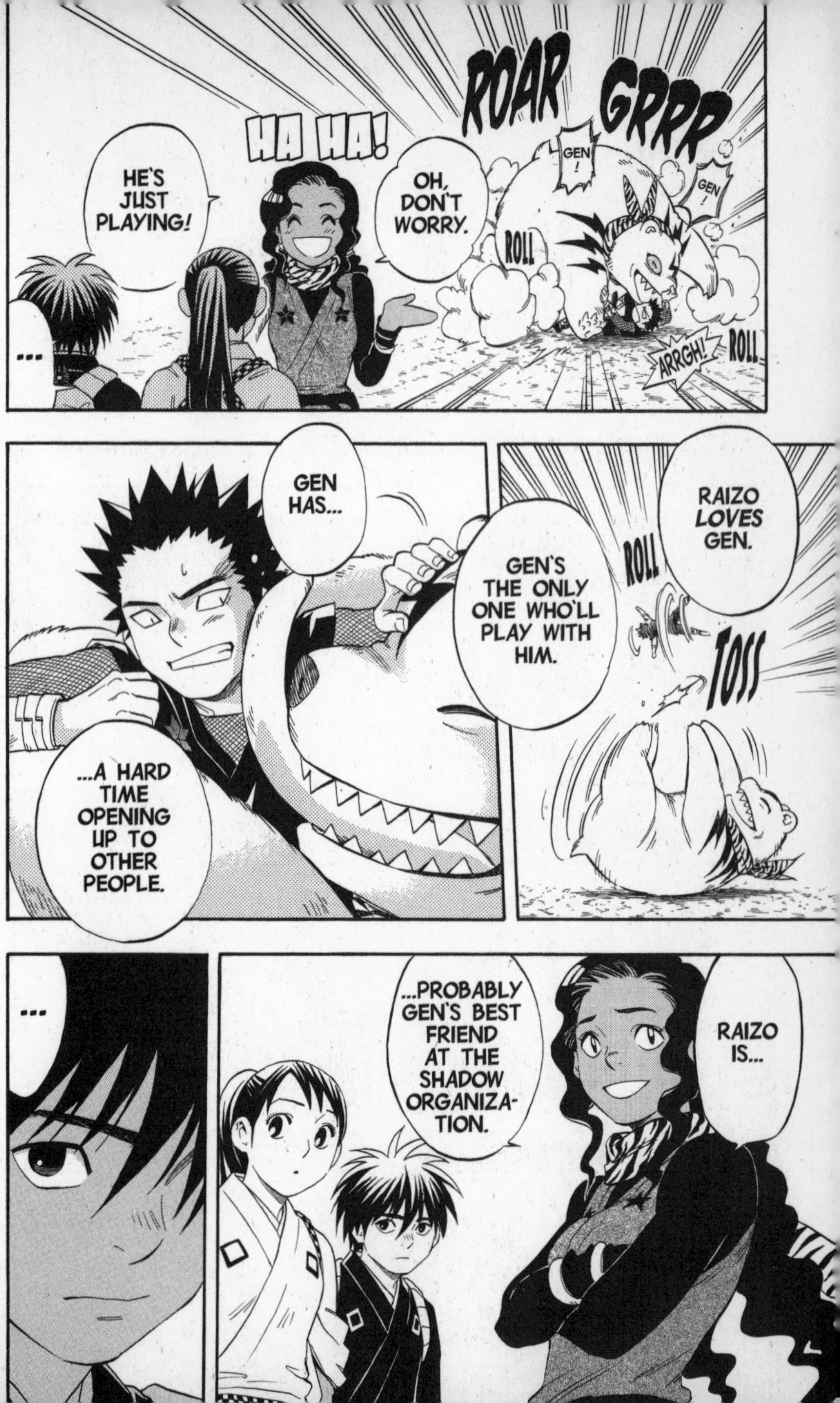
ROAR
GRRR
GEN!
GEN!
OH, DON'T WORRY.
HA HA!
HE'S JUST PLAYING!
ROLL
ROLL
ARRGH!
...
RAIZO LOVES GEN.
ROLL
GEN'S THE ONLY ONE WHO'LL PLAY WITH HIM.
TOSS
GEN HAS...
...A HARD TIME OPENING UP TO OTHER PEOPLE.
RAIZO IS...
...PROBABLY GEN'S BEST FRIEND AT THE SHADOW ORGANIZA-TION.
...

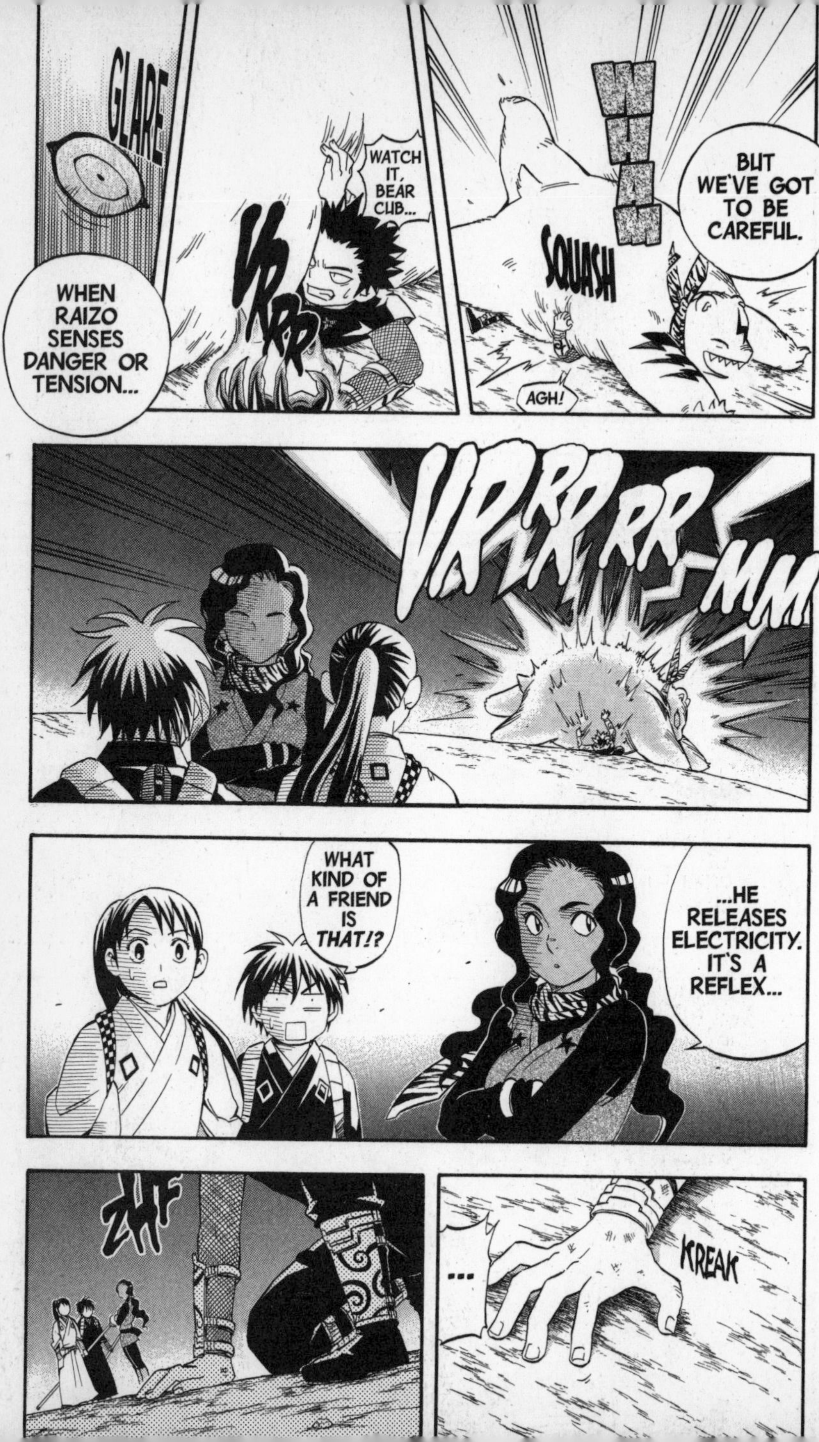
WHAM
BUT WE'VE GOT TO BE CAREFUL.
SQUASH
AGH!
WATCH IT, BEAR CUB...
VRRR
GLARE
WHEN RAIZO SENSES DANGER OR TENSION...
VRRRRRR-MM
...HE RELEASES ELECTRICITY. IT'S A REFLEX...
WHAT KIND OF A FRIEND IS *THAT!?*
KREAK
...
ZHF

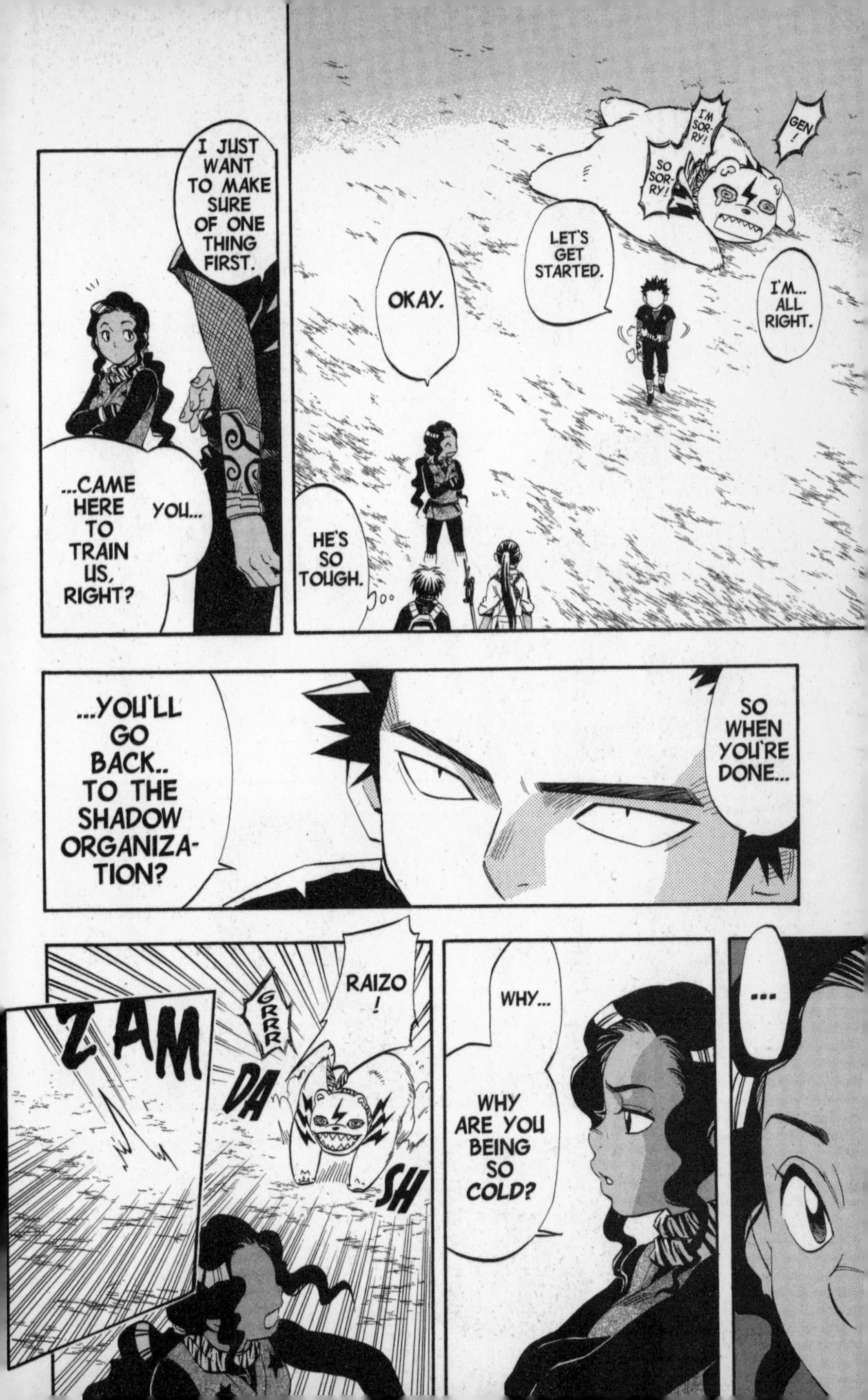
GEN!
I'M SORRY!
SO SORRY!
I'M... ALL RIGHT.
LET'S GET STARTED.
OKAY.
HE'S SO TOUGH.
I JUST WANT TO MAKE SURE OF ONE THING FIRST.
YOU...
...CAME HERE TO TRAIN US, RIGHT?
SO WHEN YOU'RE DONE...
...YOU'LL GO BACK.. TO THE SHADOW ORGANIZATION?
...
WHY...
WHY ARE YOU BEING SO COLD?
RAIZO!
GRRR
ZAM
DA
SH

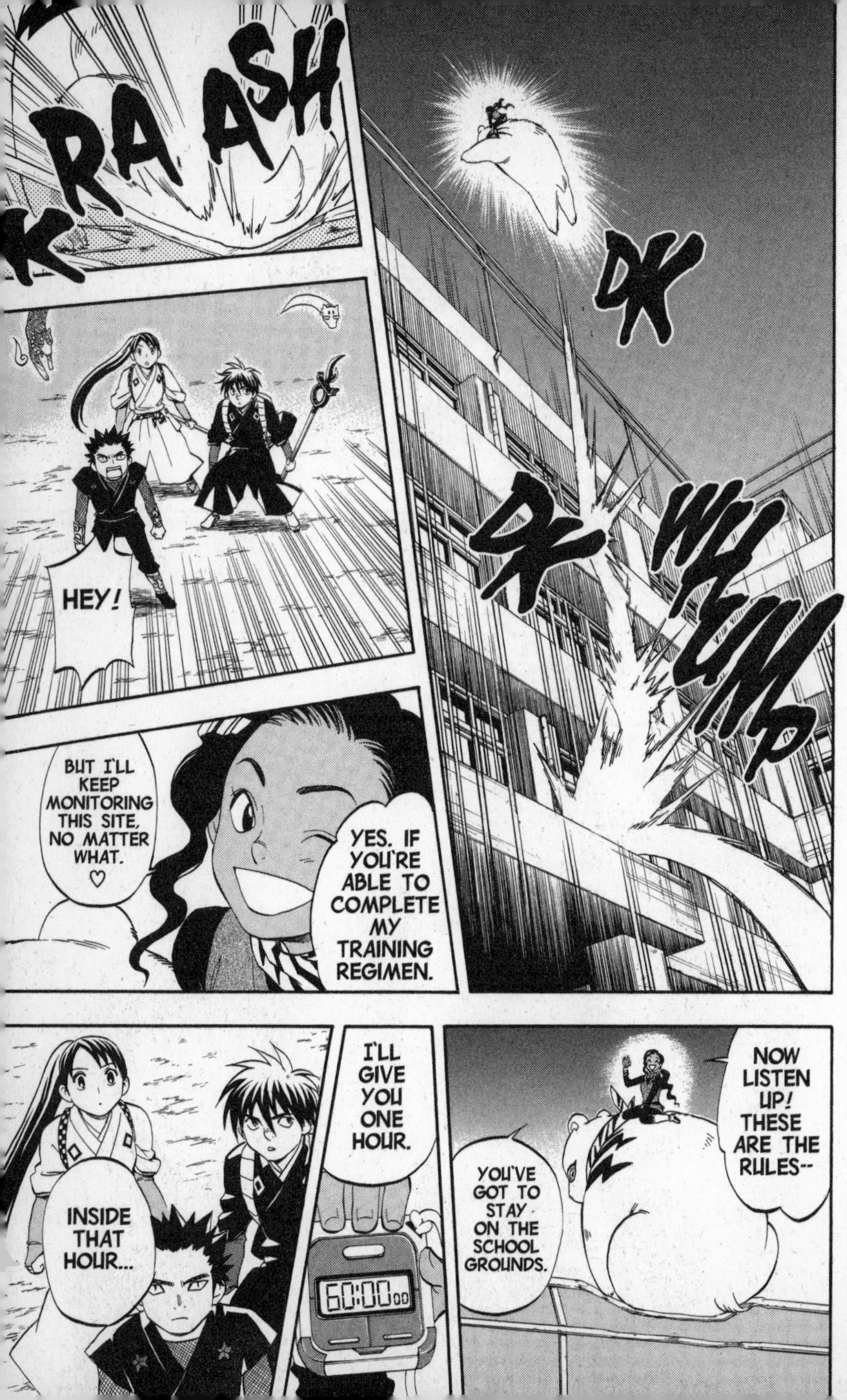
DK
DK
WHUMP
KRASH
HEY!
YES. IF YOU'RE ABLE TO COMPLETE MY TRAINING REGIMEN.
BUT I'LL KEEP MONITORING THIS SITE, NO MATTER WHAT. ♡
NOW LISTEN UP! THESE ARE THE RULES--
YOU'VE GOT TO STAY ON THE SCHOOL GROUNDS.
I'LL GIVE YOU ONE HOUR.
60:00 00
INSIDE THAT HOUR...

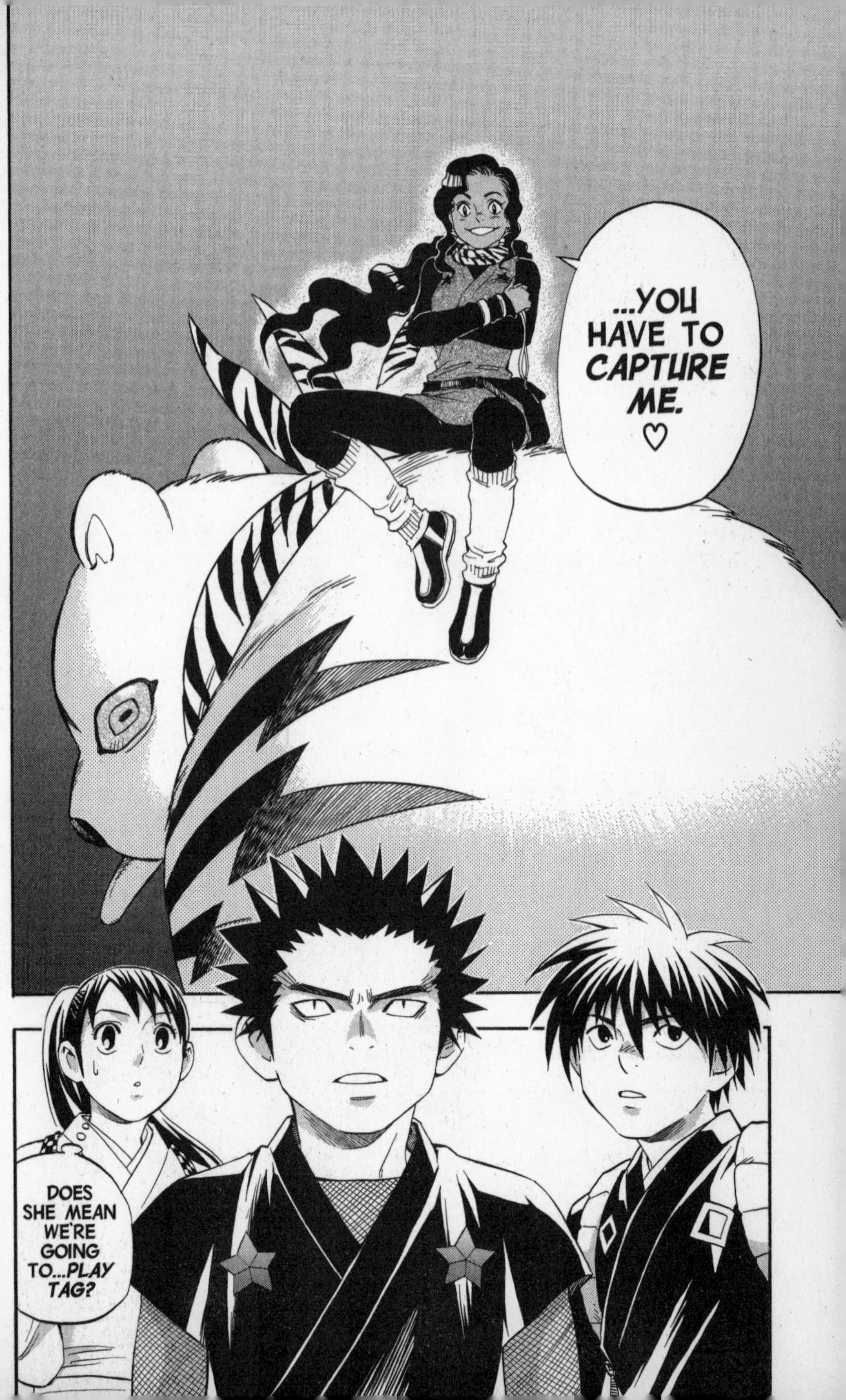
...YOU HAVE TO CAPTURE ME. ♡
DOES SHE MEAN WE'RE GOING TO...PLAY TAG?

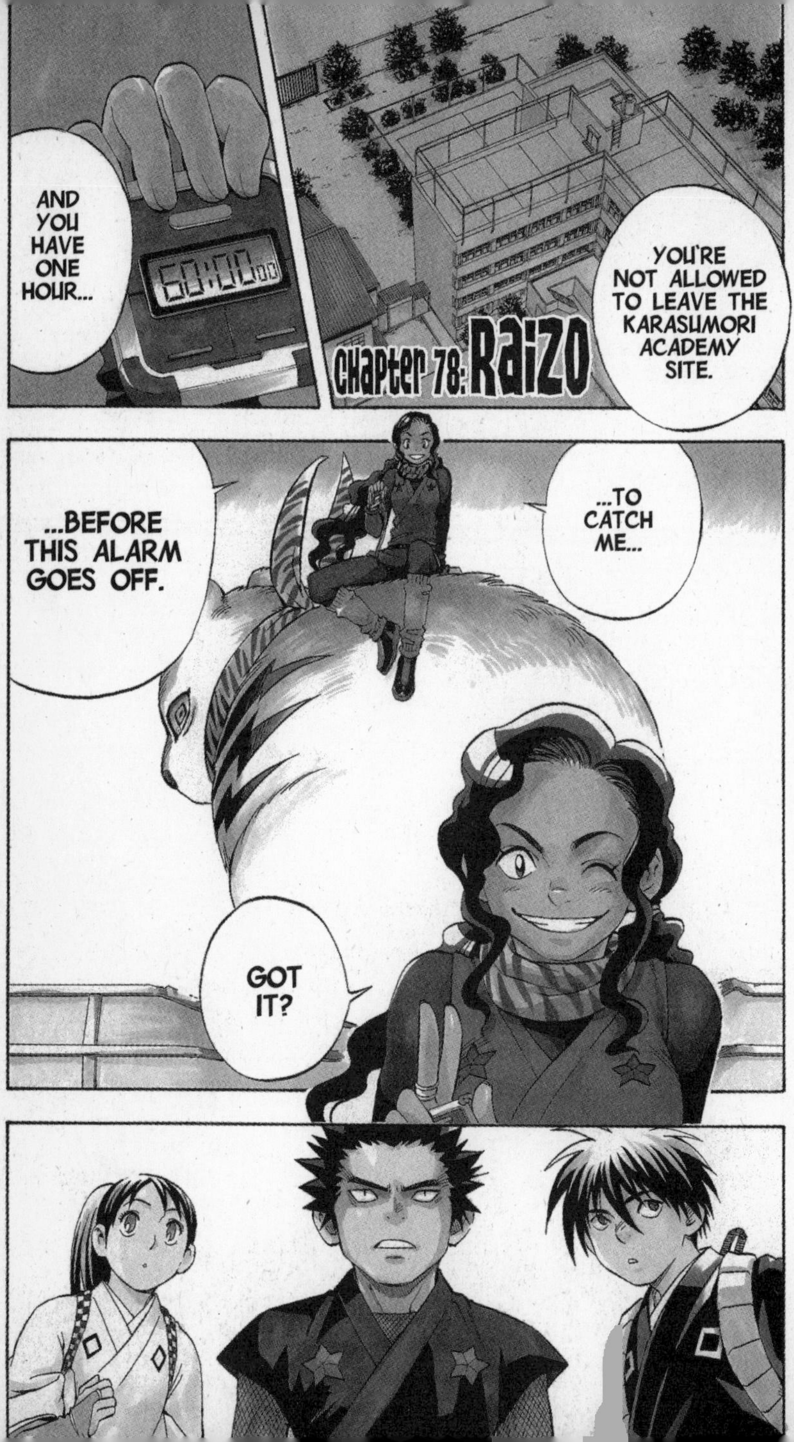
Chapter 78: Raizo
YOU'RE NOT ALLOWED TO LEAVE THE KARASUMORI ACADEMY SITE.
AND YOU HAVE ONE HOUR...
60:00 00
...TO CATCH ME...
...BEFORE THIS ALARM GOES OFF.
GOT IT?

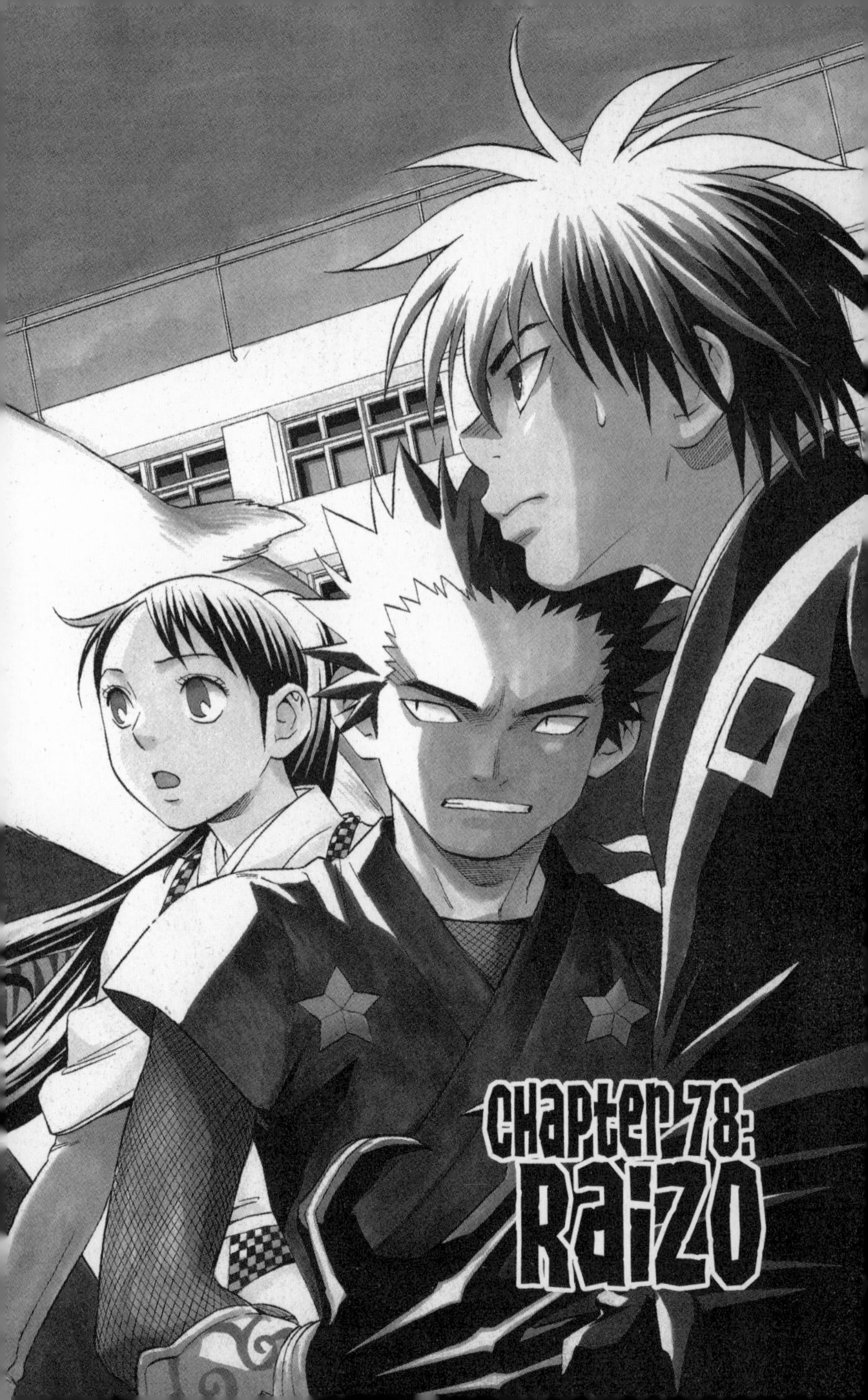
CHAPTER 78:
RAIZO

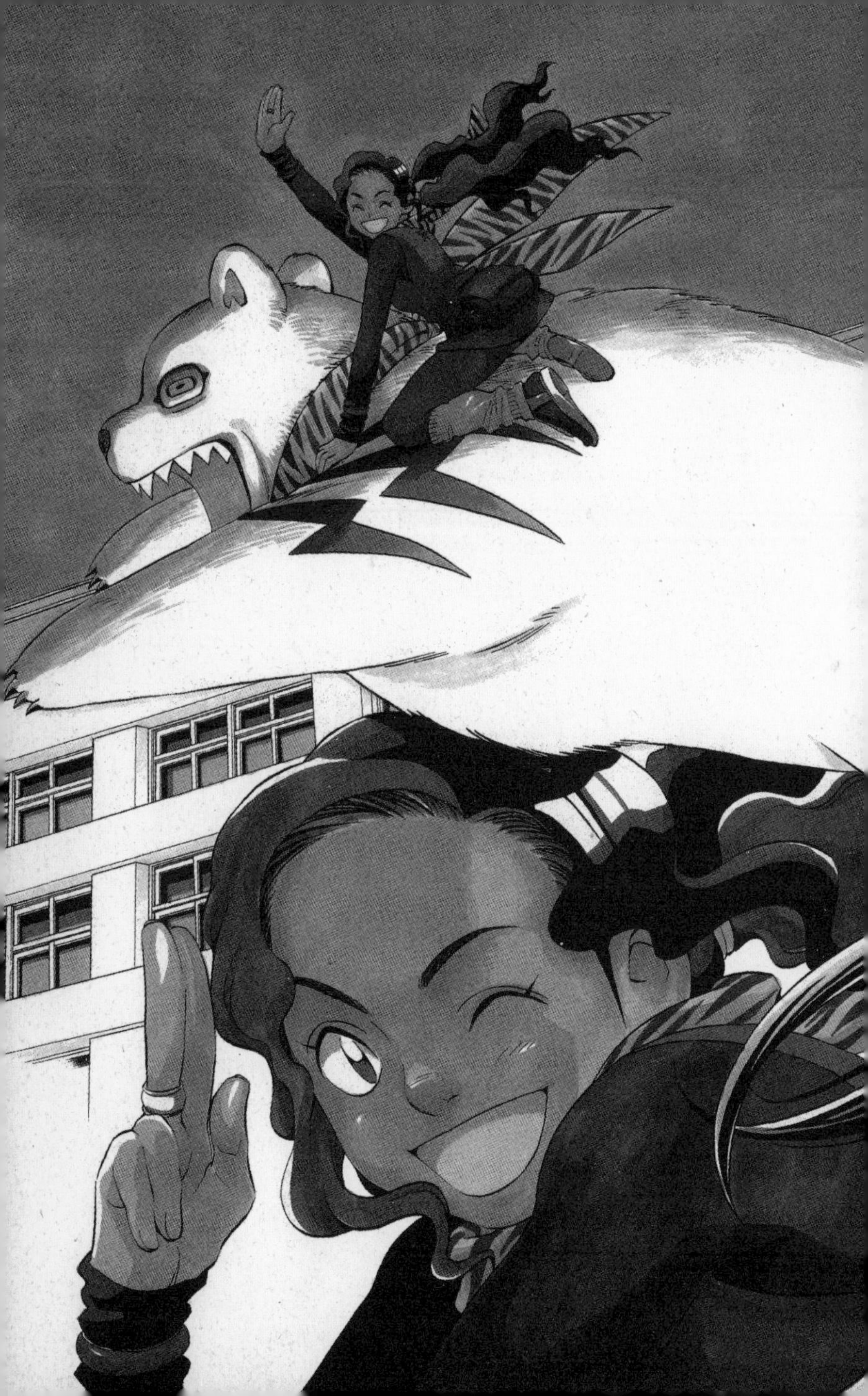

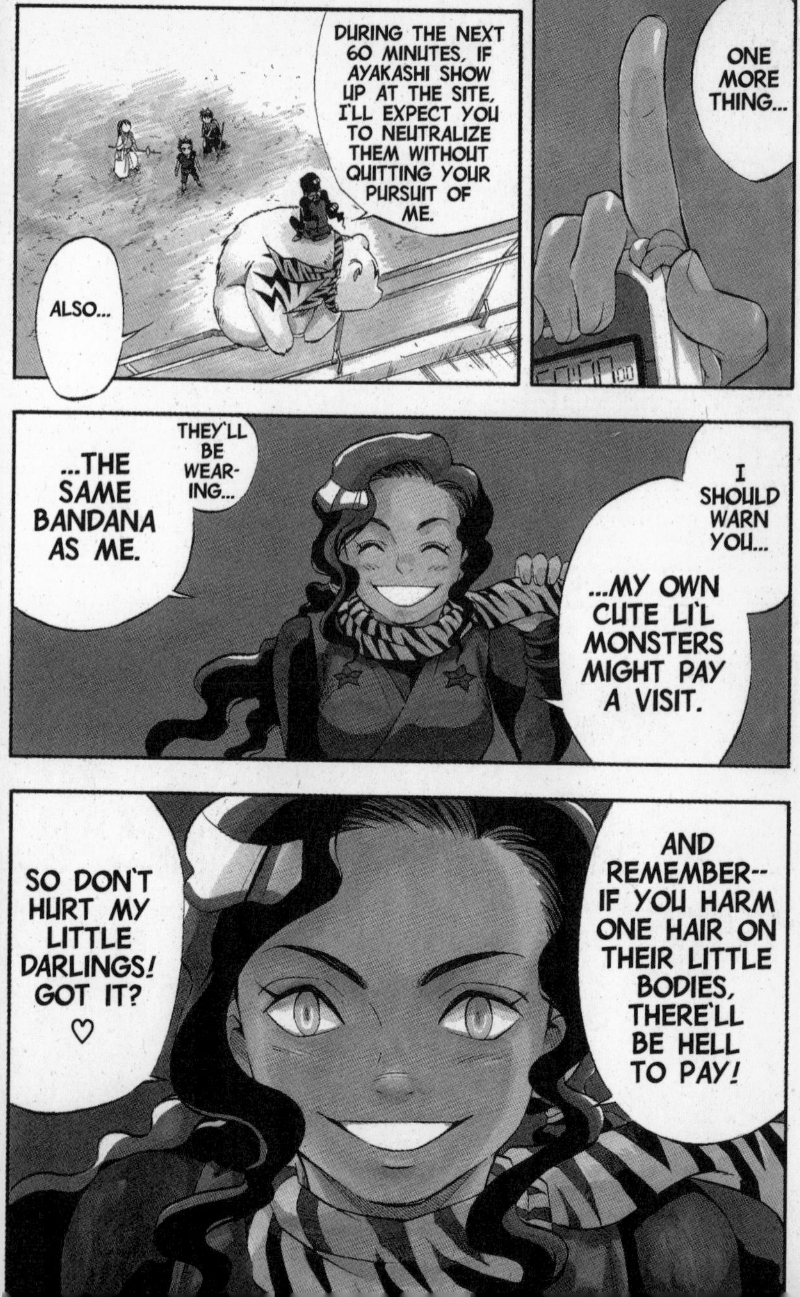
ONE MORE THING...
DURING THE NEXT 60 MINUTES, IF AYAKASHI SHOW UP AT THE SITE, I'LL EXPECT YOU TO NEUTRALIZE THEM WITHOUT QUITTING YOUR PURSUIT OF ME.
ALSO...
I SHOULD WARN YOU...
...MY OWN CUTE LI'L MONSTERS MIGHT PAY A VISIT.
THEY'LL BE WEAR-ING...
...THE SAME BANDANA AS ME.
AND REMEMBER-- IF YOU HARM ONE HAIR ON THEIR LITTLE BODIES, THERE'LL BE HELL TO PAY!
SO DON'T HURT MY LITTLE DARLINGS! GOT IT? ♡

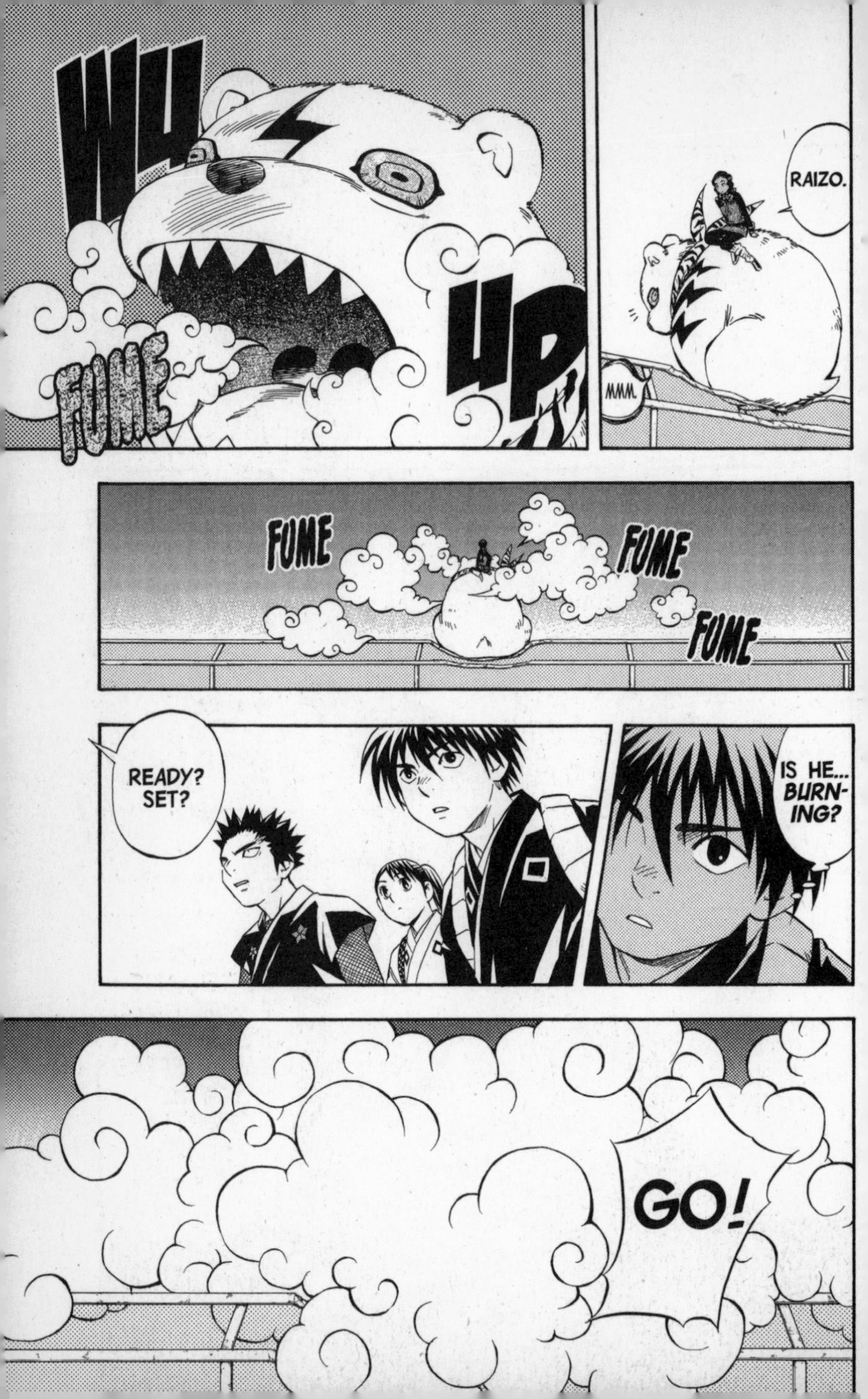
RAIZO.
MMM
WHU
UP
FUME
FUME
FUME
FUME
IS HE... BURN-ING?
READY? SET?
GO!

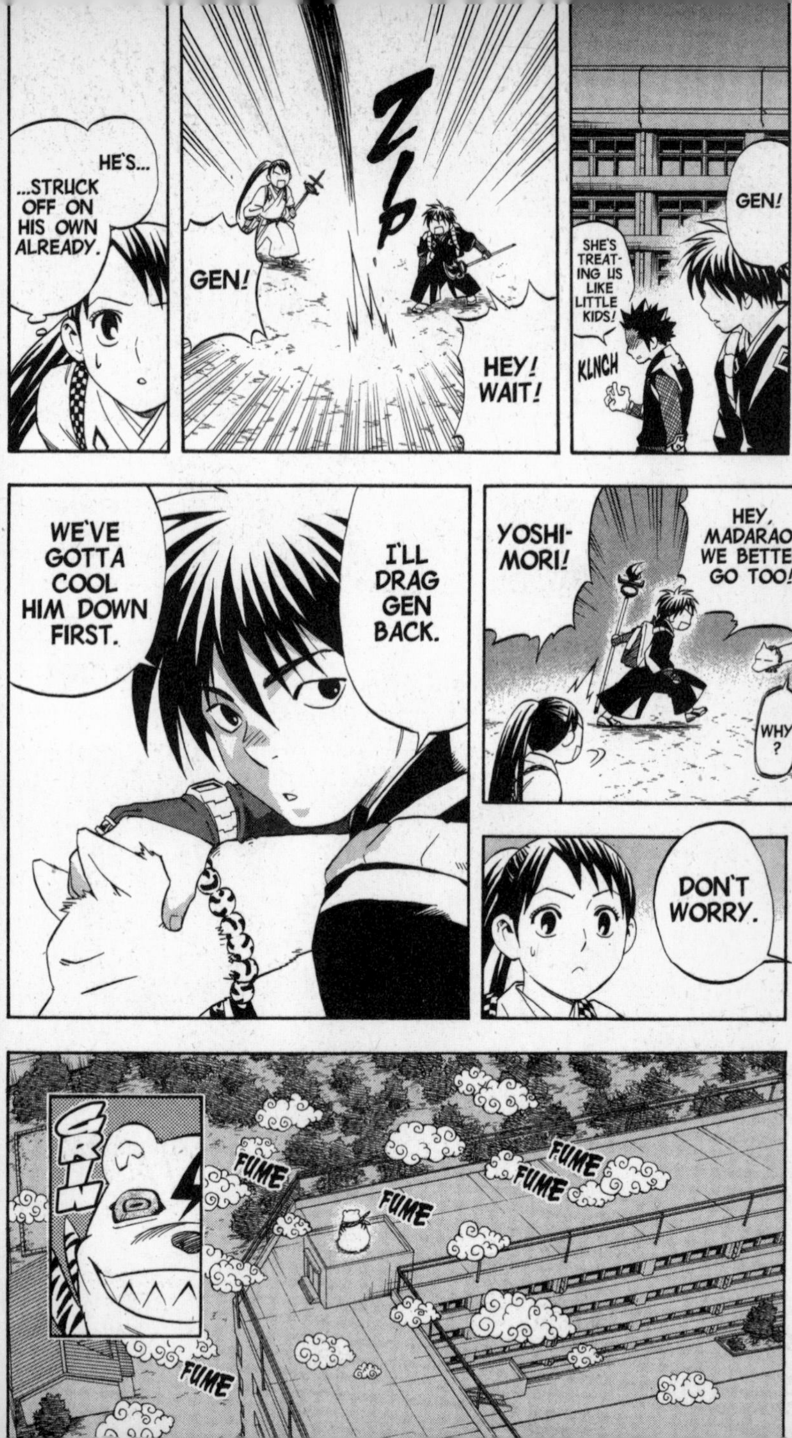
GEN!
SHE'S TREATING US LIKE LITTLE KIDS!
KLNCH
ZIP
GEN!
HEY! WAIT!
HE'S...
...STRUCK OFF ON HIS OWN ALREADY.
HEY, MADARAO! WE BETTER GO TOO!
YOSHIMORI!
WHY?
DON'T WORRY.
I'LL DRAG GEN BACK.
WE'VE GOTTA COOL HIM DOWN FIRST.
FUME
FUME
FUME
FUME
GRIN
FUME

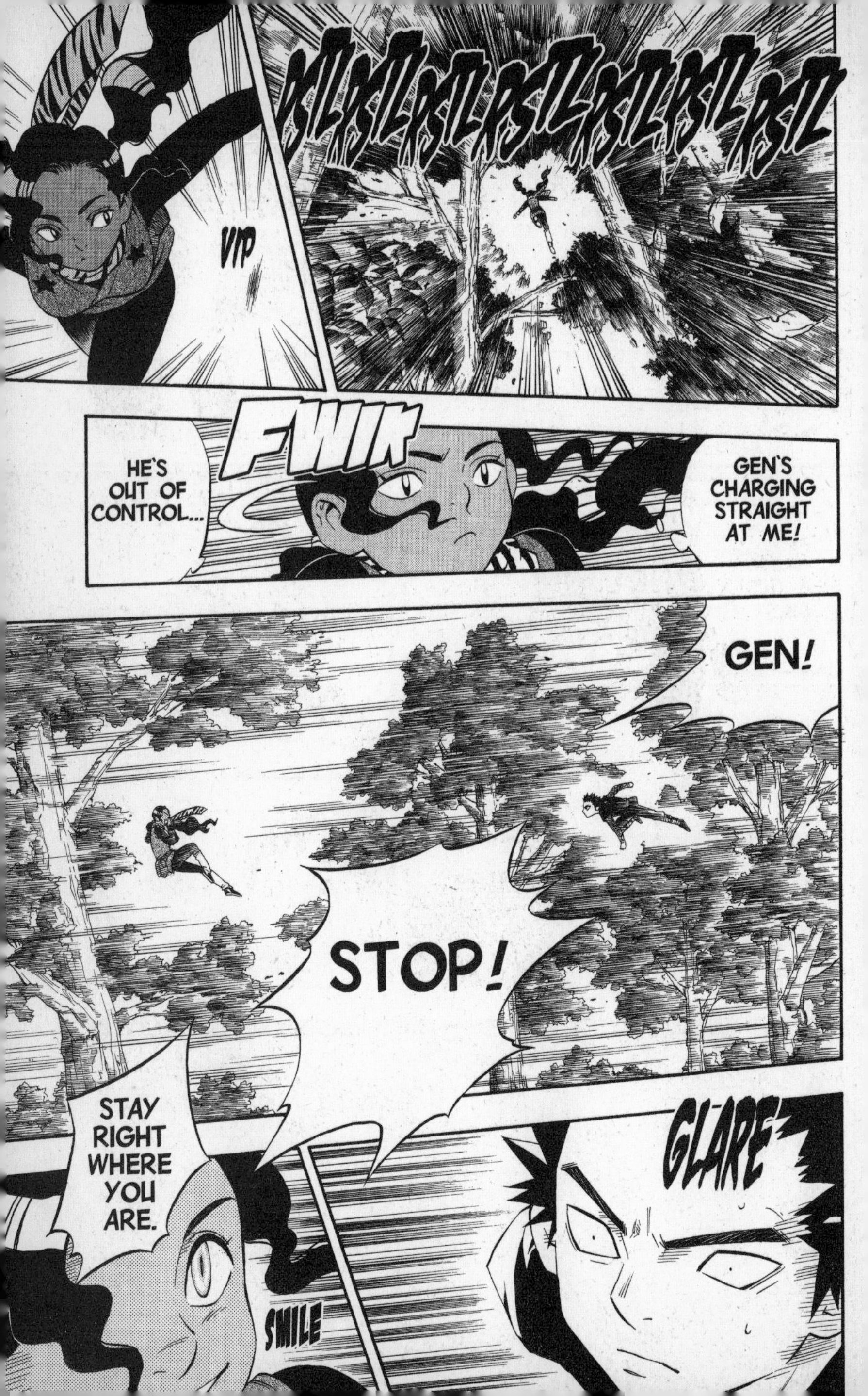
VIP
GEN'S CHARGING STRAIGHT AT ME!
F'WIK
HE'S OUT OF CONTROL...
GEN!
STOP!
GLARE
STAY RIGHT WHERE YOU ARE.
SMILE

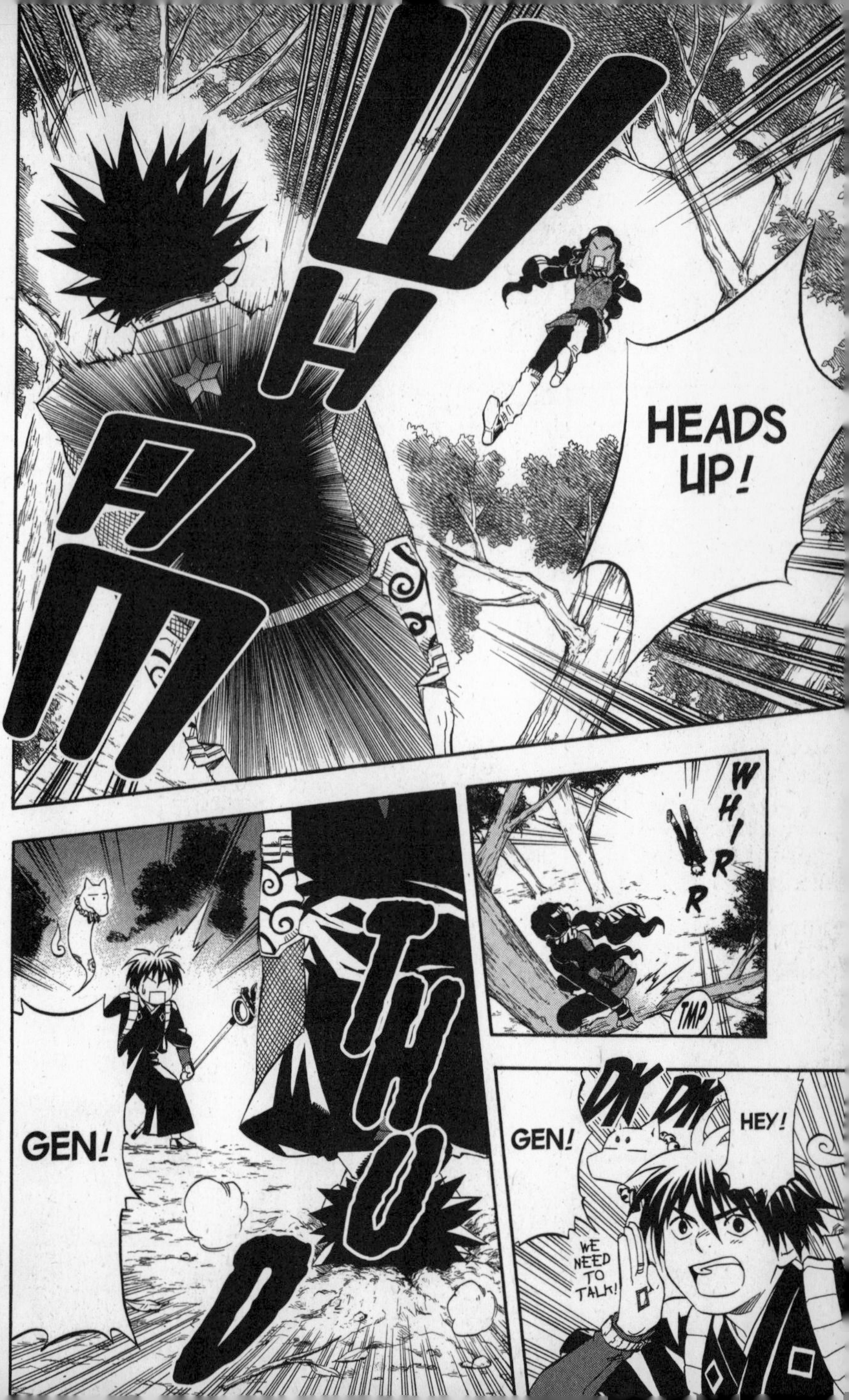
WHAM
HEADS UP!
WHIRR
TMP
DK DK
GEN!
HEY!
WE NEED TO TALK!
GEN!
THUD

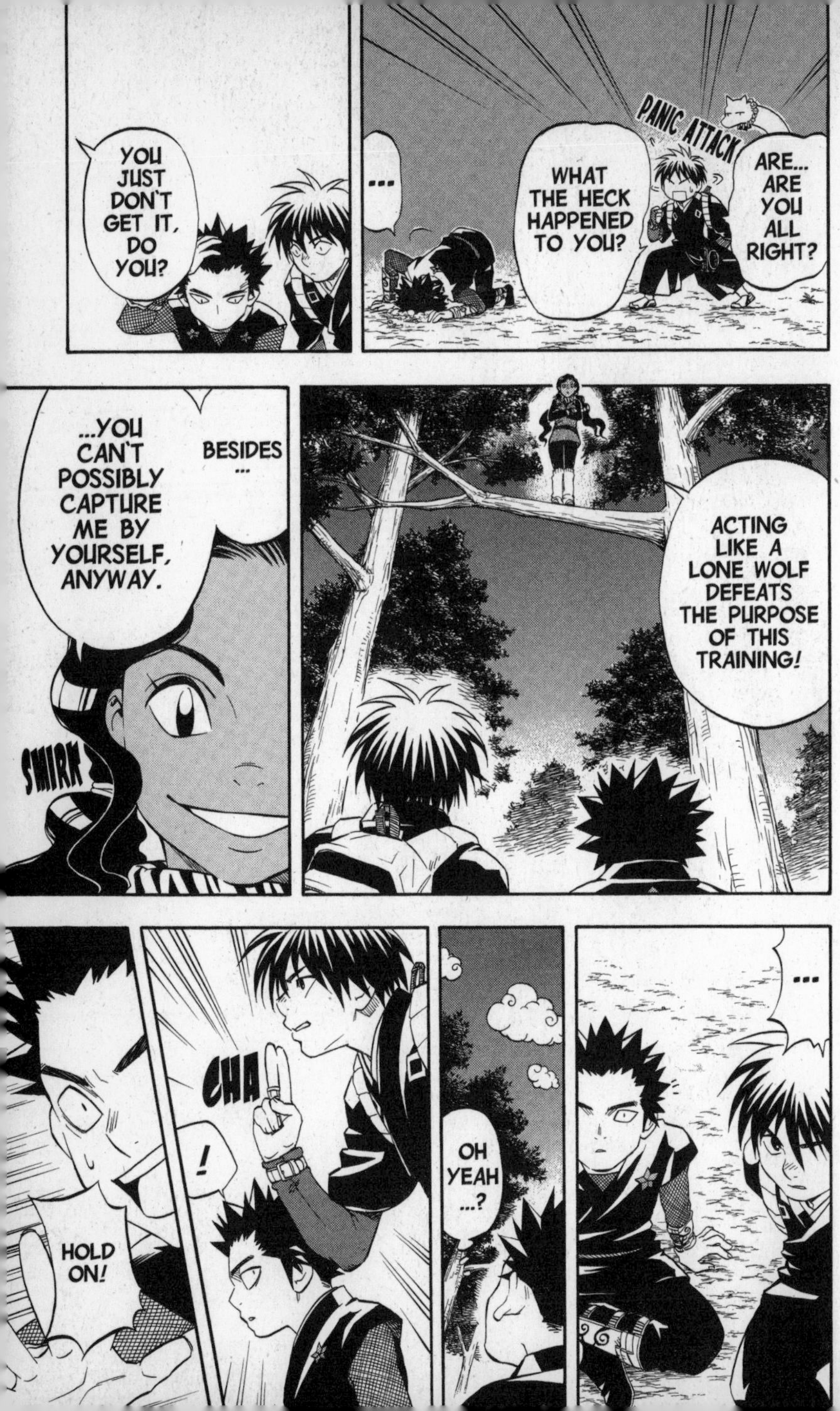
PANIC ATTACK
ARE... ARE YOU ALL RIGHT?
WHAT THE HECK HAPPENED TO YOU?
...
YOU JUST DON'T GET IT, DO YOU?
ACTING LIKE A LONE WOLF DEFEATS THE PURPOSE OF THIS TRAINING!
BESIDES...
...YOU CAN'T POSSIBLY CAPTURE ME BY YOURSELF, ANYWAY.
SMIRK
...
OH YEAH...?
CHA
!
HOLD ON!

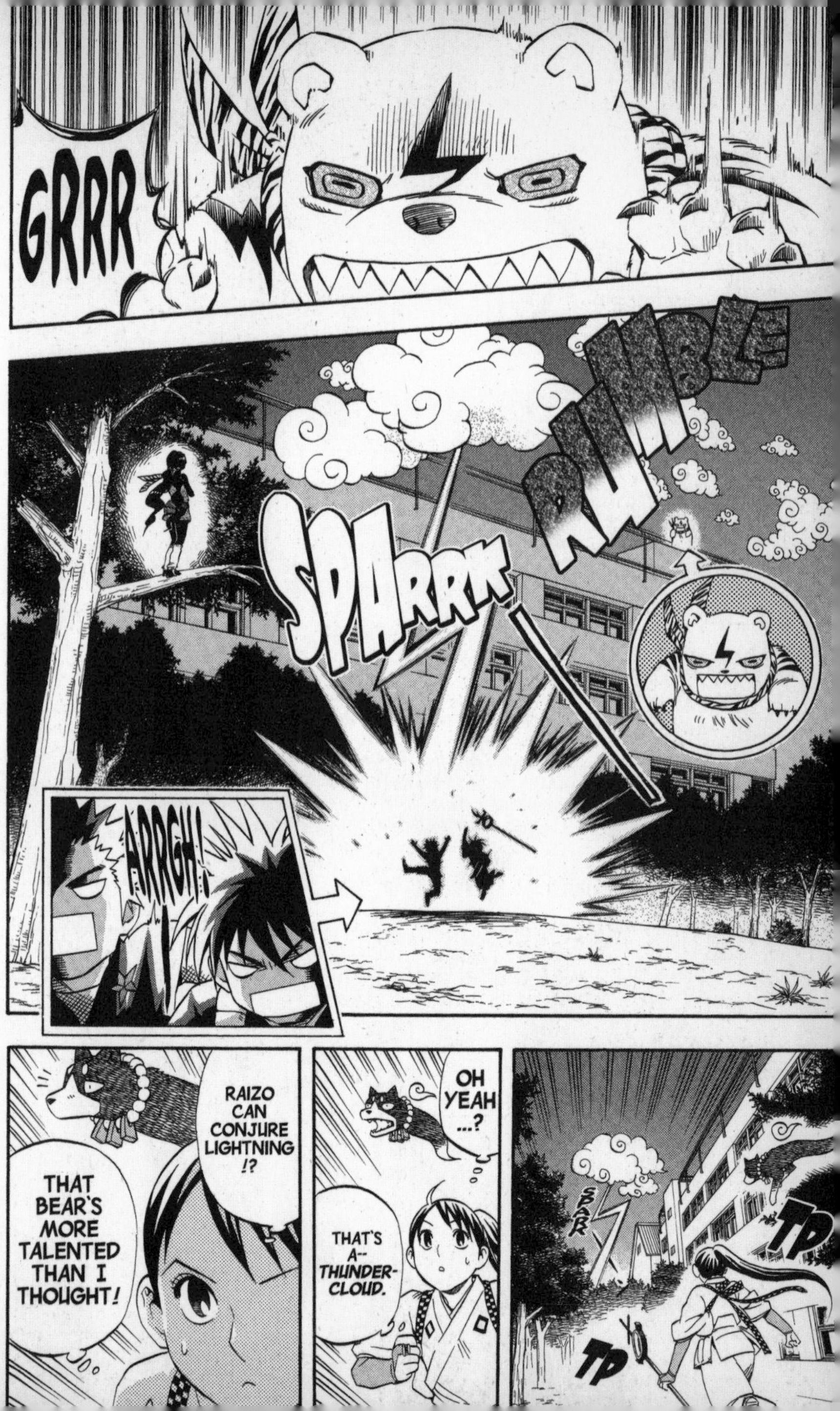
GRRR
RUMBLE
SPARRK
ARRGH!
SPARK
TP
TP
OH YEAH ...?
THAT'S A-- THUNDER-CLOUD.
RAIZO CAN CONJURE LIGHTNING !?
THAT BEAR'S MORE TALENTED THAN I THOUGHT!

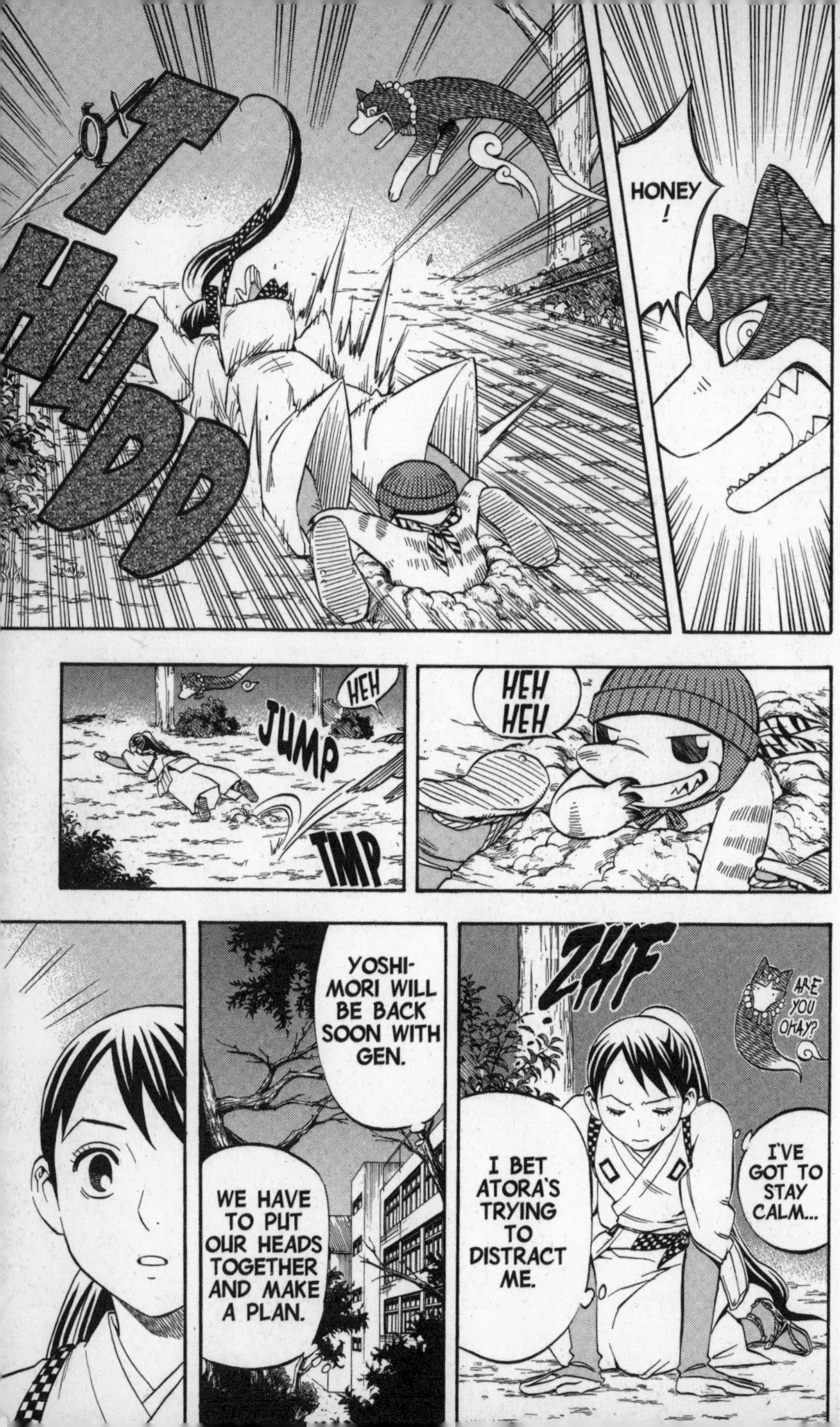
HONEY!
THUDD
HEH HEH
HEH
JUMP
TMP
ZHF
ARE YOU OKAY?
I'VE GOT TO STAY CALM...
I BET ATORA'S TRYING TO DISTRACT ME.
YOSHI-MORI WILL BE BACK SOON WITH GEN.
WE HAVE TO PUT OUR HEADS TOGETHER AND MAKE A PLAN.

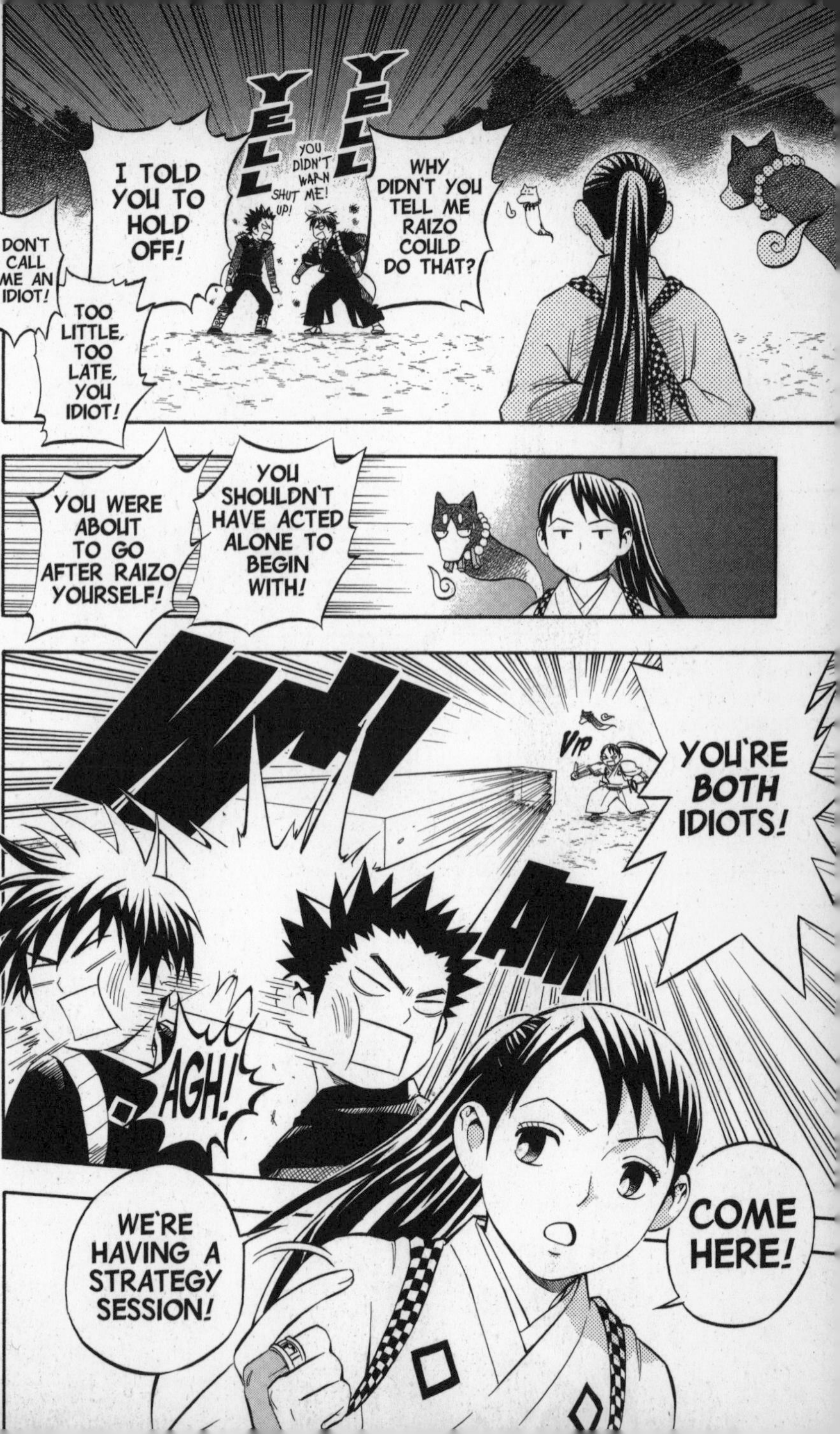
YELL
YELL
WHY DIDN'T YOU TELL ME RAIZO COULD DO THAT?
YOU DIDN'T WARN ME!
SHUT UP!
I TOLD YOU TO HOLD OFF!
DON'T CALL ME AN IDIOT!
TOO LITTLE, TOO LATE, YOU IDIOT!
YOU SHOULDN'T HAVE ACTED ALONE TO BEGIN WITH!
YOU WERE ABOUT TO GO AFTER RAIZO YOURSELF!
YOU'RE BOTH IDIOTS!
VIP
WHAM
AGH!
COME HERE!
WE'RE HAVING A STRATEGY SESSION!

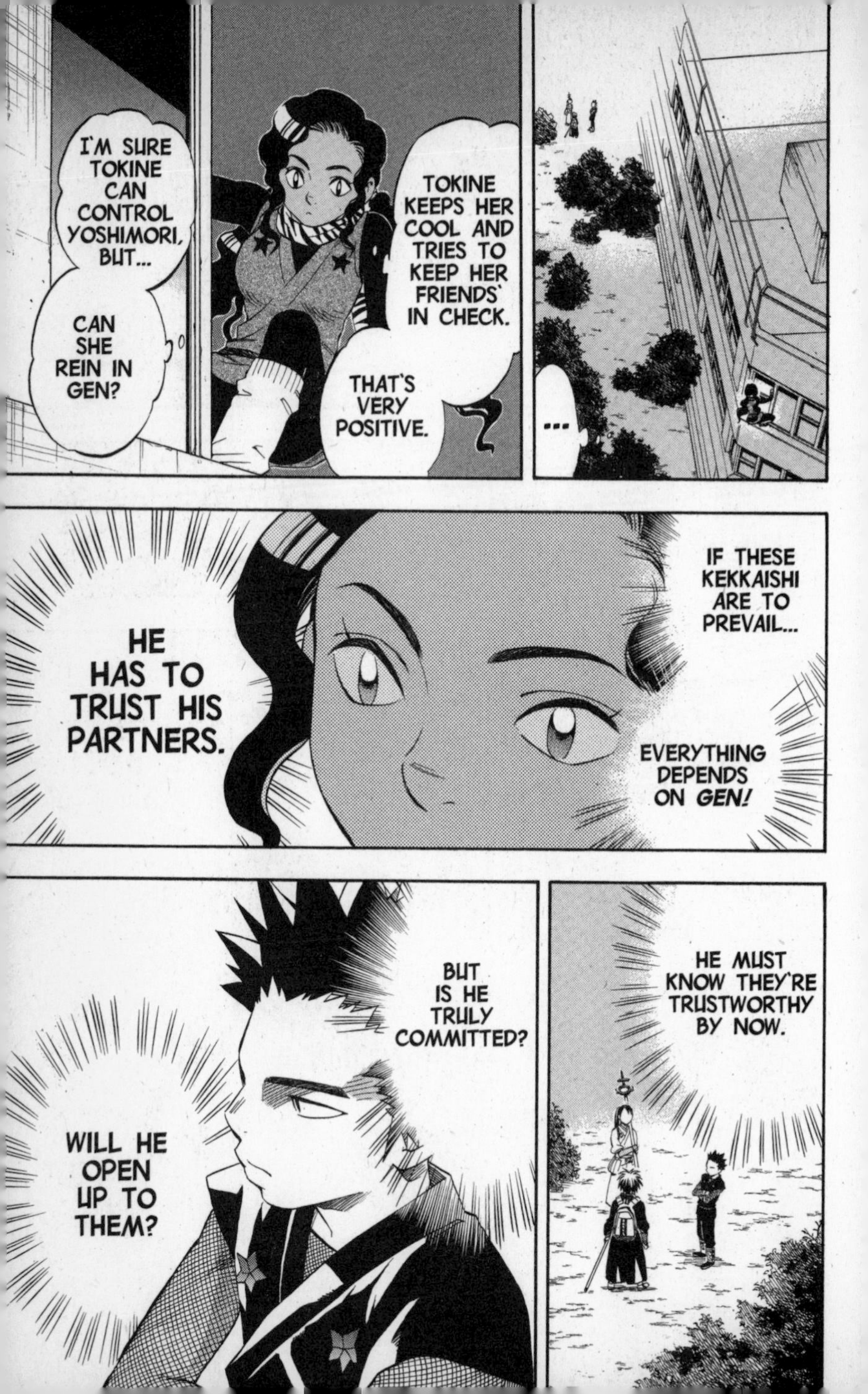
...
TOKINE KEEPS HER COOL AND TRIES TO KEEP HER FRIENDS' IN CHECK.
THAT'S VERY POSITIVE.
I'M SURE TOKINE CAN CONTROL YOSHIMORI, BUT...
CAN SHE REIN IN GEN?
IF THESE KEKKAISHI ARE TO PREVAIL...
EVERYTHING DEPENDS ON *GEN!*
HE HAS TO TRUST HIS PARTNERS.
HE MUST KNOW THEY'RE TRUSTWORTHY BY NOW.
BUT IS HE TRULY COMMITTED?
WILL HE OPEN UP TO THEM?

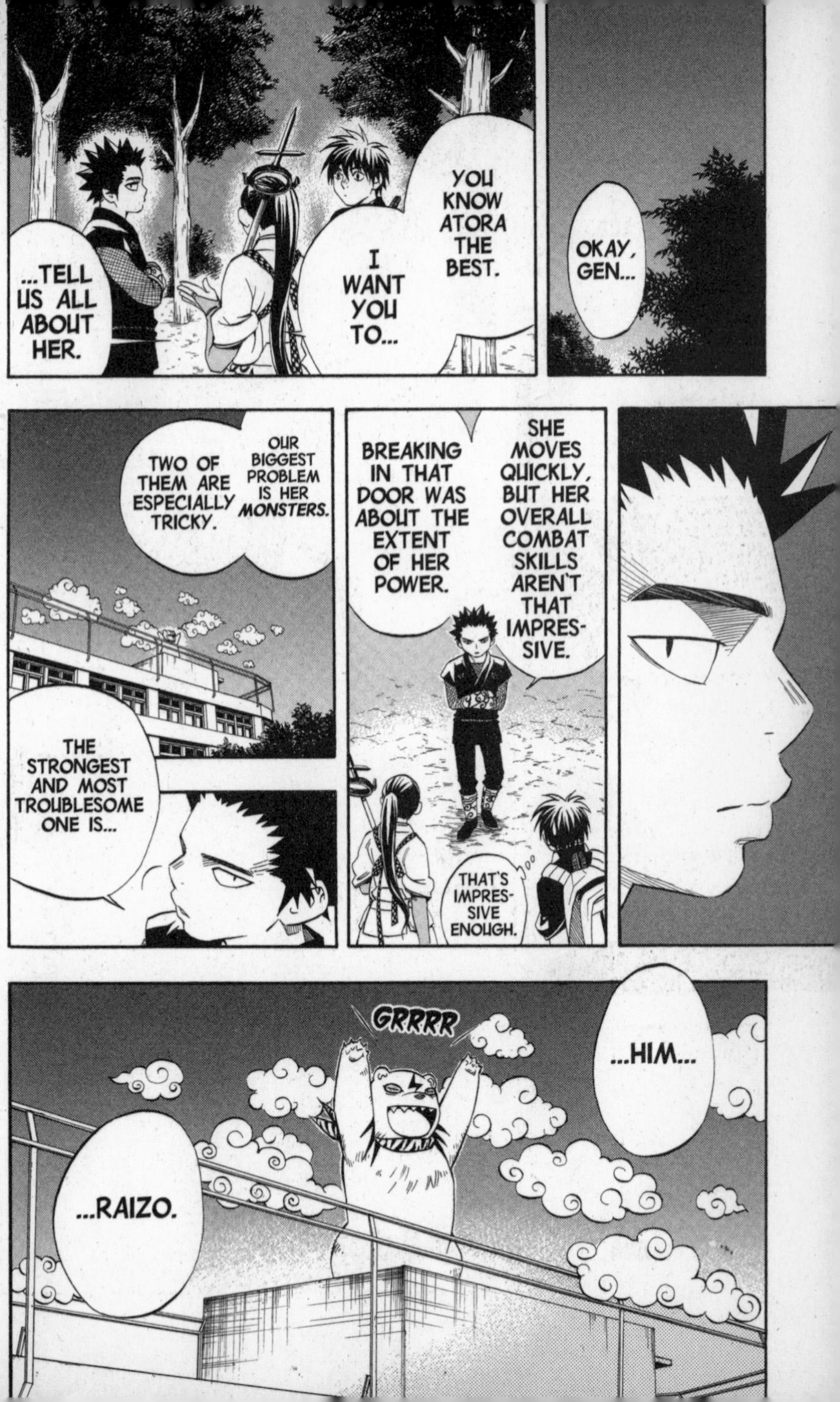
OKAY, GEN...
YOU KNOW ATORA THE BEST.
I WANT YOU TO...
...TELL US ALL ABOUT HER.
SHE MOVES QUICKLY, BUT HER OVERALL COMBAT SKILLS AREN'T THAT IMPRES-SIVE.
BREAKING IN THAT DOOR WAS ABOUT THE EXTENT OF HER POWER.
THAT'S IMPRES-SIVE ENOUGH.
OUR BIGGEST PROBLEM IS HER *MONSTERS.*
TWO OF THEM ARE ESPECIALLY TRICKY.
THE STRONGEST AND MOST TROUBLESOME ONE IS...
...HIM...
GRRRR
...RAIZO.

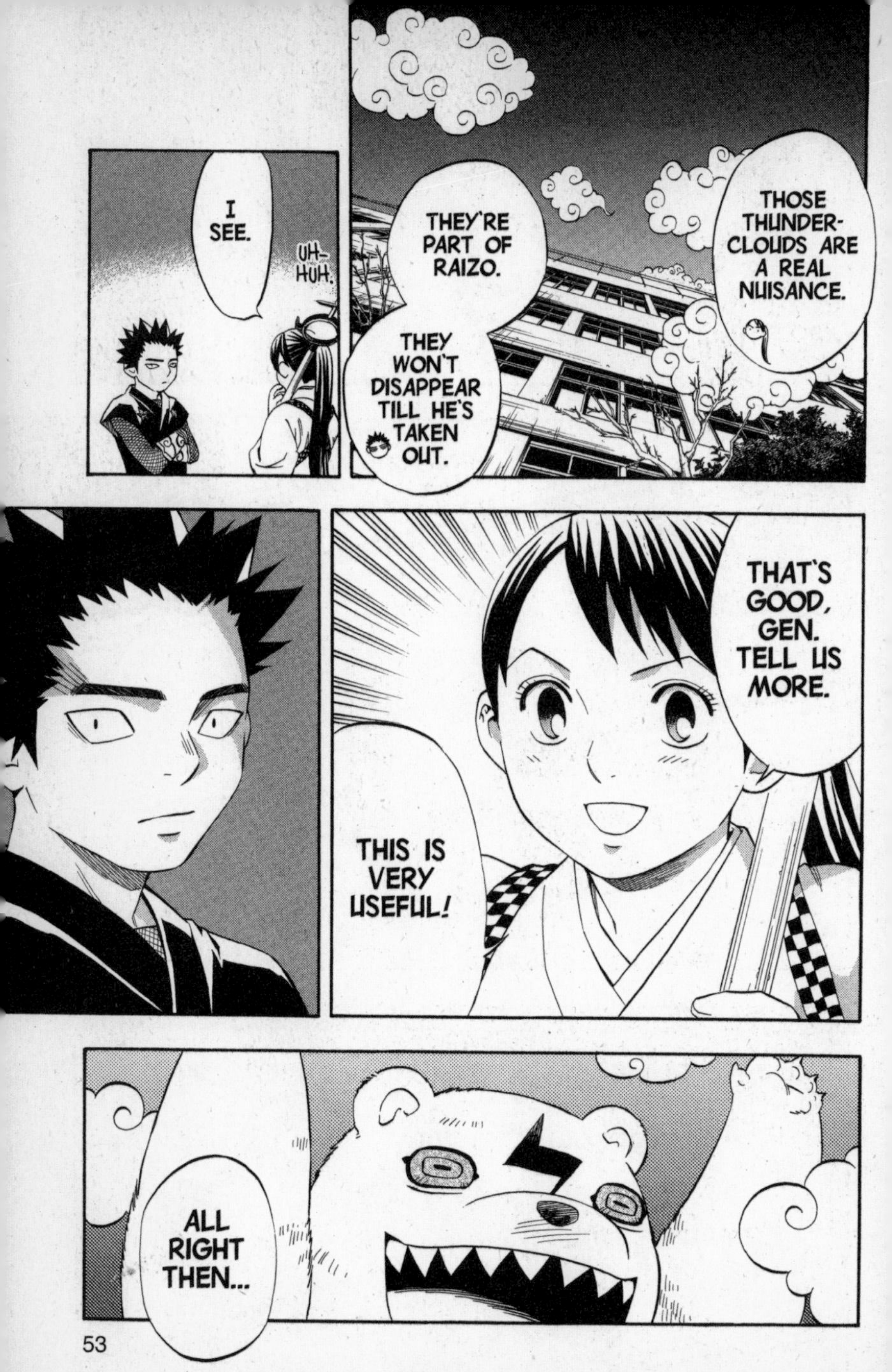

THOSE THUNDER-CLOUDS ARE A REAL NUISANCE.
THEY'RE PART OF RAIZO.
THEY WON'T DISAPPEAR TILL HE'S TAKEN OUT.
I SEE.
UH-HUH.
THAT'S GOOD, GEN. TELL US MORE.
THIS IS VERY USEFUL!
ALL RIGHT THEN...

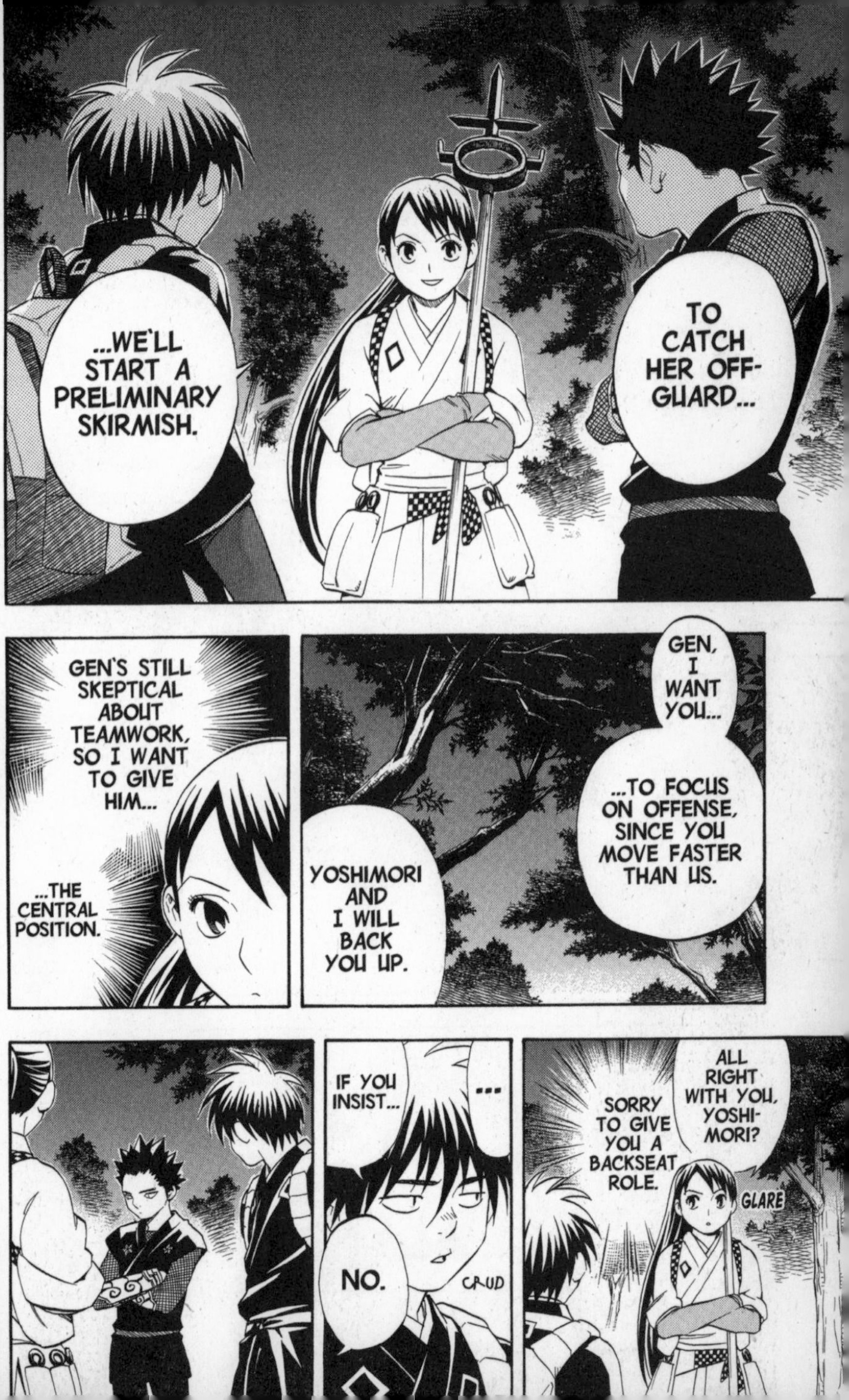
TO CATCH HER OFF-GUARD...
...WE'LL START A PRELIMINARY SKIRMISH.
GEN, I WANT YOU...
...TO FOCUS ON OFFENSE, SINCE YOU MOVE FASTER THAN US.
YOSHIMORI AND I WILL BACK YOU UP.
GEN'S STILL SKEPTICAL ABOUT TEAMWORK, SO I WANT TO GIVE HIM...
...THE CENTRAL POSITION.
ALL RIGHT WITH YOU, YOSHIMORI?
SORRY TO GIVE YOU A BACKSEAT ROLE.
GLARE
...
IF YOU INSIST...
NO.
CRUD

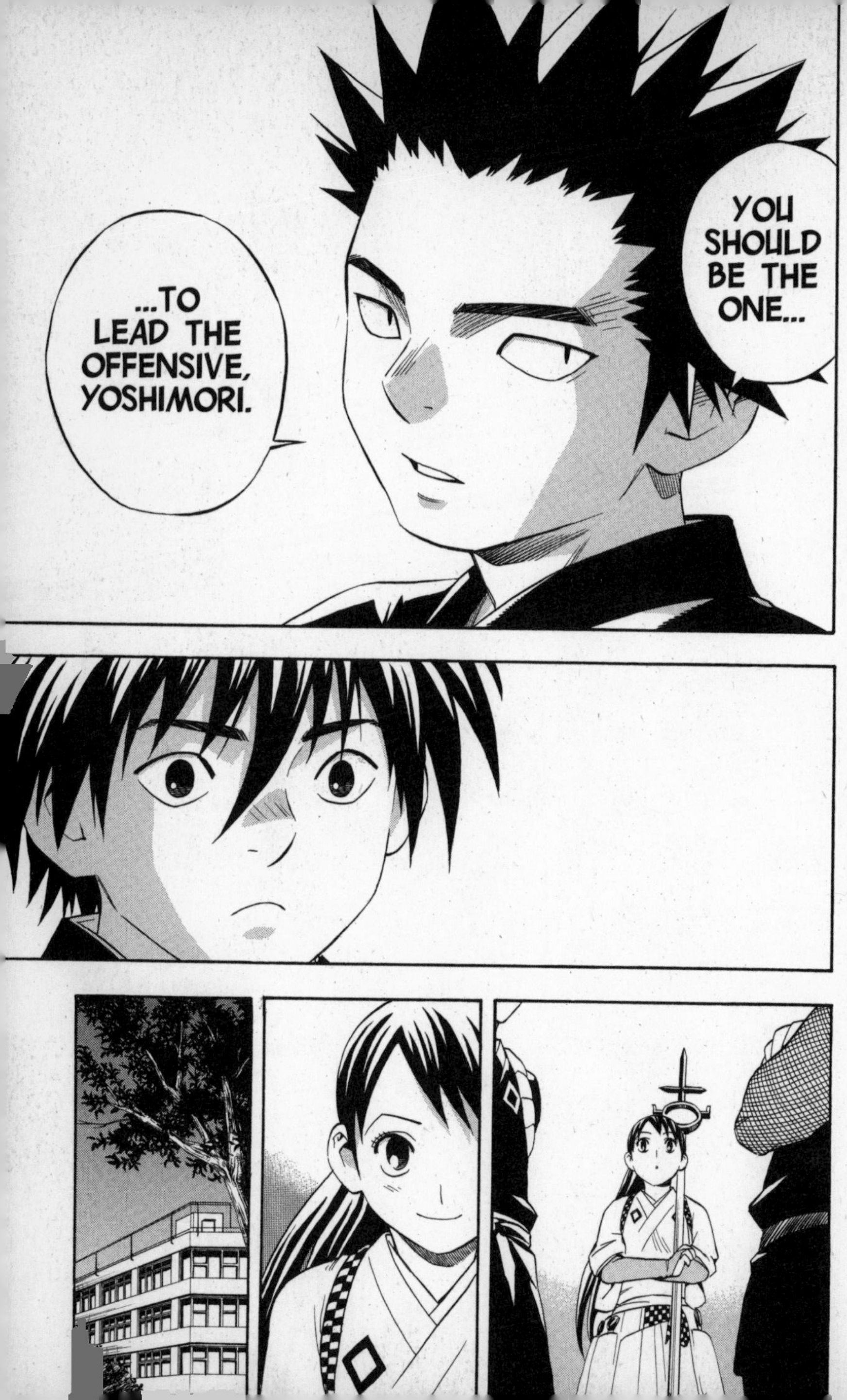
YOU SHOULD BE THE ONE...
...TO LEAD THE OFFENSIVE, YOSHIMORI.

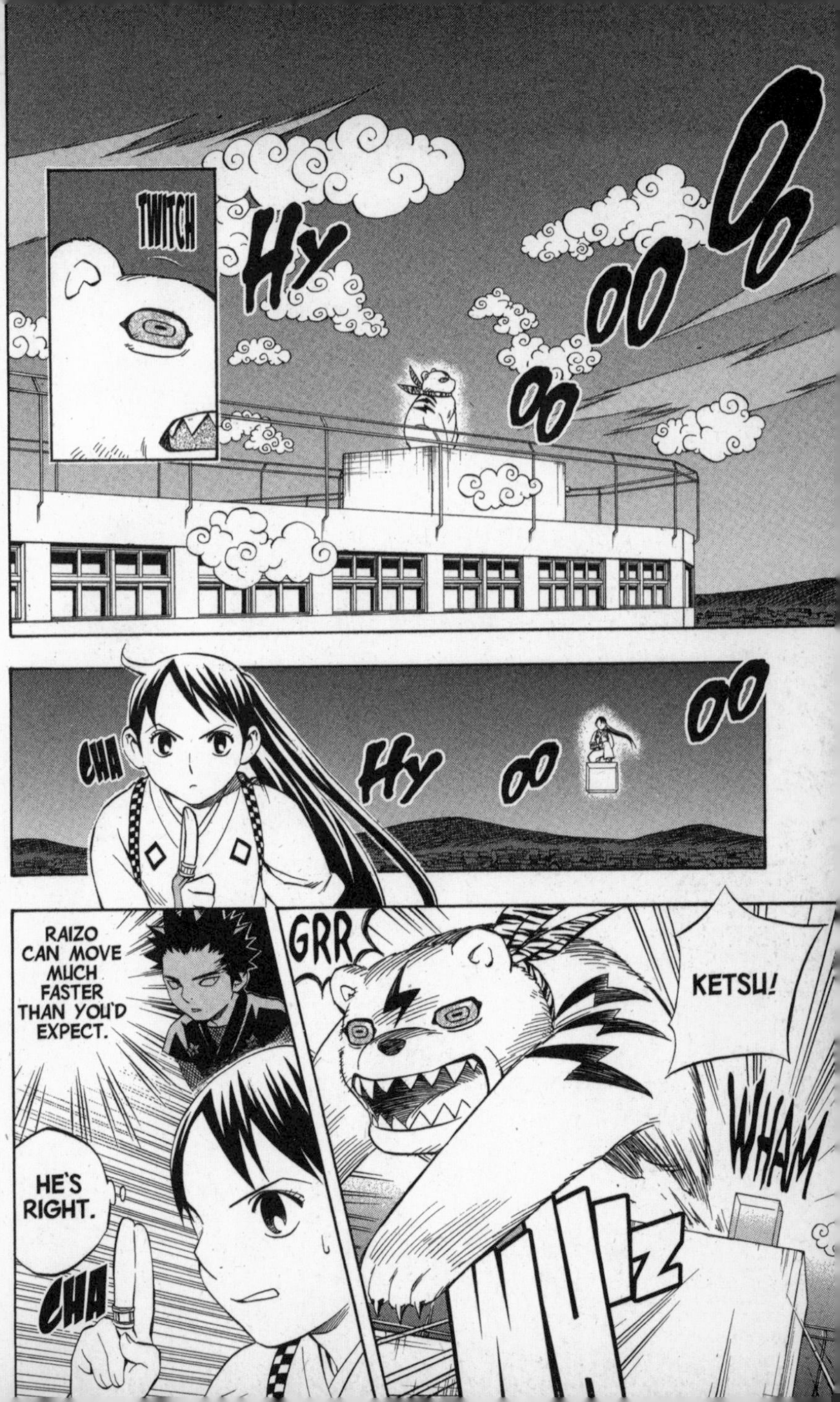

HYOOOOOOOO
TWITCH
HYOOOO
CHA
KETSU!
GRR
WHAM
RAIZO CAN MOVE MUCH FASTER THAN YOU'D EXPECT.
HE'S RIGHT.
CHA

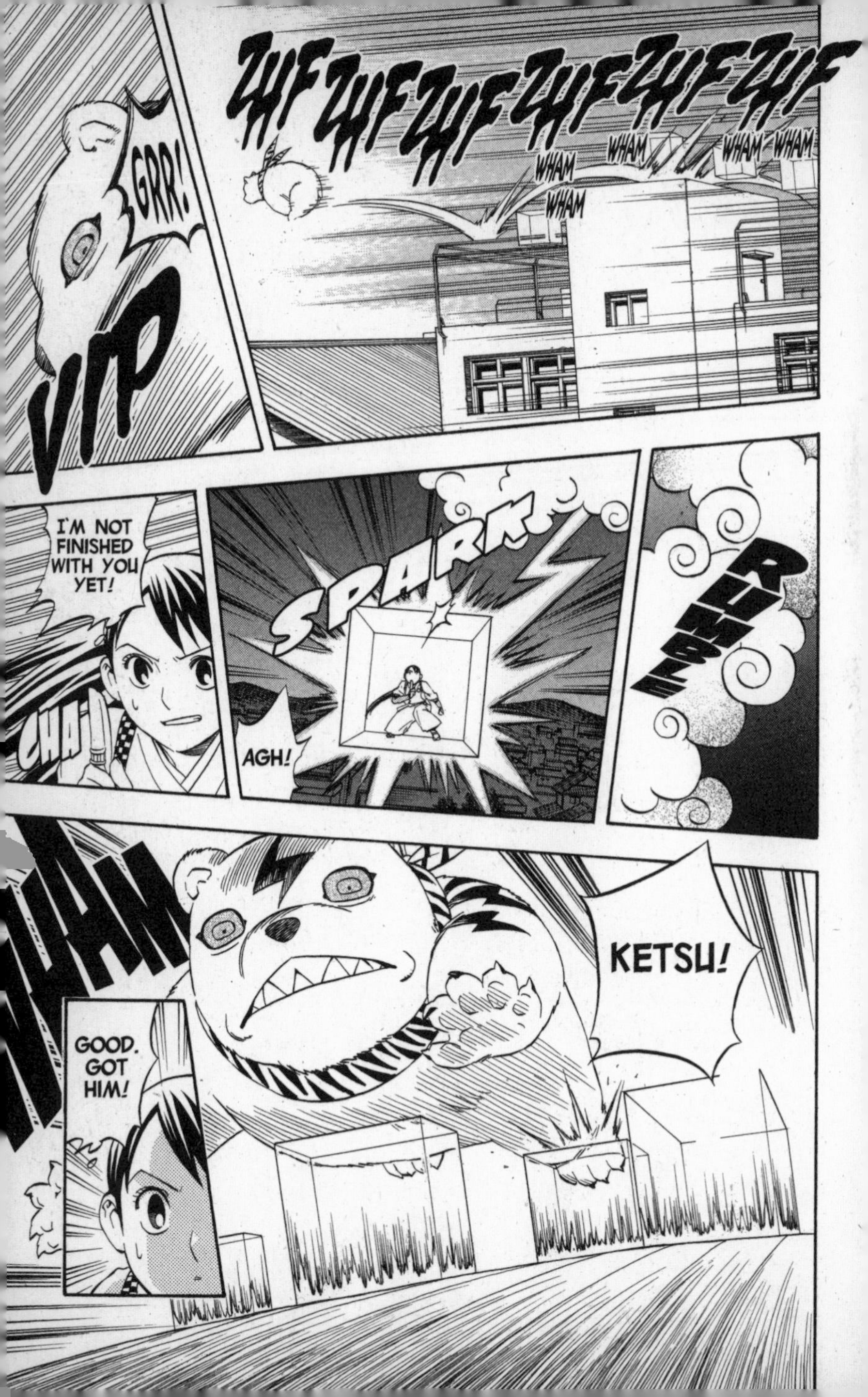
ZHF ZHF ZHF ZHF ZHF ZHF ZHF
WHAM
WHAM
WHAM
WHAM
WHAM
GRR!
VIP
RUMBLE
SPARK
AGH!
I'M NOT FINISHED WITH YOU YET!
CHA
KETSU!
WHAM
GOOD. GOT HIM!

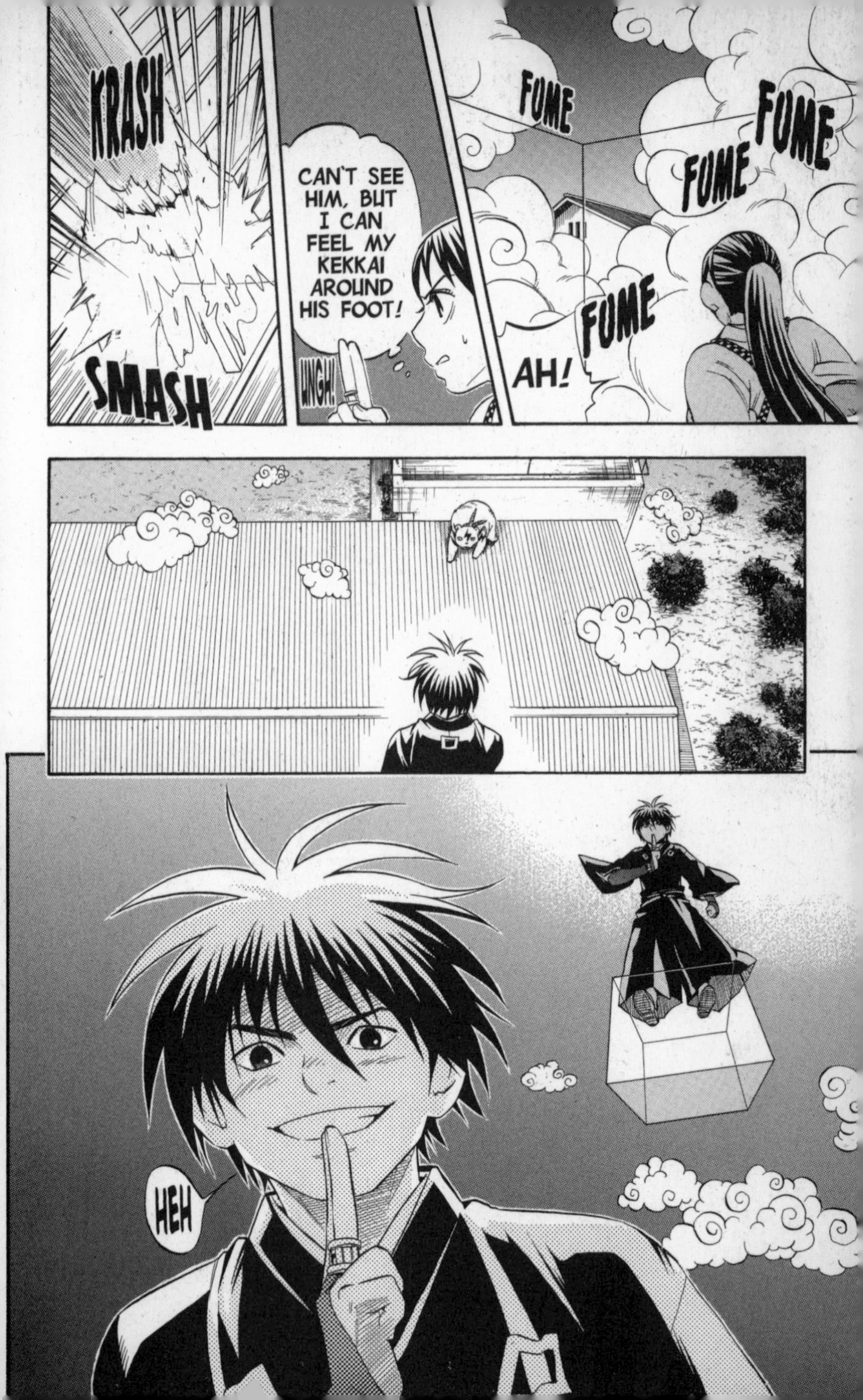
FUME
FUME
FUME
FUME
AH!
FUME
CAN'T SEE HIM, BUT I CAN FEEL MY KEKKAI AROUND HIS FOOT!
UNGH!
KRASH
SMASH
HEH

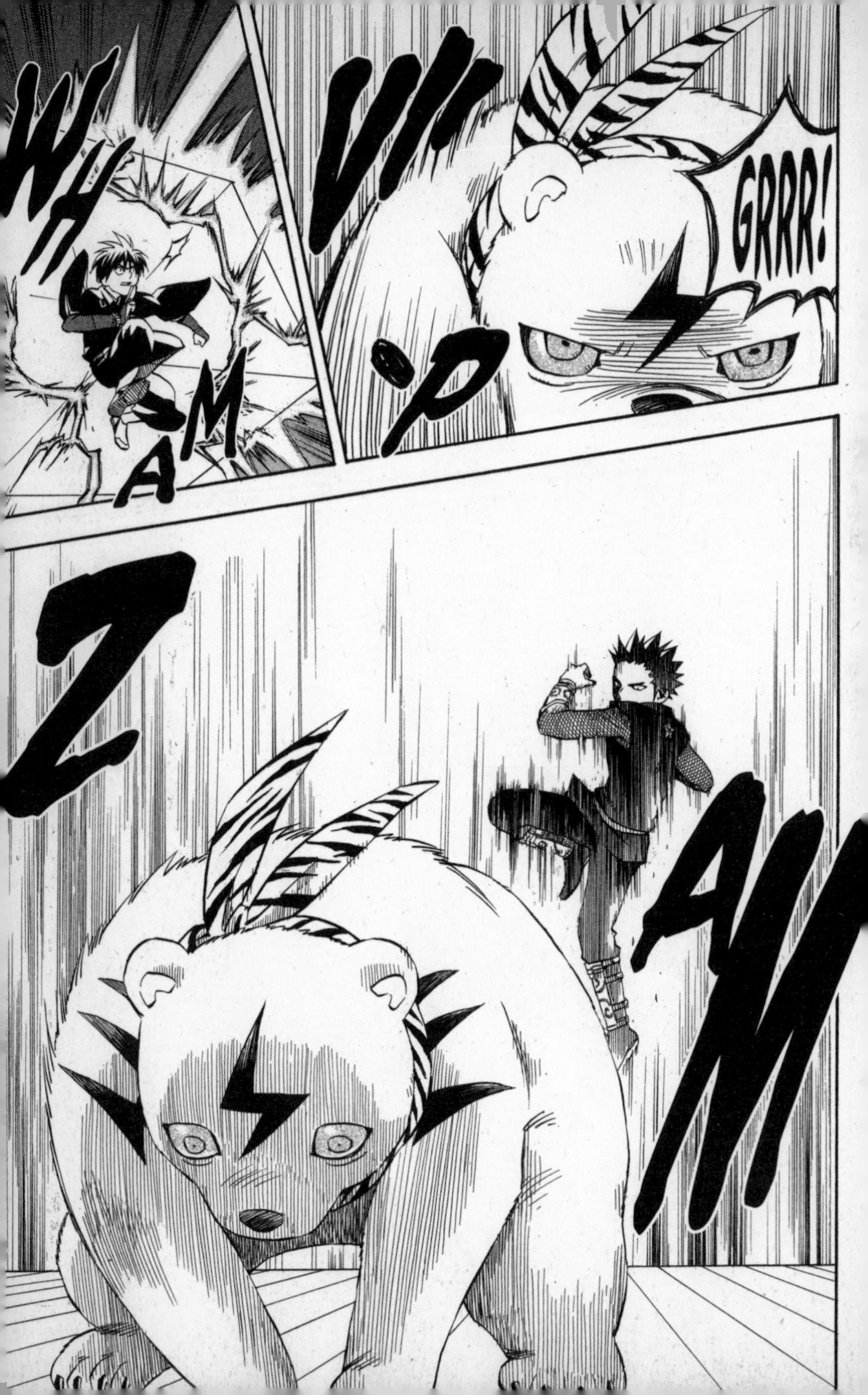
GRRR!
VWIP
WHAM
ZAM

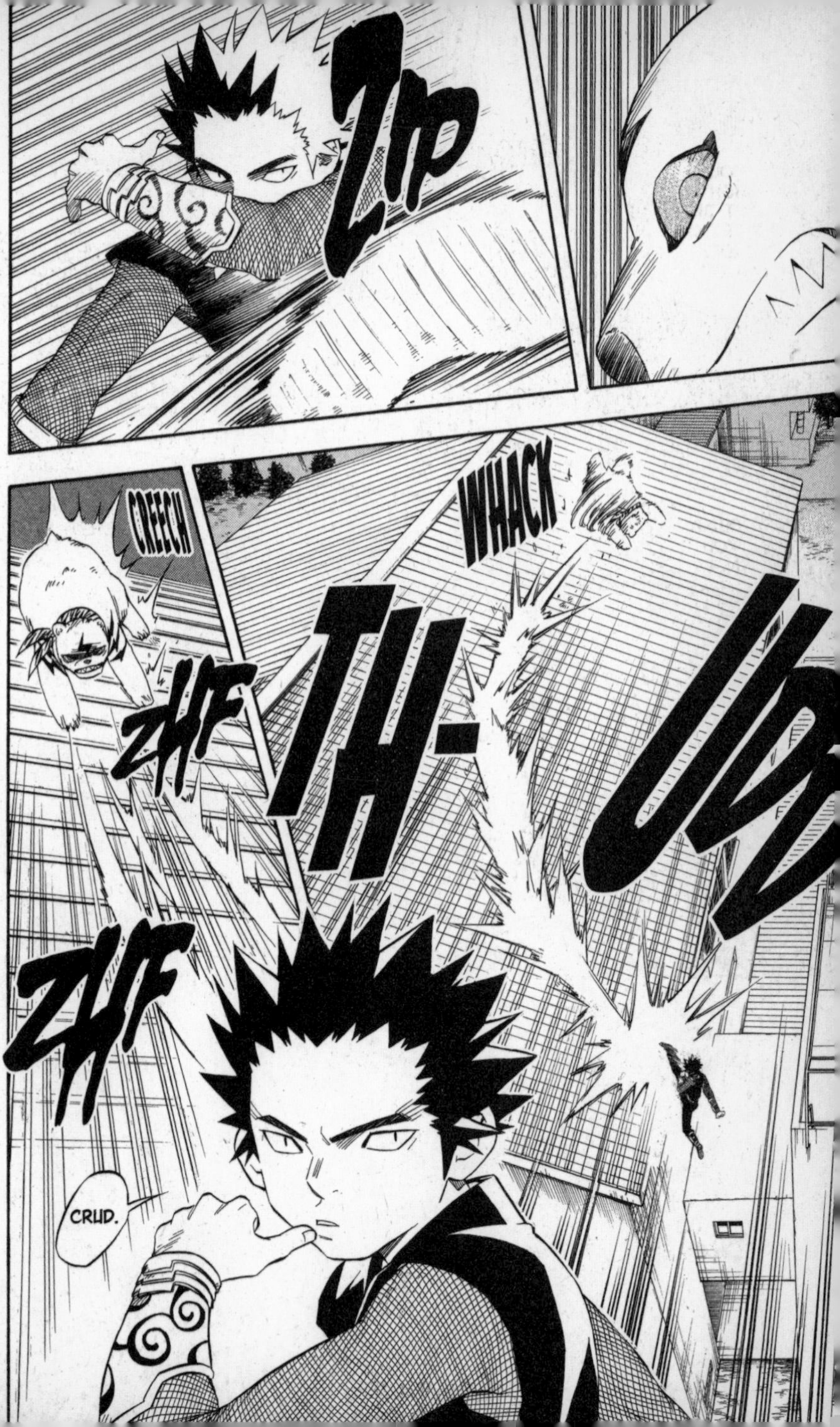
ZIP
WHACK
TH-UD
ZHF
CRUD.
CREECH
ZHF

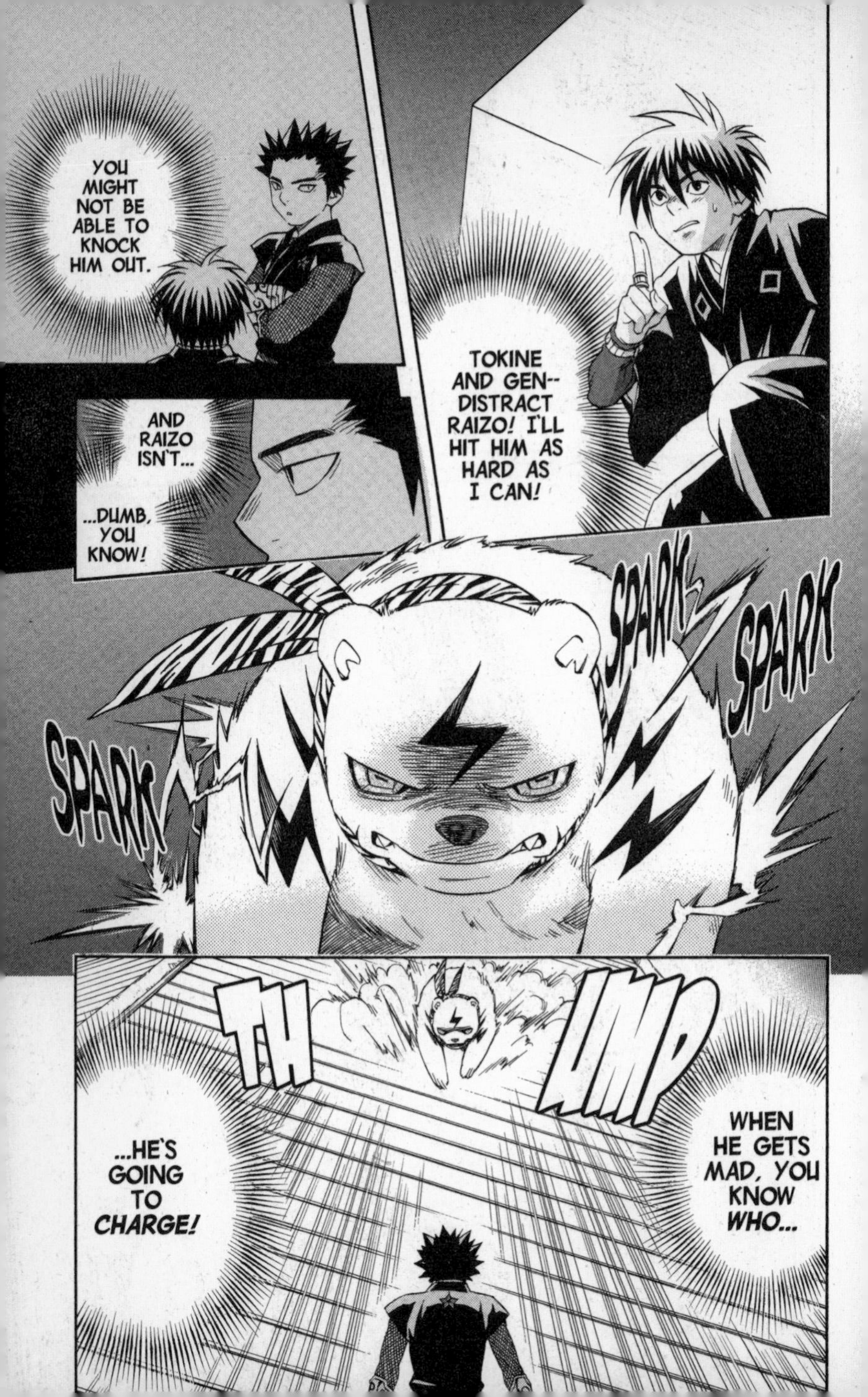
TOKINE AND GEN-- DISTRACT RAIZO! I'LL HIT HIM AS HARD AS I CAN!
YOU MIGHT NOT BE ABLE TO KNOCK HIM OUT.
AND RAIZO ISN'T...
...DUMB, YOU KNOW!
SPARK
SPARK
SPARK
WHEN HE GETS MAD, YOU KNOW *WHO*...
THUMP
...HE'S GOING TO *CHARGE!*

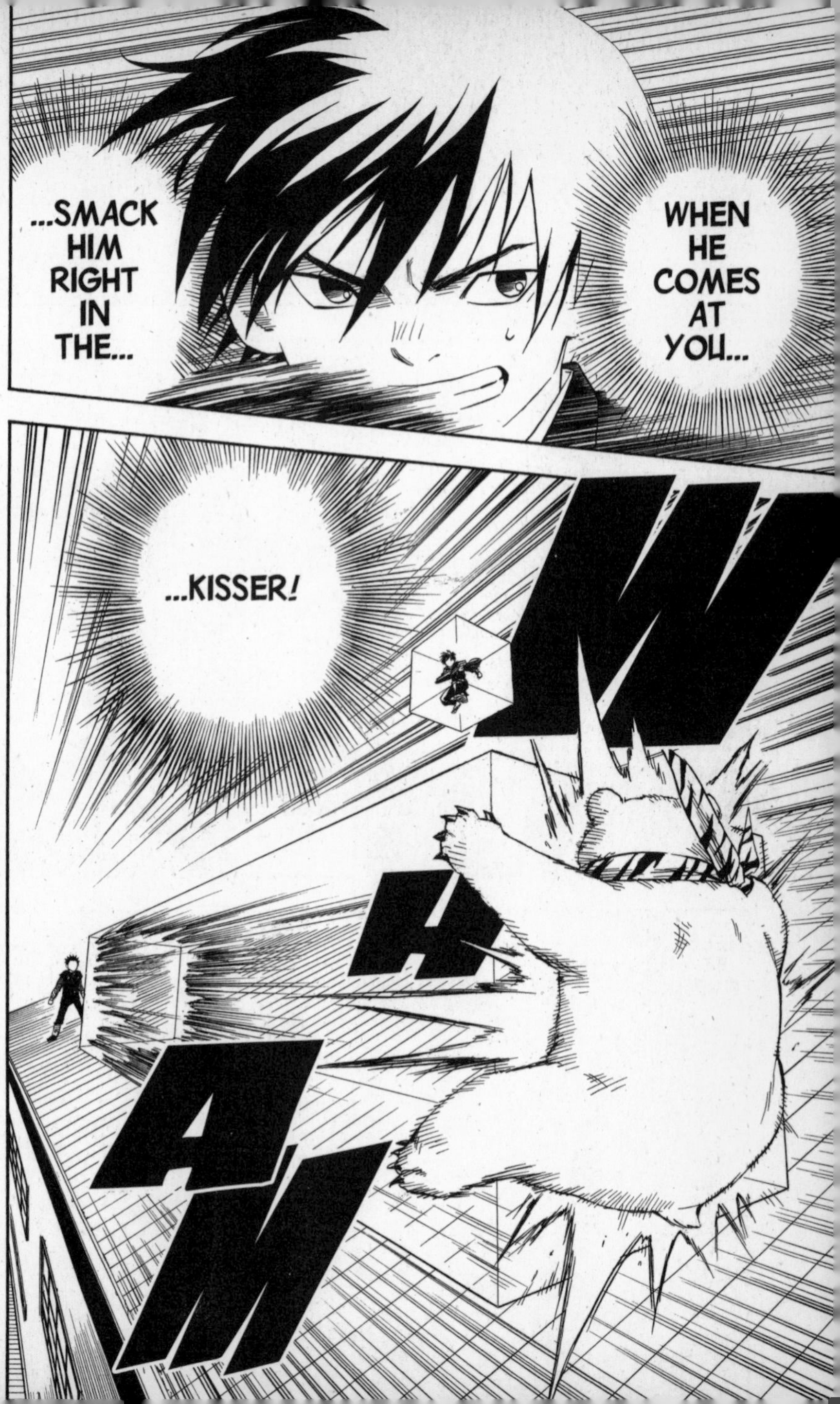
WHEN HE COMES AT YOU...
...SMACK HIM RIGHT IN THE...
...KISSER!

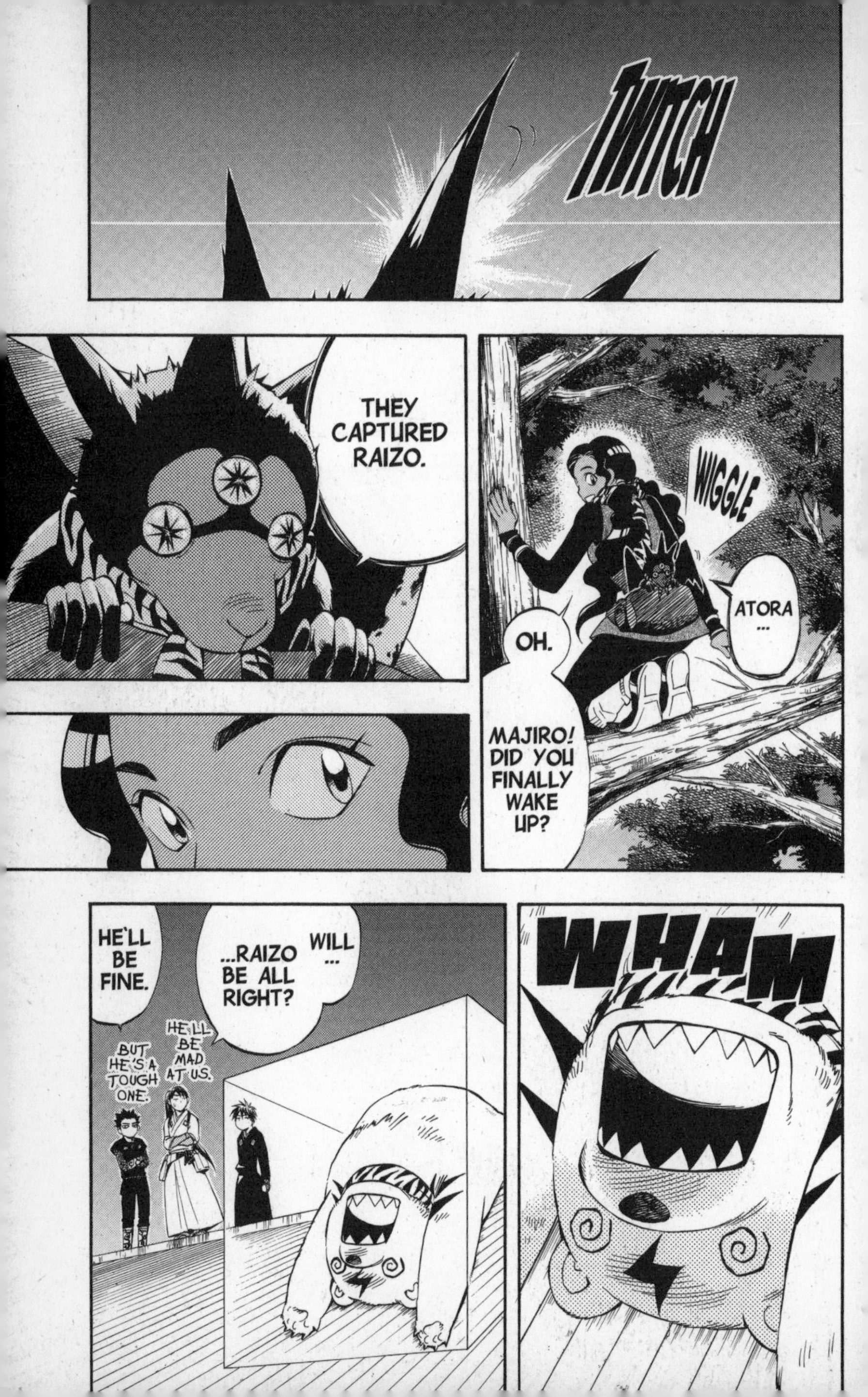
TWITCH
WIGGLE
ATORA ...
OH.
MAJIRO! DID YOU FINALLY WAKE UP?
THEY CAPTURED RAIZO.
WHAM
WILL ...
...RAIZO BE ALL RIGHT?
HE'LL BE FINE.
HE'LL BE MAD AT US.
BUT HE'S A TOUGH ONE.

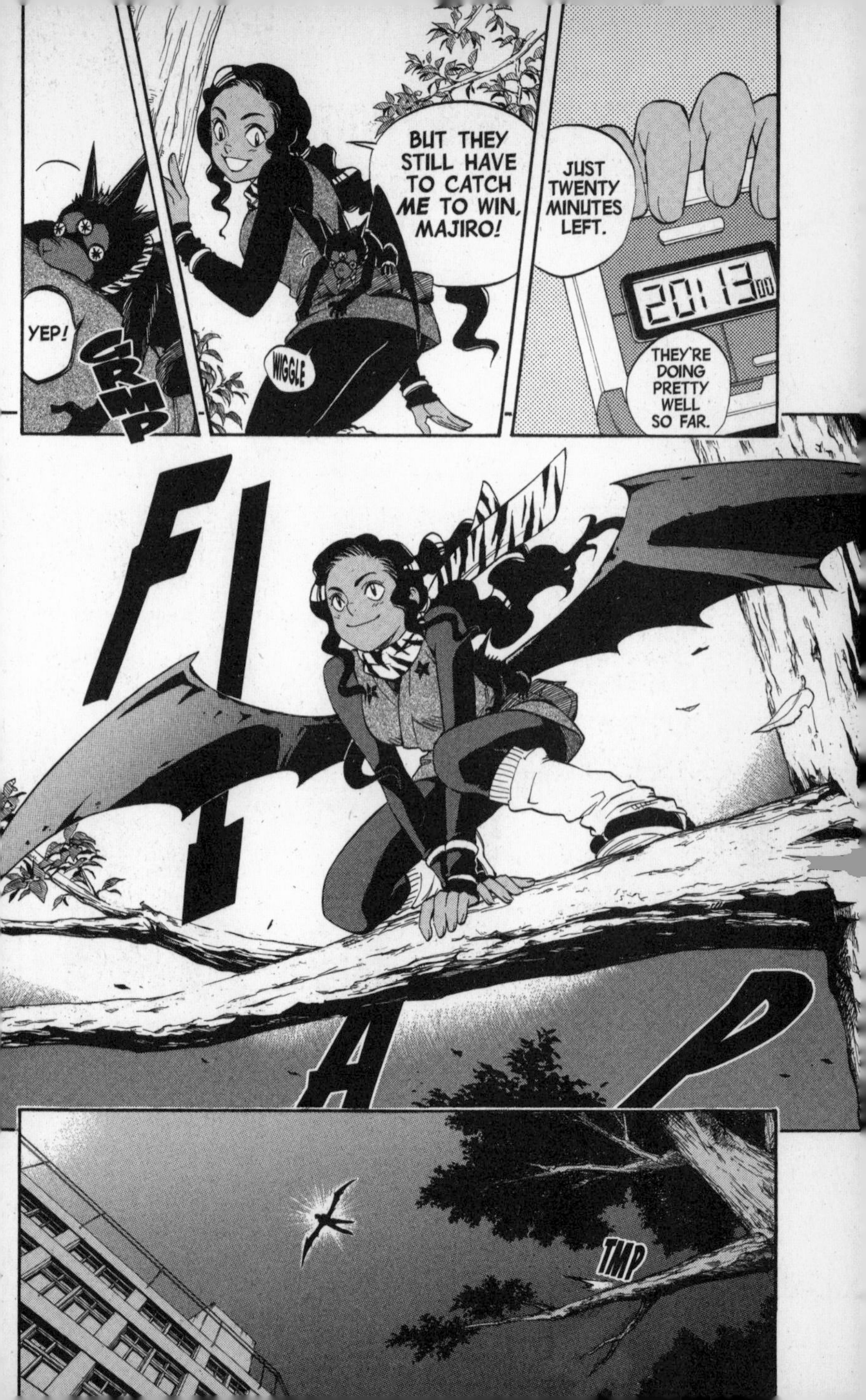
JUST TWENTY MINUTES LEFT.
THEY'RE DOING PRETTY WELL SO FAR.
BUT THEY STILL HAVE TO CATCH *ME* TO WIN, MAJIRO!
WIGGLE
YEP!
GRMP
FLAP
TMP

Chapter 79: Dog Fight

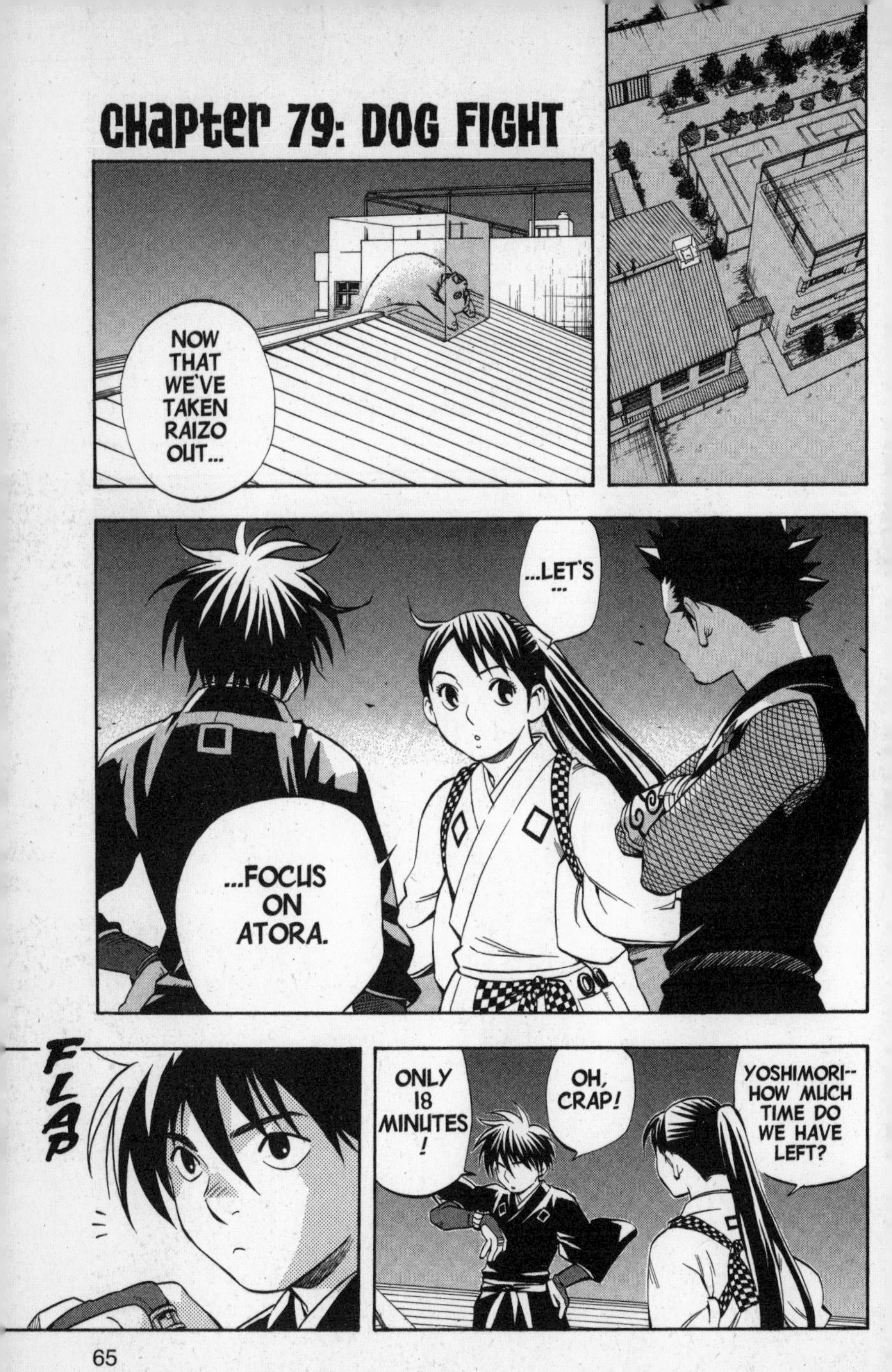
NOW THAT WE'VE TAKEN RAIZO OUT...
...LET'S ...
...FOCUS ON ATORA.
YOSHIMORI-- HOW MUCH TIME DO WE HAVE LEFT?
OH, CRAP!
ONLY 18 MINUTES!
FLAP

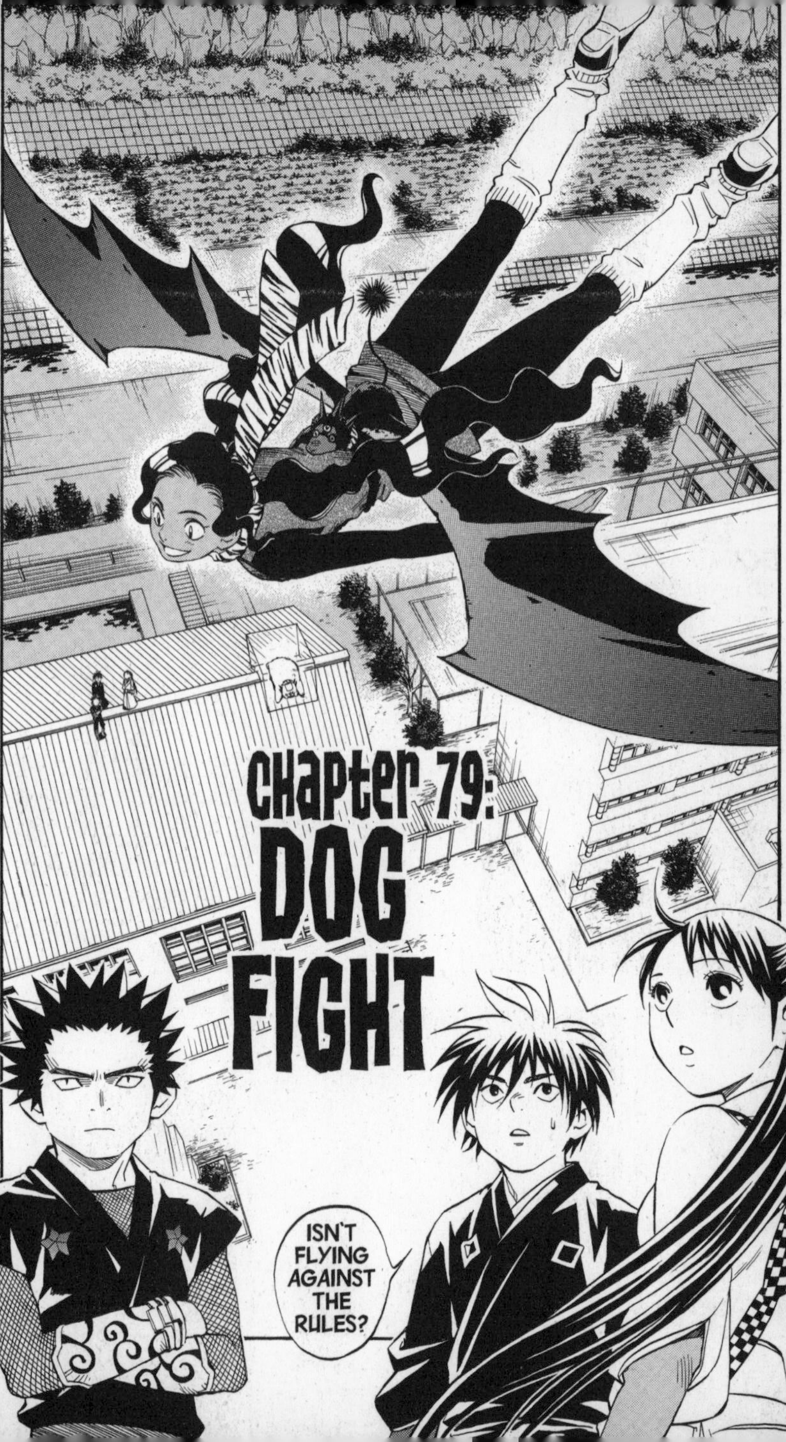
CHAPTER 79:
DOG FIGHT
ISN'T FLYING AGAINST THE RULES?

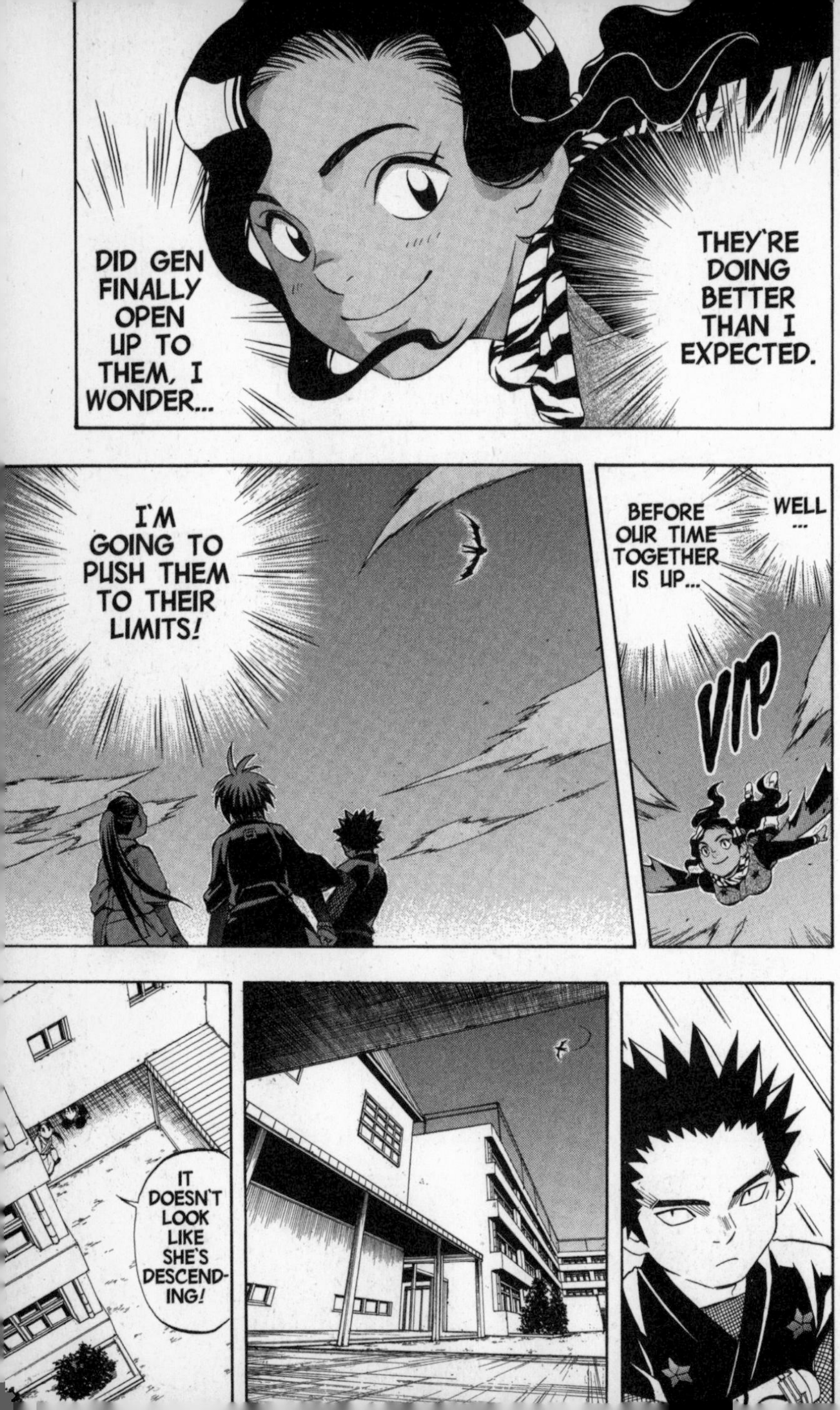
THEY'RE DOING BETTER THAN I EXPECTED.
DID GEN FINALLY OPEN UP TO THEM, I WONDER...
WELL...
BEFORE OUR TIME TOGETHER IS UP...
VIP
I'M GOING TO PUSH THEM TO THEIR LIMITS!
IT DOESN'T LOOK LIKE SHE'S DESCENDING!

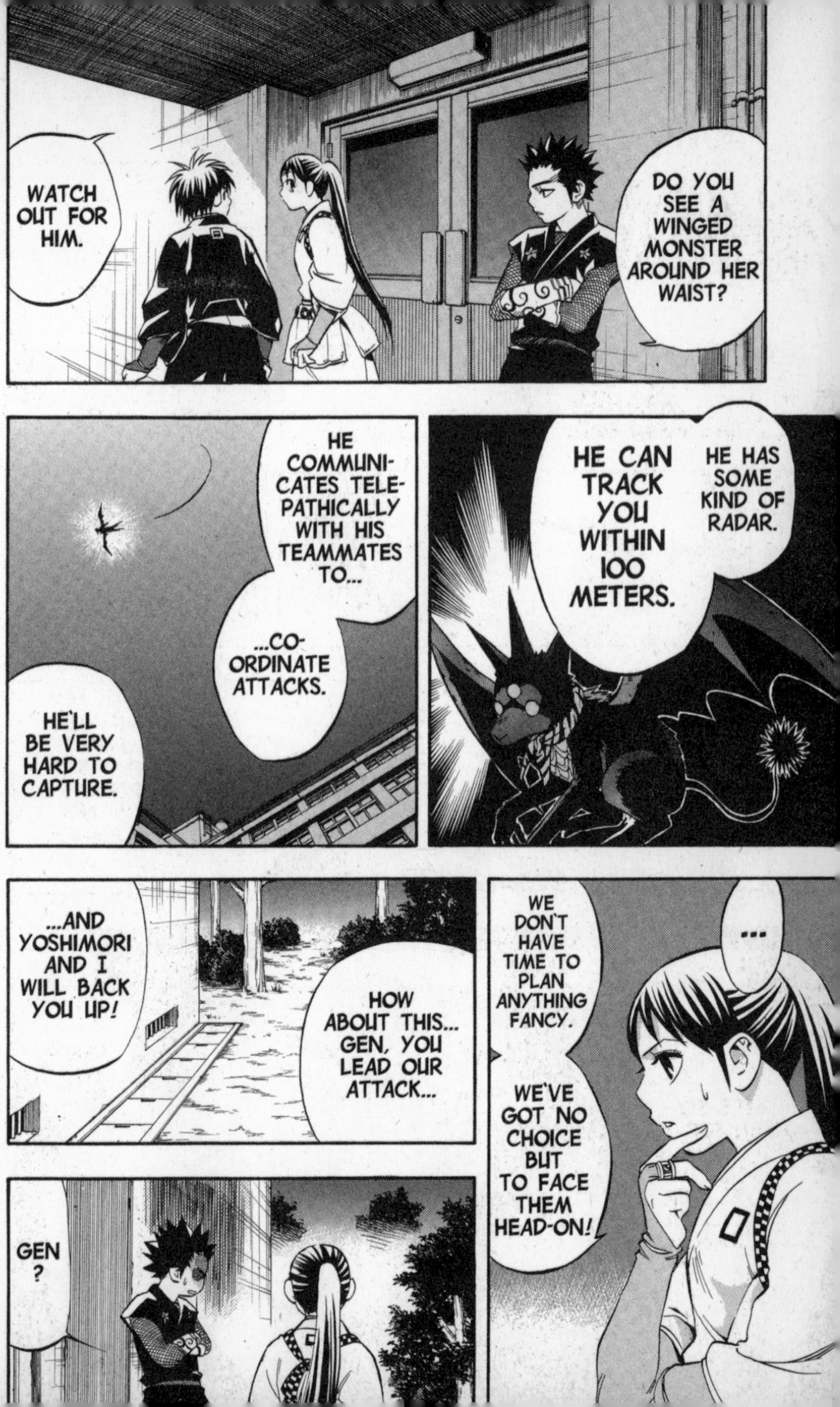
DO YOU SEE A WINGED MONSTER AROUND HER WAIST?
WATCH OUT FOR HIM.
HE HAS SOME KIND OF RADAR.
HE CAN TRACK YOU WITHIN 100 METERS.
HE COMMUNICATES TELEPATHICALLY WITH HIS TEAMMATES TO...
...CO-ORDINATE ATTACKS.
HE'LL BE VERY HARD TO CAPTURE.
...
WE DON'T HAVE TIME TO PLAN ANYTHING FANCY.
WE'VE GOT NO CHOICE BUT TO FACE THEM HEAD-ON!
HOW ABOUT THIS... GEN, YOU LEAD OUR ATTACK...
...AND YOSHIMORI AND I WILL BACK YOU UP!
GEN?

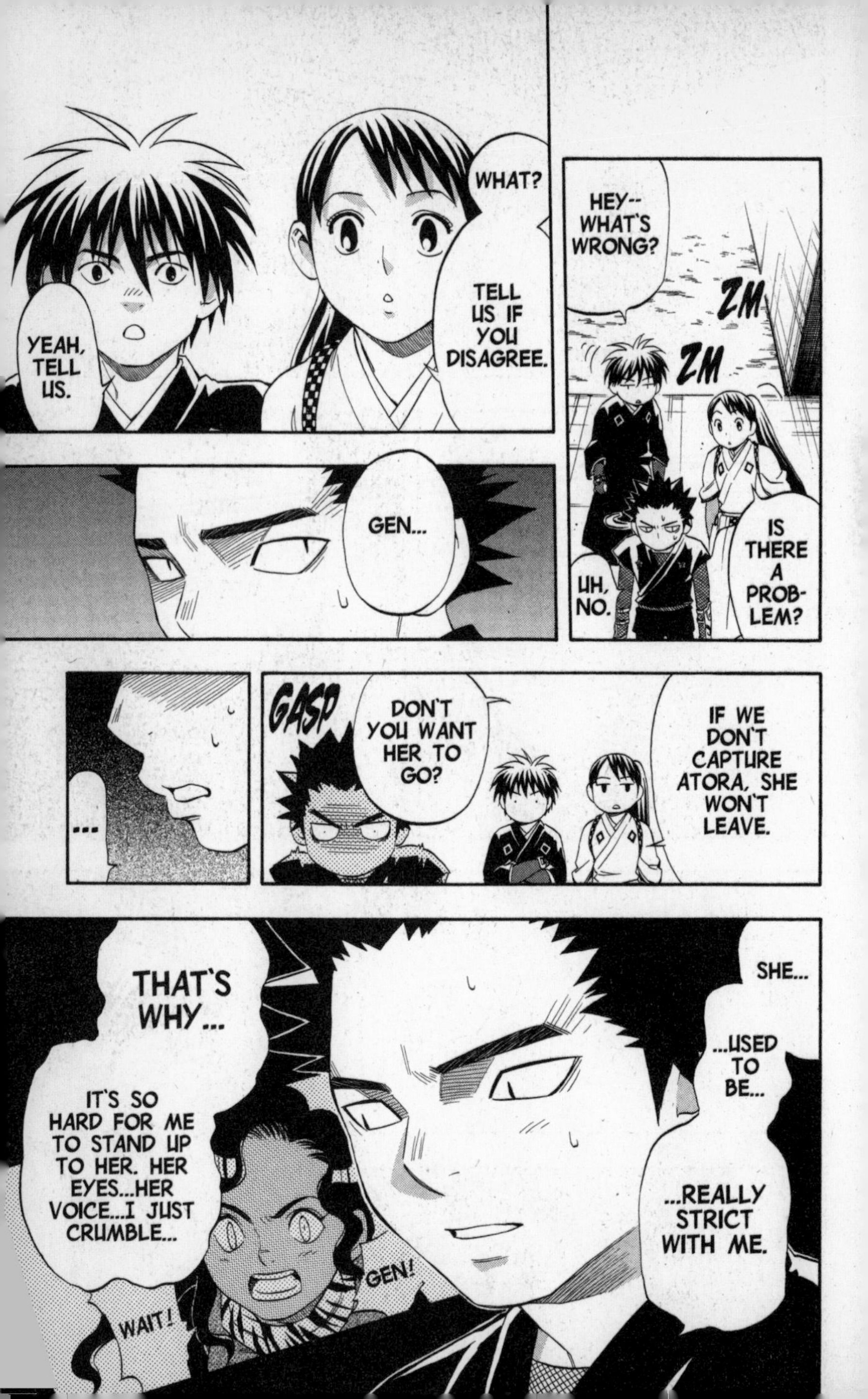
HEY-- WHAT'S WRONG?
ZM
ZM
IS THERE A PROBLEM?
UH, NO.
WHAT?
TELL US IF YOU DISAGREE.
YEAH, TELL US.
GEN...
IF WE DON'T CAPTURE ATORA, SHE WON'T LEAVE.
DON'T YOU WANT HER TO GO?
GASP
...
SHE...
...USED TO BE...
...REALLY STRICT WITH ME.
THAT'S WHY...
IT'S SO HARD FOR ME TO STAND UP TO HER. HER EYES...HER VOICE...I JUST CRUMBLE...
GEN!
WAIT!

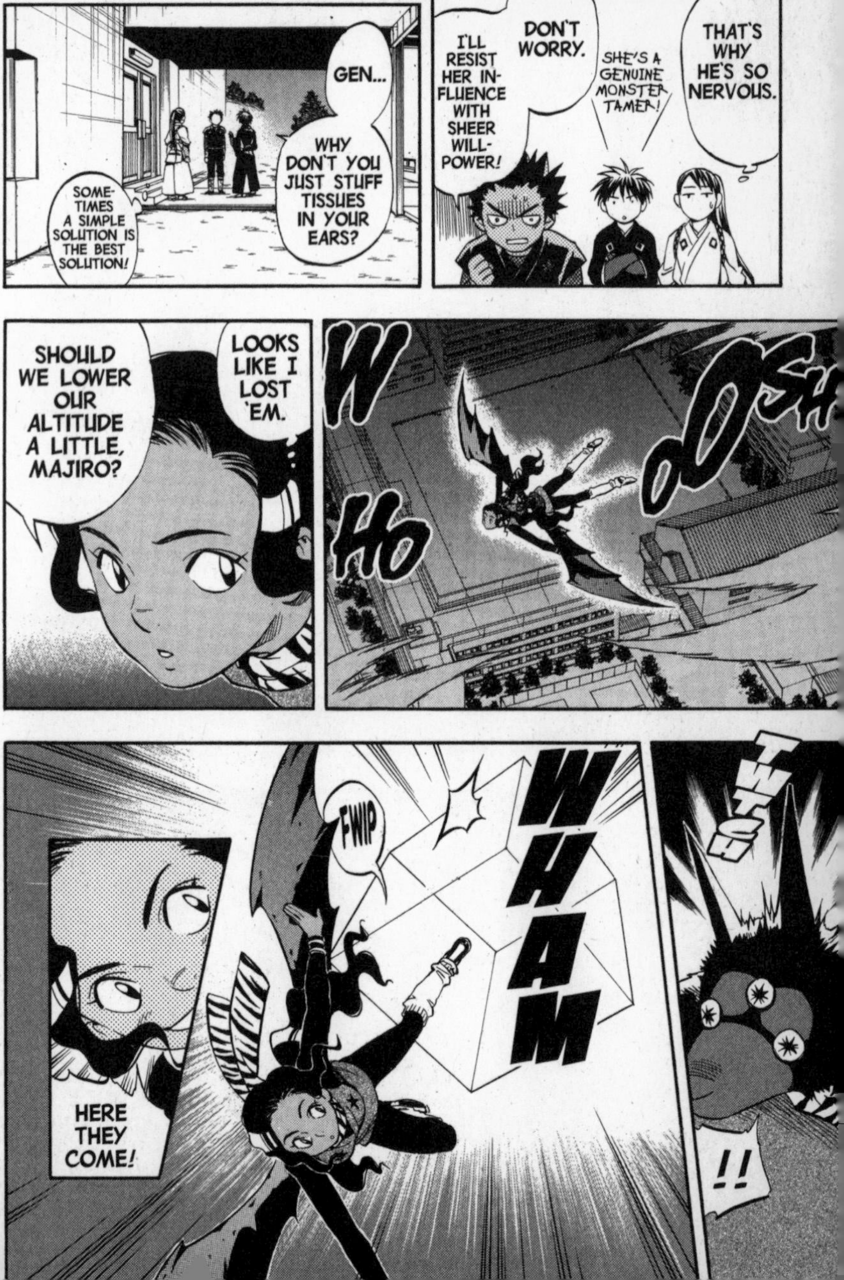
THAT'S WHY HE'S SO NERVOUS.
SHE'S A GENUINE MONSTER TAMER!
DON'T WORRY.
I'LL RESIST HER IN-FLUENCE WITH SHEER WILL-POWER!
GEN...
WHY DON'T YOU JUST STUFF TISSUES IN YOUR EARS?
SOME-TIMES A SIMPLE SOLUTION IS THE BEST SOLUTION!
WHOOSH
LOOKS LIKE I LOST 'EM.
SHOULD WE LOWER OUR ALTITUDE A LITTLE, MAJIRO?
!!
WHAM
FWIP
HERE THEY COME!

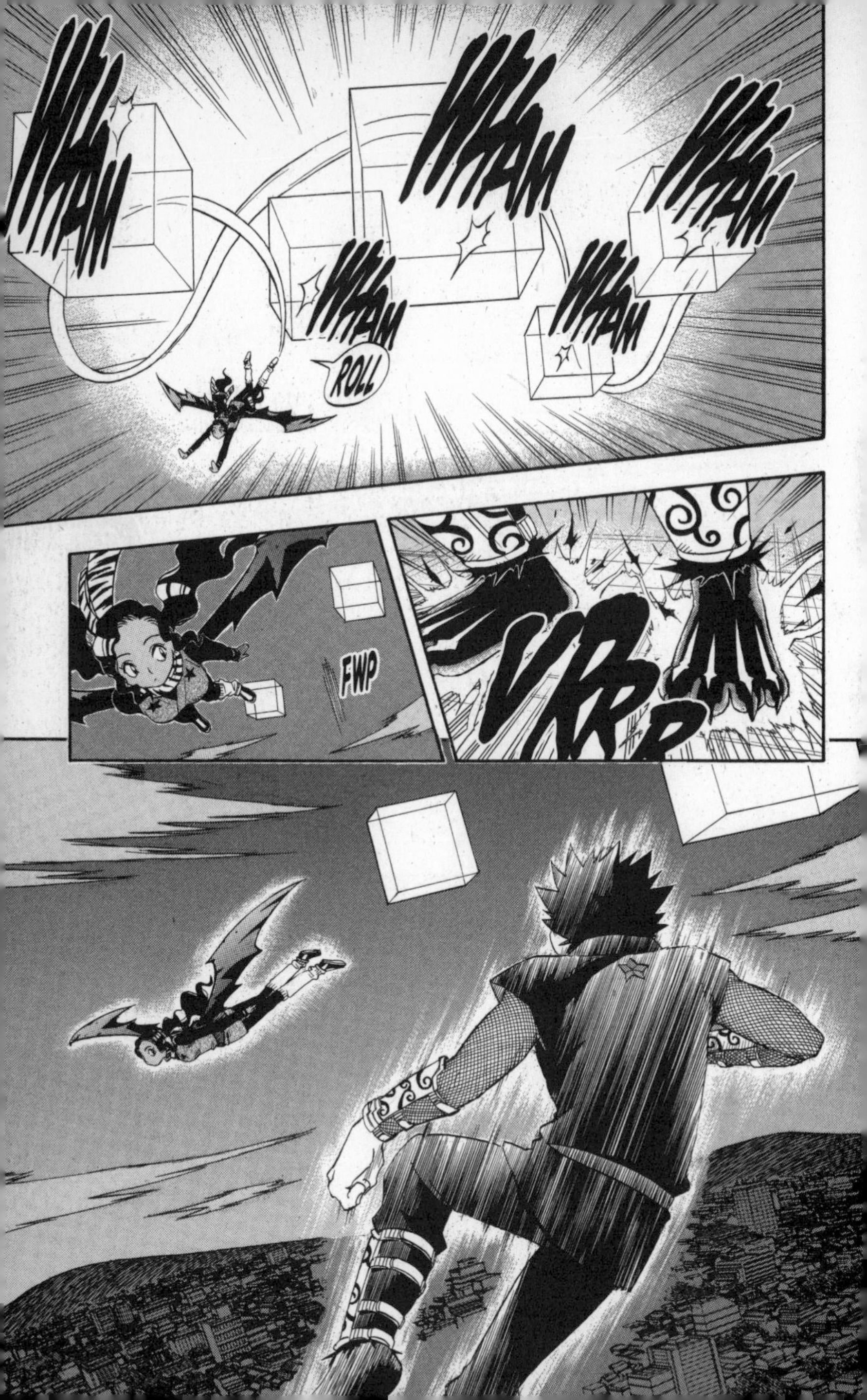
WHAM
WHAM
WHAM
WHAM
ROLL
WHAM
VRR
FWP

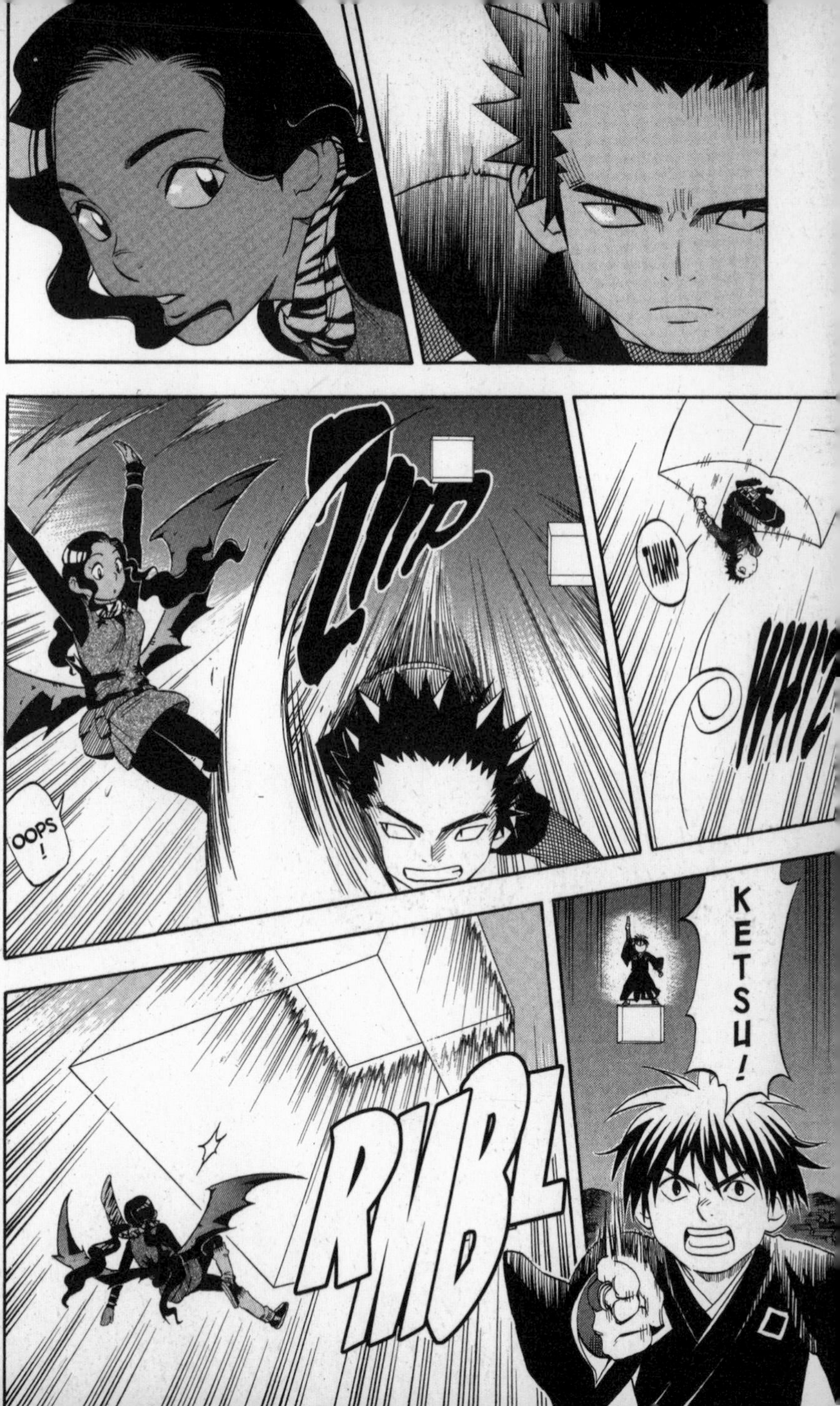
THUMP
WHI
ZWIP
OOPS!
KETSU!
RMBL

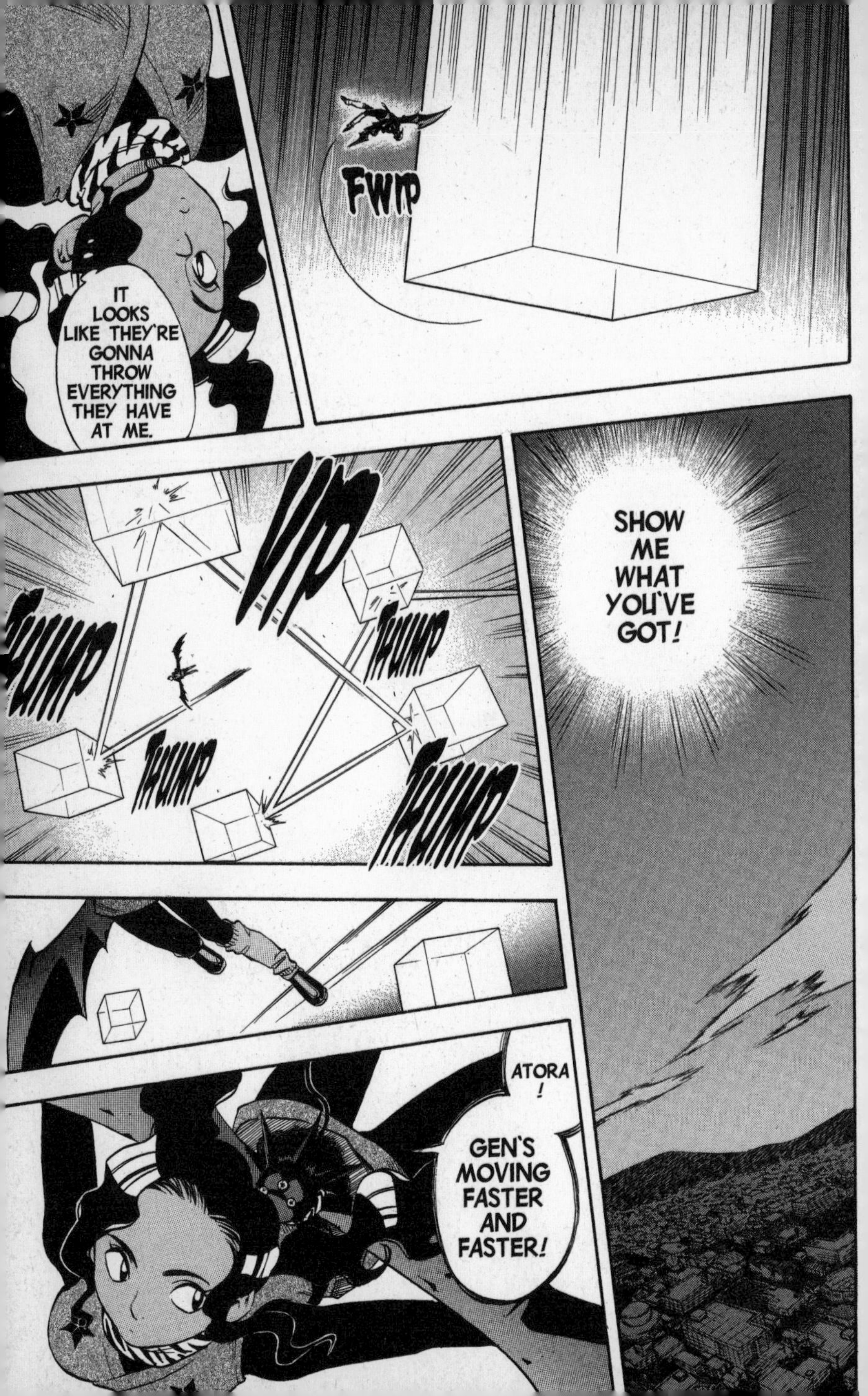
FWIP
IT LOOKS LIKE THEY'RE GONNA THROW EVERYTHING THEY HAVE AT ME.
SHOW ME WHAT YOU'VE GOT!
VIP
THUMP
THUMP
THUMP
THUMP
ATORA!
GEN'S MOVING FASTER AND FASTER!

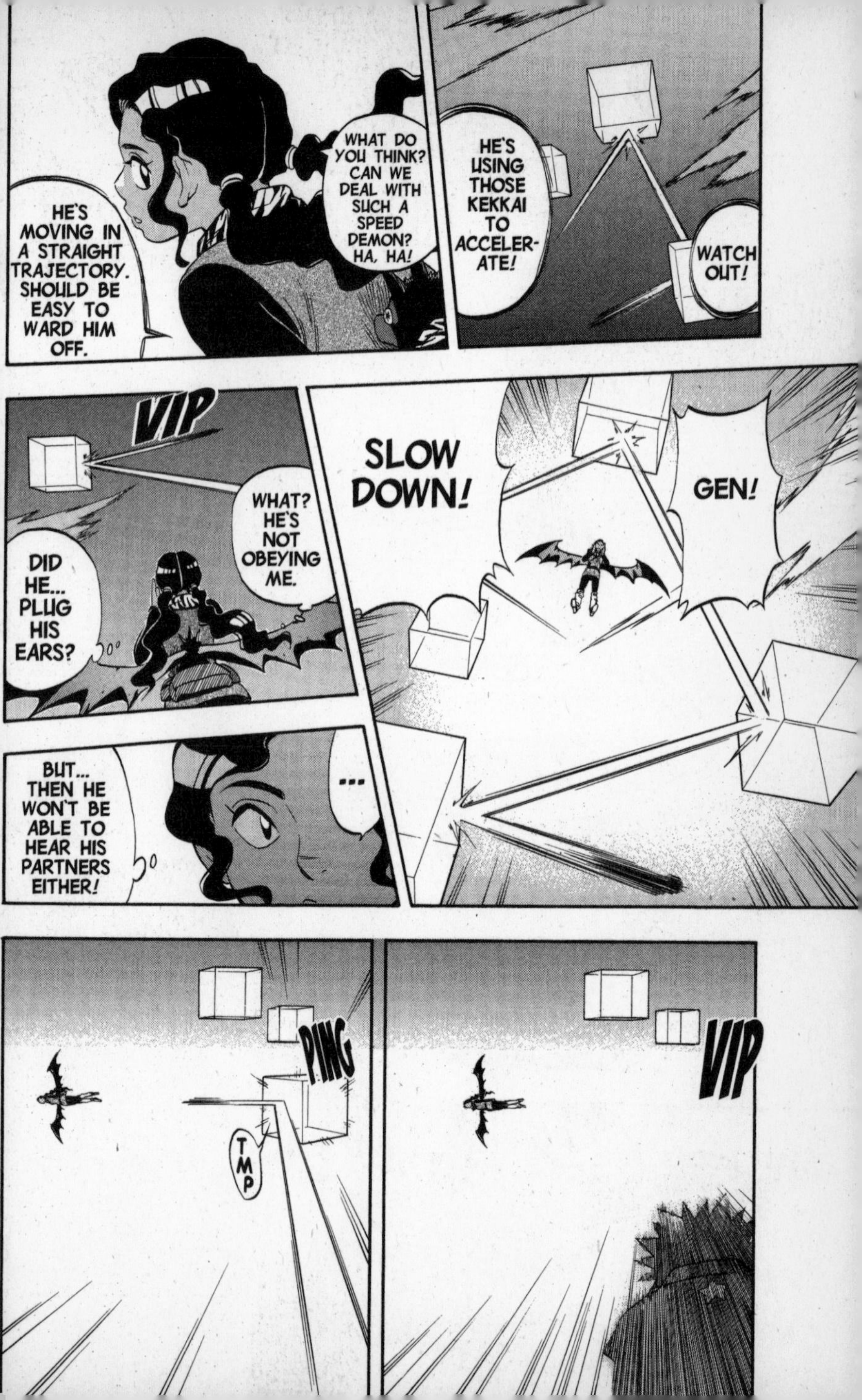
HE'S USING THOSE KEKKAI TO ACCELER-ATE!
WATCH OUT!
WHAT DO YOU THINK? CAN WE DEAL WITH SUCH A SPEED DEMON? HA, HA!
HE'S MOVING IN A STRAIGHT TRAJECTORY. SHOULD BE EASY TO WARD HIM OFF.
GEN!
SLOW DOWN!
VIP
WHAT? HE'S NOT OBEYING ME.
DID HE... PLUG HIS EARS?
...
BUT... THEN HE WON'T BE ABLE TO HEAR HIS PARTNERS EITHER!
VIP
PING
TMP

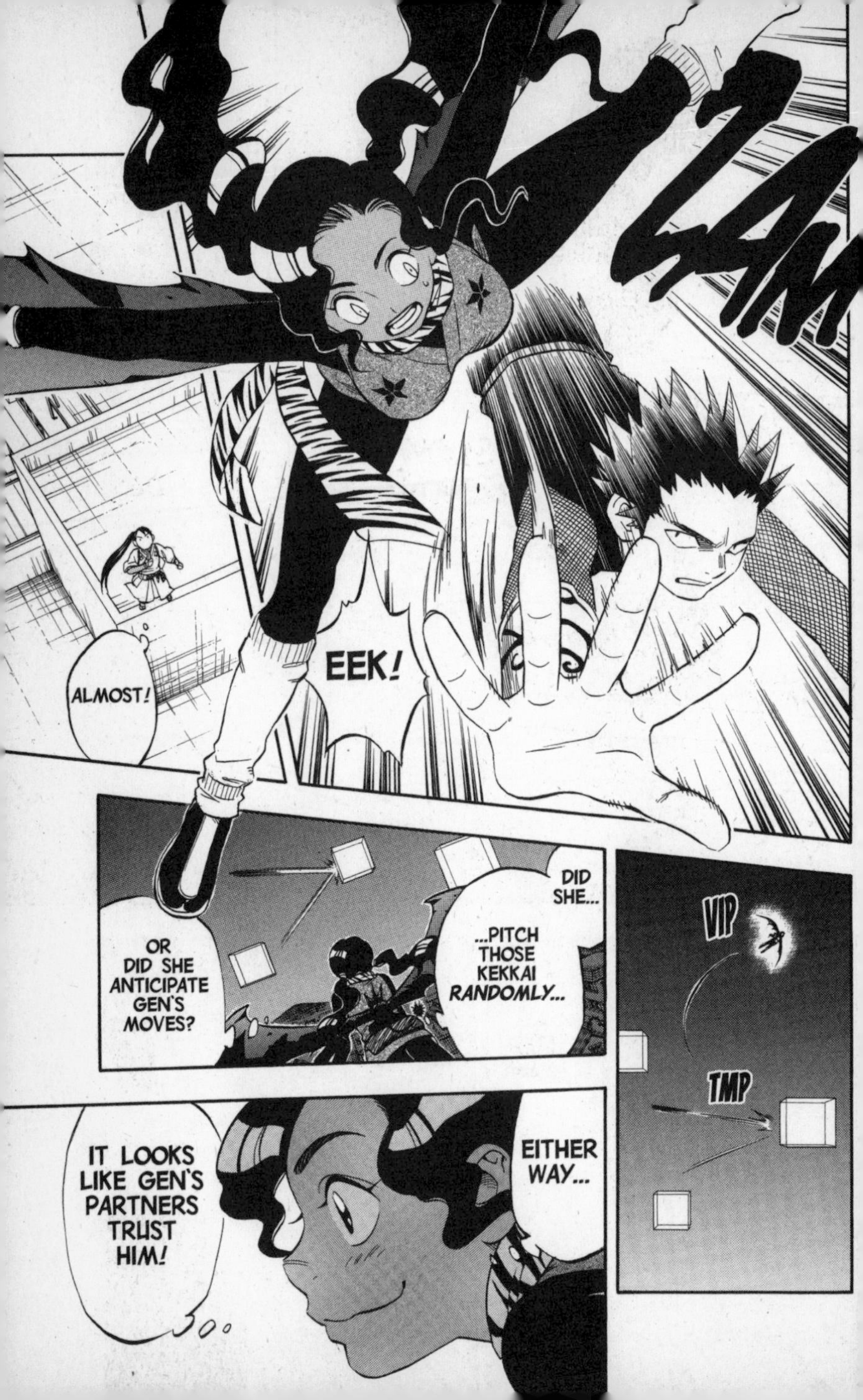
EEK!
ALMOST!
VIP
TMP
DID SHE...
...PITCH THOSE KEKKAI *RANDOMLY...*
OR DID SHE ANTICIPATE GEN'S MOVES?
EITHER WAY...
IT LOOKS LIKE GEN'S PARTNERS TRUST HIM!

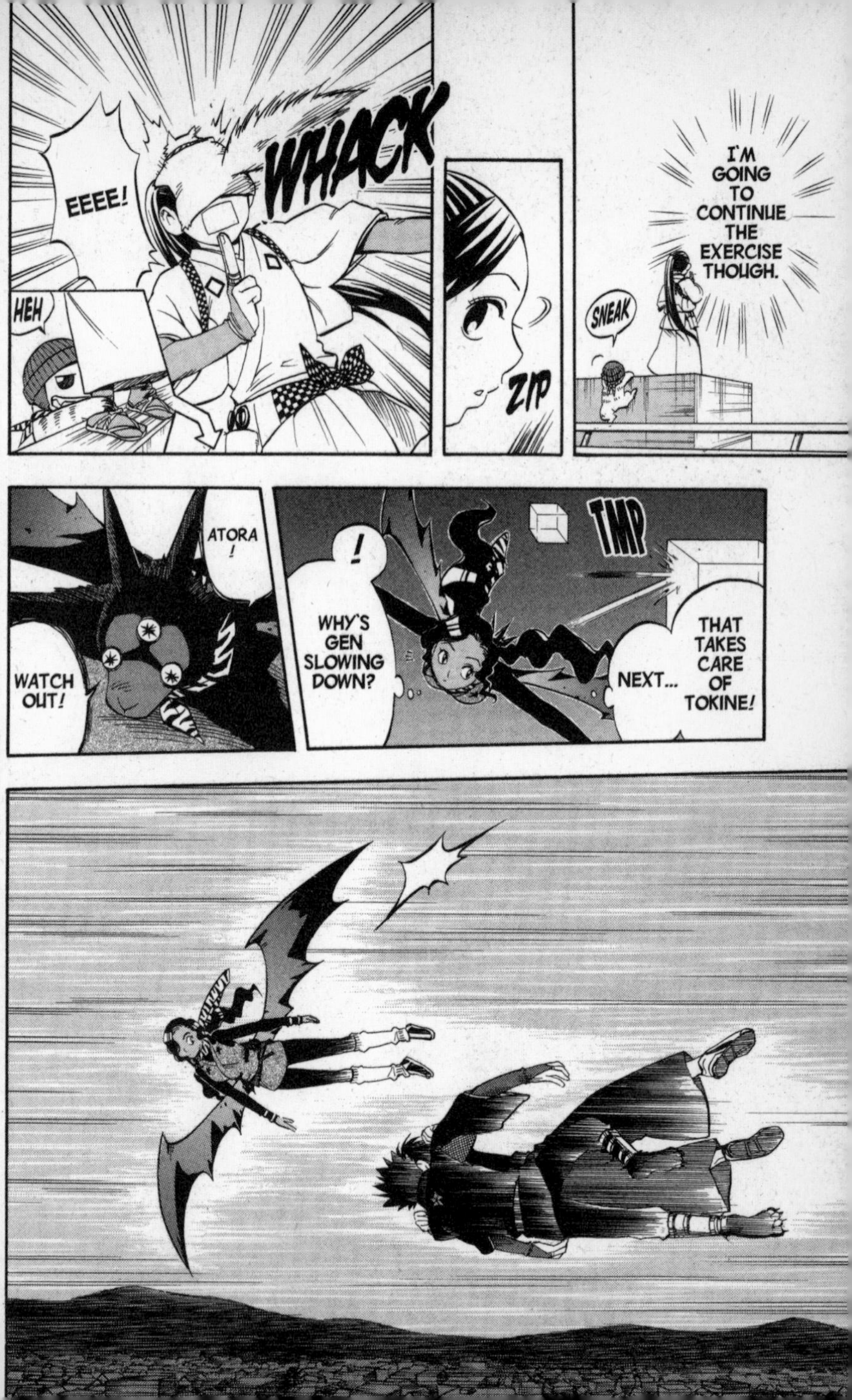

I'M GOING TO CONTINUE THE EXERCISE THOUGH.
SNEAK
ZIP
WHACK
EEEE!
HEH
TMP
THAT TAKES CARE OF TOKINE!
NEXT...
!
WHY'S GEN SLOWING DOWN?
ATORA!
WATCH OUT!

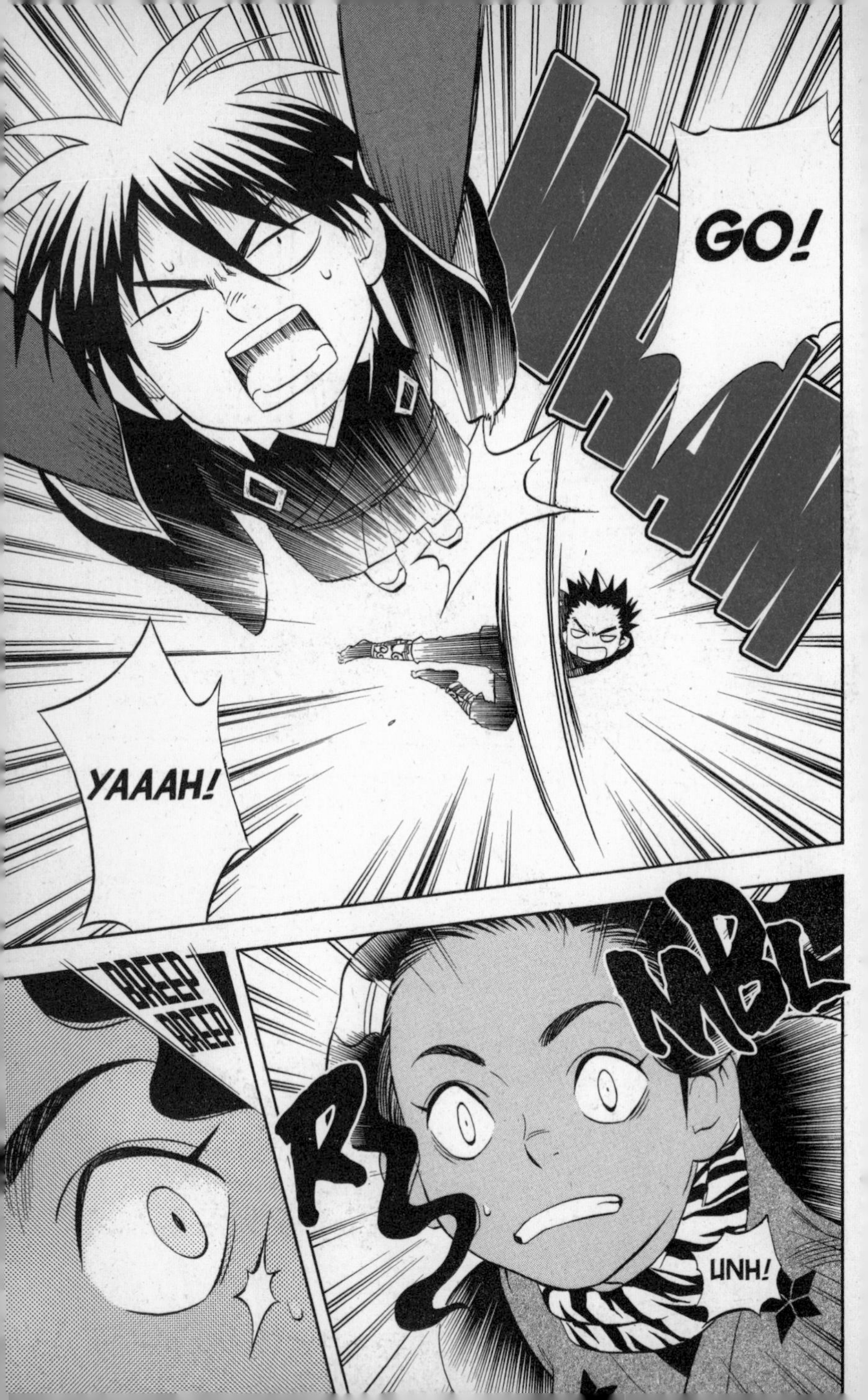
GO!
YAAAH!
UNH!
BREEP
BREEP

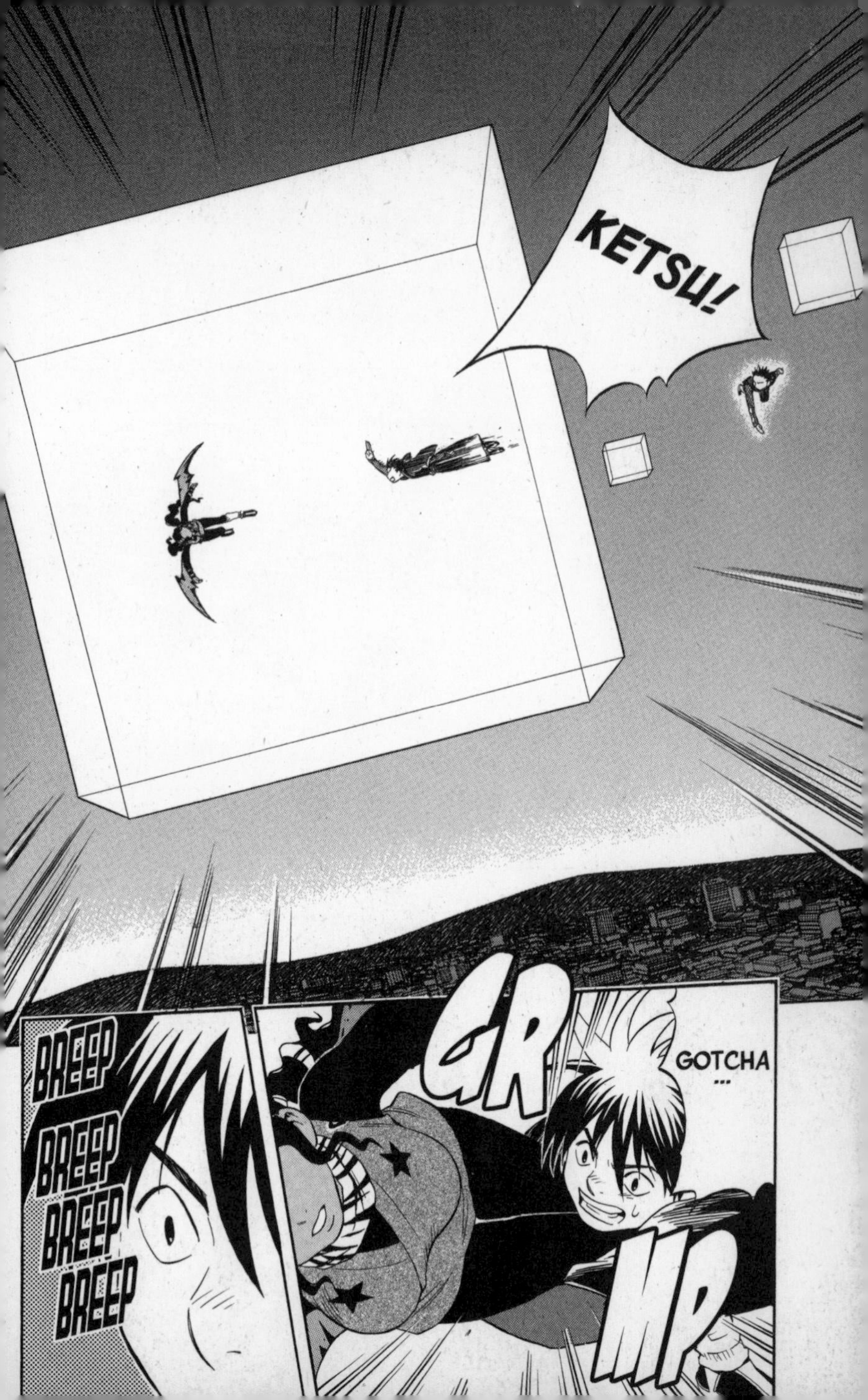
KETSU!
GOTCHA ...
GR
MP
BREEP
BREEP
BREEP
BREEP

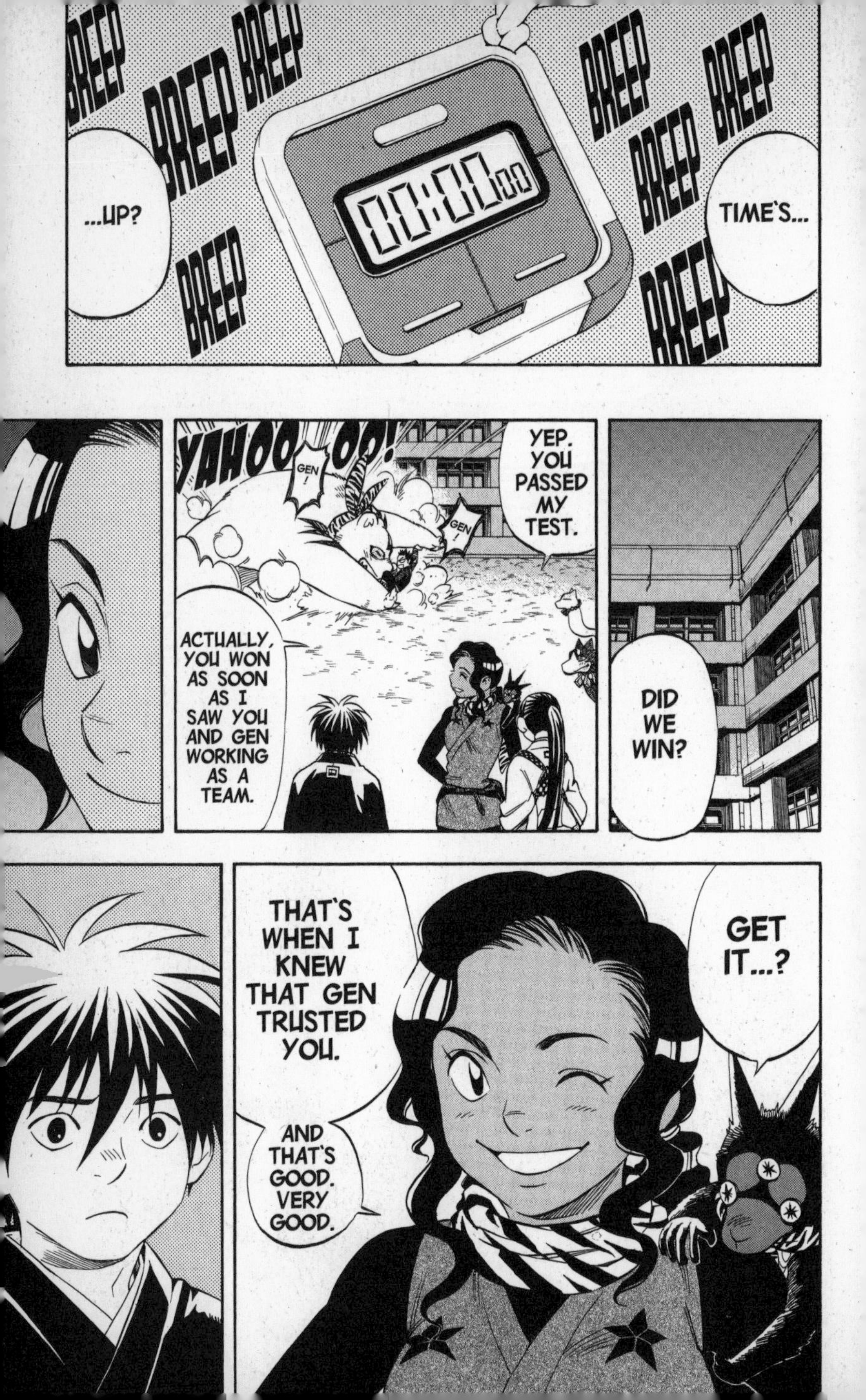
BREEP
BREEP
BREEP
TIME'S...
BREEP BREEP
BREEP
BREEP
...UP?
DID WE WIN?
YEP. YOU PASSED MY TEST.
YAHOO...OO!
GEN!
GEN!
ACTUALLY, YOU WON AS SOON AS I SAW YOU AND GEN WORKING AS A TEAM.
GET IT...?
THAT'S WHEN I KNEW THAT GEN TRUSTED YOU.
AND THAT'S GOOD. VERY GOOD.

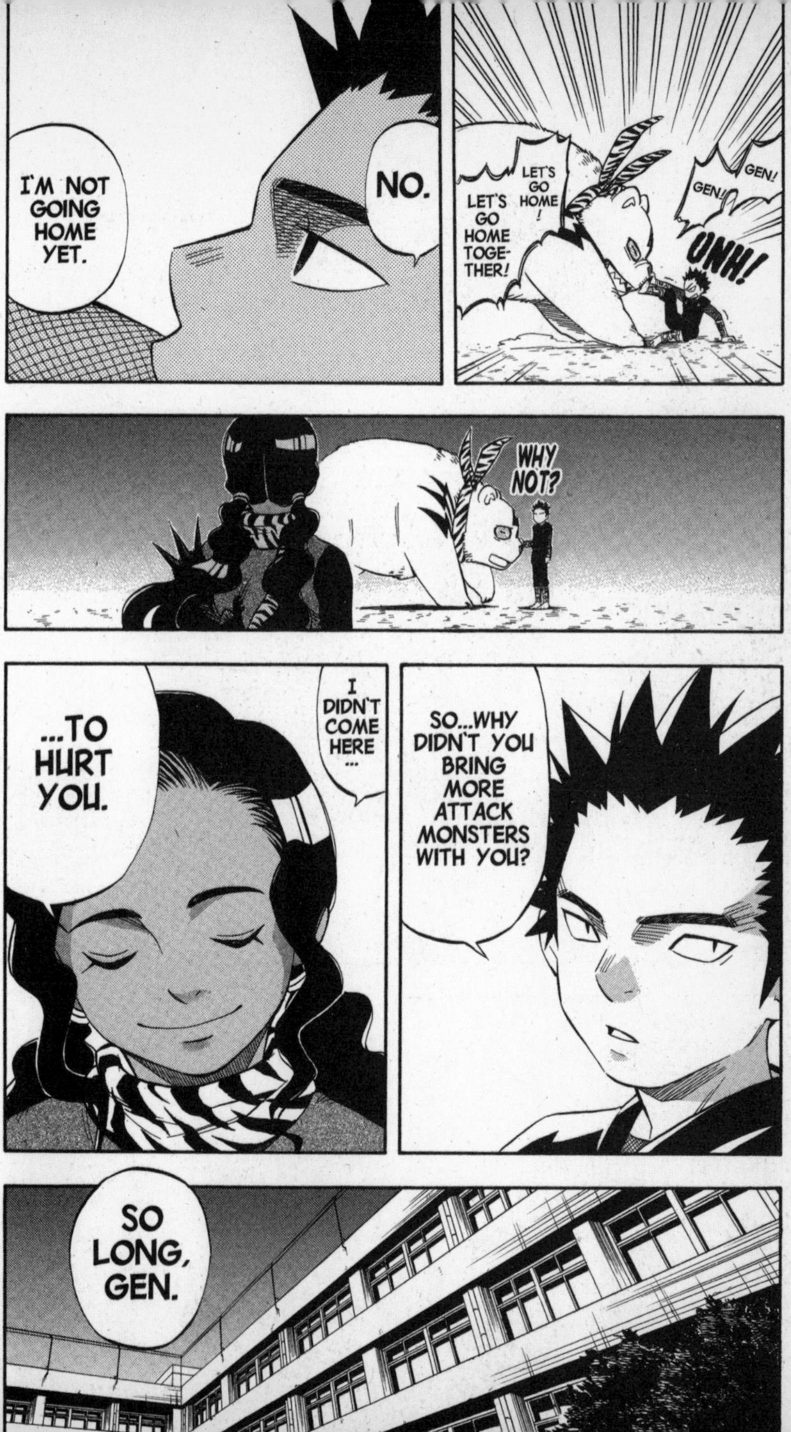
GEN!
GEN!
UNH!
LET'S GO HOME!
LET'S GO HOME TOGE-THER!
NO.
I'M NOT GOING HOME YET.
WHY NOT?
SO...WHY DIDN'T YOU BRING MORE ATTACK MONSTERS WITH YOU?
I DIDN'T COME HERE...
...TO HURT YOU.
SO LONG, GEN.

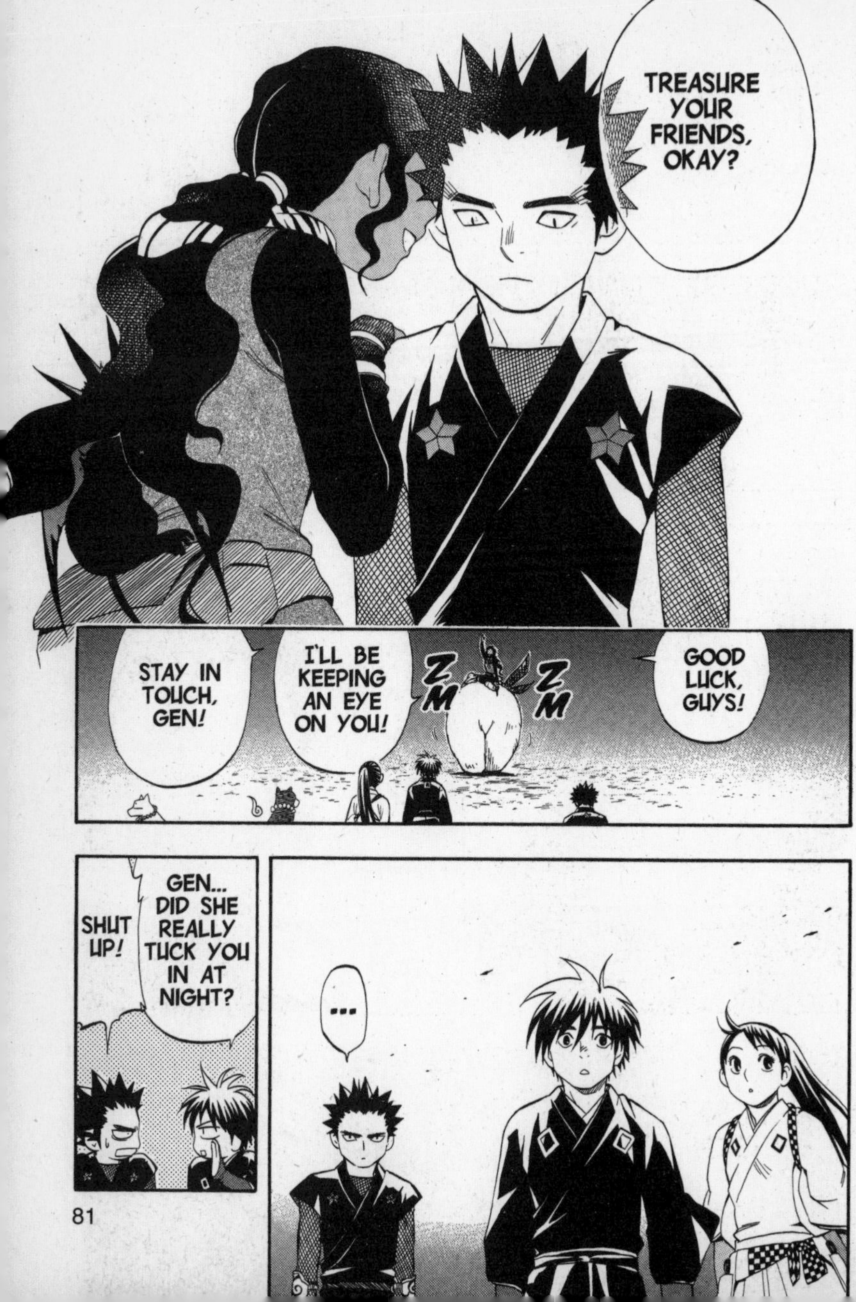
TREASURE YOUR FRIENDS, OKAY?
GOOD LUCK, GUYS!
ZM ZM
I'LL BE KEEPING AN EYE ON YOU!
STAY IN TOUCH, GEN!
...
GEN... DID SHE REALLY TUCK YOU IN AT NIGHT?
SHUT UP!

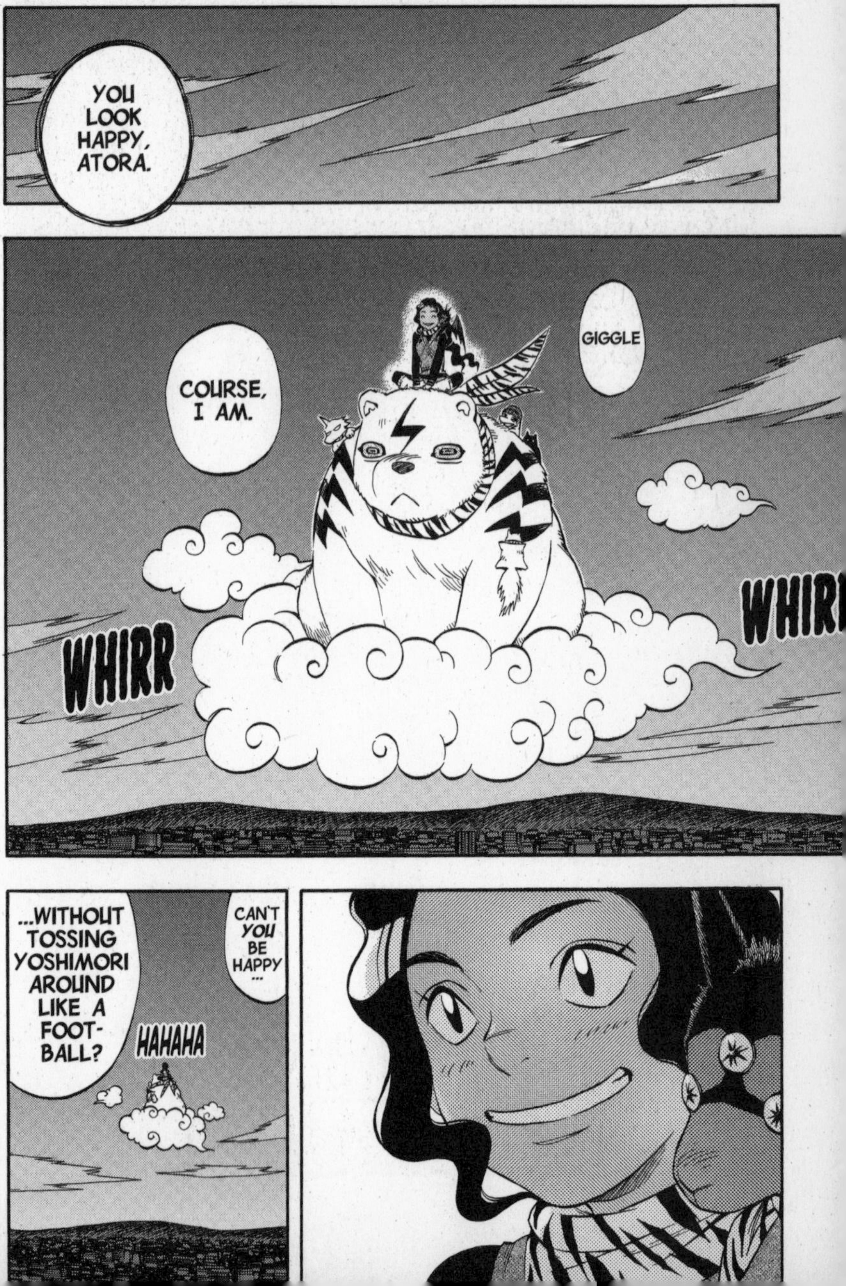
YOU LOOK HAPPY, ATORA.
GIGGLE
COURSE, I AM.
WHIR
WHIRR
CAN'T *YOU* BE HAPPY...
...WITHOUT TOSSING YOSHIMORI AROUND LIKE A FOOT-BALL?
HAHAHA

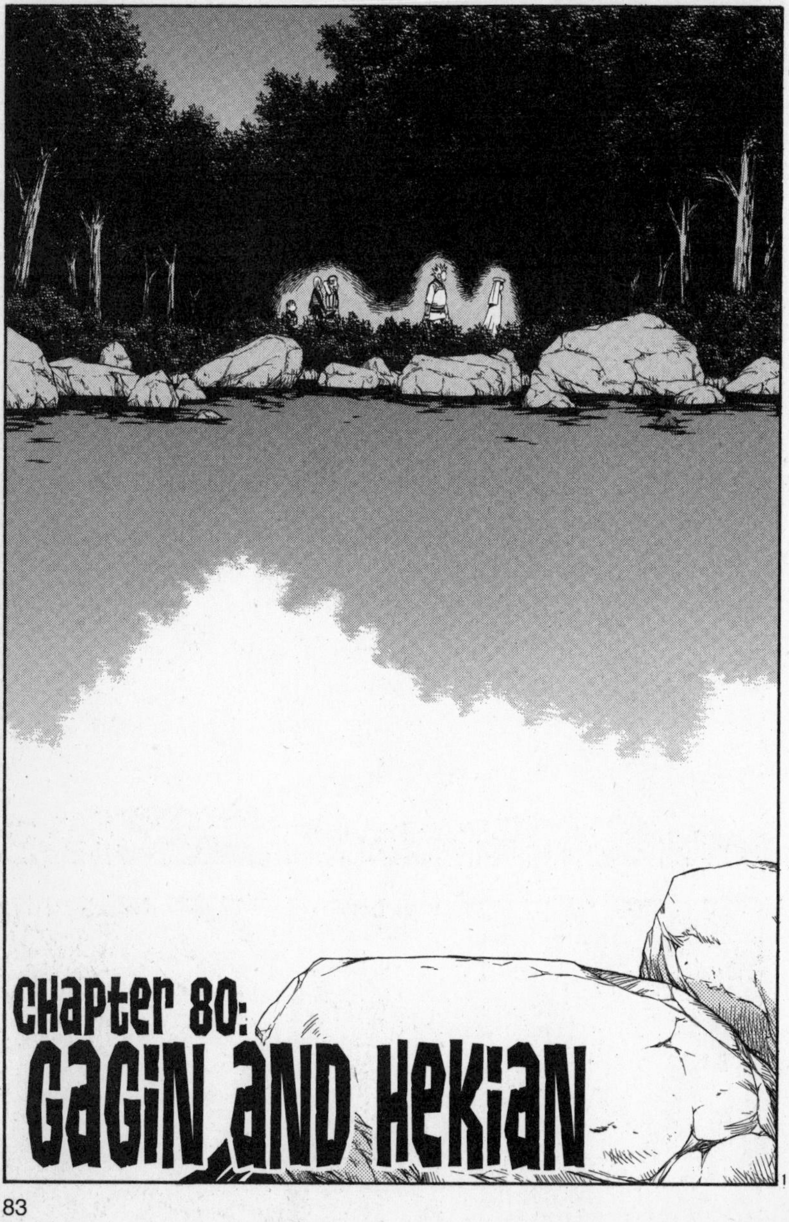
CHAPTER 80:
GAGIN AND HEKIAN

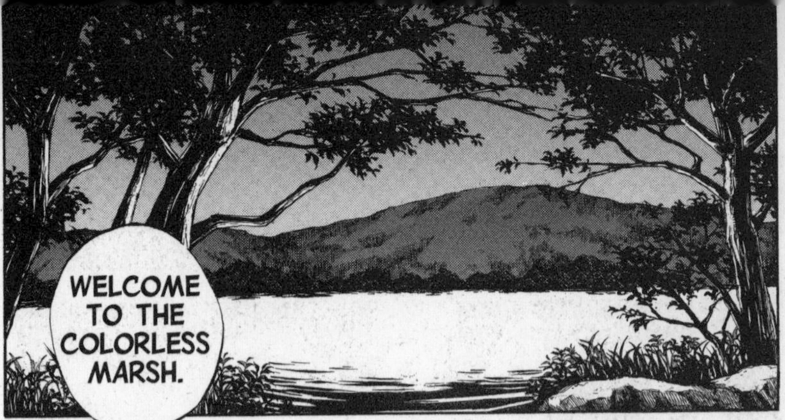
WELCOME TO THE COLORLESS MARSH.

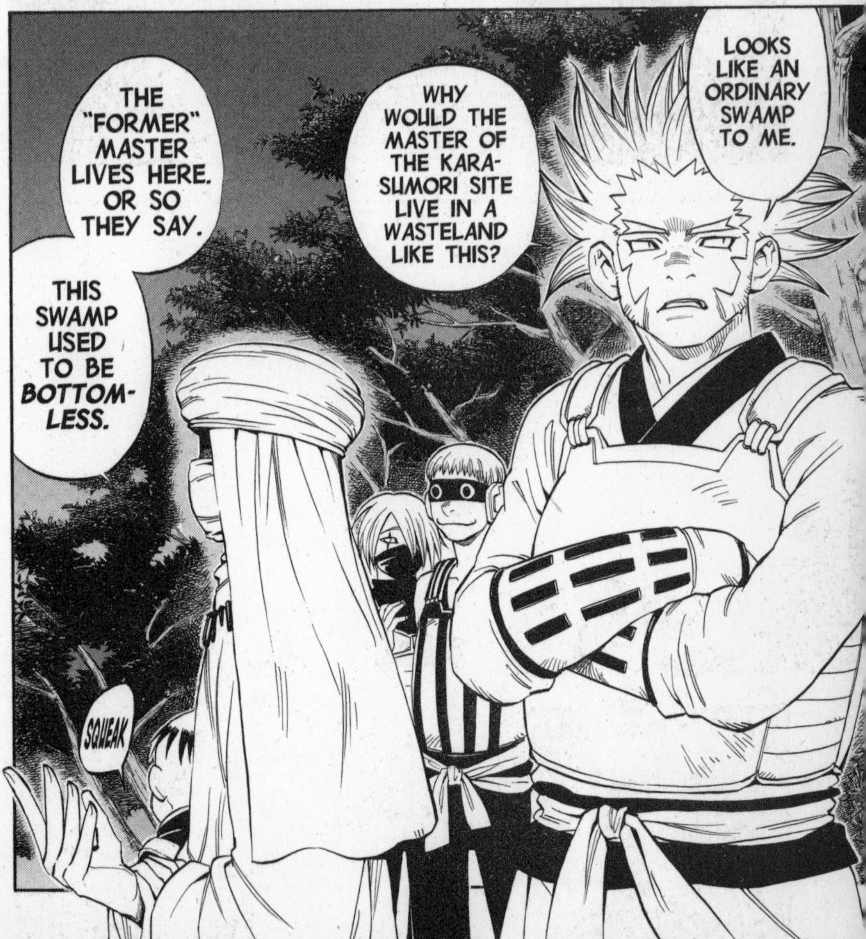
LOOKS LIKE AN ORDINARY SWAMP TO ME.
WHY WOULD THE MASTER OF THE KARA-SUMORI SITE LIVE IN A WASTELAND LIKE THIS?
THE "FORMER" MASTER LIVES HERE. OR SO THEY SAY.
THIS SWAMP USED TO BE *BOTTOM-LESS.*
SQUEAK

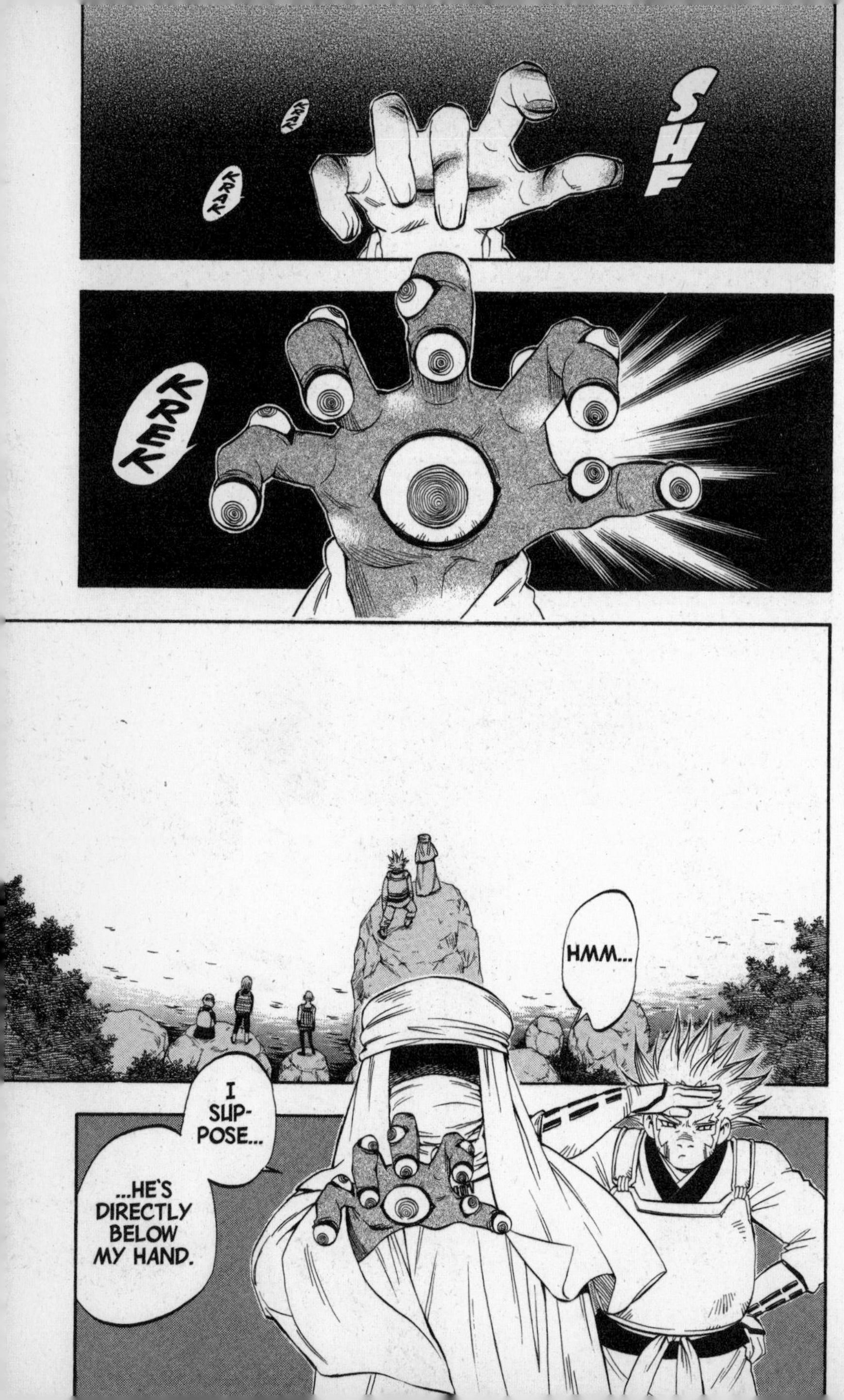
SHF
KRAK
KRAK
KREK
HMM...
I SUP-POSE...
...HE'S DIRECTLY BELOW MY HAND.

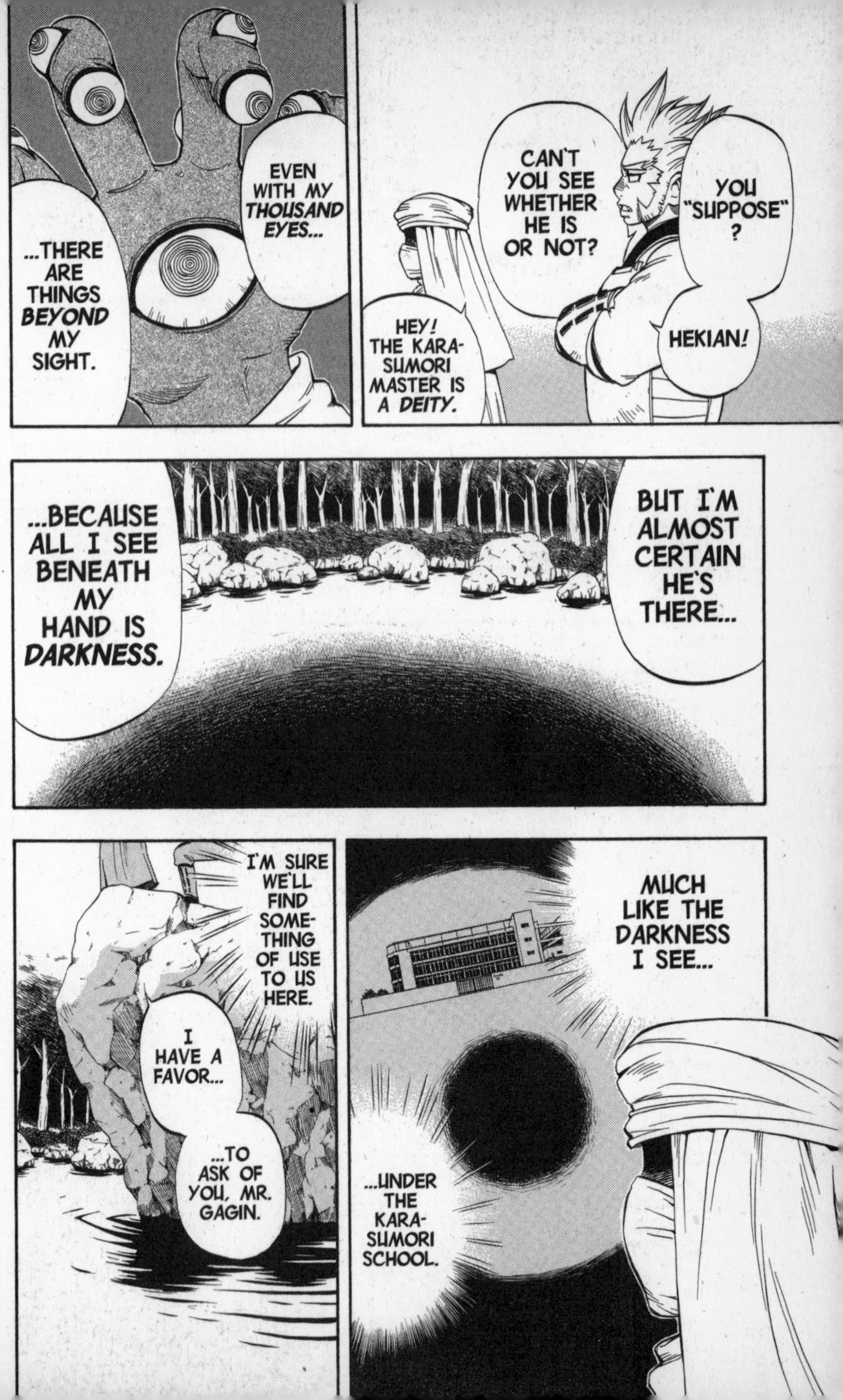
YOU "SUPPOSE"?
CAN'T YOU SEE WHETHER HE IS OR NOT?
HEKIAN!
HEY! THE KARA-SUMORI MASTER IS A *DEITY*.
EVEN WITH MY *THOUSAND EYES*...
...THERE ARE THINGS *BEYOND* MY SIGHT.
BUT I'M ALMOST CERTAIN HE'S THERE...
...BECAUSE ALL I SEE BENEATH *MY* HAND IS *DARKNESS*.
MUCH LIKE THE DARKNESS I SEE...
...UNDER THE KARA-SUMORI SCHOOL.
I'M SURE WE'LL FIND SOME-THING OF USE TO US HERE.
I HAVE A FAVOR...
...TO ASK OF YOU, MR. GAGIN.

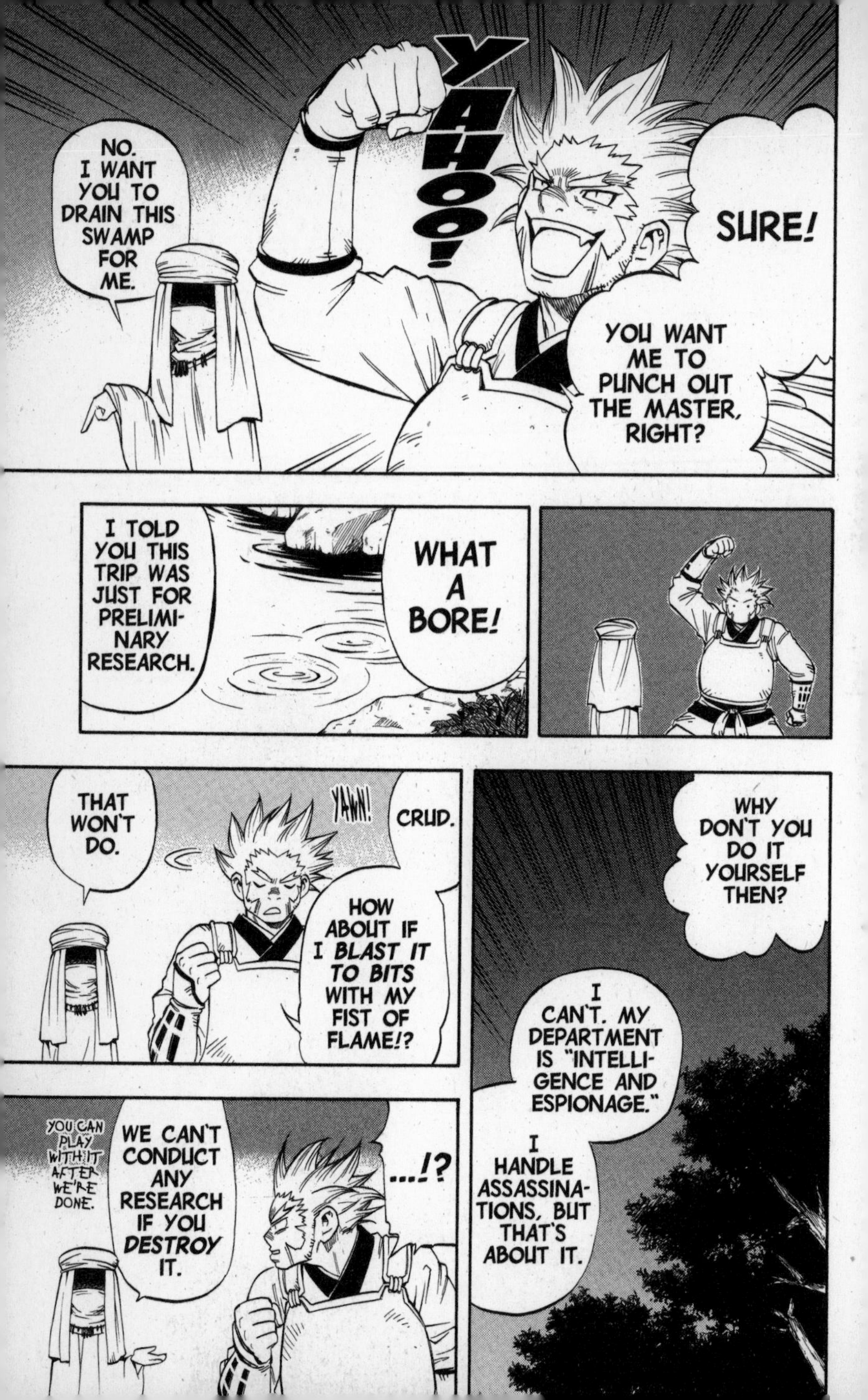
YAHOO!
SURE!
YOU WANT ME TO PUNCH OUT THE MASTER, RIGHT?
NO. I WANT YOU TO DRAIN THIS SWAMP FOR ME.
WHAT A BORE!
I TOLD YOU THIS TRIP WAS JUST FOR PRELIMINARY RESEARCH.
WHY DON'T YOU DO IT YOURSELF THEN?
I CAN'T. MY DEPARTMENT IS "INTELLIGENCE AND ESPIONAGE."
I HANDLE ASSASSINATIONS, BUT THAT'S ABOUT IT.
CRUD.
YAWN!
HOW ABOUT IF I *BLAST* IT *TO BITS* WITH MY FIST OF FLAME!?
THAT WON'T DO.
...!?
WE CAN'T CONDUCT ANY RESEARCH IF YOU *DESTROY* IT.
YOU CAN PLAY WITH IT AFTER WE'RE DONE.

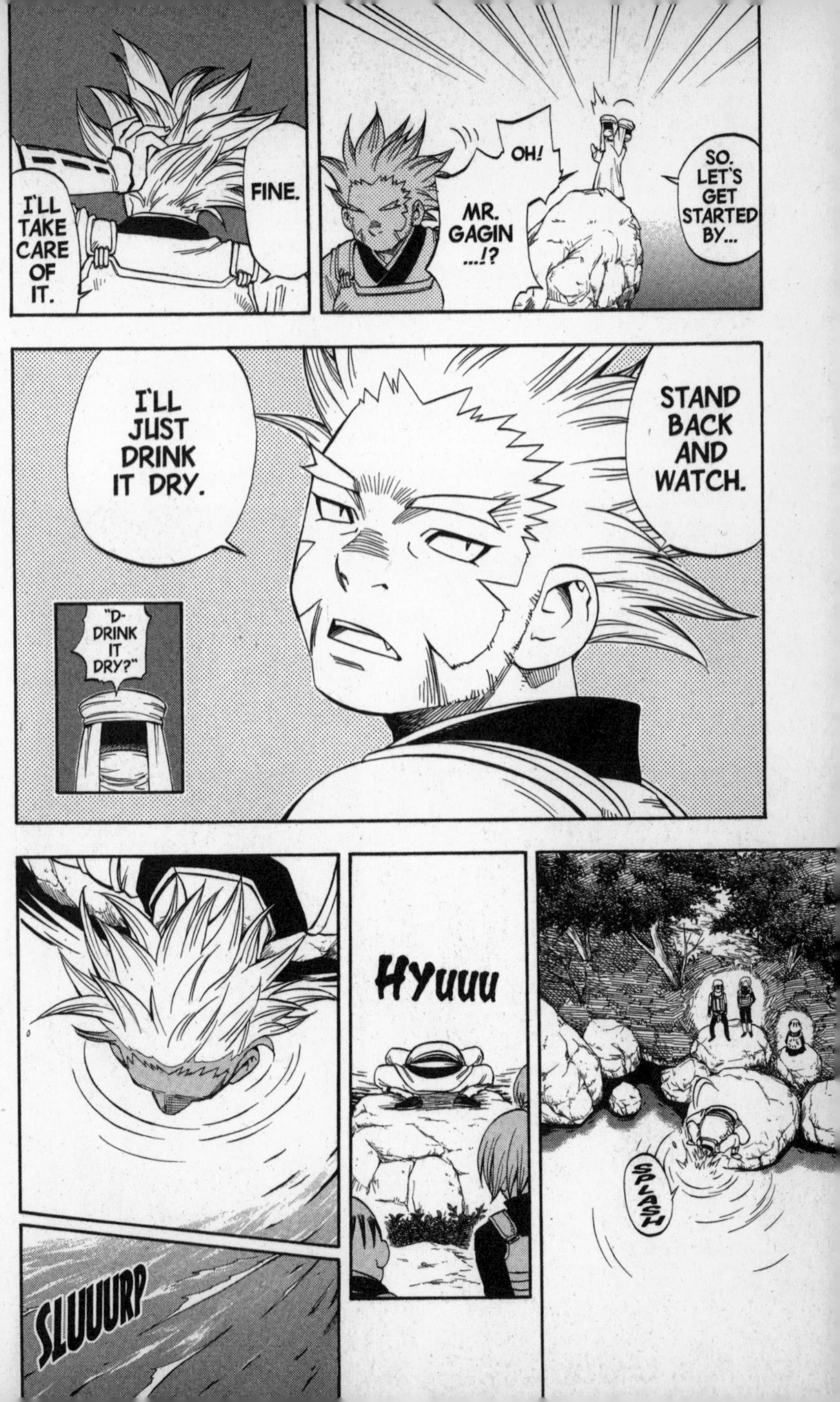
SO. LET'S GET STARTED BY...
OH!
MR. GAGIN ...!?
FINE.
I'LL TAKE CARE OF IT.
STAND BACK AND WATCH.
I'LL JUST DRINK IT DRY.
"D-DRINK IT DRY?"
SPLASH
Hyuuu
SLUUURP

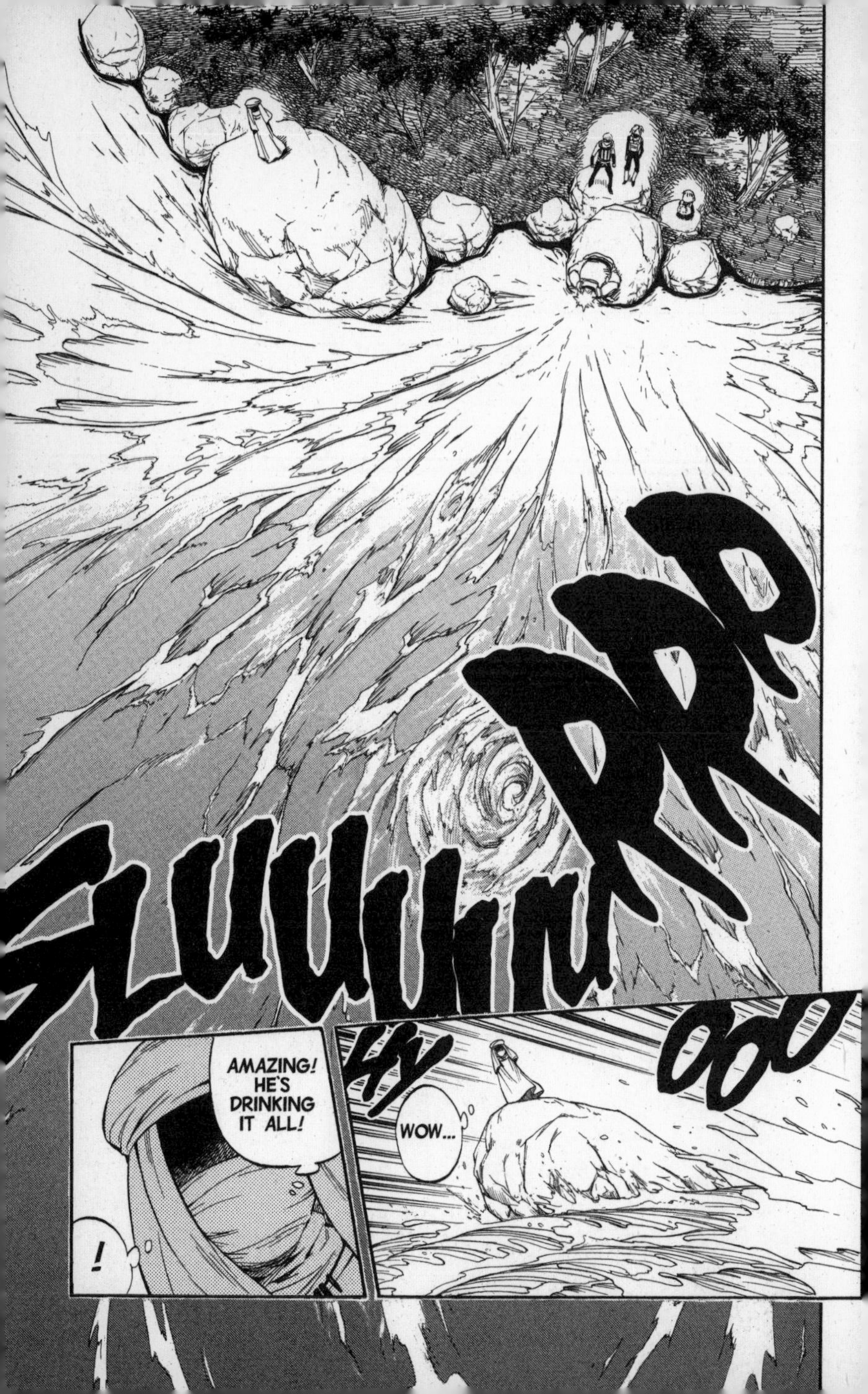
WOW...
AMAZING! HE'S DRINKING IT ALL!
!

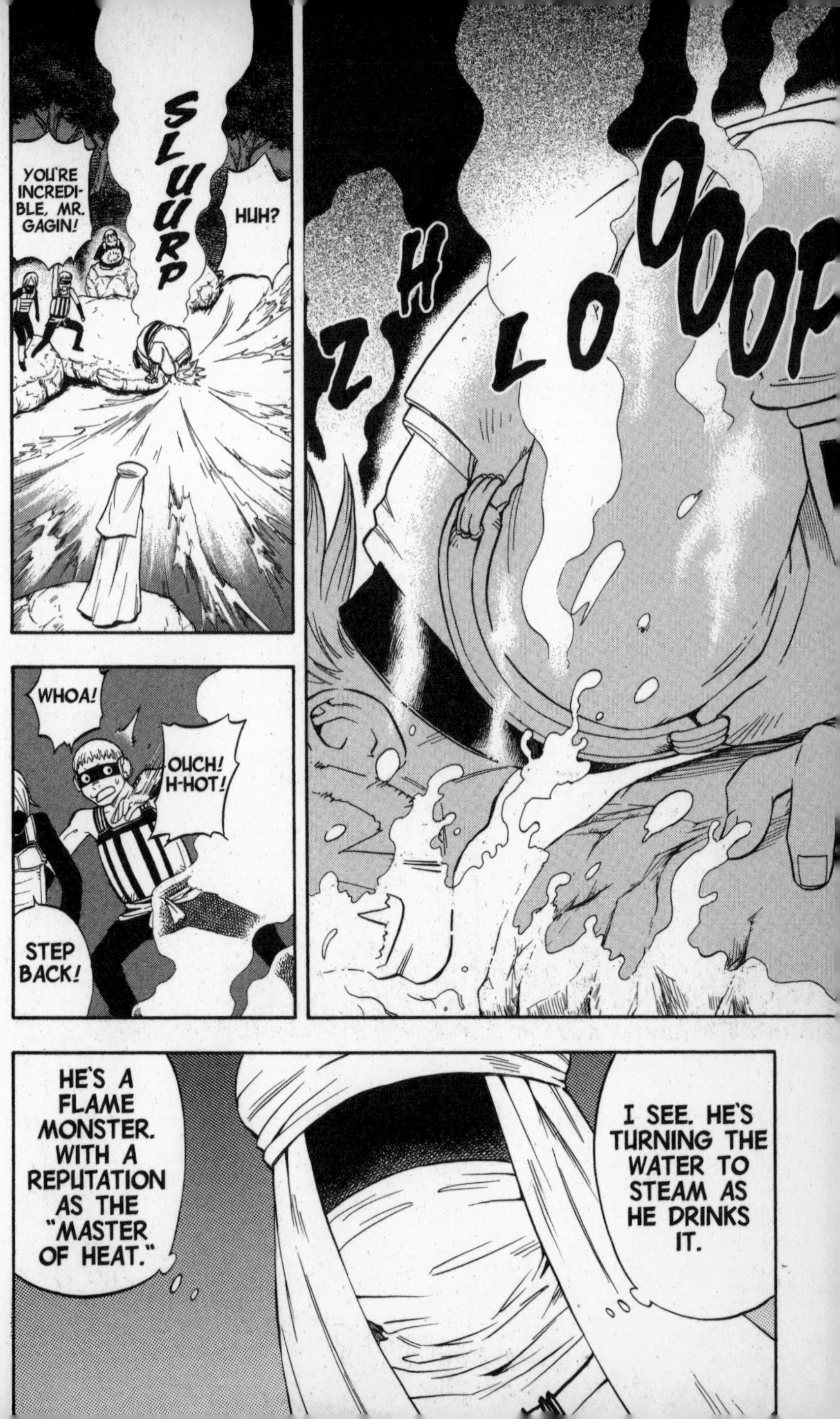
ZHLOOOOP
HUH?
SLUURP
YOU'RE INCREDIBLE, MR. GAGIN!
WHOA!
OUCH! H-HOT!
STEP BACK!
I SEE. HE'S TURNING THE WATER TO STEAM AS HE DRINKS IT.
HE'S A FLAME MONSTER. WITH A REPUTATION AS THE "MASTER OF HEAT."

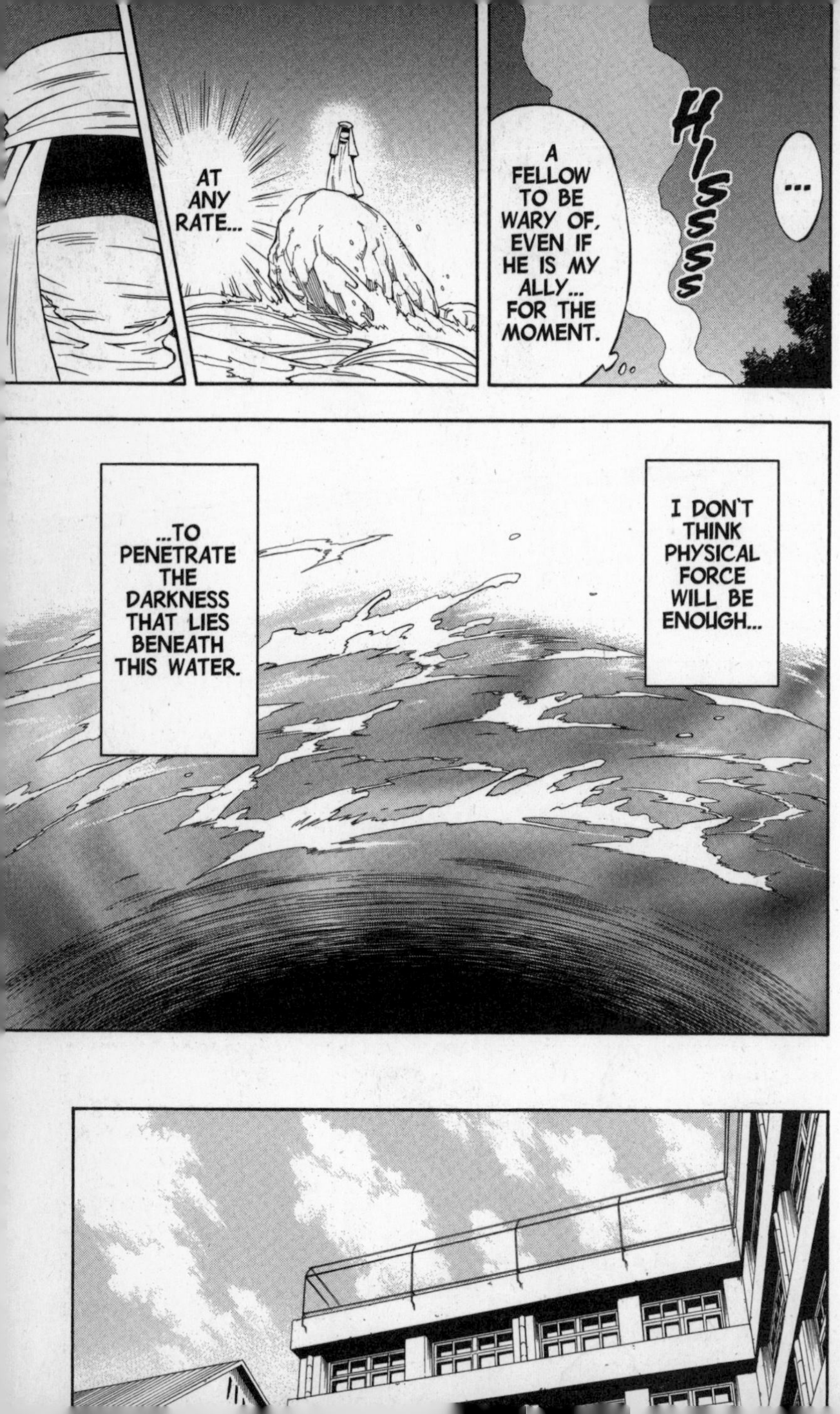
...
HISSSS
A FELLOW TO BE WARY OF, EVEN IF HE IS MY ALLY... FOR THE MOMENT.
AT ANY RATE...
I DON'T THINK PHYSICAL FORCE WILL BE ENOUGH...
...TO PENETRATE THE DARKNESS THAT LIES BENEATH THIS WATER.

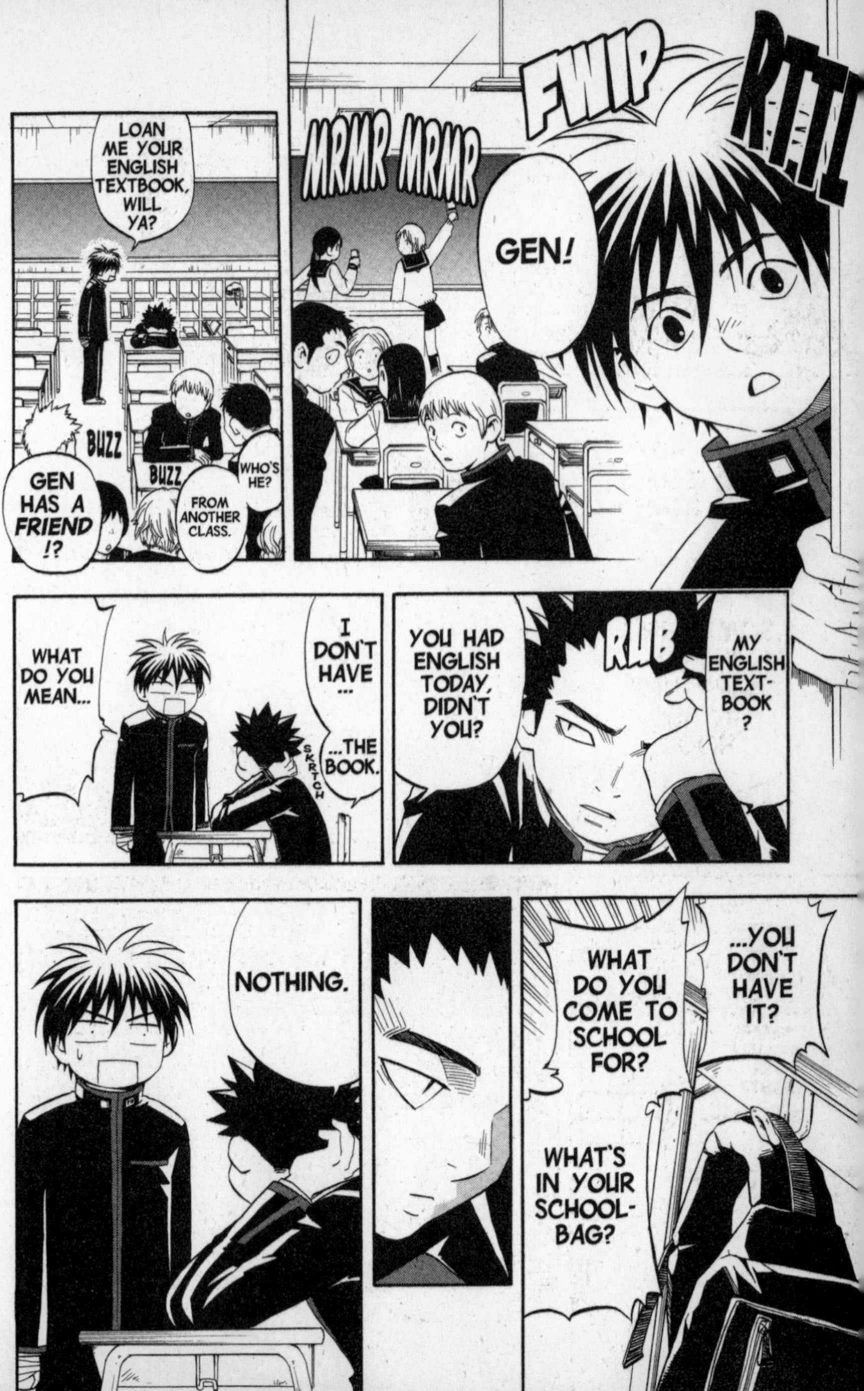
FWIP
GEN!
MRMR MRMR
LOAN ME YOUR ENGLISH TEXTBOOK, WILL YA?
BUZZ
BUZZ
WHO'S HE?
FROM ANOTHER CLASS.
GEN HAS A FRIEND!?
MY ENGLISH TEXT-BOOK?
RUB
YOU HAD ENGLISH TODAY, DIDN'T YOU?
I DON'T HAVE...
...THE BOOK.
SKRTCH
WHAT DO YOU MEAN...
...YOU DON'T HAVE IT?
WHAT DO YOU COME TO SCHOOL FOR?
WHAT'S IN YOUR SCHOOL-BAG?
NOTHING.

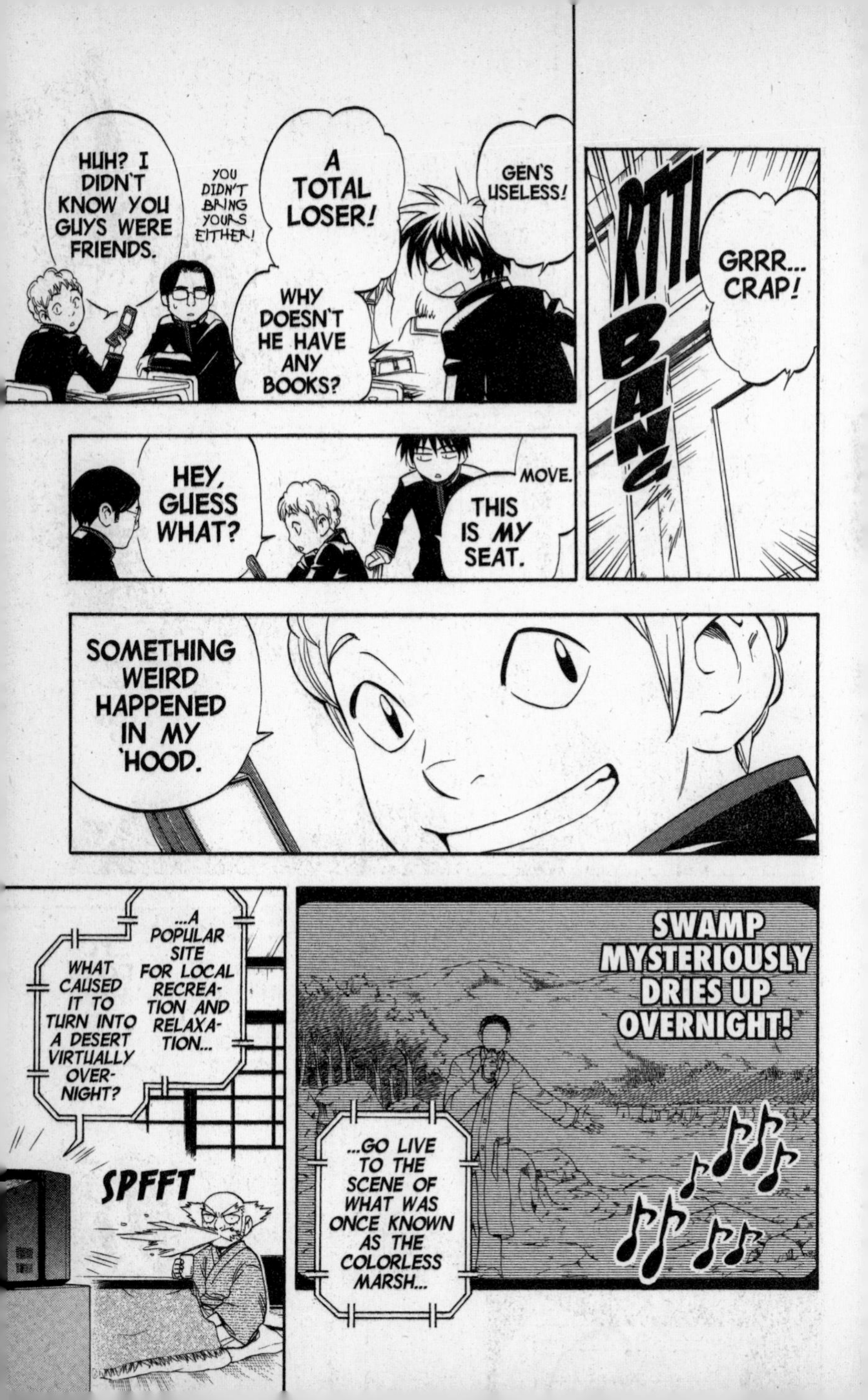
RTTI
BANG
GRRR... CRAP!
GEN'S USELESS!
A TOTAL LOSER!
WHY DOESN'T HE HAVE ANY BOOKS?
YOU DIDN'T BRING YOURS EITHER!
HUH? I DIDN'T KNOW YOU GUYS WERE FRIENDS.
MOVE.
THIS IS MY SEAT.
HEY, GUESS WHAT?
SOMETHING WEIRD HAPPENED IN MY 'HOOD.
SWAMP MYSTERIOUSLY DRIES UP OVERNIGHT!
...GO LIVE TO THE SCENE OF WHAT WAS ONCE KNOWN AS THE COLORLESS MARSH...
...A POPULAR SITE FOR LOCAL RECREATION AND RELAXATION...
WHAT CAUSED IT TO TURN INTO A DESERT VIRTUALLY OVERNIGHT?
SPFFT

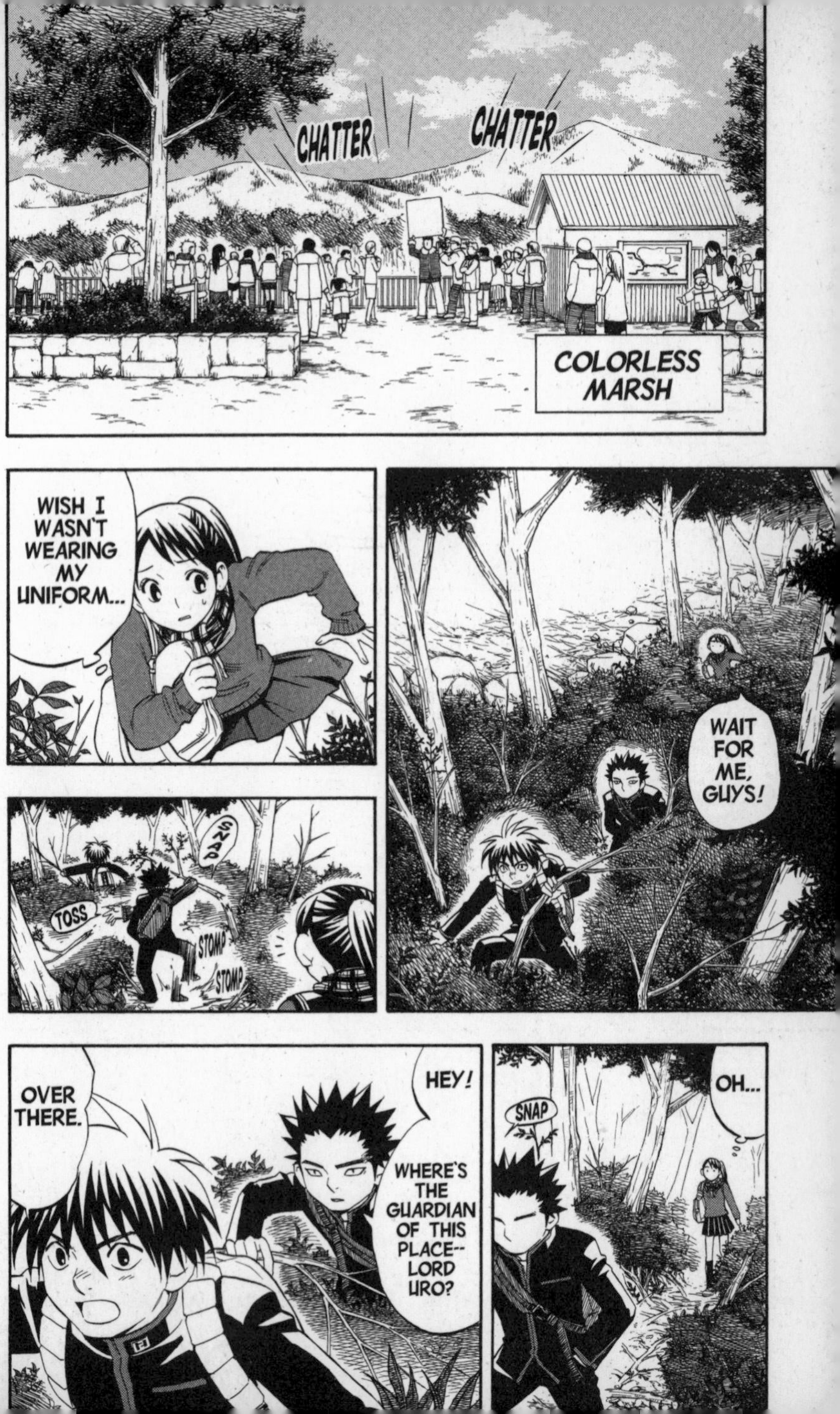
CHATTER
CHATTER
COLORLESS MARSH
WAIT FOR ME, GUYS!
WISH I WASN'T WEARING MY UNIFORM...
SNAP
TOSS
STOMP
STOMP
OH...
SNAP
HEY!
WHERE'S THE GUARDIAN OF THIS PLACE--LORD URO?
OVER THERE.

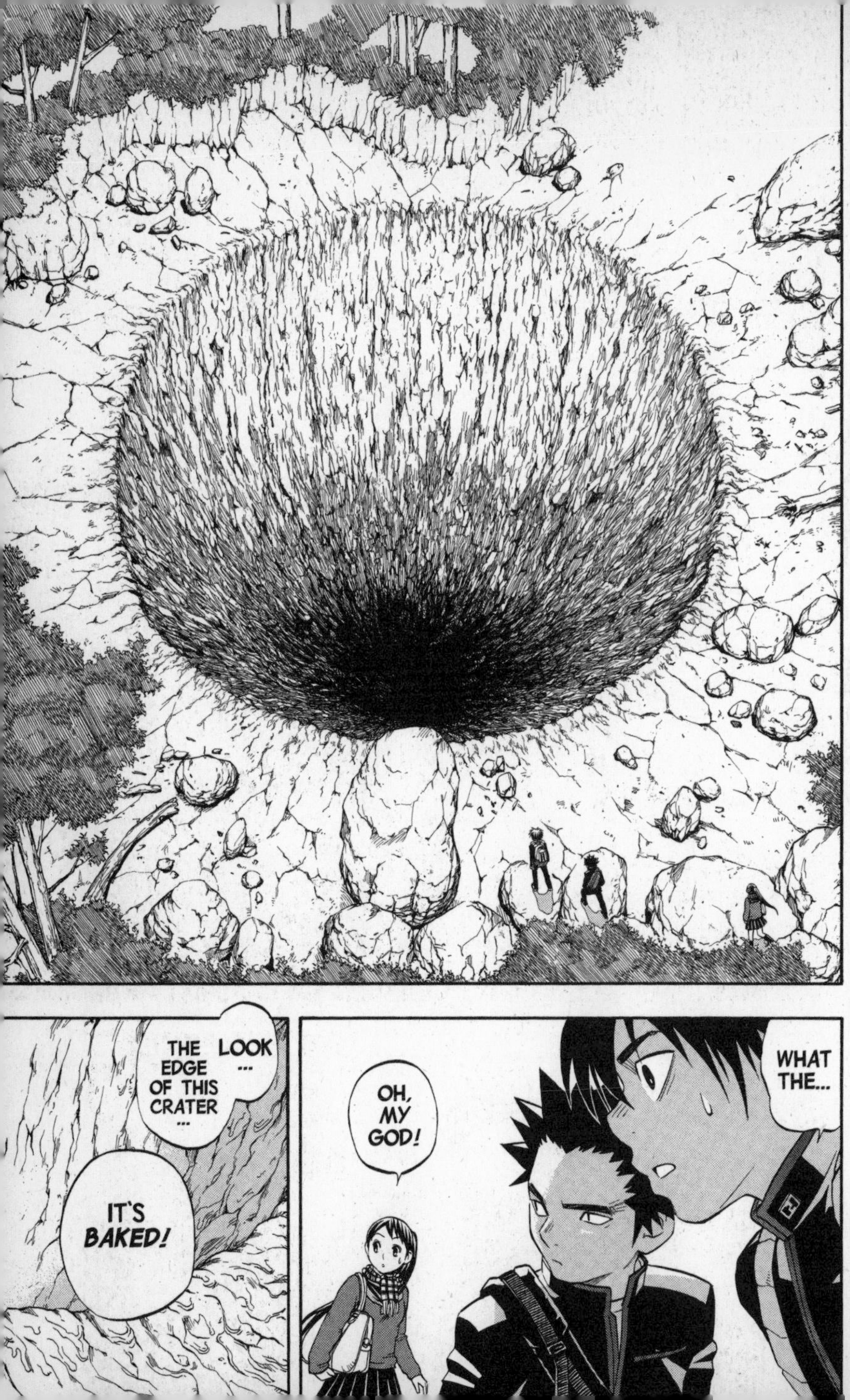
WHAT THE...
OH, MY GOD!
LOOK...
THE EDGE OF THIS CRATER...
IT'S BAKED!

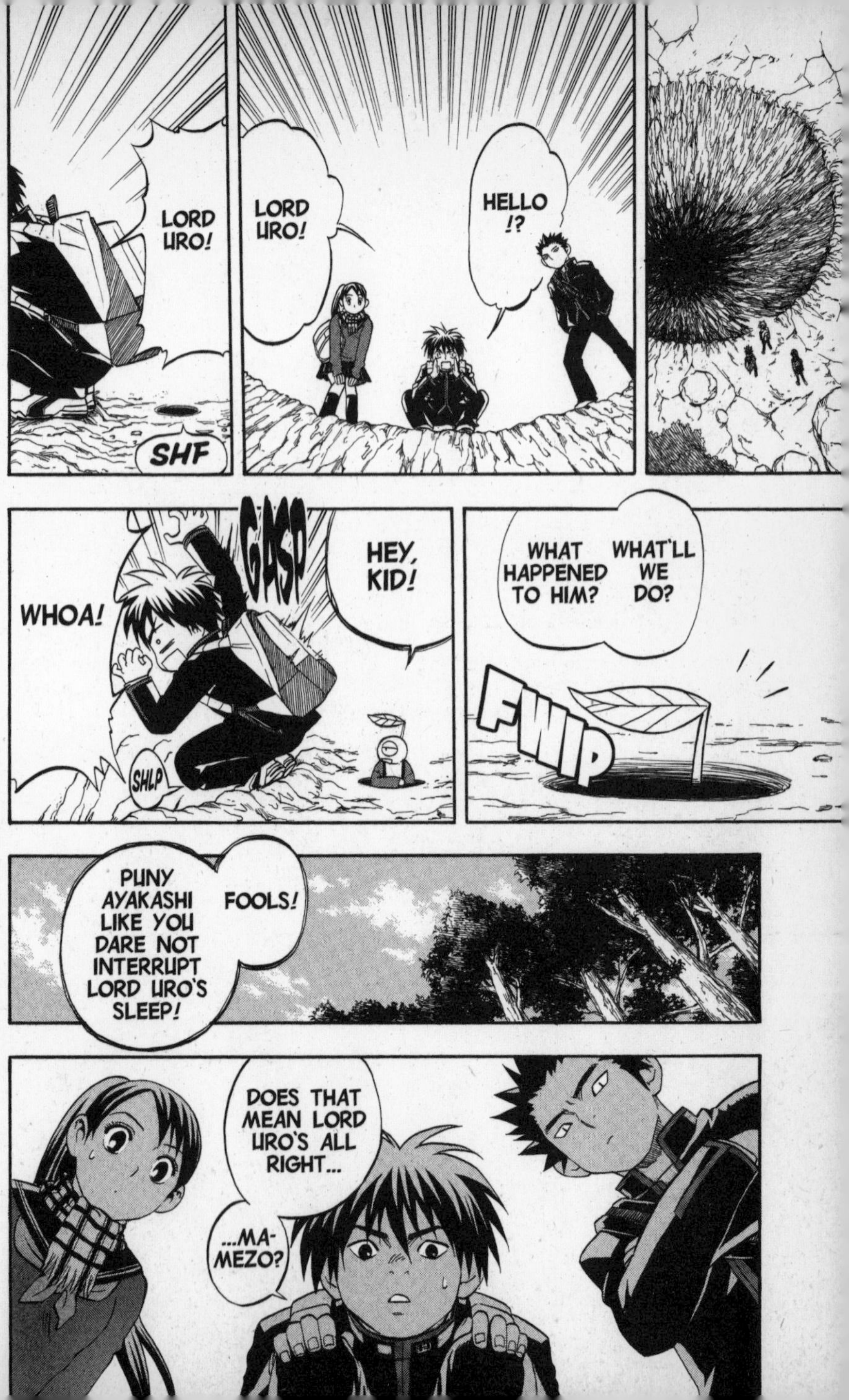
HELLO!?
LORD URO!
LORD URO!
SHF
WHAT'LL WE DO?
WHAT HAPPENED TO HIM?
FWIP
HEY, KID!
GASP
WHOA!
SHLP
FOOLS!
PUNY AYAKASHI LIKE YOU DARE NOT INTERRUPT LORD URO'S SLEEP!
DOES THAT MEAN LORD URO'S ALL RIGHT...
...MA-MEZO?

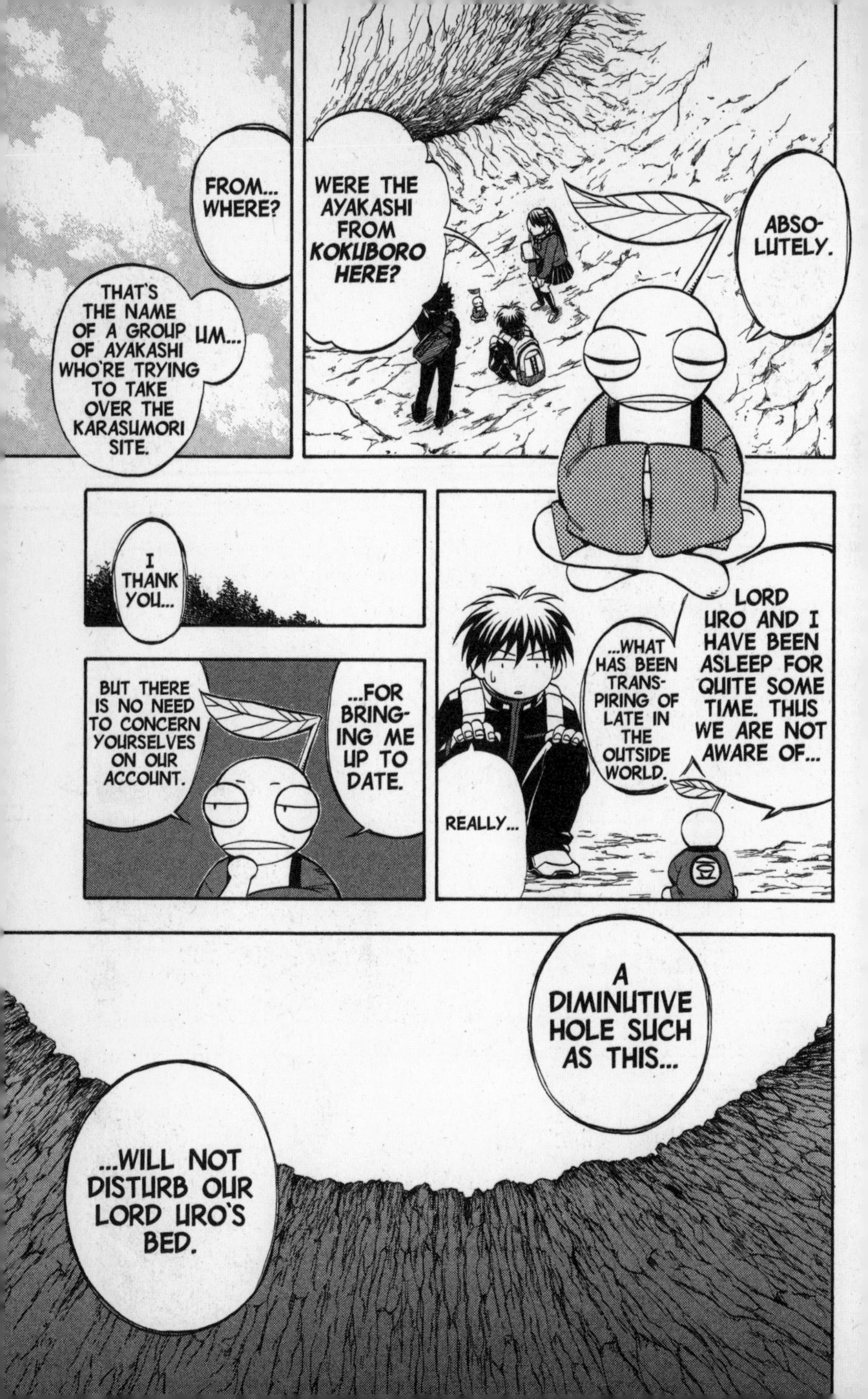

WERE THE AYAKASHI FROM KOKUBORO HERE?
ABSO-LUTELY.
FROM... WHERE?
UM...
THAT'S THE NAME OF A GROUP OF AYAKASHI WHO'RE TRYING TO TAKE OVER THE KARASUMORI SITE.
LORD URO AND I HAVE BEEN ASLEEP FOR QUITE SOME TIME. THUS WE ARE NOT AWARE OF...
...WHAT HAS BEEN TRANS-PIRING OF LATE IN THE OUTSIDE WORLD.
REALLY...
I THANK YOU...
...FOR BRING-ING ME UP TO DATE.
BUT THERE IS NO NEED TO CONCERN YOURSELVES ON OUR ACCOUNT.
A DIMINUTIVE HOLE SUCH AS THIS...
...WILL NOT DISTURB OUR LORD URO'S BED.

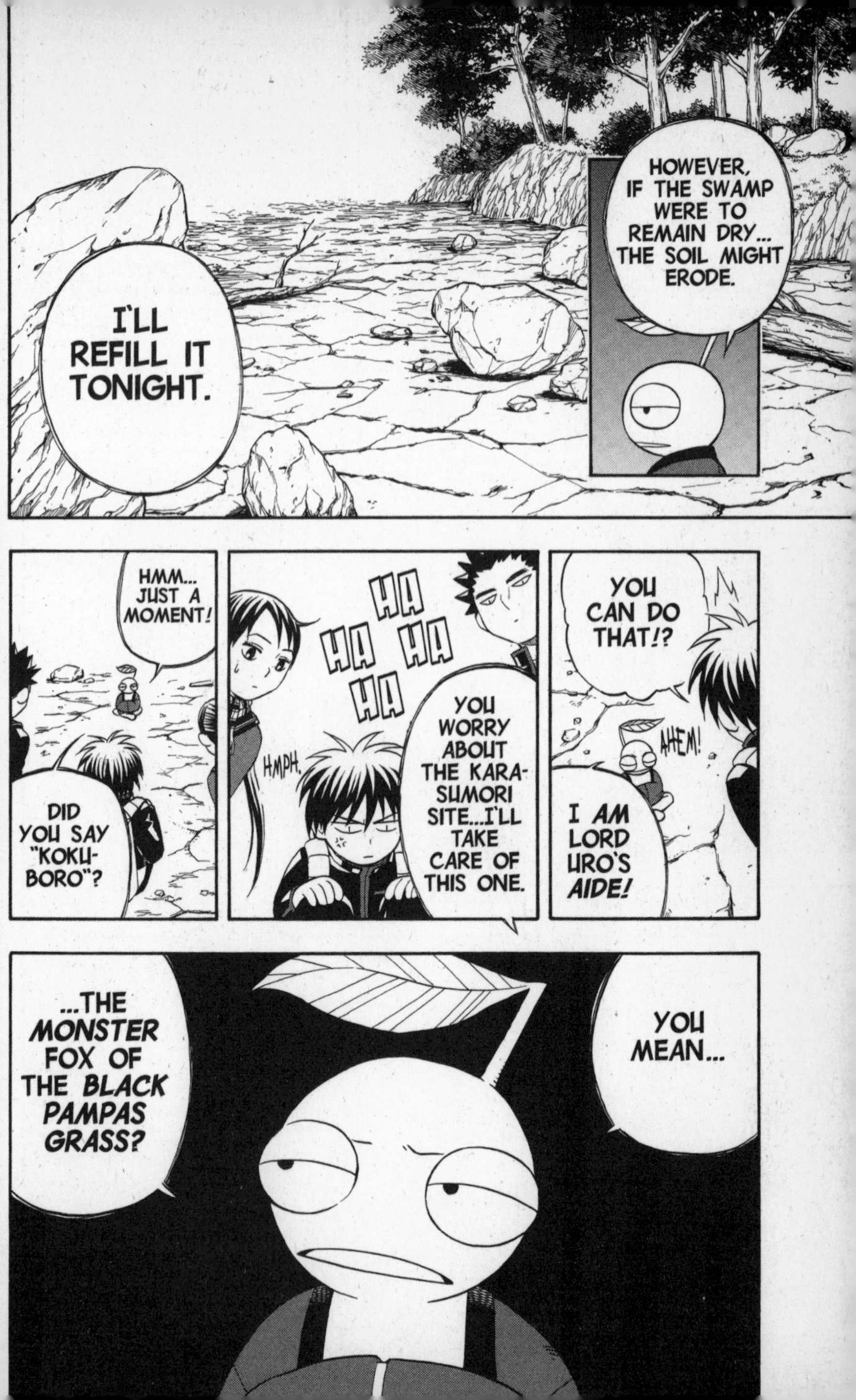
HOWEVER, IF THE SWAMP WERE TO REMAIN DRY... THE SOIL MIGHT ERODE.
I'LL REFILL IT TONIGHT.
YOU CAN DO THAT!?
AHEM!
I AM LORD URO'S AIDE!
HA HA HA HA
YOU WORRY ABOUT THE KARA-SUMORI SITE...I'LL TAKE CARE OF THIS ONE.
HMPH.
HMM... JUST A MOMENT!
DID YOU SAY "KOKU-BORO"?
YOU MEAN...
...THE MONSTER FOX OF THE BLACK PAMPAS GRASS?

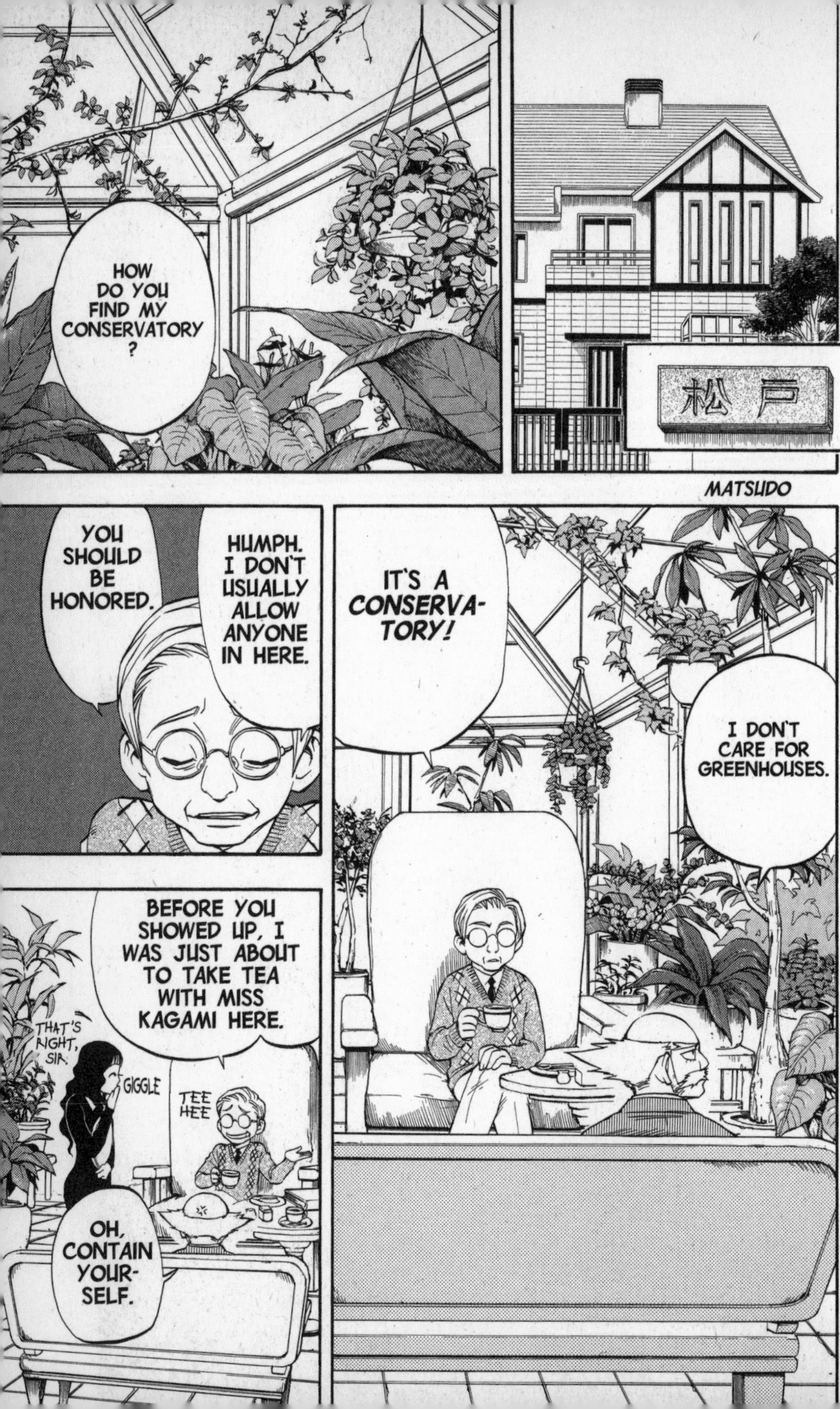
松戸
MATSUDO
HOW DO YOU FIND MY CONSERVATORY?
I DON'T CARE FOR GREENHOUSES.
IT'S A CONSERVATORY!
HUMPH. I DON'T USUALLY ALLOW ANYONE IN HERE.
YOU SHOULD BE HONORED.
BEFORE YOU SHOWED UP, I WAS JUST ABOUT TO TAKE TEA WITH MISS KAGAMI HERE.
THAT'S RIGHT, SIR.
GIGGLE
TEE HEE
OH, CONTAIN YOURSELF.

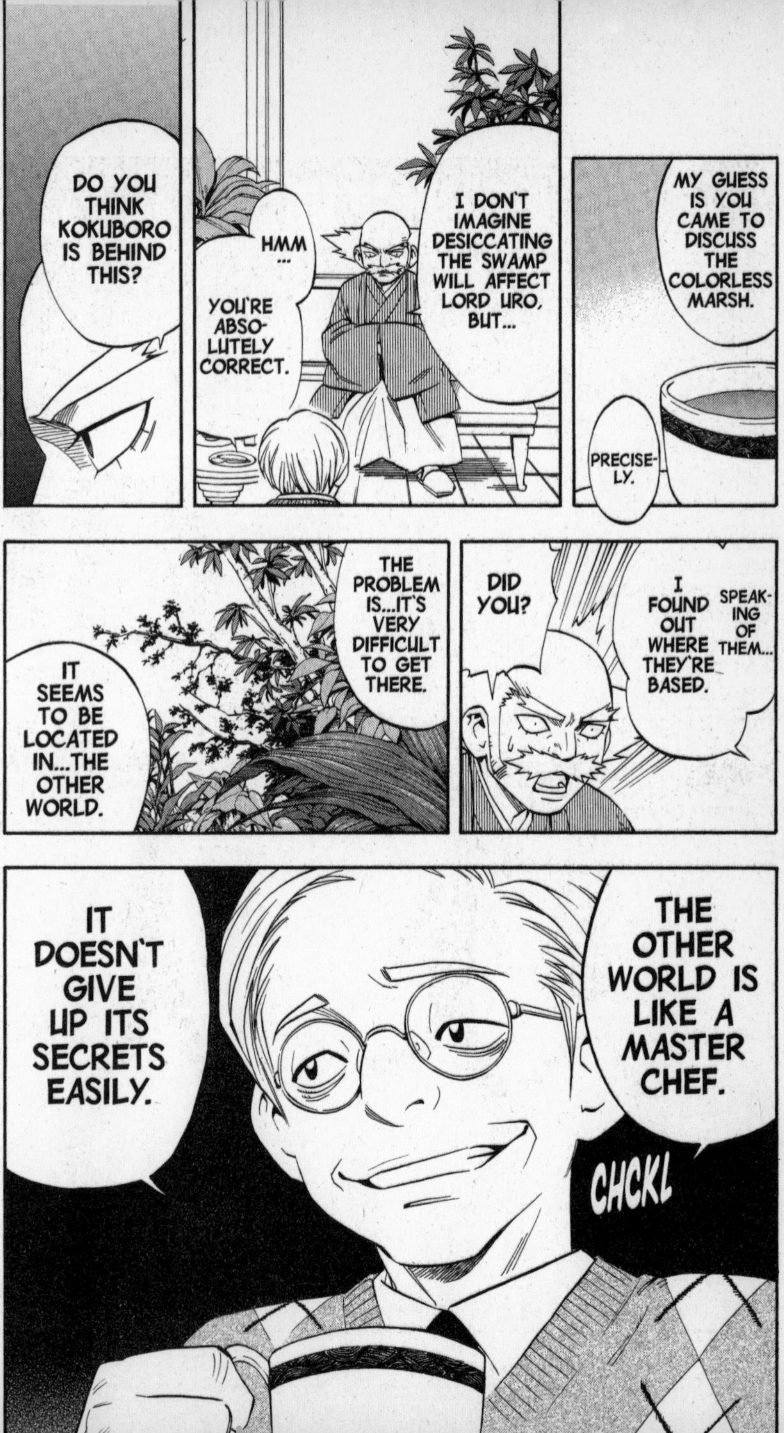
MY GUESS IS YOU CAME TO DISCUSS THE COLORLESS MARSH.
PRECISE-LY.
I DON'T IMAGINE DESICCATING THE SWAMP WILL AFFECT LORD URO, BUT...
HMM ...
YOU'RE ABSO-LUTELY CORRECT.
DO YOU THINK KOKUBORO IS BEHIND THIS?
SPEAK-ING OF THEM...
I FOUND OUT WHERE THEY'RE BASED.
DID YOU?
THE PROBLEM IS...IT'S VERY DIFFICULT TO GET THERE.
IT SEEMS TO BE LOCATED IN...THE OTHER WORLD.
THE OTHER WORLD IS LIKE A MASTER CHEF.
CHCKL
IT DOESN'T GIVE UP ITS SECRETS EASILY.

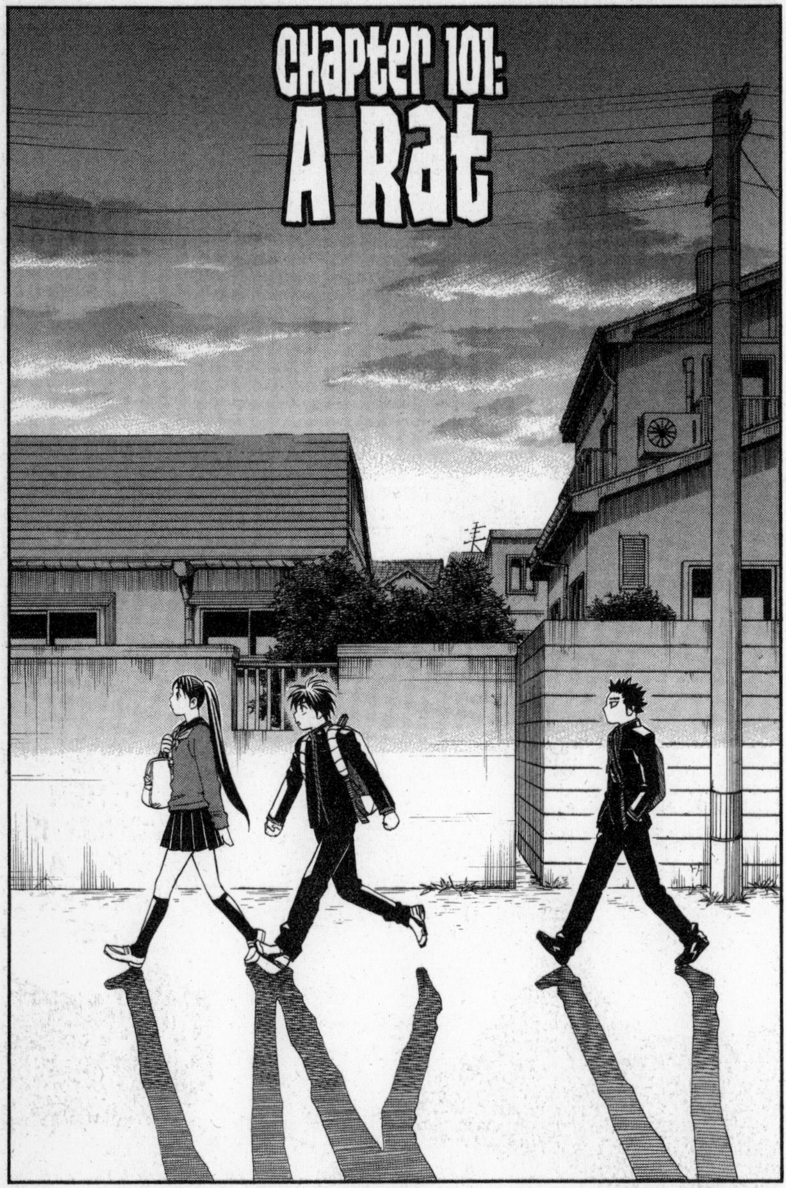
Chapter 101:
A Rat

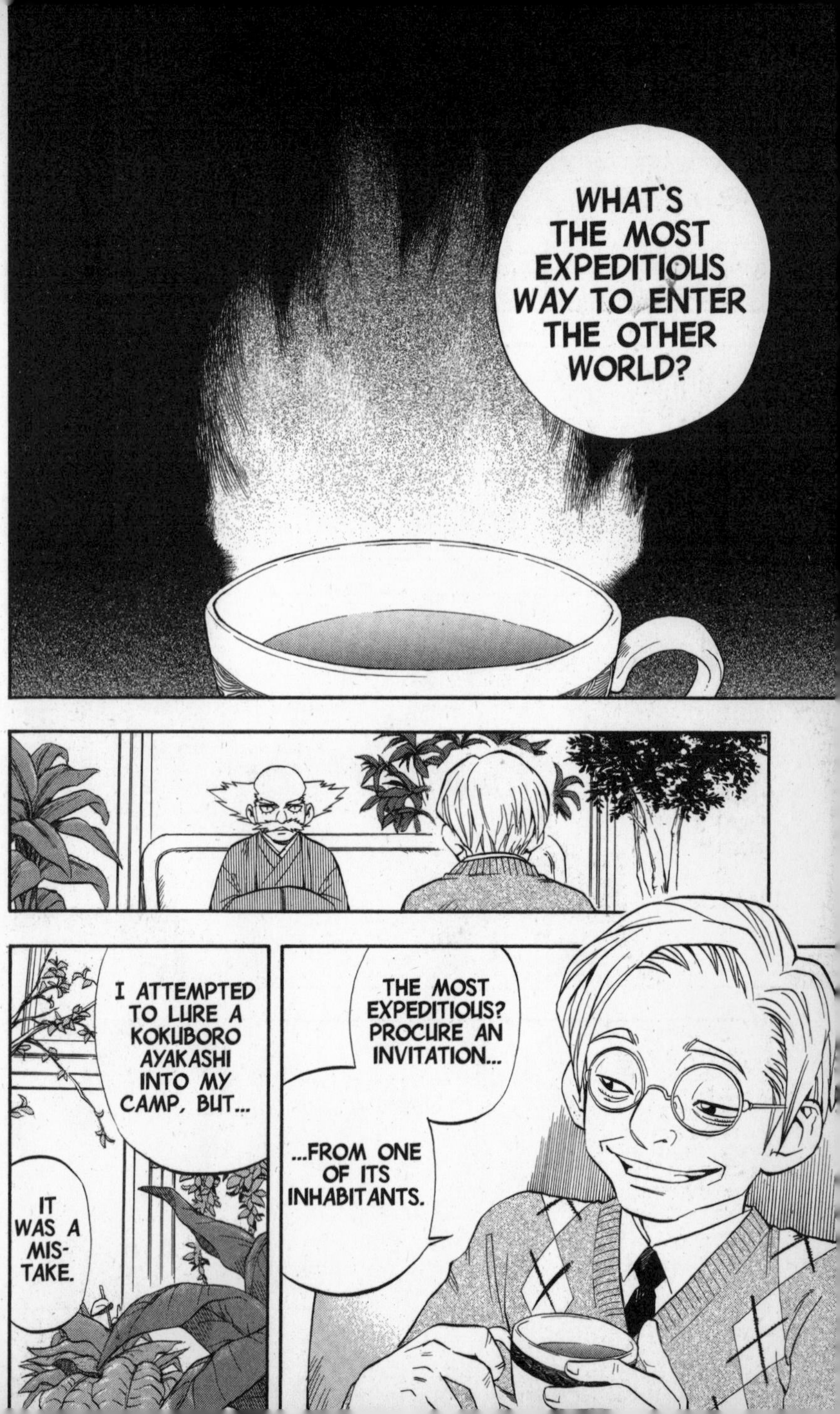
WHAT'S THE MOST EXPEDITIOUS WAY TO ENTER THE OTHER WORLD?
THE MOST EXPEDITIOUS? PROCURE AN INVITATION...
...FROM ONE OF ITS INHABITANTS.
I ATTEMPTED TO LURE A KOKUBORO AYAKASHI INTO MY CAMP, BUT...
IT WAS A MIS-TAKE.

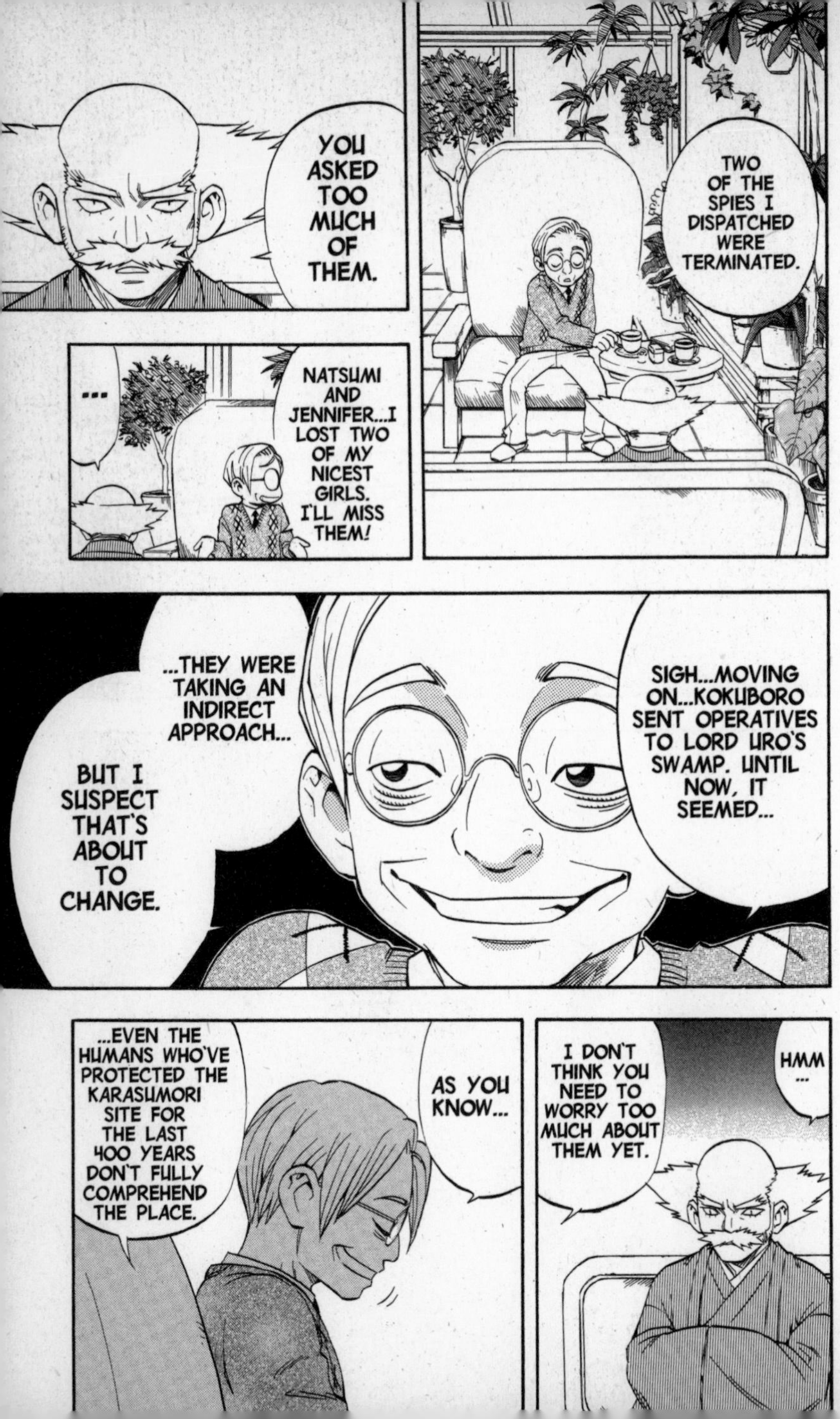
TWO OF THE SPIES I DISPATCHED WERE TERMINATED.
YOU ASKED TOO MUCH OF THEM.
NATSUMI AND JENNIFER...I LOST TWO OF MY NICEST GIRLS. I'LL MISS THEM!
...
SIGH...MOVING ON...KOKUBORO SENT OPERATIVES TO LORD URO'S SWAMP. UNTIL NOW, IT SEEMED...
...THEY WERE TAKING AN INDIRECT APPROACH...
BUT I SUSPECT THAT'S ABOUT TO CHANGE.
HMM...
I DON'T THINK YOU NEED TO WORRY TOO MUCH ABOUT THEM YET.
AS YOU KNOW...
...EVEN THE HUMANS WHO'VE PROTECTED THE KARASUMORI SITE FOR THE LAST 400 YEARS DON'T FULLY COMPREHEND THE PLACE.

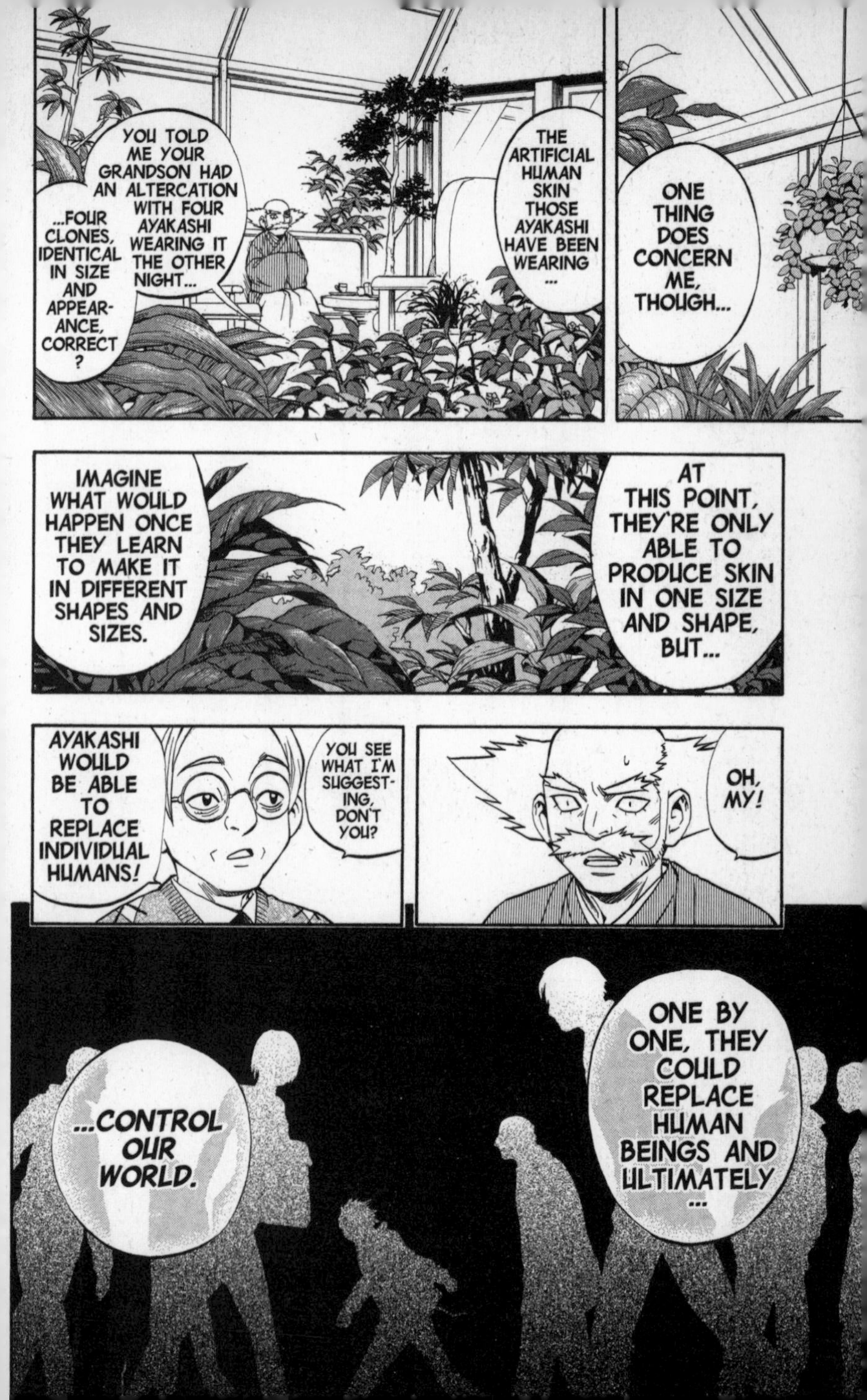
ONE THING DOES CONCERN ME, THOUGH...
THE ARTIFICIAL HUMAN SKIN THOSE AYAKASHI HAVE BEEN WEARING ...
YOU TOLD ME YOUR GRANDSON HAD AN ALTERCATION WITH FOUR AYAKASHI WEARING IT THE OTHER NIGHT...
...FOUR CLONES, IDENTICAL IN SIZE AND APPEARANCE, CORRECT?
AT THIS POINT, THEY'RE ONLY ABLE TO PRODUCE SKIN IN ONE SIZE AND SHAPE, BUT...
IMAGINE WHAT WOULD HAPPEN ONCE THEY LEARN TO MAKE IT IN DIFFERENT SHAPES AND SIZES.
OH, MY!
YOU SEE WHAT I'M SUGGESTING, DON'T YOU?
AYAKASHI WOULD BE ABLE TO REPLACE INDIVIDUAL HUMANS!
ONE BY ONE, THEY COULD REPLACE HUMAN BEINGS AND ULTIMATELY ...
...CONTROL OUR WORLD.

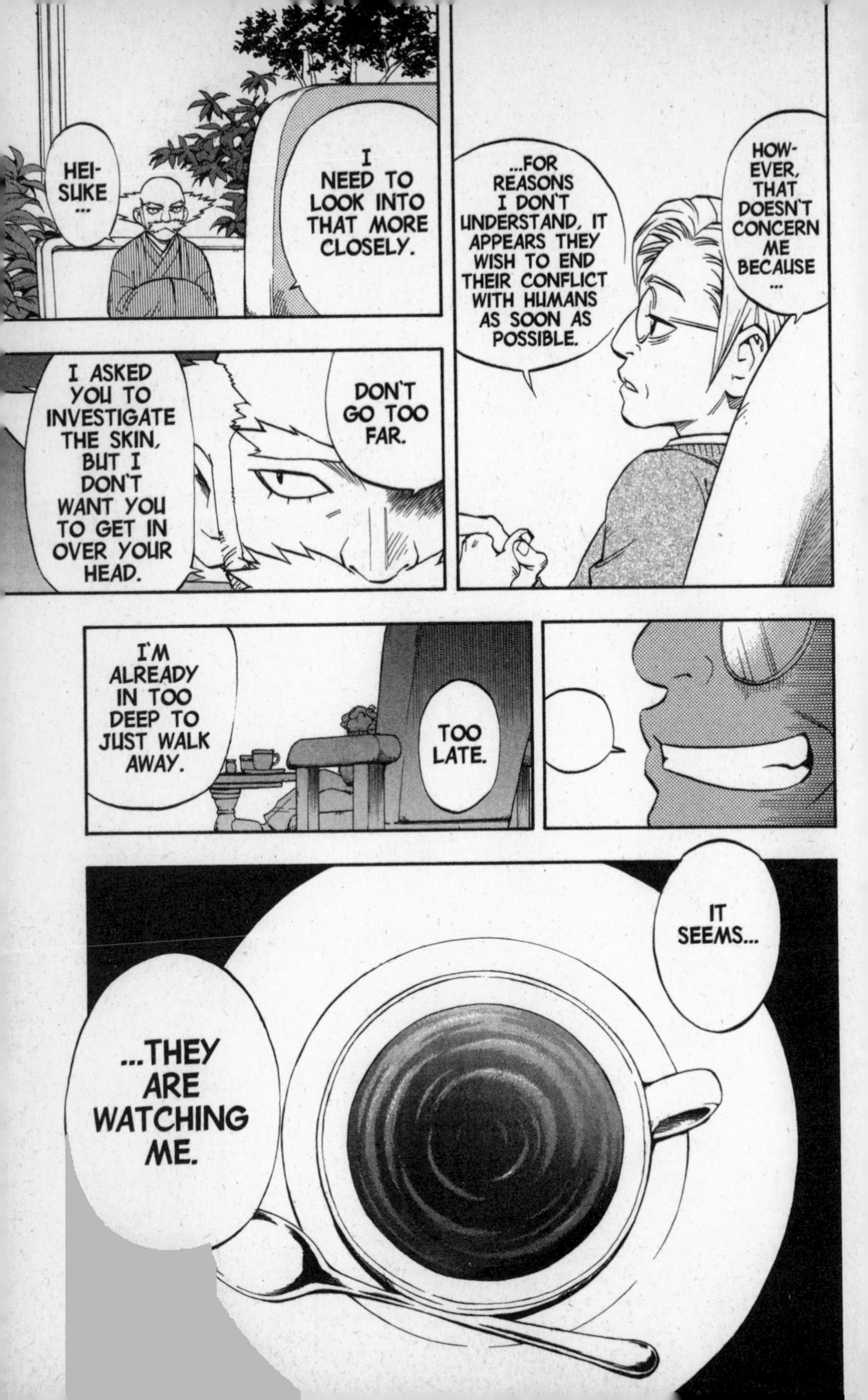
HOWEVER, THAT DOESN'T CONCERN ME BECAUSE...
...FOR REASONS I DON'T UNDERSTAND, IT APPEARS THEY WISH TO END THEIR CONFLICT WITH HUMANS AS SOON AS POSSIBLE.
I NEED TO LOOK INTO THAT MORE CLOSELY.
HEISUKE...
DON'T GO TOO FAR.
I ASKED YOU TO INVESTIGATE THE SKIN, BUT I DON'T WANT YOU TO GET IN OVER YOUR HEAD.
TOO LATE.
I'M ALREADY IN TOO DEEP TO JUST WALK AWAY.
IT SEEMS...
...THEY ARE WATCHING ME.

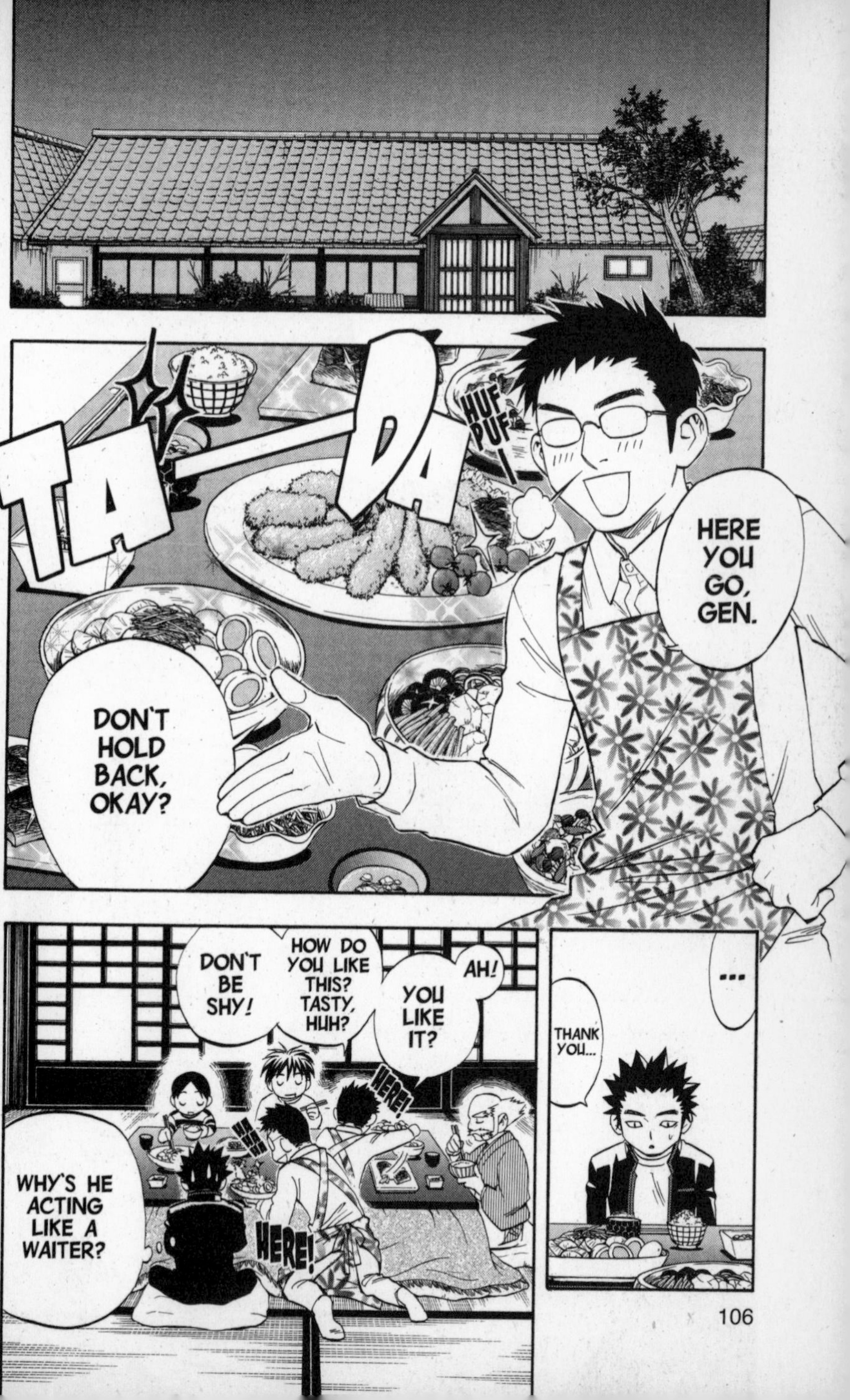
HERE YOU GO, GEN.
TA DA
HUF PUF
DON'T HOLD BACK, OKAY?
...
THANK YOU...
AH!
YOU LIKE IT?
HOW DO YOU LIKE THIS? TASTY, HUH?
DON'T BE SHY!
HERE!
HERE!
WHY'S HE ACTING LIKE A WAITER?

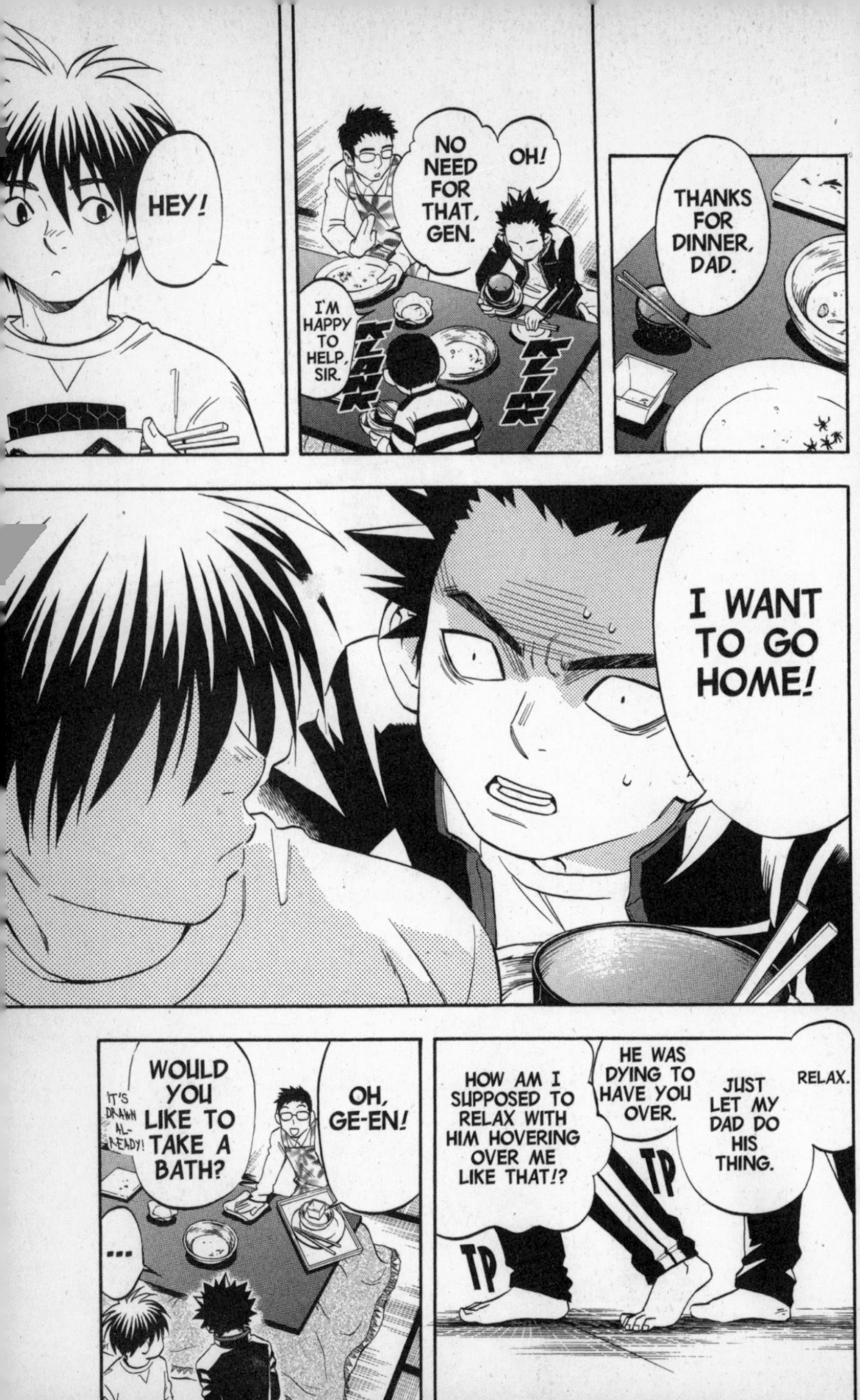
THANKS FOR DINNER, DAD.
OH!
NO NEED FOR THAT, GEN.
KLINK
I'M HAPPY TO HELP, SIR.
KLANK
HEY!
I WANT TO GO HOME!
RELAX.
JUST LET MY DAD DO HIS THING.
HE WAS DYING TO HAVE YOU OVER.
HOW AM I SUPPOSED TO RELAX WITH HIM HOVERING OVER ME LIKE THAT!?
TP
TP
OH, GE-EN!
WOULD YOU LIKE TO TAKE A BATH?
IT'S DRAWN AL-READY!
...

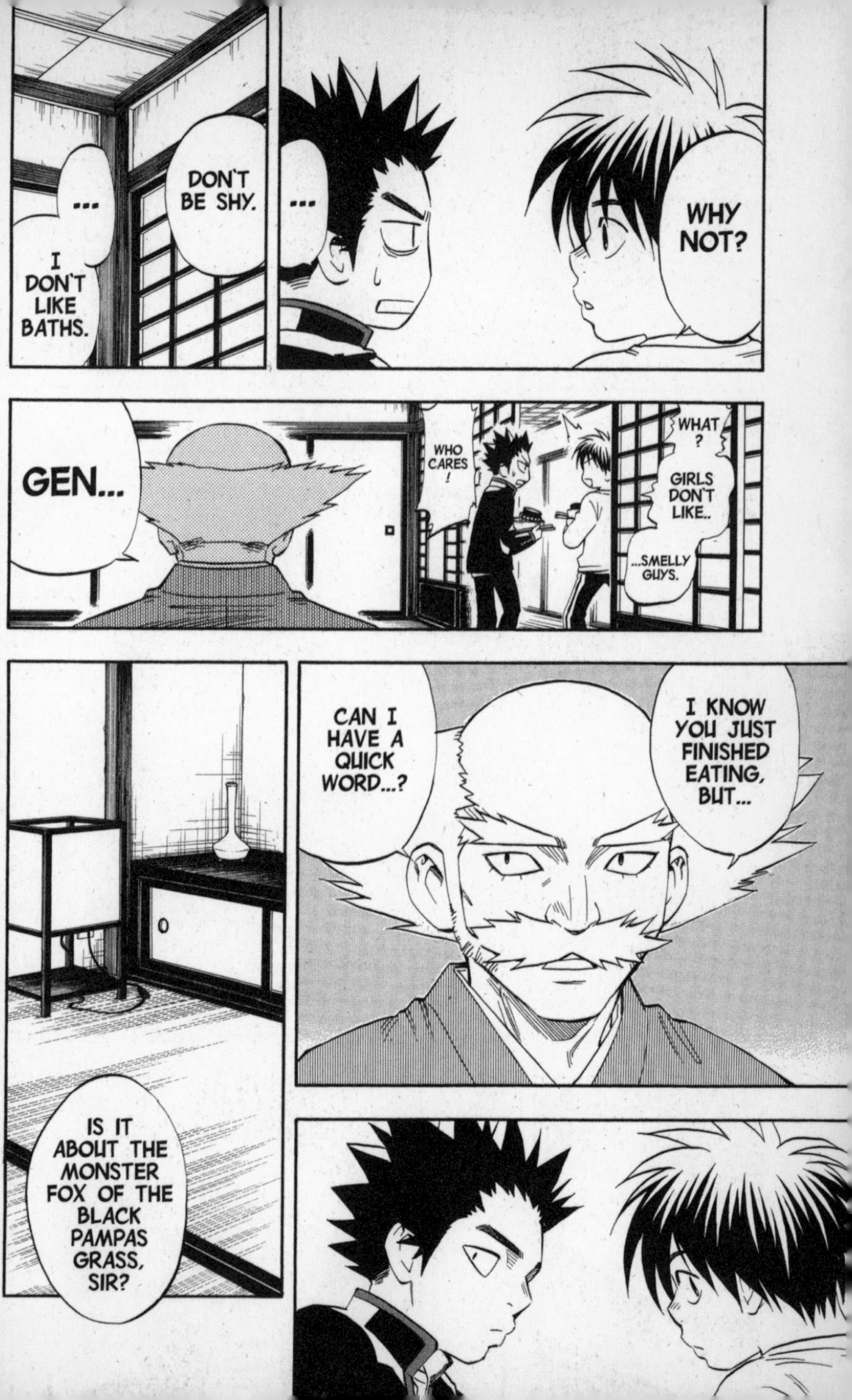
WHY NOT?
...
DON'T BE SHY.
...
I DON'T LIKE BATHS.
WHAT?
GIRLS DON'T LIKE..
...SMELLY GUYS.
WHO CARES!
GEN...
I KNOW YOU JUST FINISHED EATING, BUT...
CAN I HAVE A QUICK WORD...?
IS IT ABOUT THE MONSTER FOX OF THE BLACK PAMPAS GRASS, SIR?

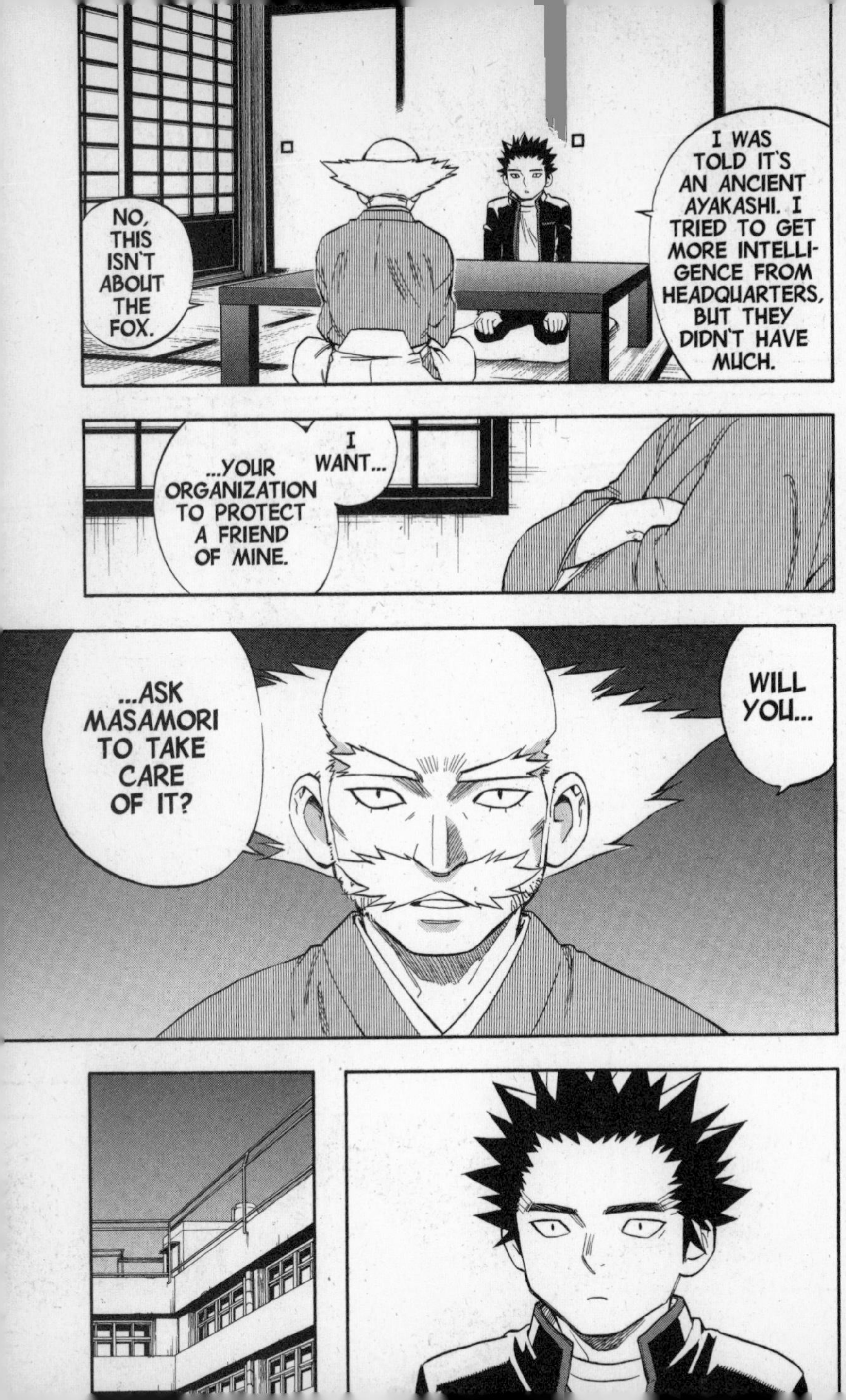
I WAS TOLD IT'S AN ANCIENT AYAKASHI. I TRIED TO GET MORE INTELLIGENCE FROM HEADQUARTERS, BUT THEY DIDN'T HAVE MUCH.
NO, THIS ISN'T ABOUT THE FOX.
I WANT...
...YOUR ORGANIZATION TO PROTECT A FRIEND OF MINE.
WILL YOU...
...ASK MASAMORI TO TAKE CARE OF IT?

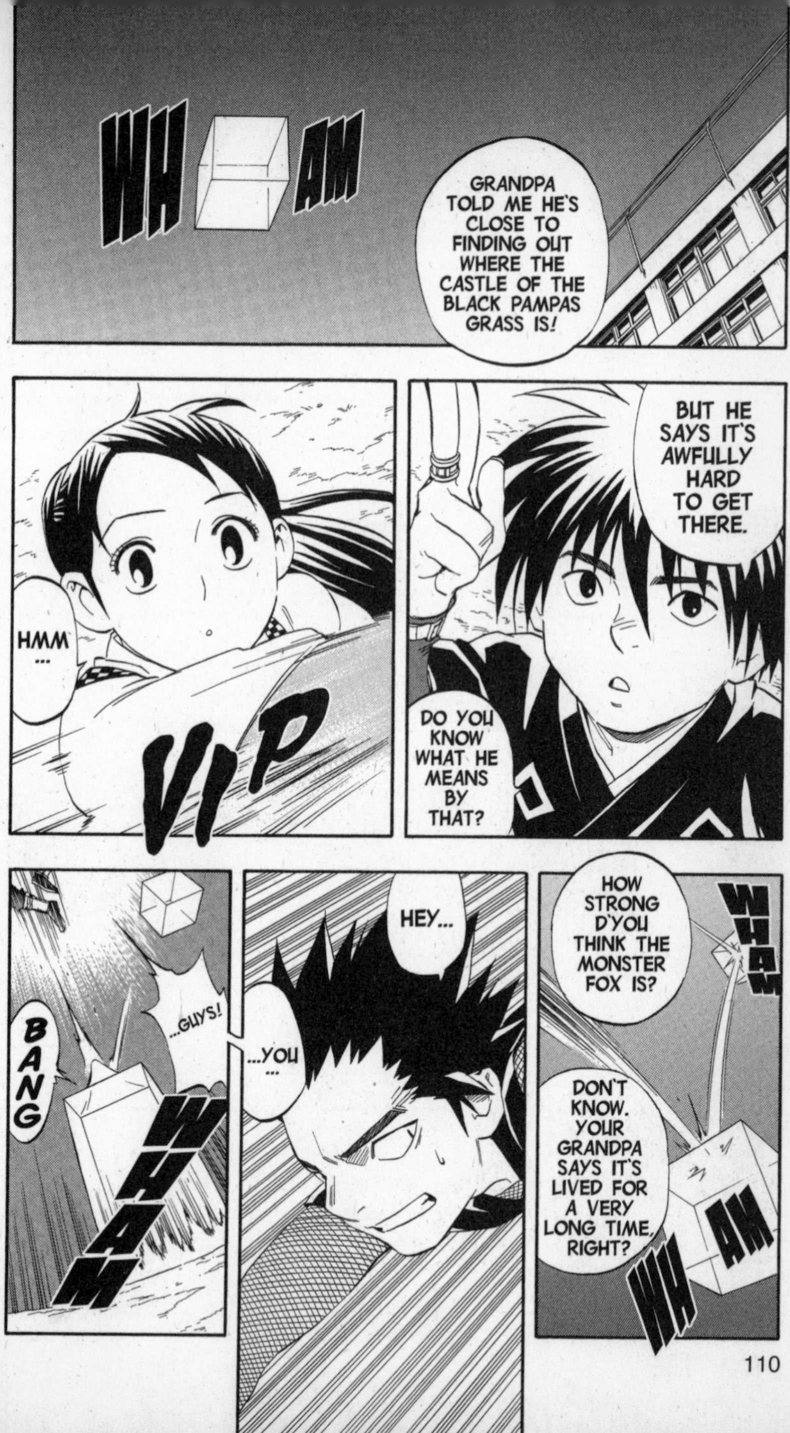
WHAM
GRANDPA TOLD ME HE'S CLOSE TO FINDING OUT WHERE THE CASTLE OF THE BLACK PAMPAS GRASS IS!
BUT HE SAYS IT'S AWFULLY HARD TO GET THERE.
DO YOU KNOW WHAT HE MEANS BY THAT?
HMM...
VIP
HOW STRONG D'YOU THINK THE MONSTER FOX IS?
WHAM
DON'T KNOW. YOUR GRANDPA SAYS IT'S LIVED FOR A VERY LONG TIME, RIGHT?
WHAM
HEY...
...YOU...
...GUYS!
BANG
WHAM

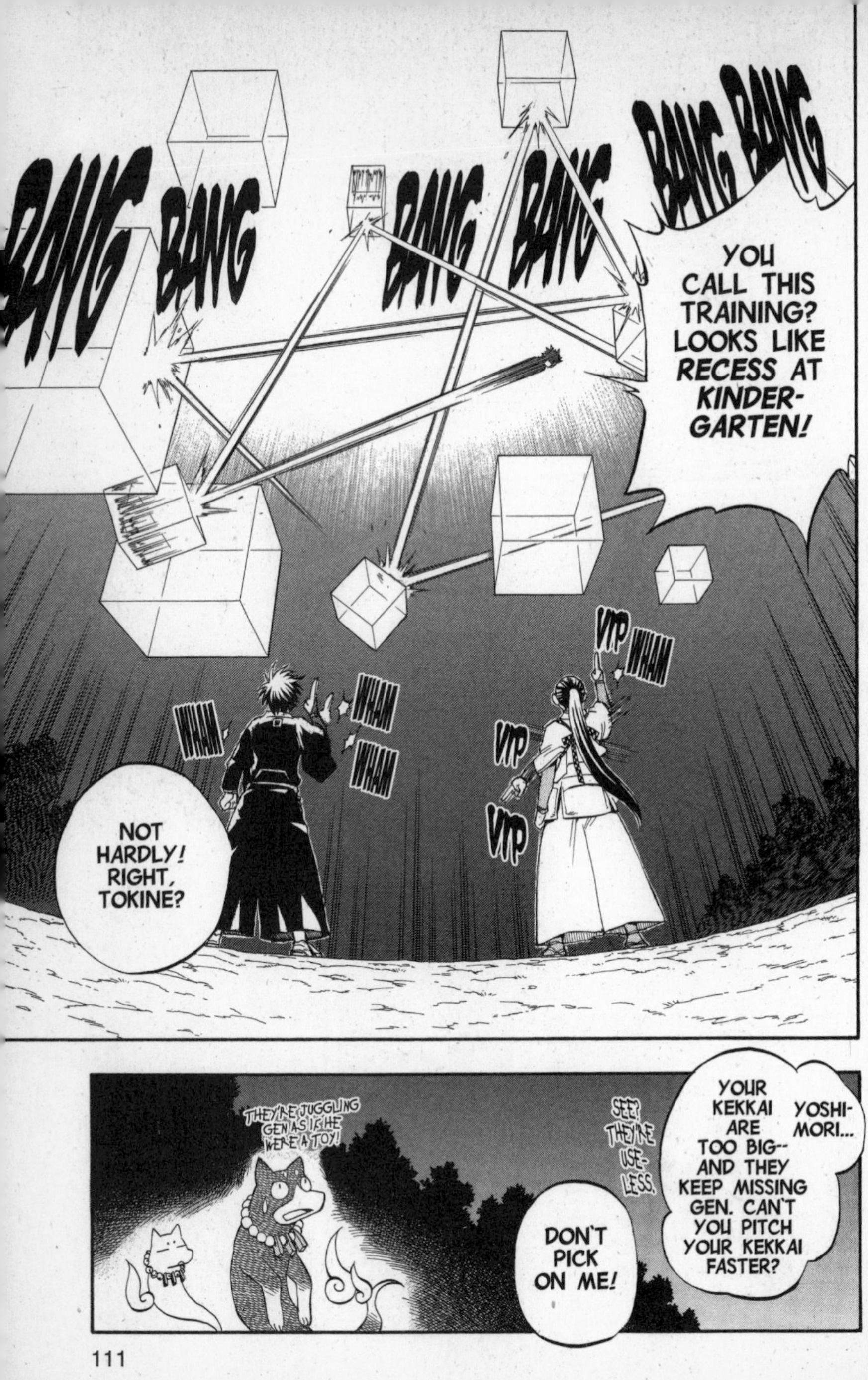
BANG BANG BANG BANG BANG BANG
YOU CALL THIS TRAINING? LOOKS LIKE *RECESS* AT *KINDERGARTEN!*
VIP WHAM
WHAM WHAM WHAM
VIP VIP
NOT HARDLY! RIGHT, TOKINE?
YOSHIMORI... YOUR KEKKAI ARE TOO BIG-- AND THEY KEEP MISSING GEN. CAN'T YOU PITCH YOUR KEKKAI FASTER?
SEE? THEY'RE USELESS.
DON'T PICK ON ME!
THEY'RE JUGGLING GEN AS IF HE WERE A TOY!

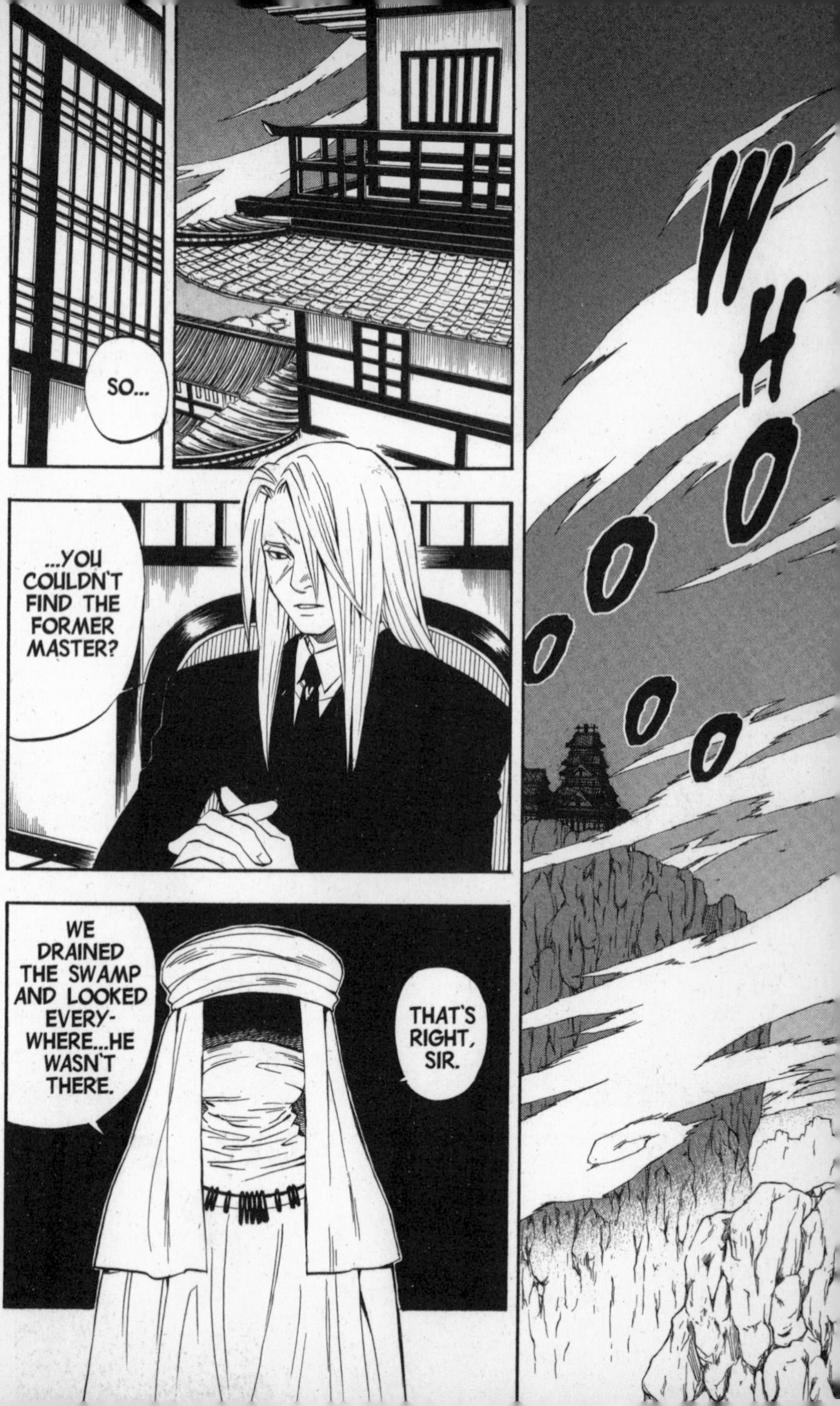
WHOOOOOOO
SO...
...YOU COULDN'T FIND THE FORMER MASTER?
THAT'S RIGHT, SIR.
WE DRAINED THE SWAMP AND LOOKED EVERY-WHERE...HE WASN'T THERE.

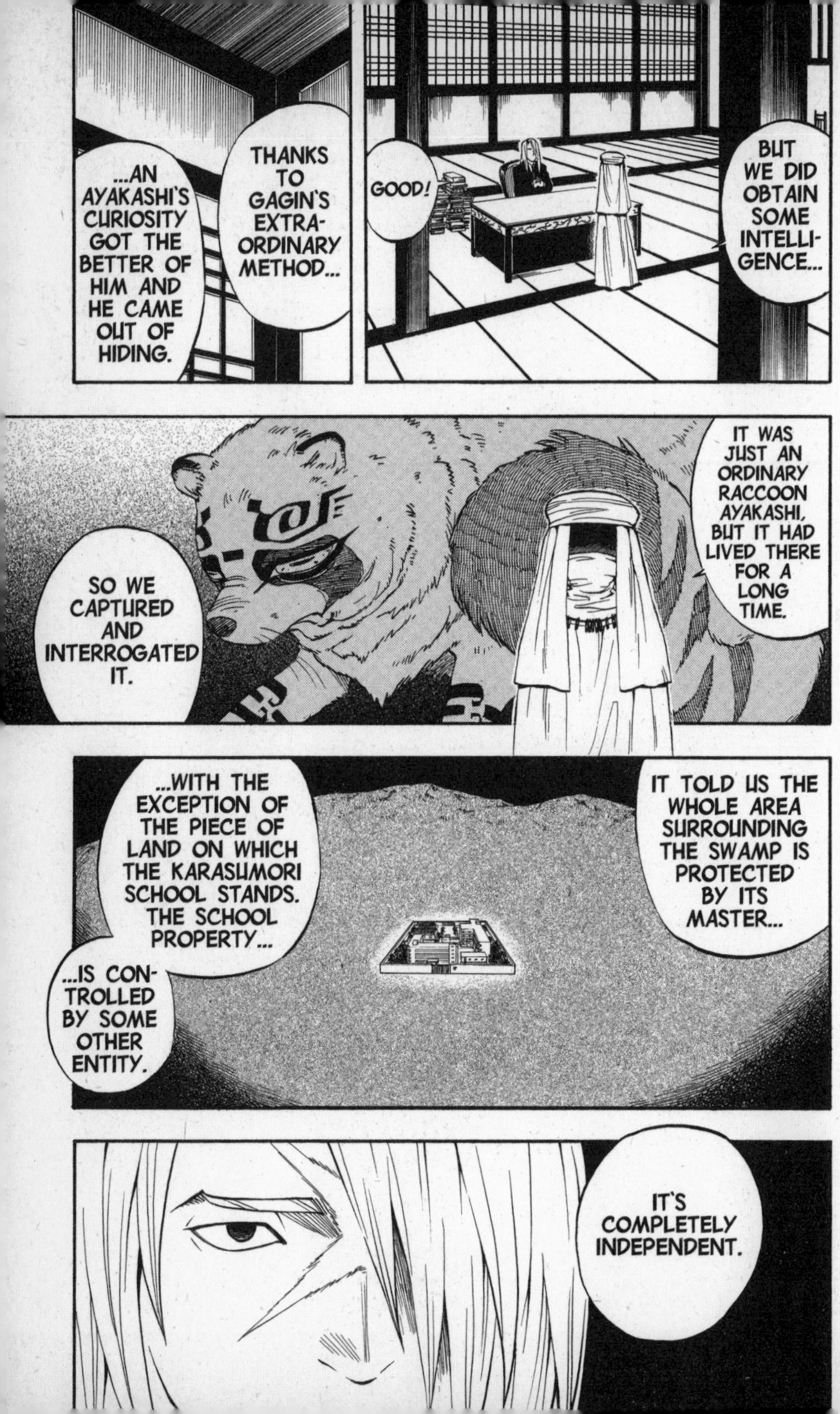
BUT WE DID OBTAIN SOME INTELLIGENCE...
GOOD!
THANKS TO GAGIN'S EXTRA-ORDINARY METHOD...
...AN AYAKASHI'S CURIOSITY GOT THE BETTER OF HIM AND HE CAME OUT OF HIDING.
IT WAS JUST AN ORDINARY RACCOON AYAKASHI, BUT IT HAD LIVED THERE FOR A LONG TIME.
SO WE CAPTURED AND INTERROGATED IT.
IT TOLD US THE WHOLE AREA SURROUNDING THE SWAMP IS PROTECTED BY ITS MASTER...
...WITH THE EXCEPTION OF THE PIECE OF LAND ON WHICH THE KARASUMORI SCHOOL STANDS. THE SCHOOL PROPERTY...
...IS CONTROLLED BY SOME OTHER ENTITY.
IT'S COMPLETELY INDEPENDENT.

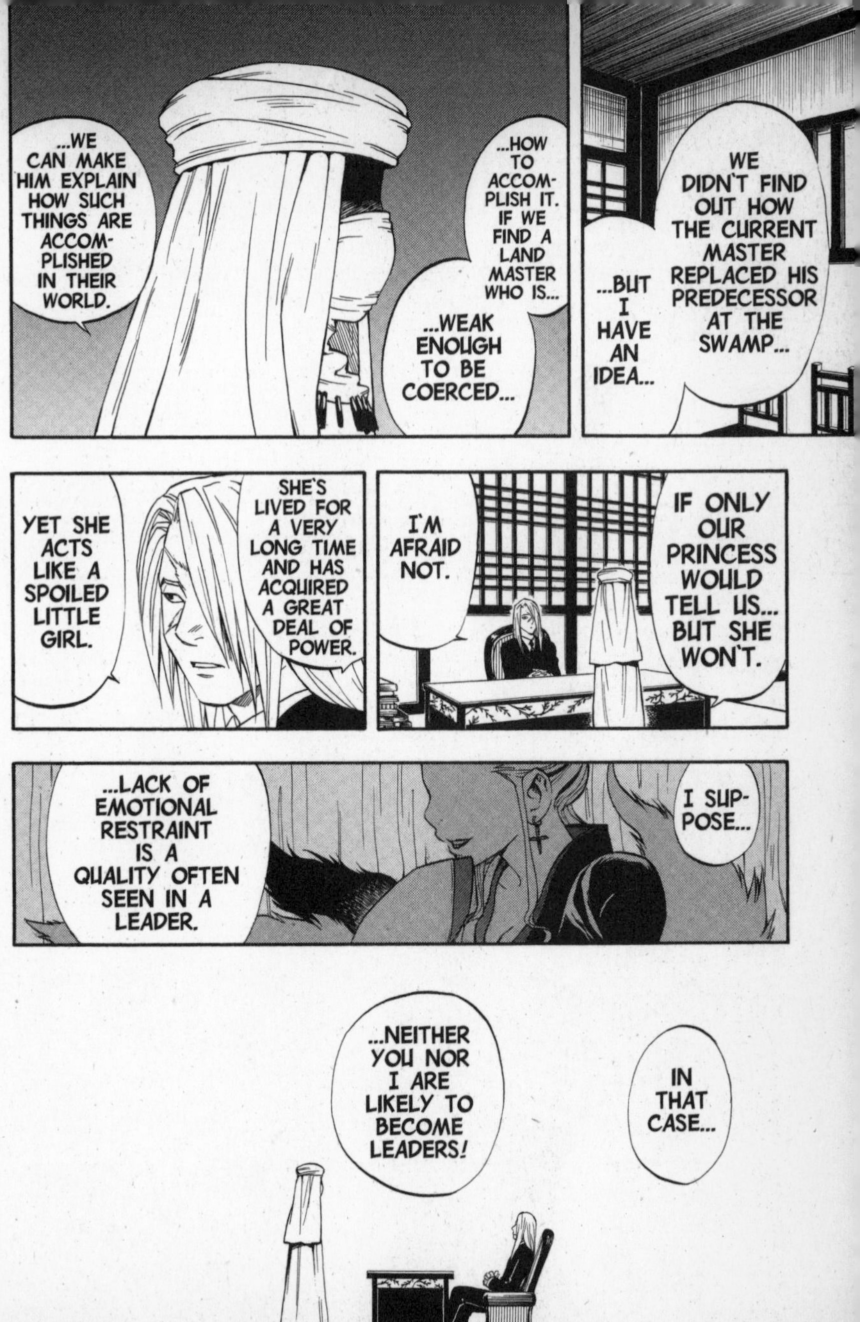
WE DIDN'T FIND OUT HOW THE CURRENT MASTER REPLACED HIS PREDECESSOR AT THE SWAMP...
...BUT I HAVE AN IDEA...
...HOW TO ACCOMPLISH IT. IF WE FIND A LAND MASTER WHO IS...
...WEAK ENOUGH TO BE COERCED...
...WE CAN MAKE HIM EXPLAIN HOW SUCH THINGS ARE ACCOMPLISHED IN THEIR WORLD.
IF ONLY OUR PRINCESS WOULD TELL US... BUT SHE WON'T.
I'M AFRAID NOT.
SHE'S LIVED FOR A VERY LONG TIME AND HAS ACQUIRED A GREAT DEAL OF POWER.
YET SHE ACTS LIKE A SPOILED LITTLE GIRL.
I SUPPOSE...
...LACK OF EMOTIONAL RESTRAINT IS A QUALITY OFTEN SEEN IN A LEADER.
IN THAT CASE...
...NEITHER YOU NOR I ARE LIKELY TO BECOME LEADERS!

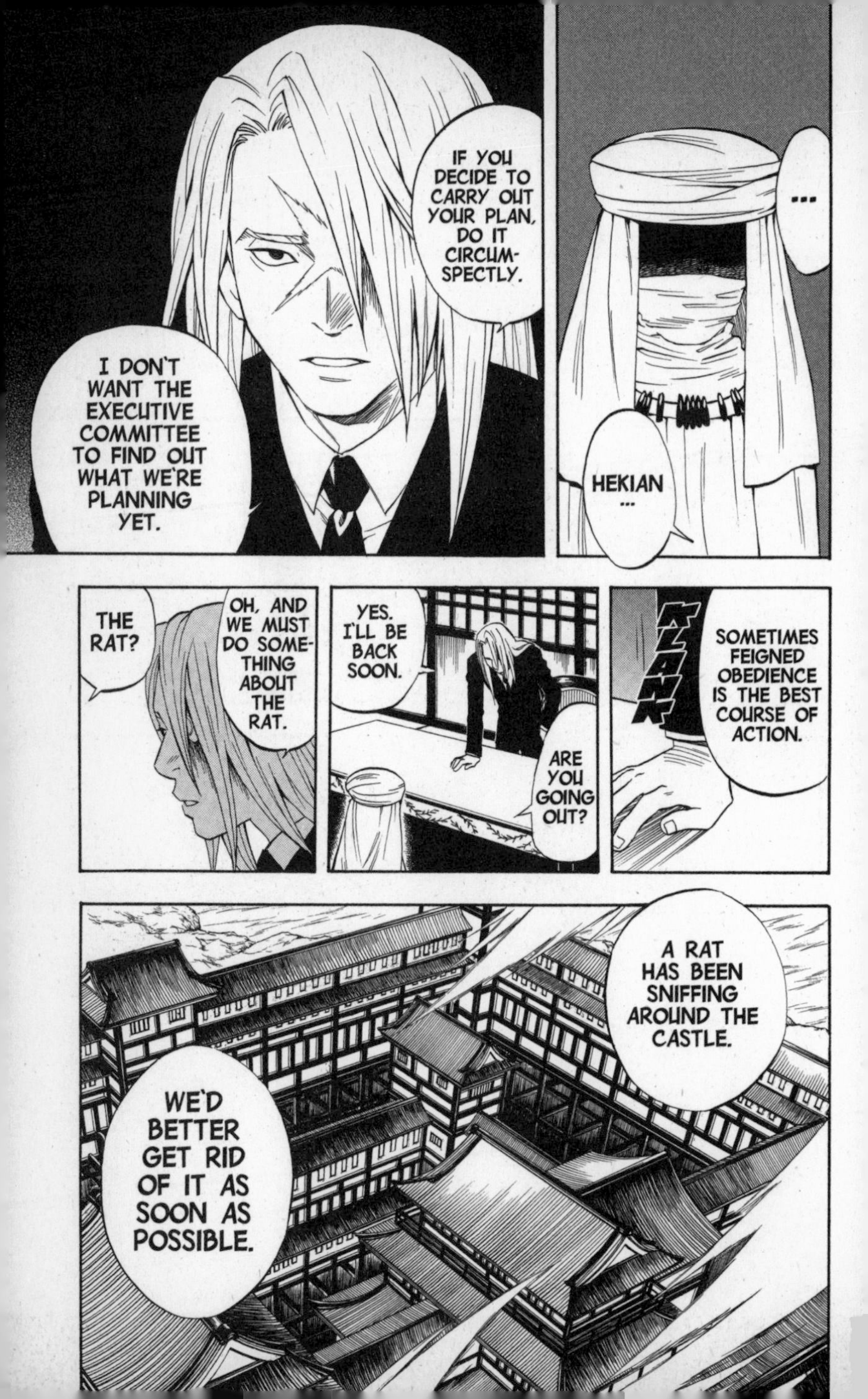
...
HEKIAN ...
IF YOU DECIDE TO CARRY OUT YOUR PLAN, DO IT CIRCUM-SPECTLY.
I DON'T WANT THE EXECUTIVE COMMITTEE TO FIND OUT WHAT WE'RE PLANNING YET.
KLANK
SOMETIMES FEIGNED OBEDIENCE IS THE BEST COURSE OF ACTION.
ARE YOU GOING OUT?
YES. I'LL BE BACK SOON.
OH, AND WE MUST DO SOME-THING ABOUT THE RAT.
THE RAT?
A RAT HAS BEEN SNIFFING AROUND THE CASTLE.
WE'D BETTER GET RID OF IT AS SOON AS POSSIBLE.

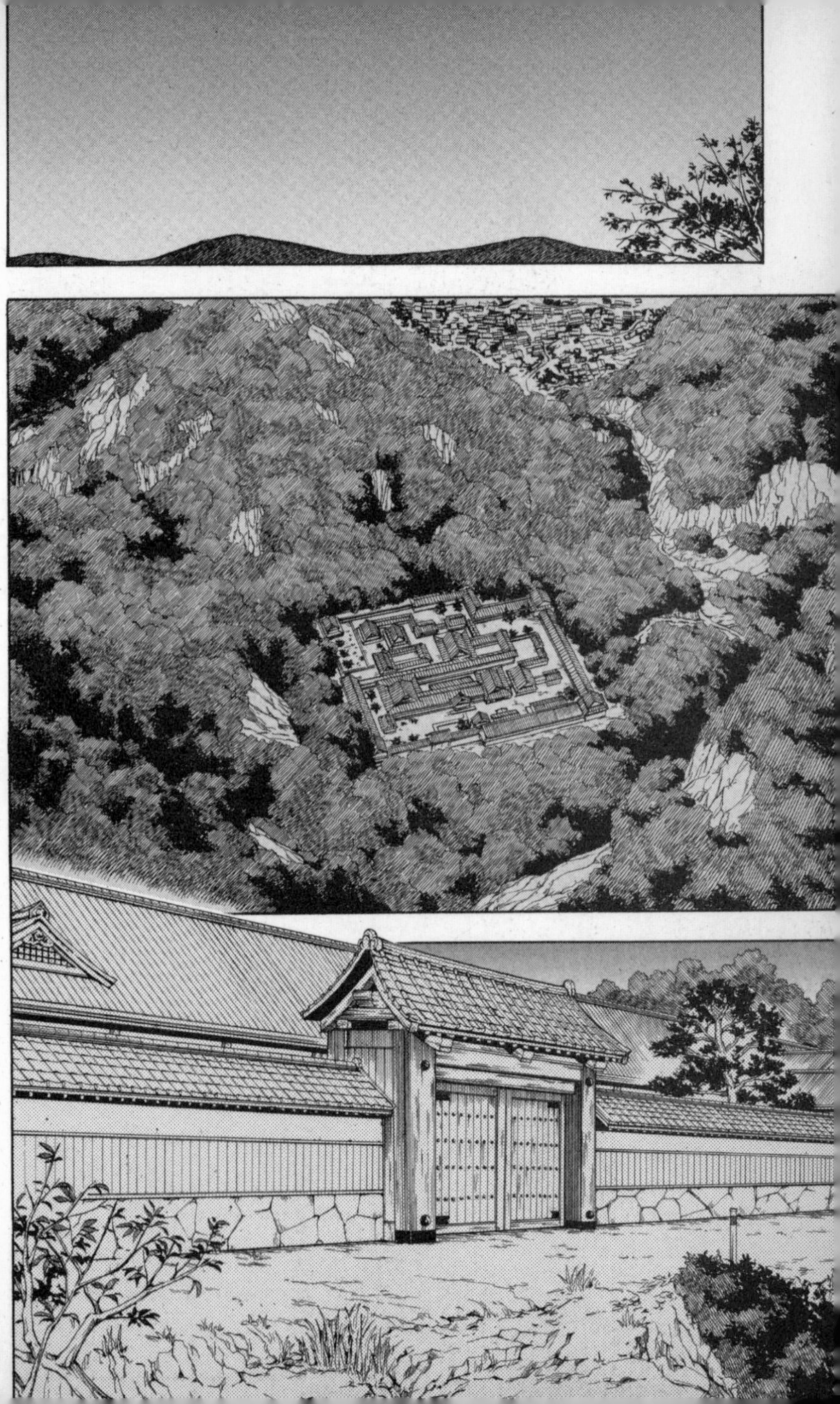

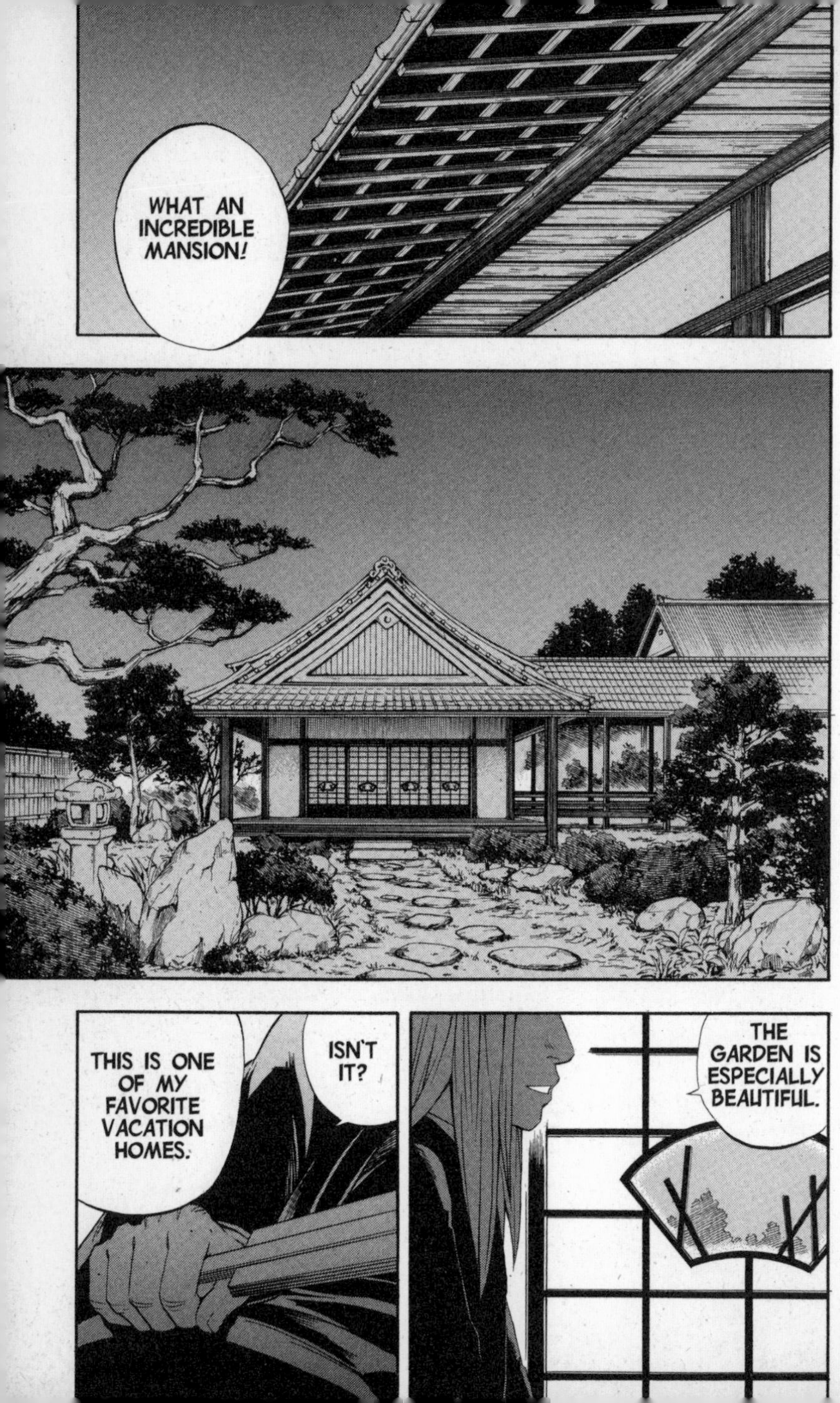
WHAT AN INCREDIBLE MANSION!
THE GARDEN IS ESPECIALLY BEAUTIFUL.
ISN'T IT?
THIS IS ONE OF MY FAVORITE VACATION HOMES.

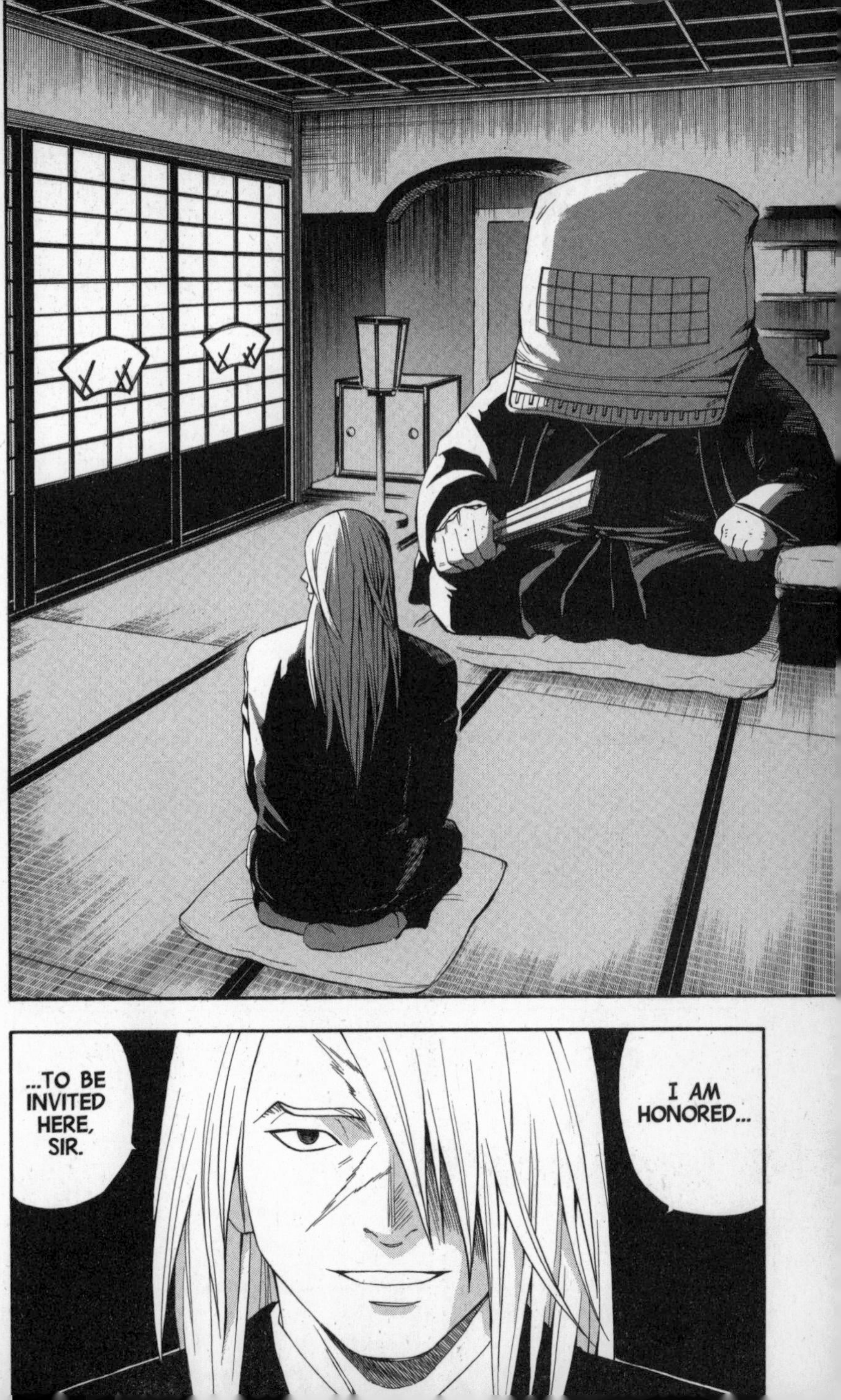
I AM HONORED...
...TO BE INVITED HERE, SIR.

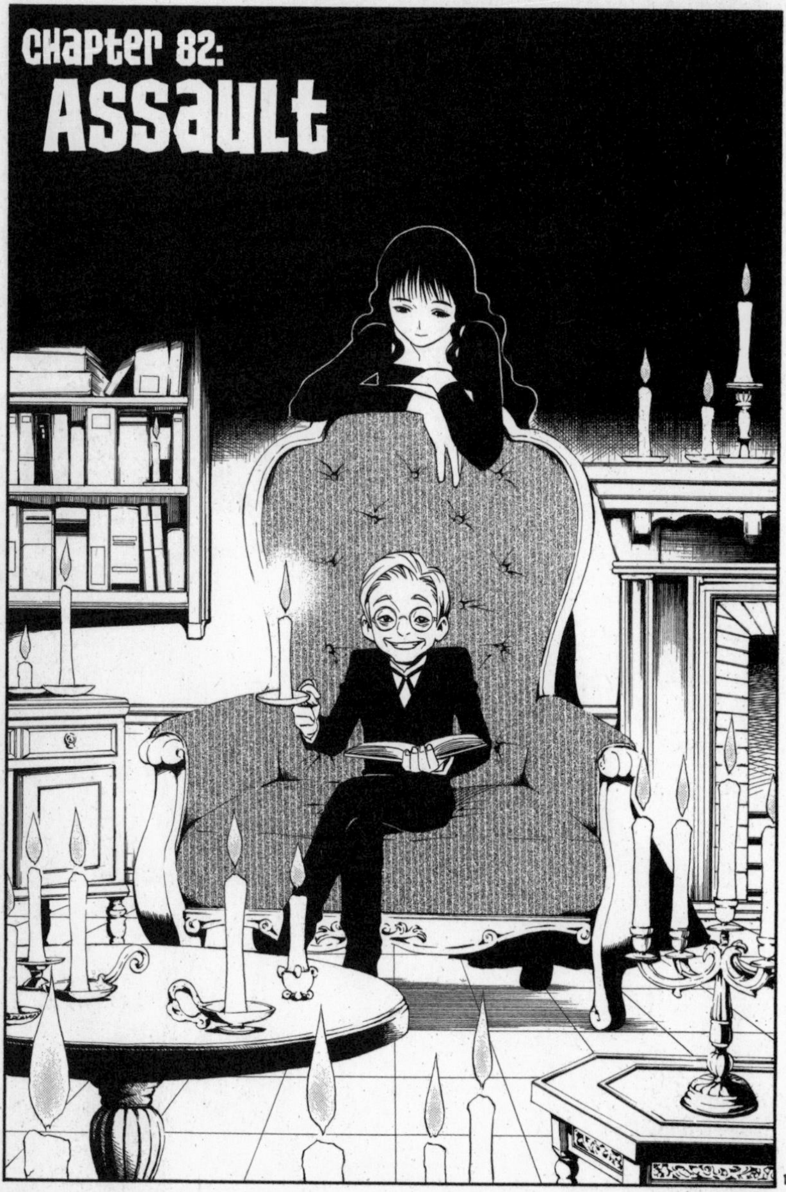
Chapter 82:
Assault

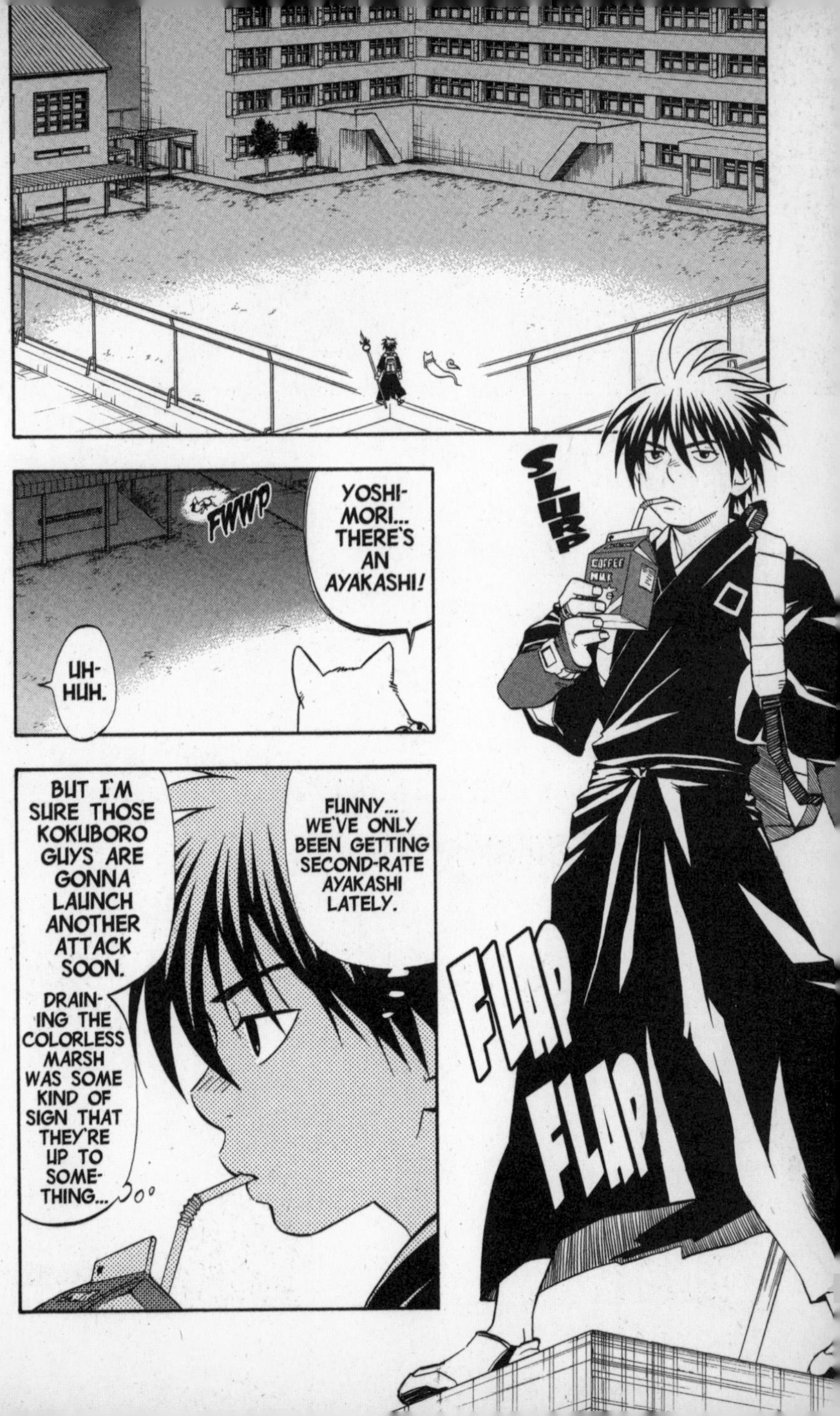
SLURP
FLAP
FLAP
YOSHI-MORI... THERE'S AN AYAKASHI!
FWWP
UH-HUH.
FUNNY... WE'VE ONLY BEEN GETTING SECOND-RATE AYAKASHI LATELY.
BUT I'M SURE THOSE KOKUBORO GUYS ARE GONNA LAUNCH ANOTHER ATTACK SOON.
DRAIN-ING THE COLORLESS MARSH WAS SOME KIND OF SIGN THAT THEY'RE UP TO SOME-THING...

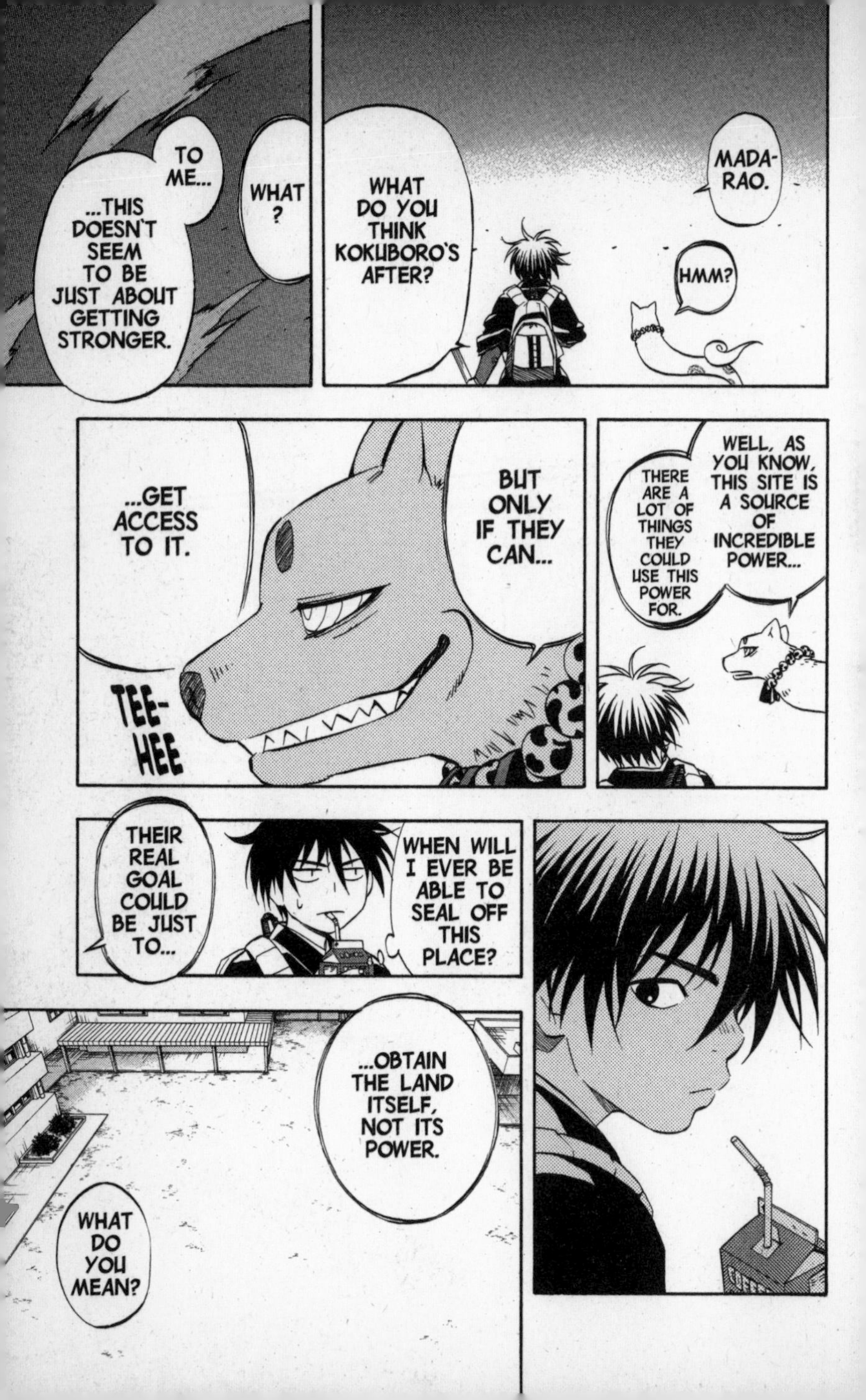
MADARAO.
HMM?
WHAT DO YOU THINK KOKUBORO'S AFTER?
WHAT?
TO ME...
...THIS DOESN'T SEEM TO BE JUST ABOUT GETTING STRONGER.
WELL, AS YOU KNOW, THIS SITE IS A SOURCE OF INCREDIBLE POWER...
THERE ARE A LOT OF THINGS THEY COULD USE THIS POWER FOR.
BUT ONLY IF THEY CAN...
...GET ACCESS TO IT.
TEE-HEE
WHEN WILL I EVER BE ABLE TO SEAL OFF THIS PLACE?
THEIR REAL GOAL COULD BE JUST TO...
...OBTAIN THE LAND ITSELF, NOT ITS POWER.
WHAT DO YOU MEAN?

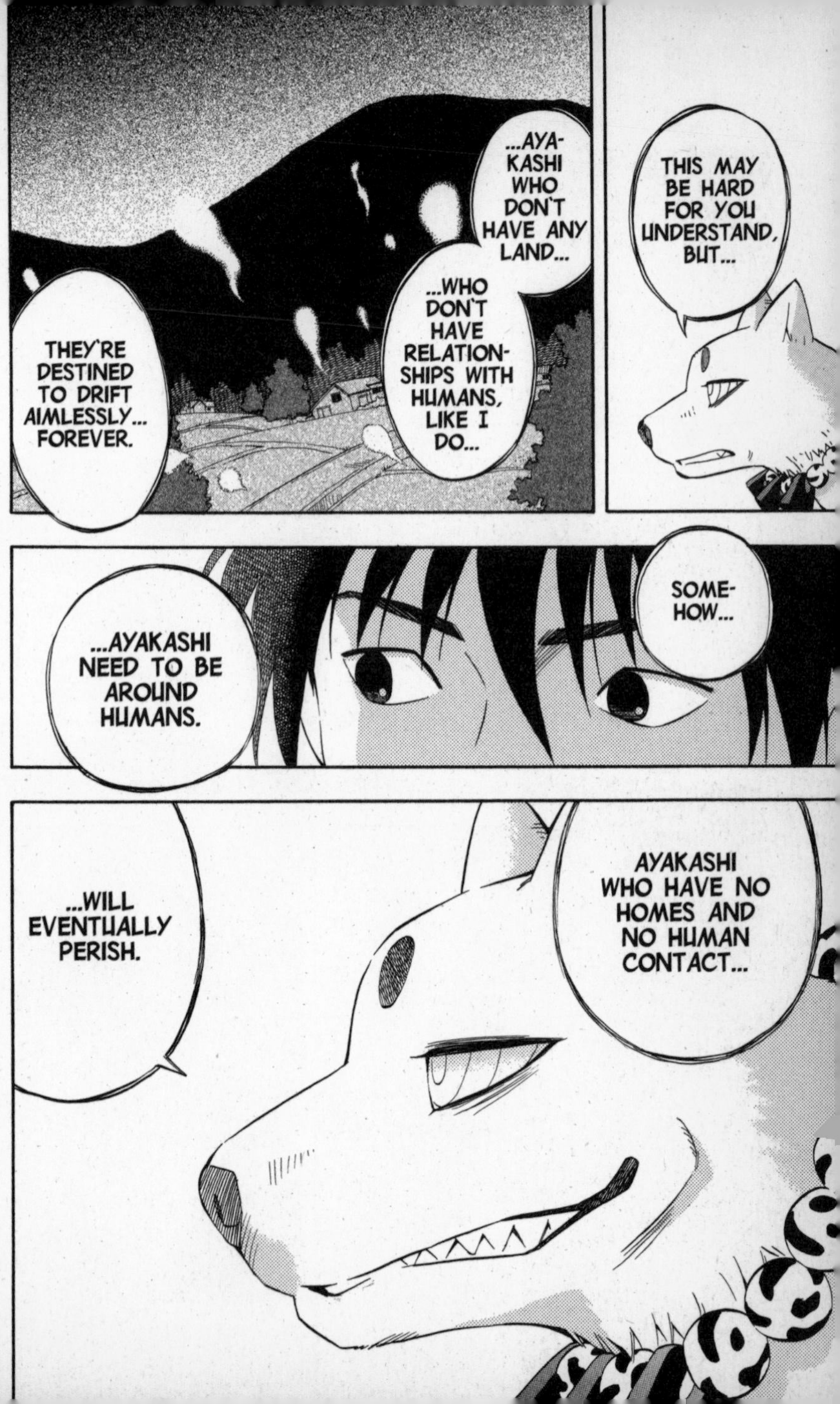
THIS MAY BE HARD FOR YOU UNDERSTAND, BUT...
...AYA-KASHI WHO DON'T HAVE ANY LAND...
...WHO DON'T HAVE RELATION-SHIPS WITH HUMANS, LIKE I DO...
THEY'RE DESTINED TO DRIFT AIMLESSLY... FOREVER.
SOME-HOW...
...AYAKASHI NEED TO BE AROUND HUMANS.
AYAKASHI WHO HAVE NO HOMES AND NO HUMAN CONTACT...
...WILL EVENTUALLY PERISH.

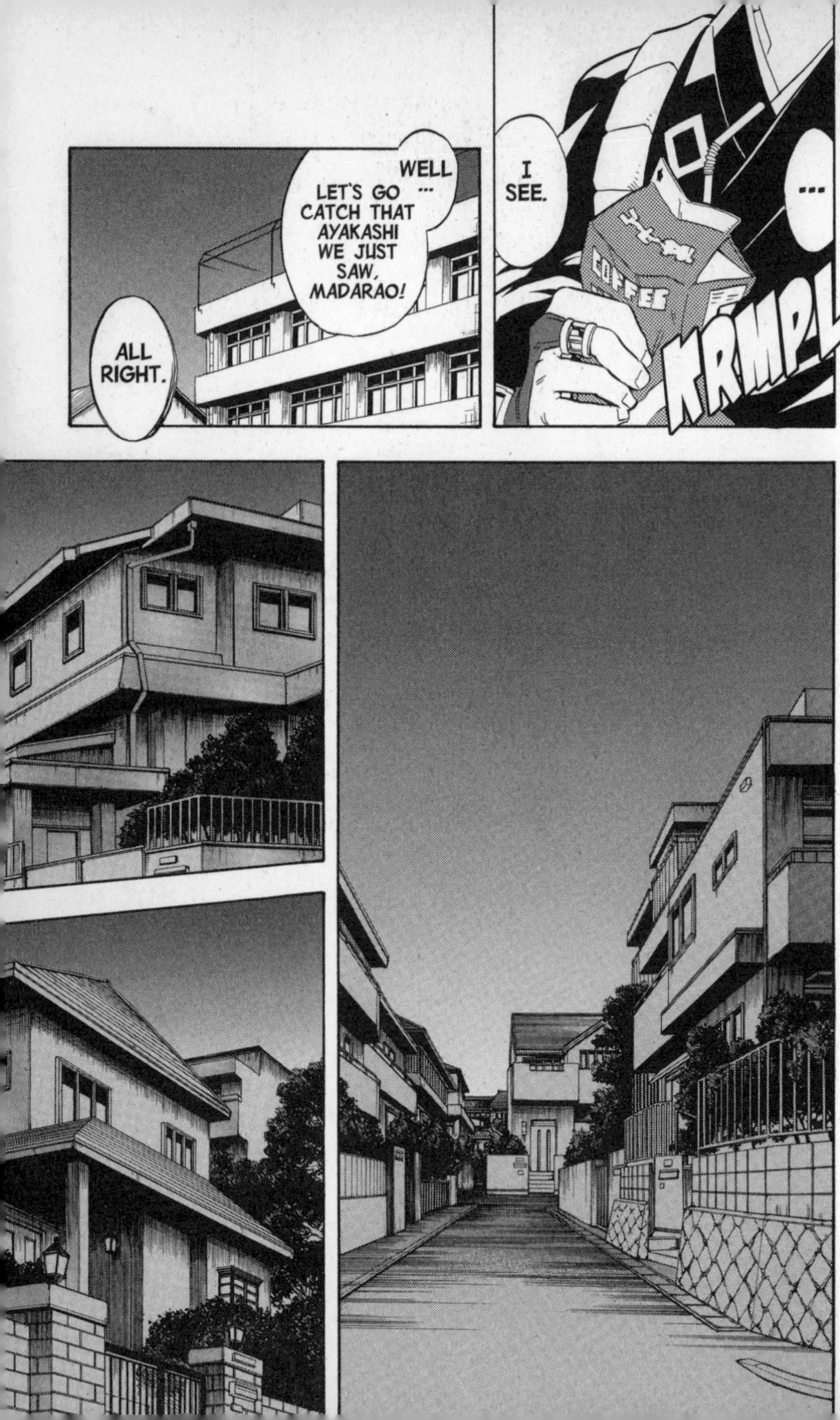
...
I SEE.
COFFEE
KRMPL
WELL ... LET'S GO CATCH THAT AYAKASHI WE JUST SAW, MADARAO!
ALL RIGHT.

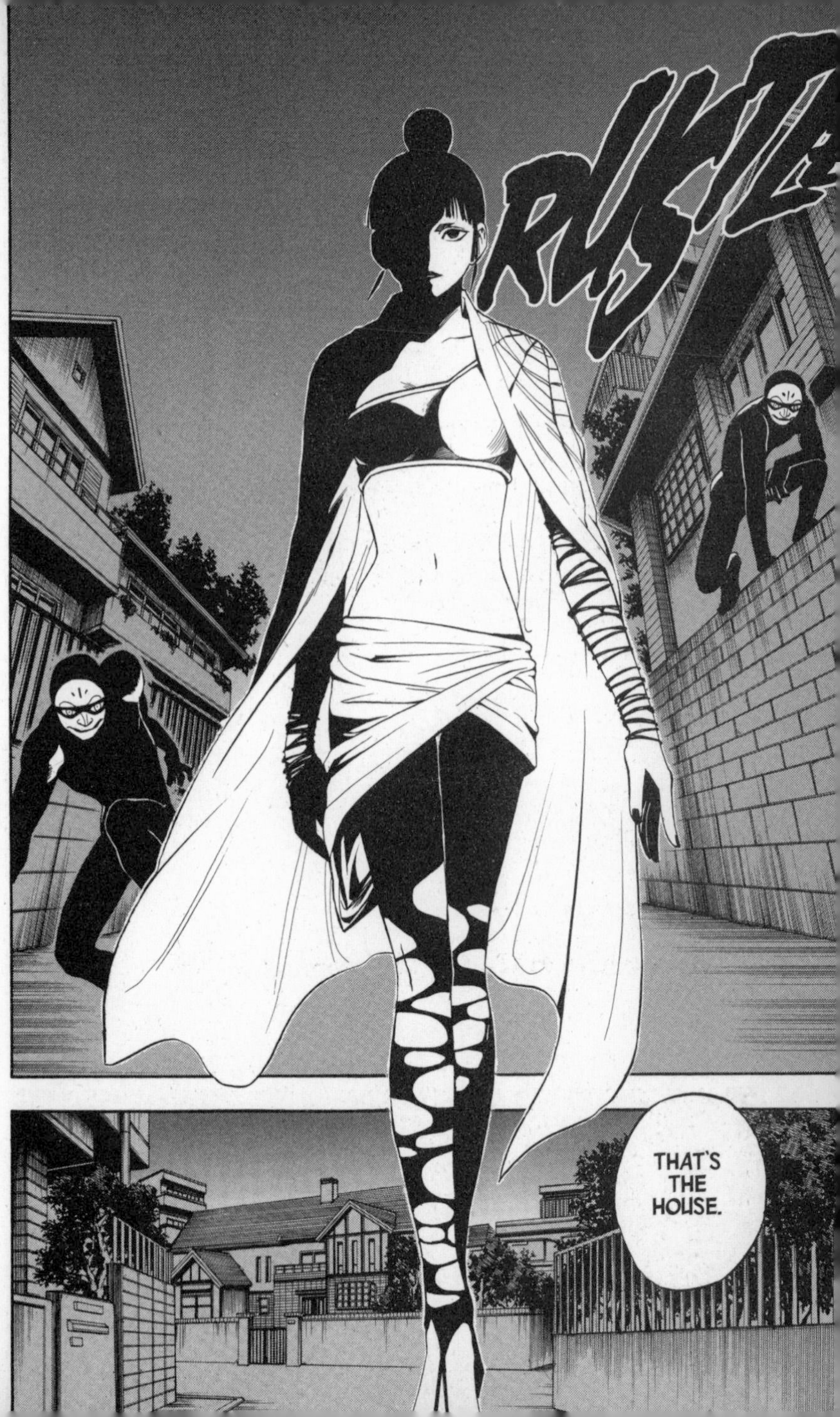
RUSTLE
THAT'S THE HOUSE.

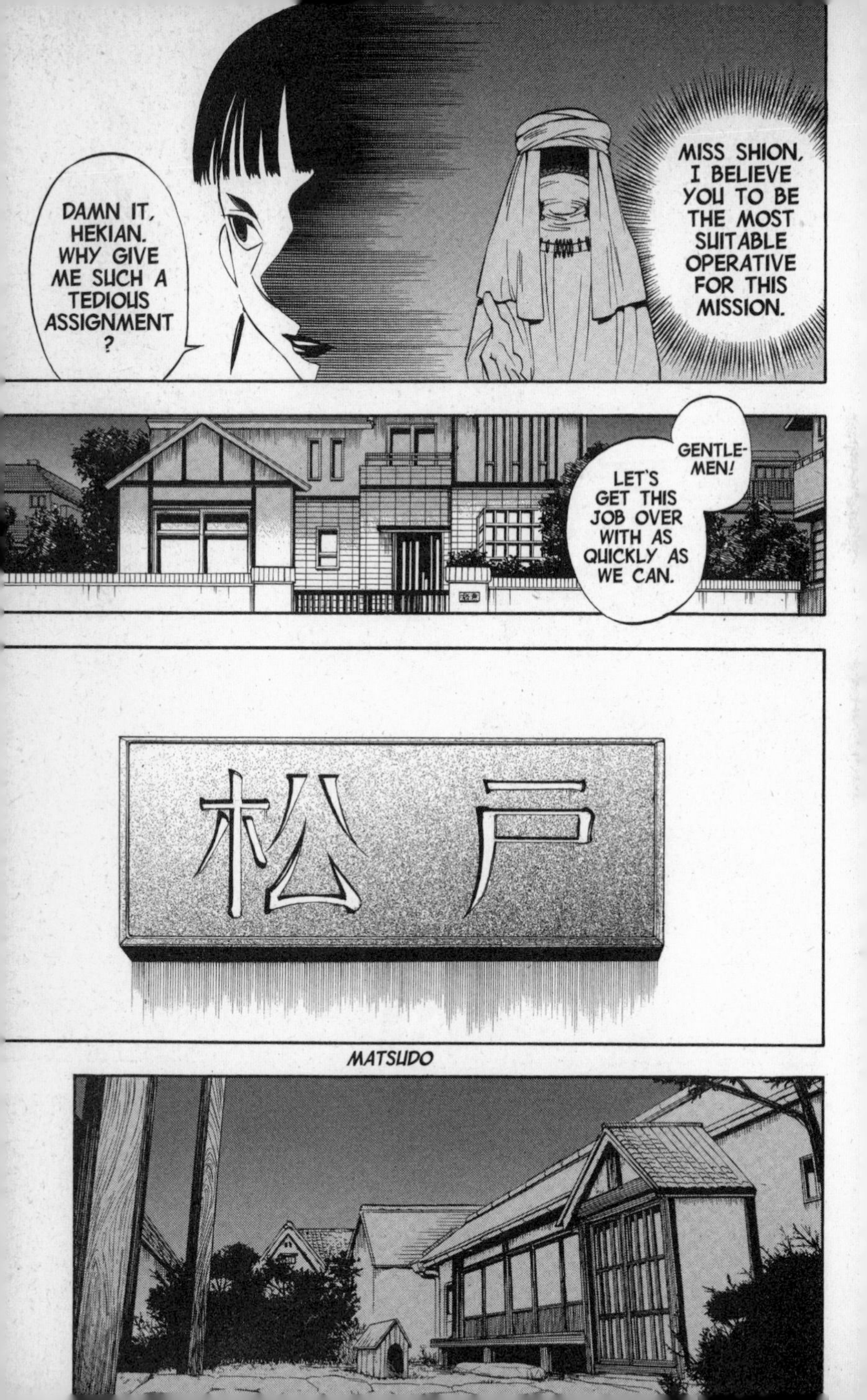
MISS SHION, I BELIEVE YOU TO BE THE MOST SUITABLE OPERATIVE FOR THIS MISSION.
DAMN IT, HEKIAN. WHY GIVE ME SUCH A TEDIOUS ASSIGNMENT?
GENTLE-MEN!
LET'S GET THIS JOB OVER WITH AS QUICKLY AS WE CAN.
松戸
MATSUDO

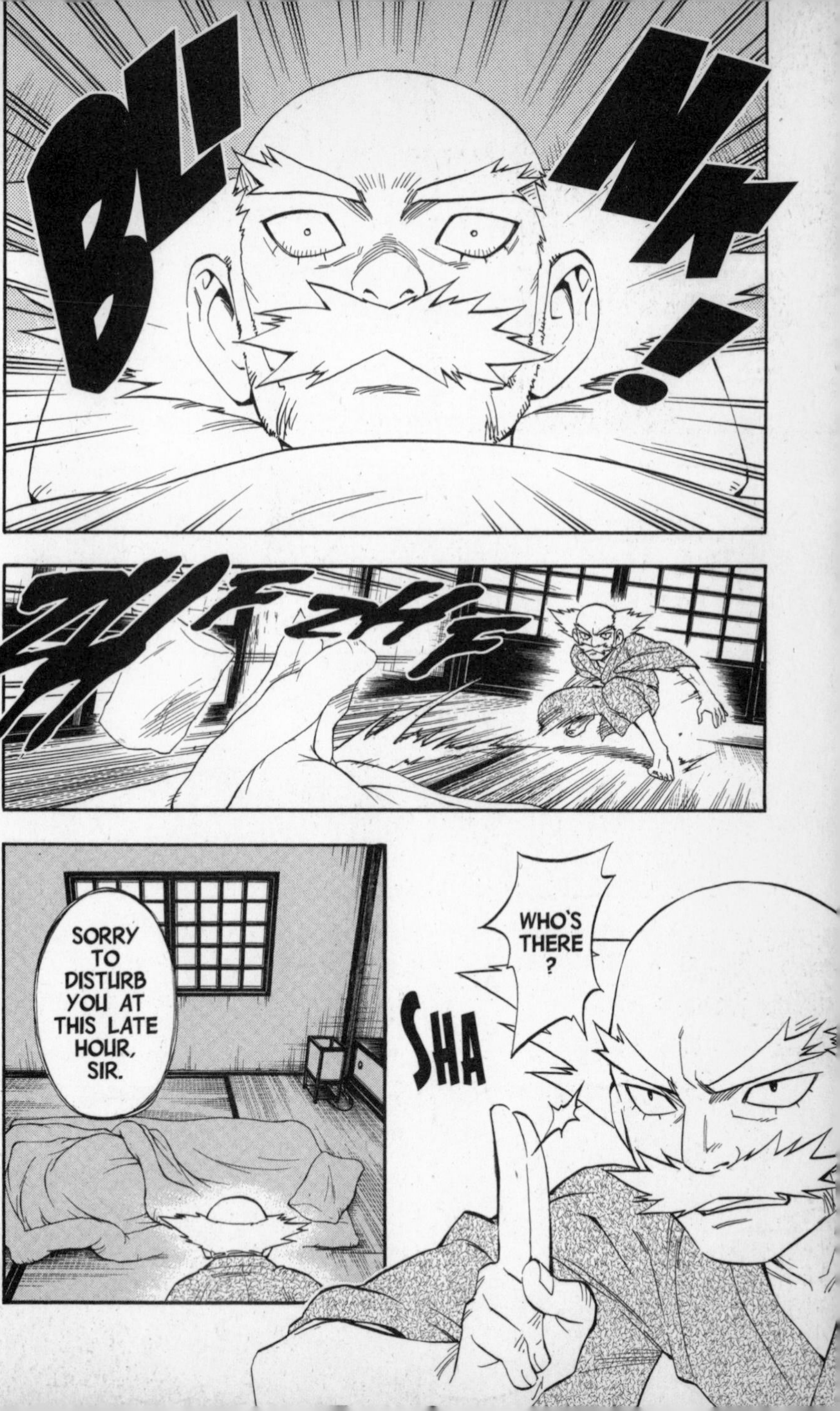
BLINK!
WHO'S THERE?
SHA
SORRY TO DISTURB YOU AT THIS LATE HOUR, SIR.

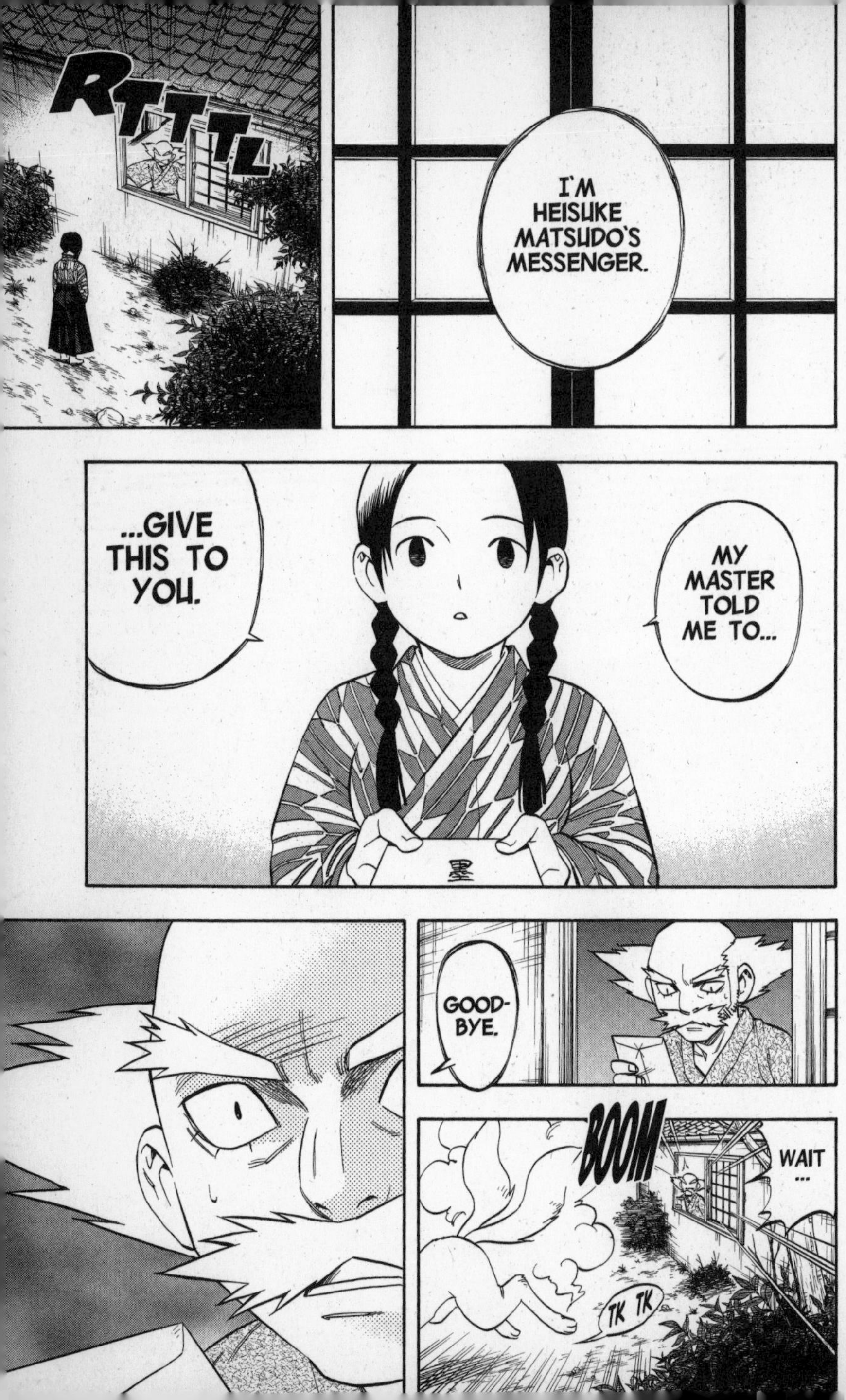
I'M HEISUKE MATSUDO'S MESSENGER.
RTTTL
MY MASTER TOLD ME TO...
...GIVE THIS TO YOU.
GOOD-BYE.
BOOM
WAIT ...
TK TK

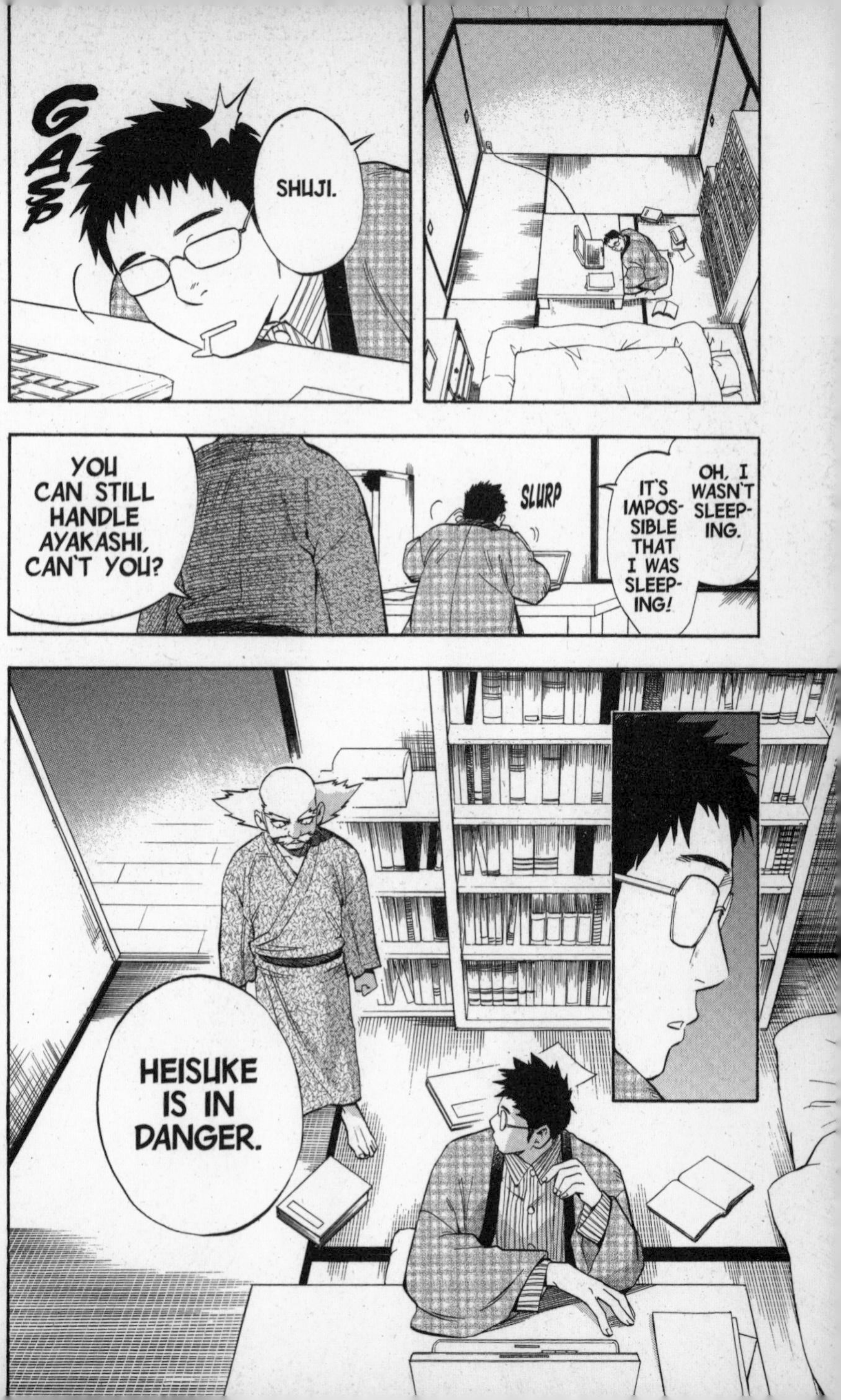
SHUJI.
GASP
OH, I WASN'T SLEEP-ING.
IT'S IMPOS-SIBLE THAT I WAS SLEEP-ING!
SLURP
YOU CAN STILL HANDLE AYAKASHI, CAN'T YOU?
HEISUKE IS IN DANGER.

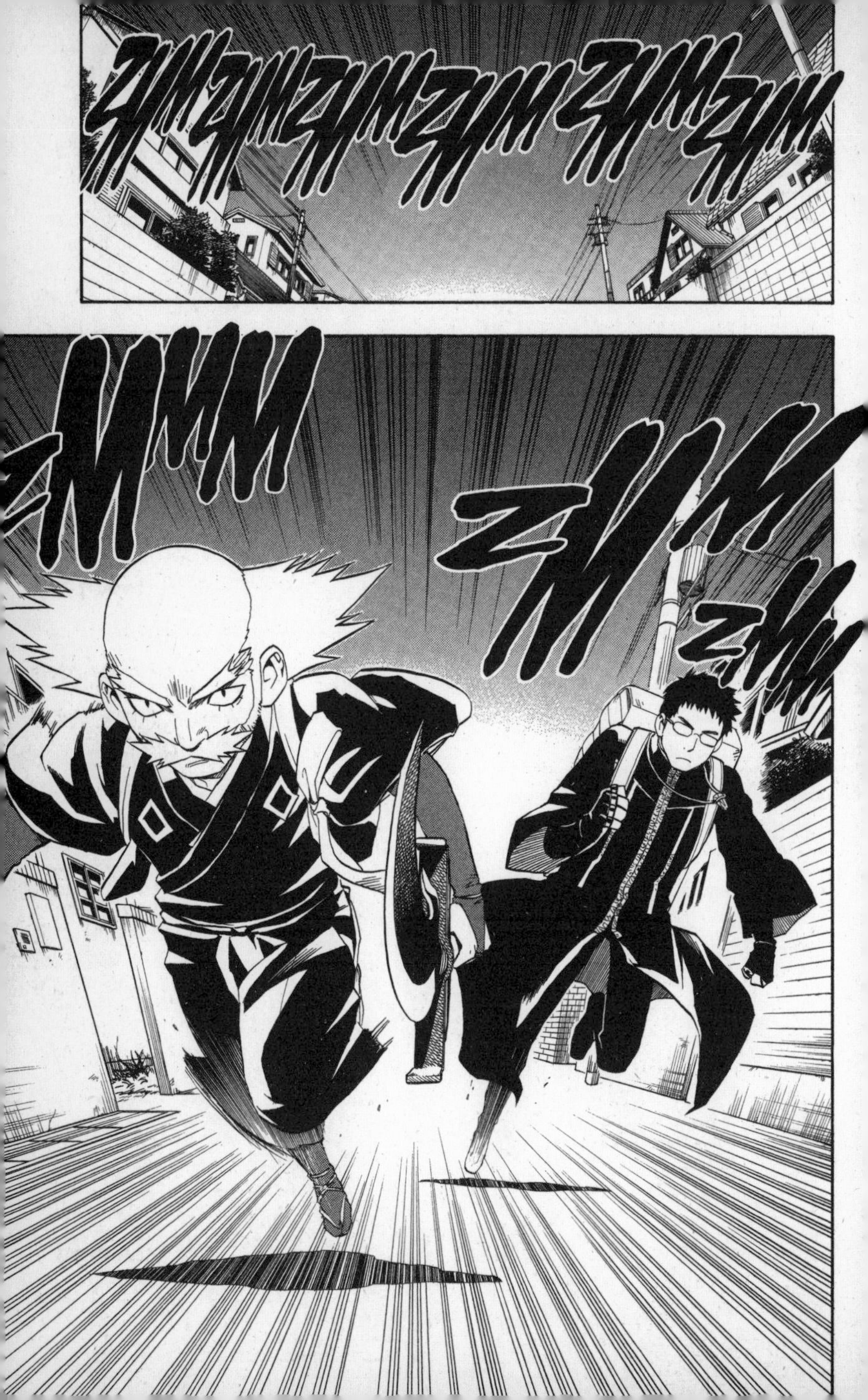
ZMMM
ZMMM
ZMM

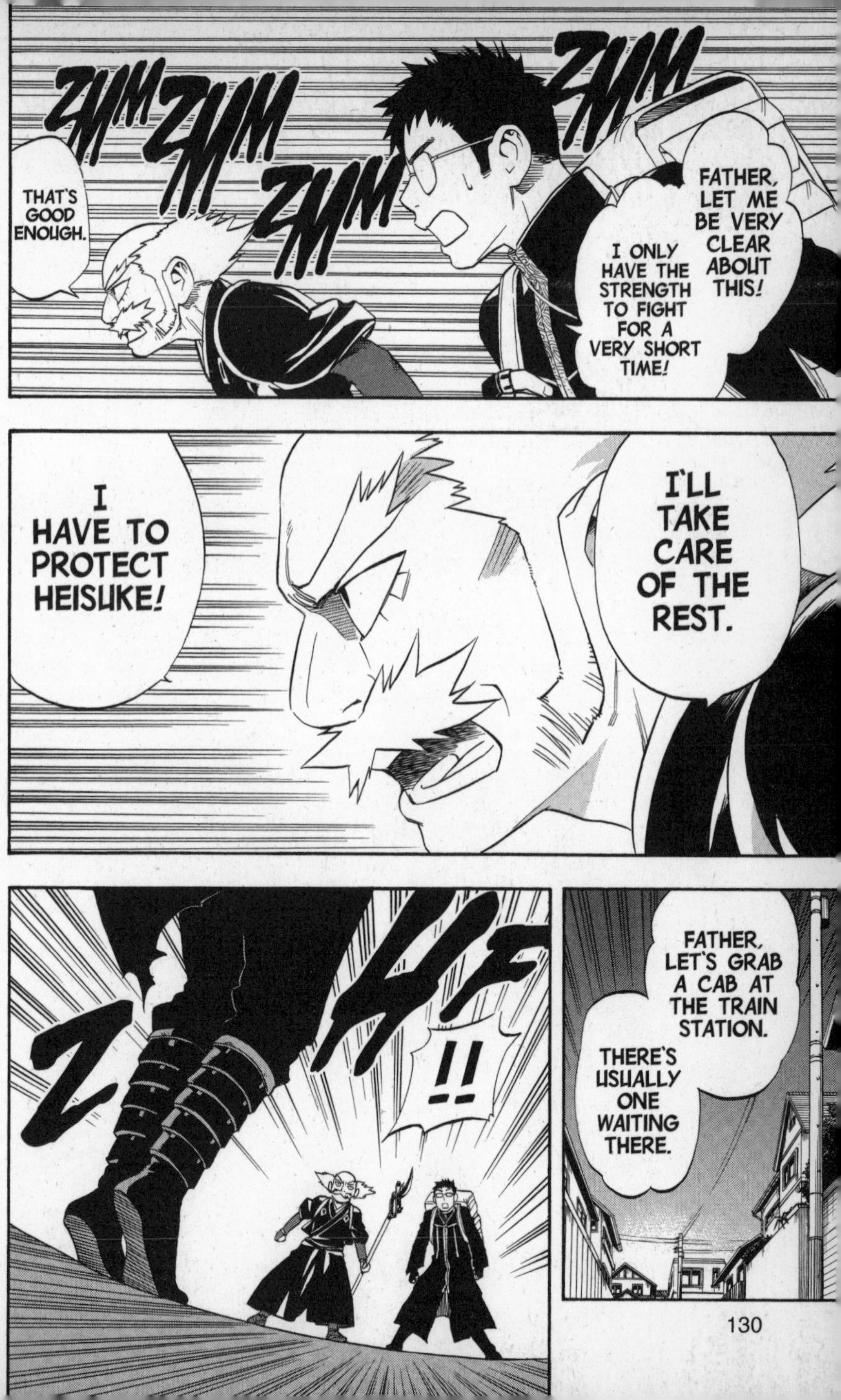
FATHER, LET ME BE VERY CLEAR ABOUT THIS!
I ONLY HAVE THE STRENGTH TO FIGHT FOR A VERY SHORT TIME!
ZMM
ZMM ZMM ZMM
THAT'S GOOD ENOUGH.
I'LL TAKE CARE OF THE REST.
I HAVE TO PROTECT HEISUKE!
FATHER, LET'S GRAB A CAB AT THE TRAIN STATION.
THERE'S USUALLY ONE WAITING THERE.
!!

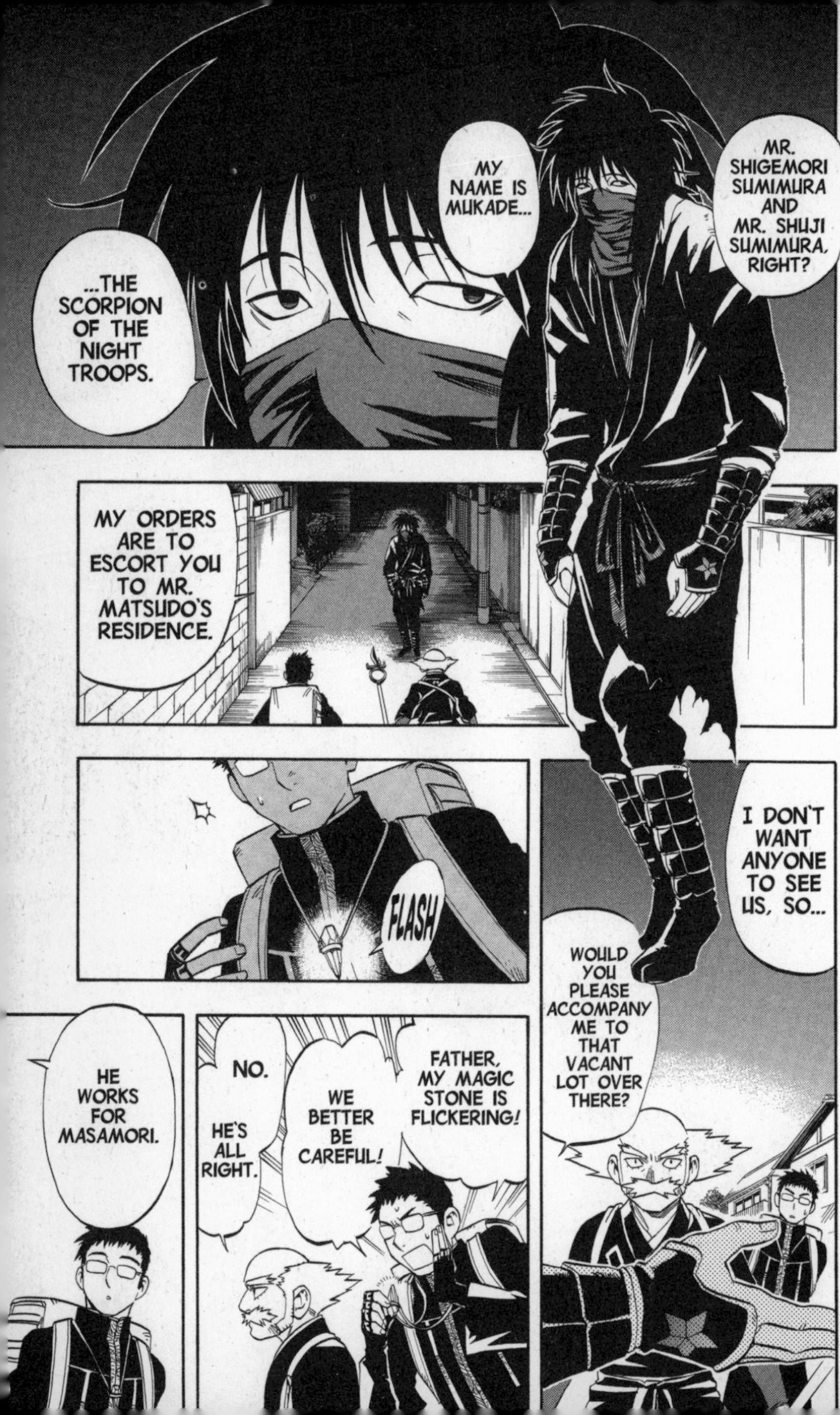
MR. SHIGEMORI SUMIMURA AND MR. SHUJI SUMIMURA, RIGHT?
MY NAME IS MUKADE...
...THE SCORPION OF THE NIGHT TROOPS.
MY ORDERS ARE TO ESCORT YOU TO MR. MATSUDO'S RESIDENCE.
I DON'T WANT ANYONE TO SEE US, SO...
WOULD YOU PLEASE ACCOMPANY ME TO THAT VACANT LOT OVER THERE?
FLASH
FATHER, MY MAGIC STONE IS FLICKERING!
WE BETTER BE CAREFUL!
NO.
HE'S ALL RIGHT.
HE WORKS FOR MASAMORI.

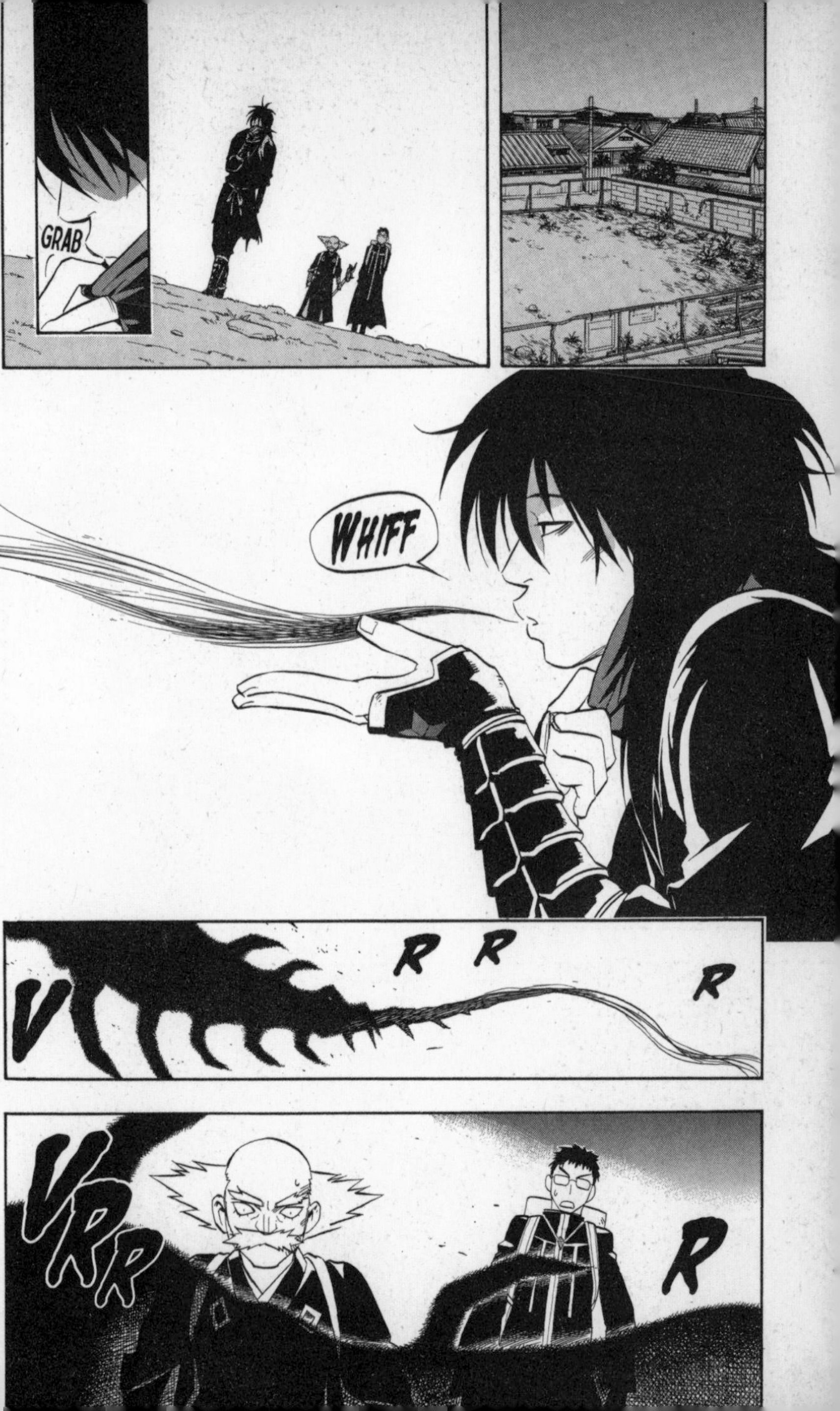

GRAB
WHIFF
V R R R
VRR R

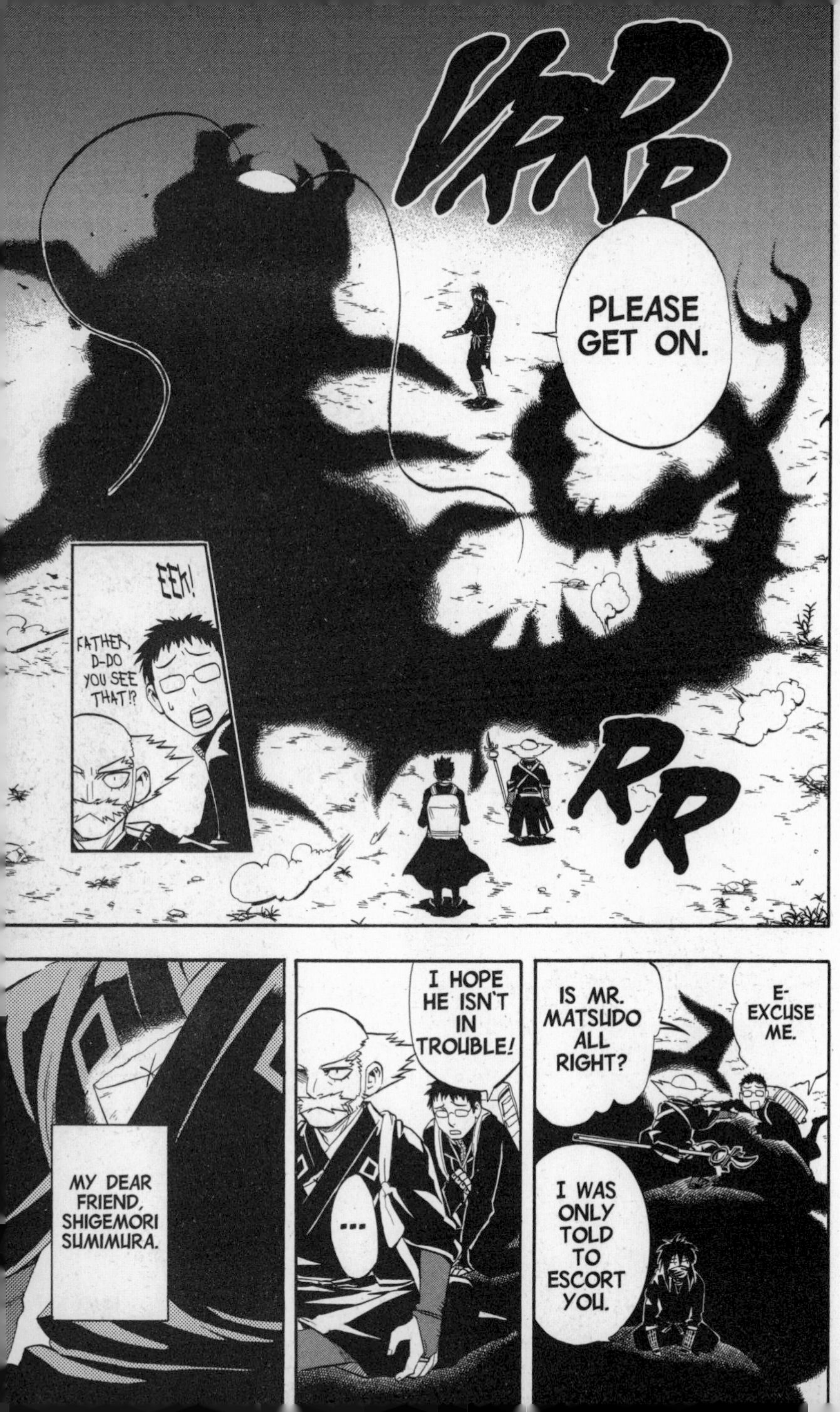
VRRR
PLEASE GET ON.
EEK!
FATHER, D-DO YOU SEE THAT!?
RR
E-EXCUSE ME.
IS MR. MATSUDO ALL RIGHT?
I WAS ONLY TOLD TO ESCORT YOU.
I HOPE HE ISN'T IN TROUBLE!
...
MY DEAR FRIEND, SHIGEMORI SUMIMURA.

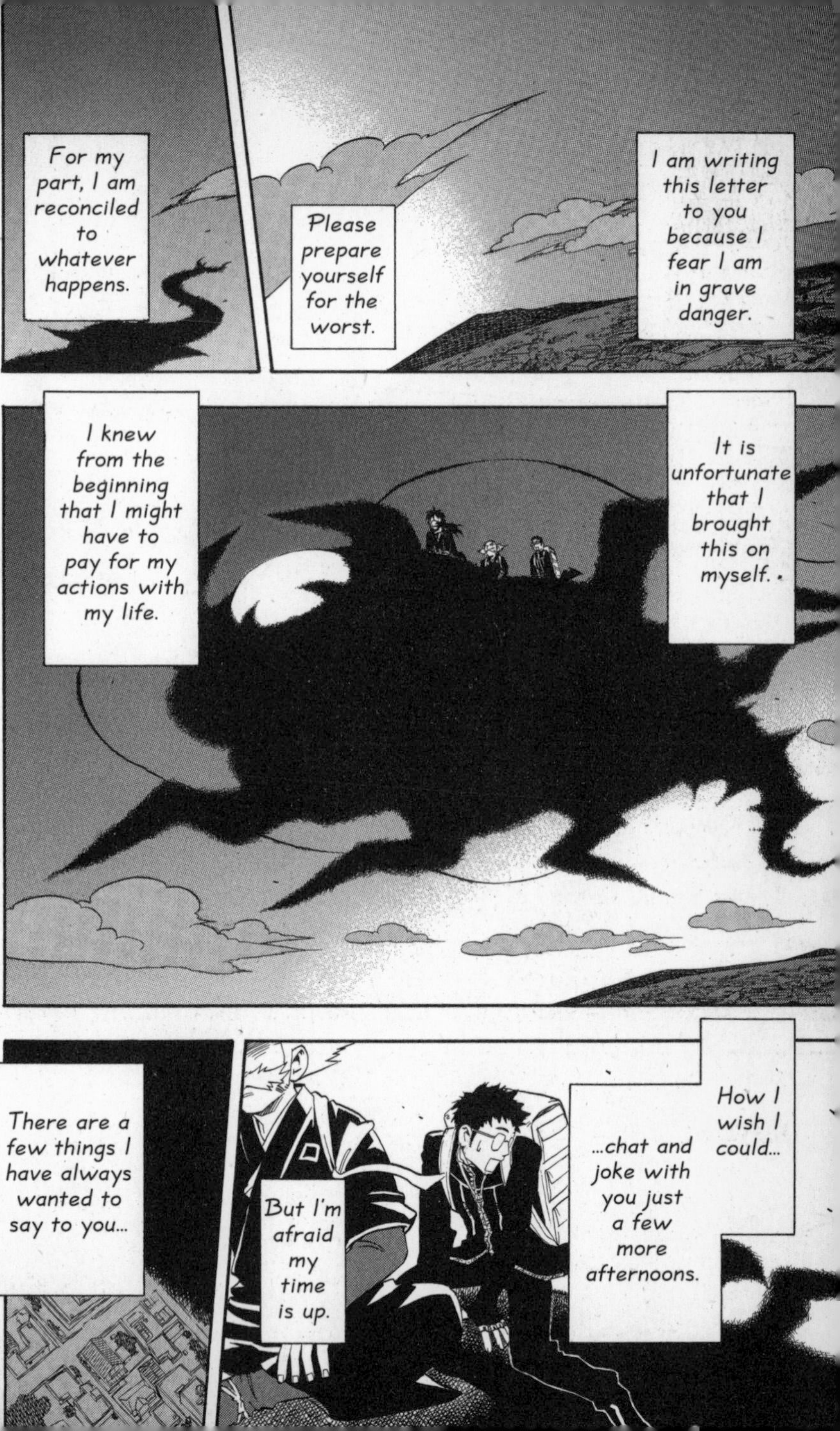
I am writing this letter to you because I fear I am in grave danger.
Please prepare yourself for the worst.
For my part, I am reconciled to whatever happens.
It is unfortunate that I brought this on myself.
I knew from the beginning that I might have to pay for my actions with my life.
How I wish I could...
...chat and joke with you just a few more afternoons.
But I'm afraid my time is up.
There are a few things I have always wanted to say to you...

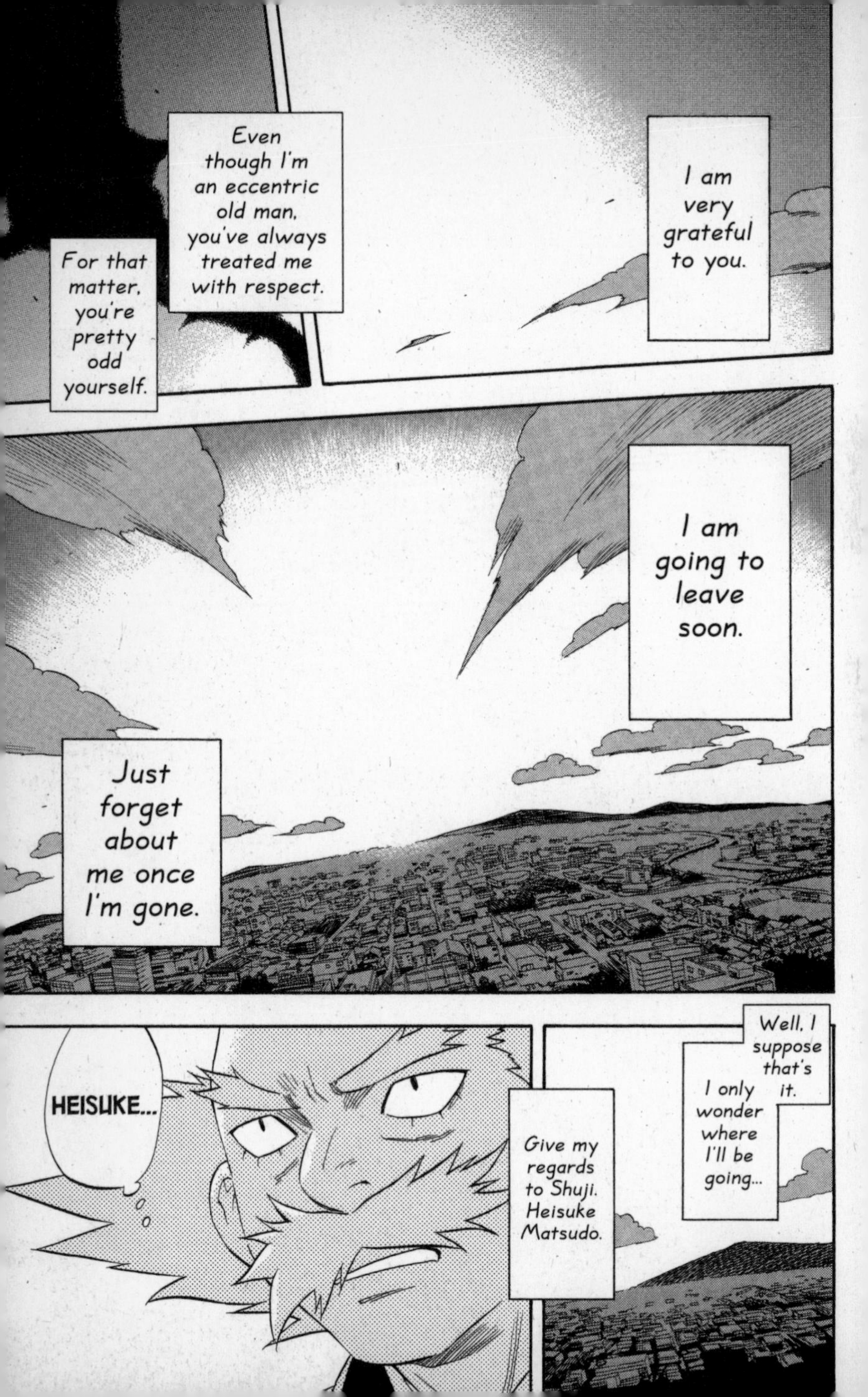
I am very grateful to you.
Even though I'm an eccentric old man, you've always treated me with respect.
For that matter, you're pretty odd yourself.
I am going to leave soon.
Just forget about me once I'm gone.
Well, I suppose that's it.
I only wonder where I'll be going...
Give my regards to Shuji. Heisuke Matsudo.
HEISUKE...

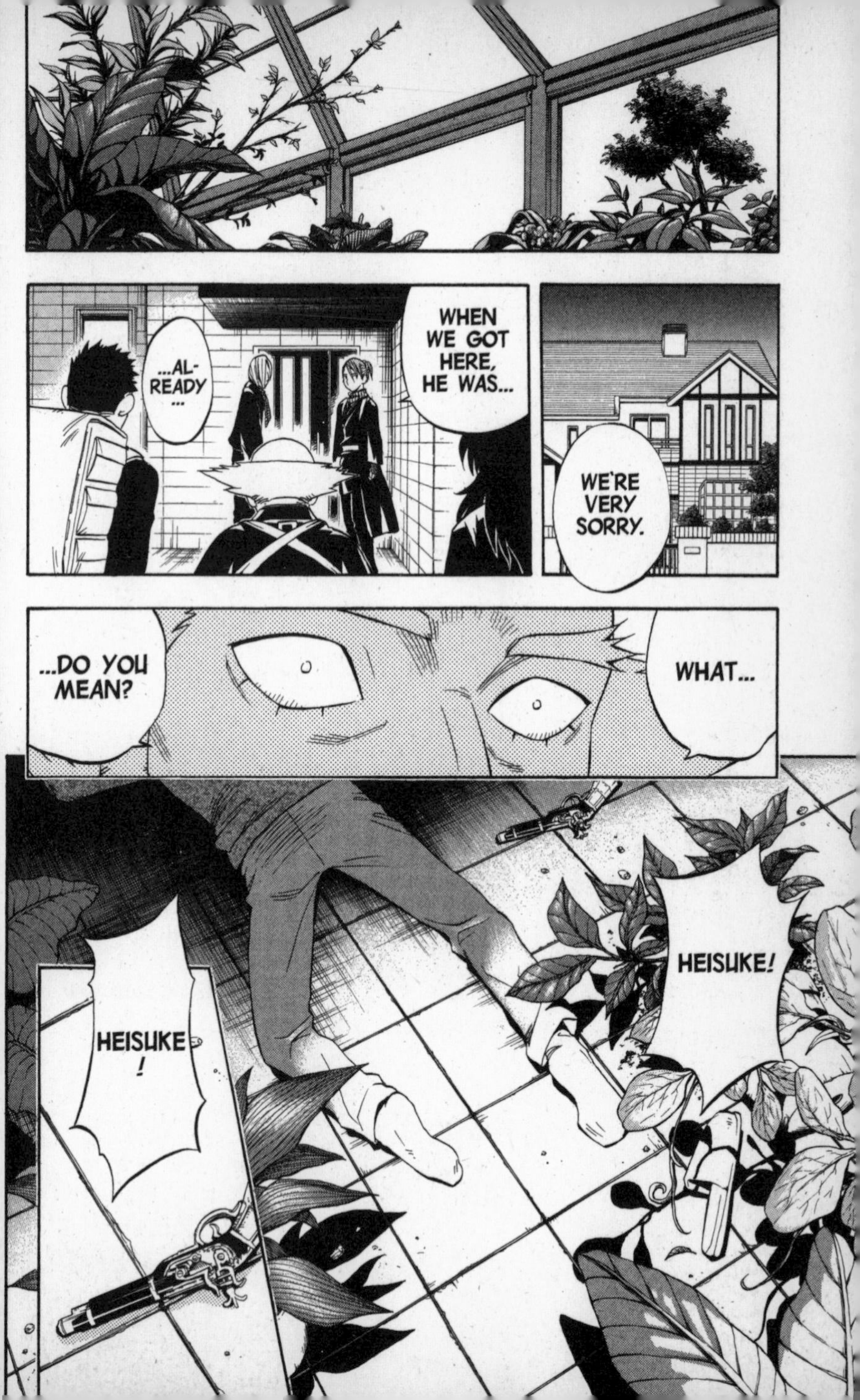
WE'RE VERY SORRY.
WHEN WE GOT HERE, HE WAS...
...AL-READY...
WHAT...
...DO YOU MEAN?
HEISUKE!
HEISUKE!

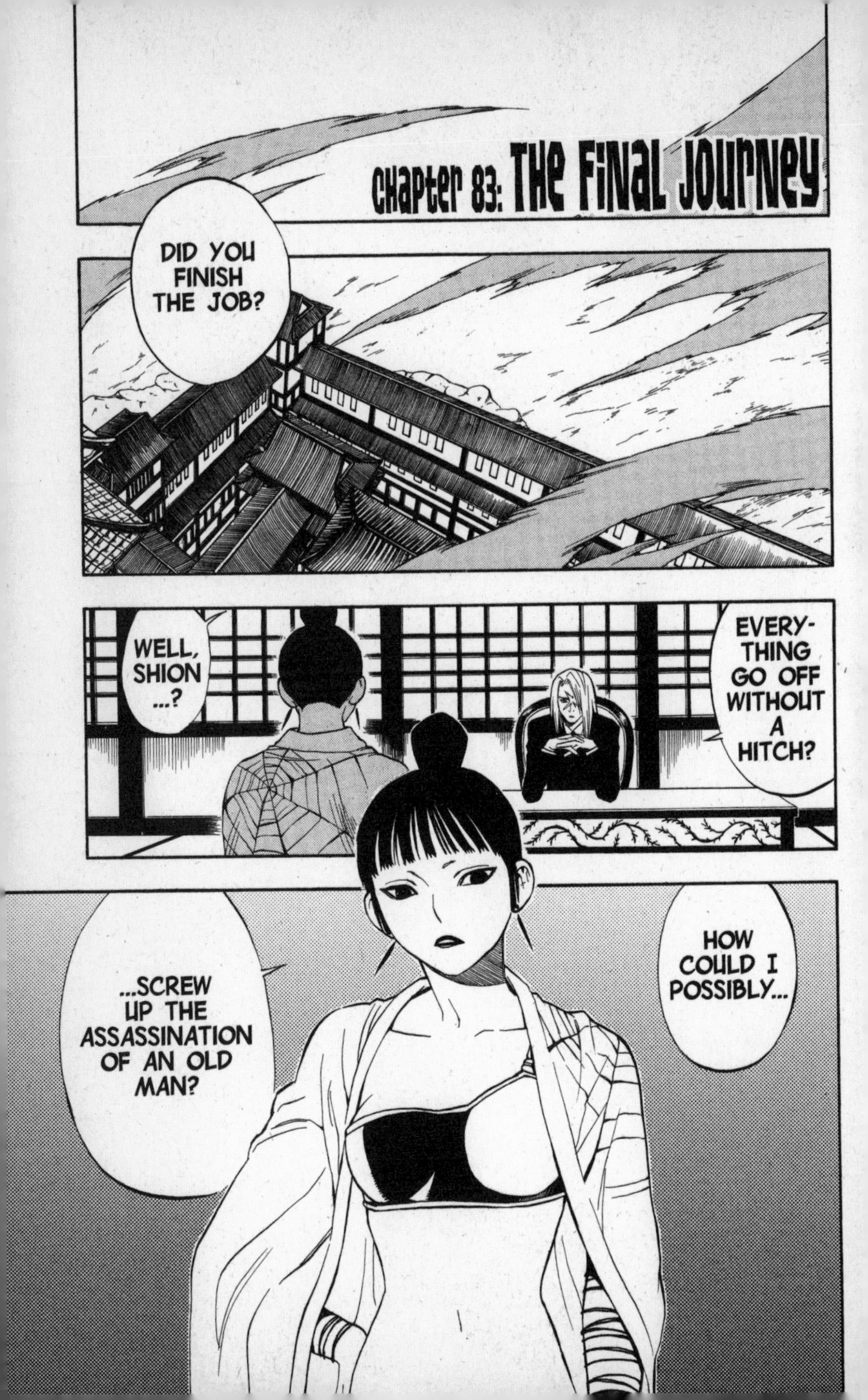
Chapter 83: The Final Journey
DID YOU FINISH THE JOB?
EVERY-THING GO OFF WITHOUT A HITCH?
WELL, SHION ...?
HOW COULD I POSSIBLY...
...SCREW UP THE ASSASSINATION OF AN OLD MAN?

Chapter 83: The Final Journey

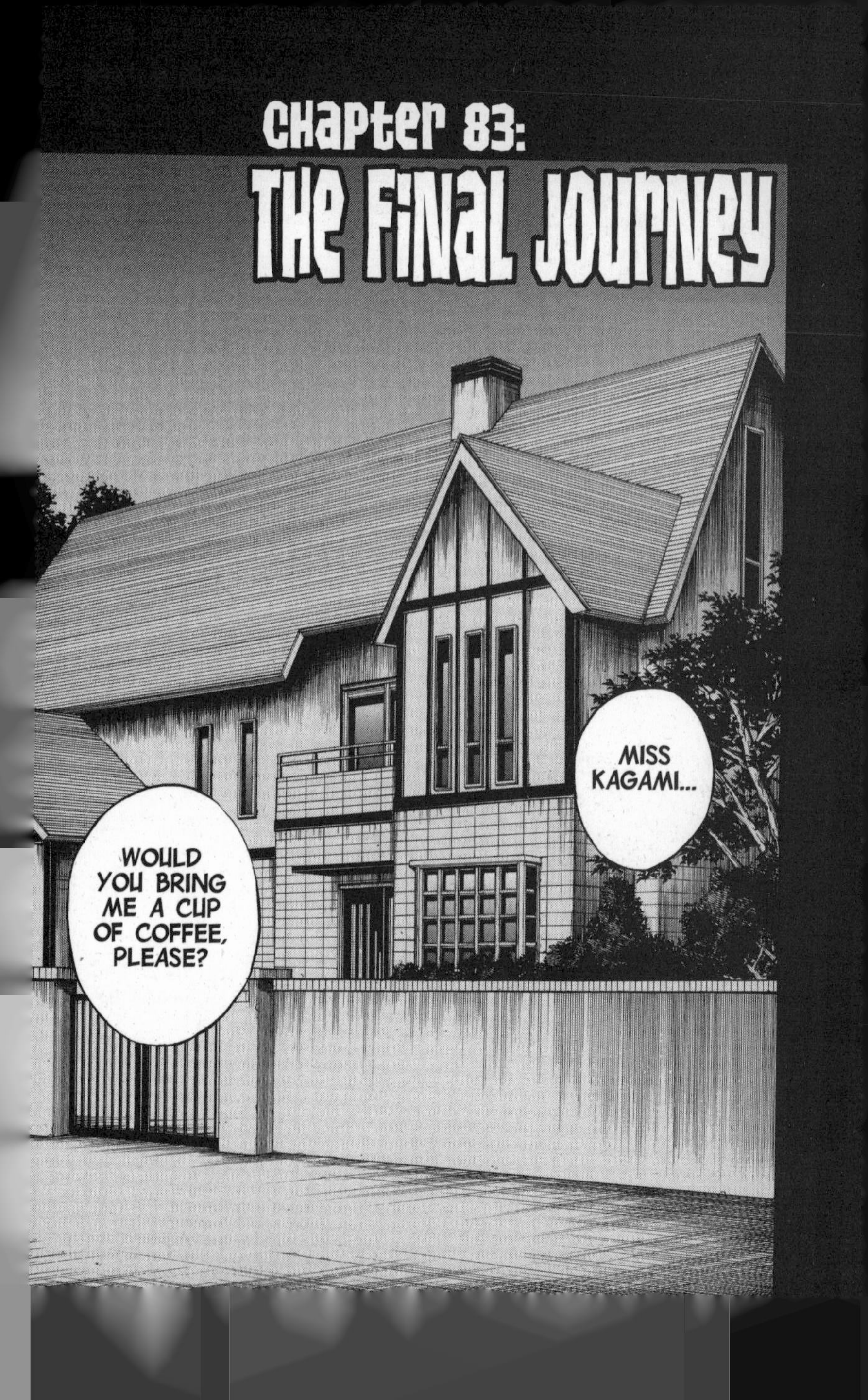
MISS KAGAMI...
WOULD YOU BRING ME A CUP OF COFFEE, PLEASE?

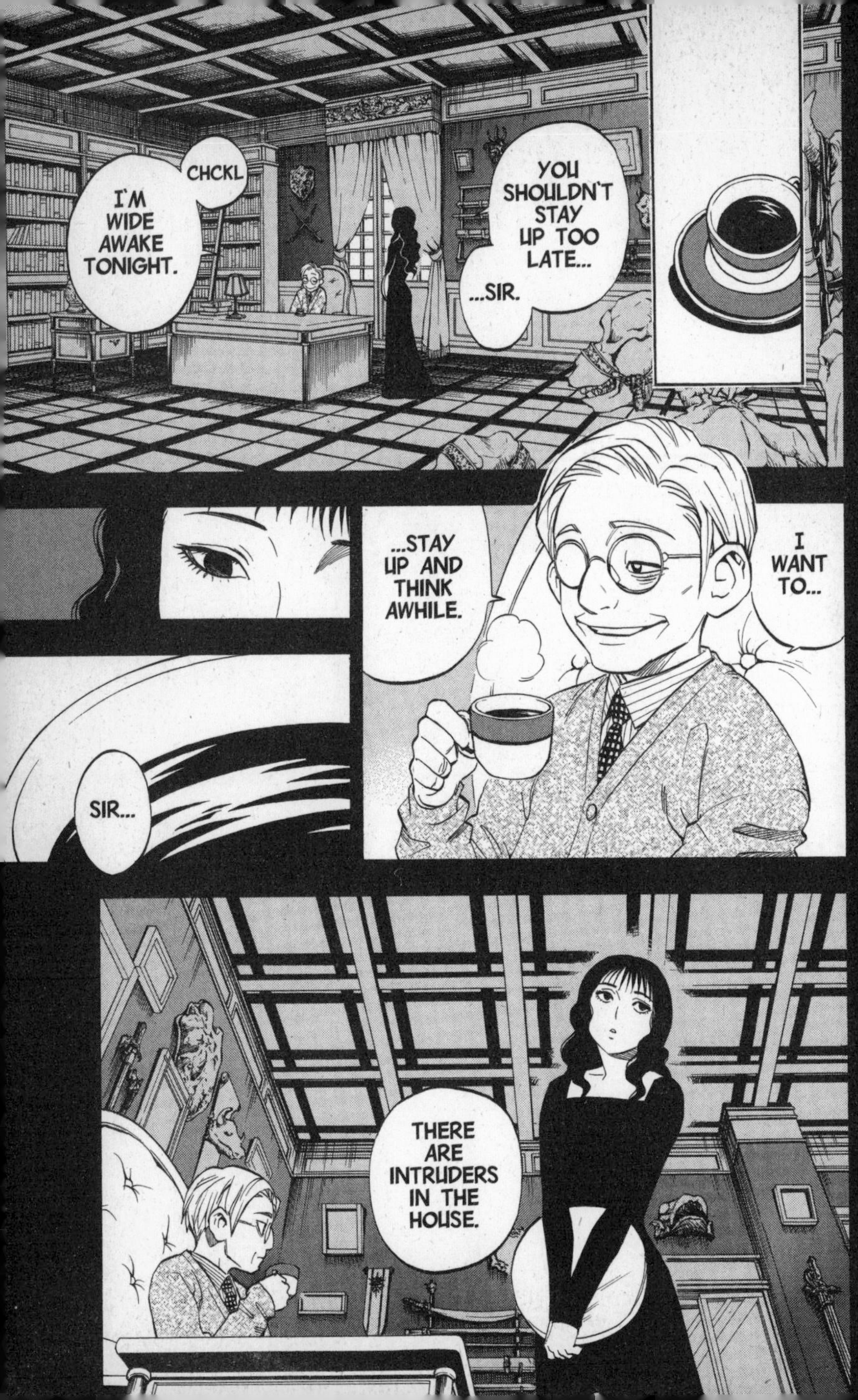
YOU SHOULDN'T STAY UP TOO LATE...
...SIR.
CHCKL
I'M WIDE AWAKE TONIGHT.
I WANT TO...
...STAY UP AND THINK AWHILE.
SIR...
THERE ARE INTRUDERS IN THE HOUSE.

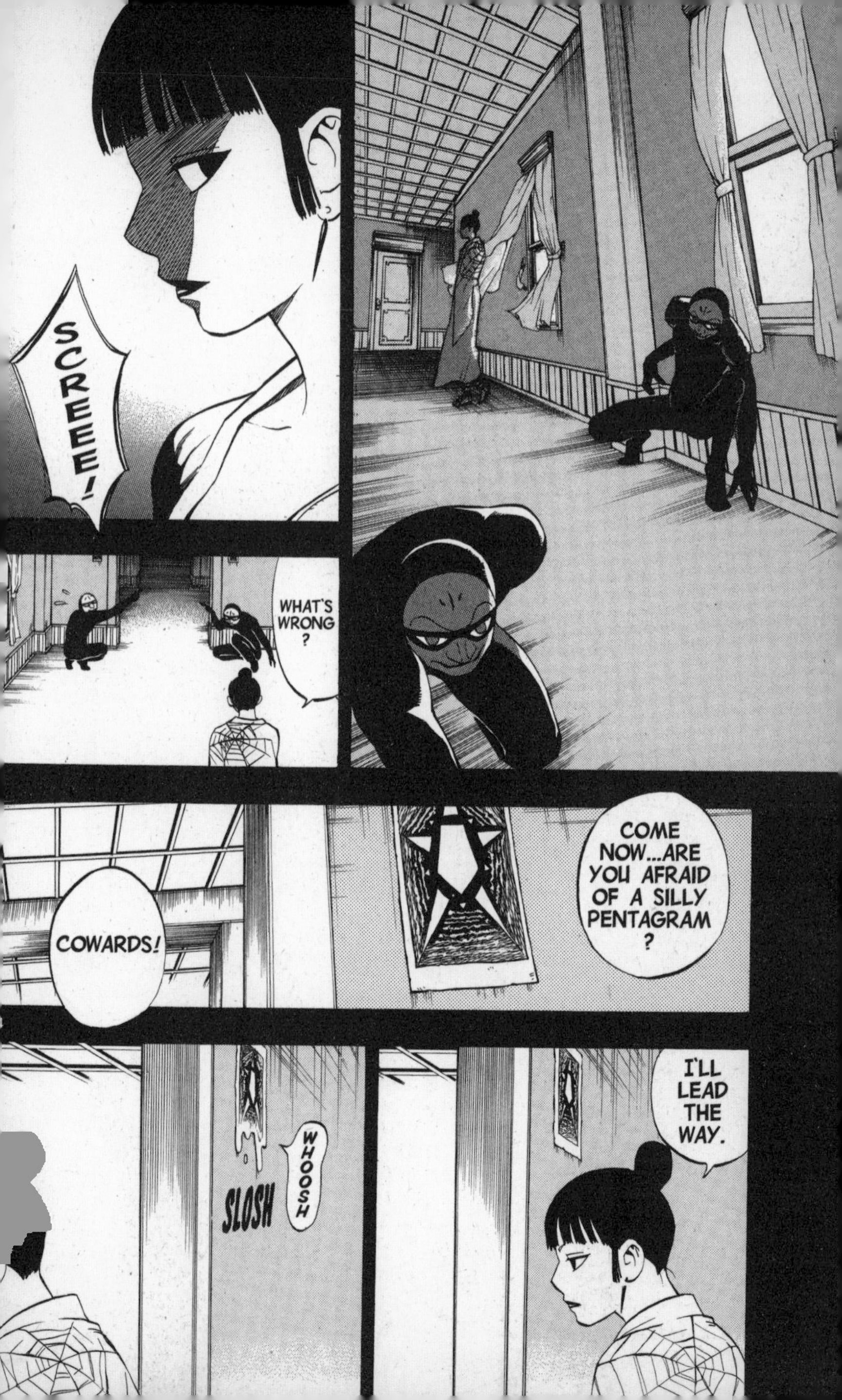
SCREEE!
WHAT'S WRONG?
COME NOW...ARE YOU AFRAID OF A SILLY PENTAGRAM?
COWARDS!
I'LL LEAD THE WAY.
WHOOSH
SLOSH

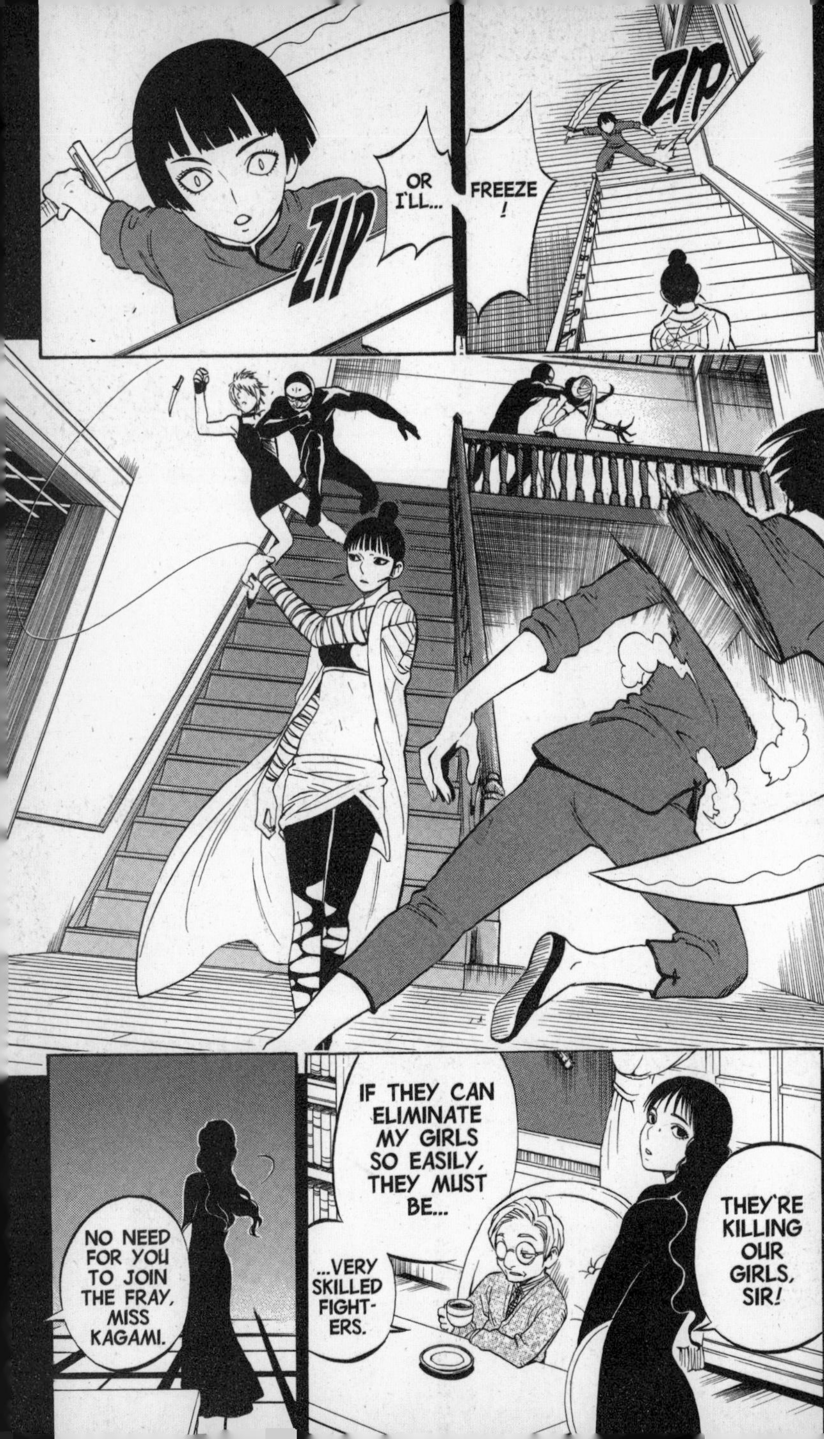
ZIP
FREEZE!
OR I'LL...
ZIP
THEY'RE KILLING OUR GIRLS, SIR!
IF THEY CAN ELIMINATE MY GIRLS SO EASILY, THEY MUST BE...
...VERY SKILLED FIGHTERS.
NO NEED FOR YOU TO JOIN THE FRAY, MISS KAGAMI.

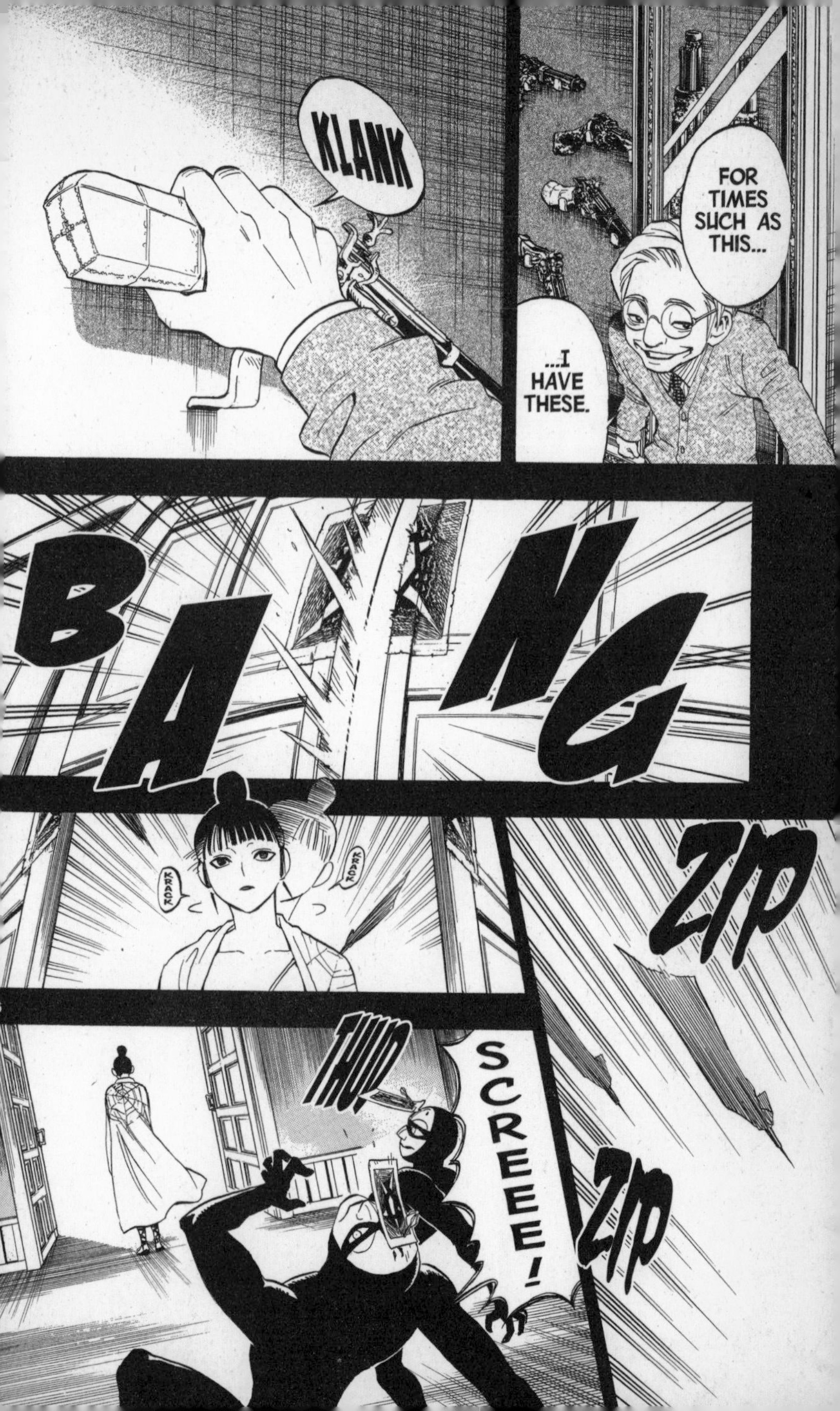
FOR TIMES SUCH AS THIS...
...I HAVE THESE.
KLANK
BANG
ZIP
KRACK
KRACK
SCREEE!
THUD
ZIP

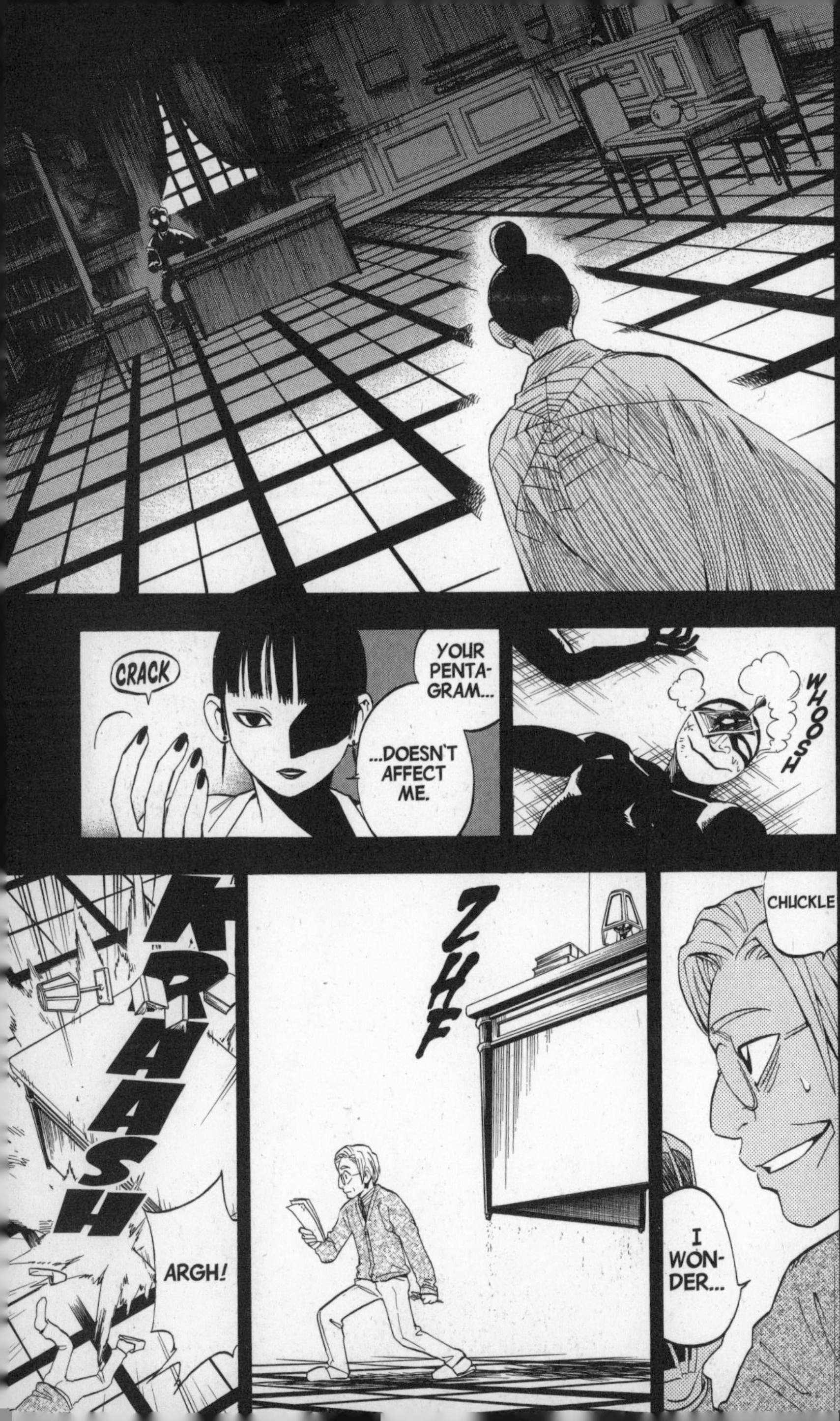
WHOOSH
YOUR PENTA-GRAM...
CRACK
...DOESN'T AFFECT ME.
CHUCKLE
I WON-DER...
ZHF
KRAASH
ARGH!

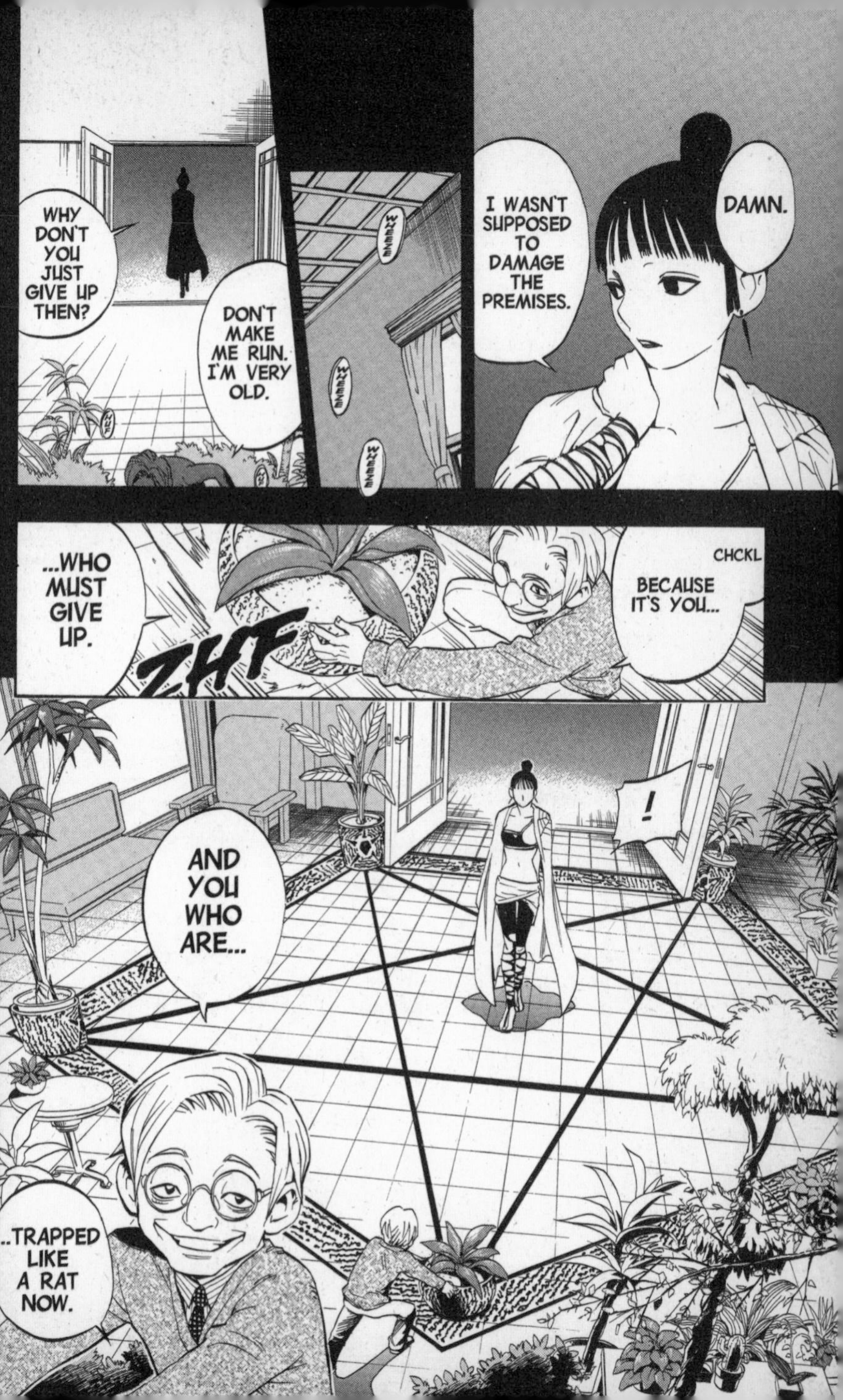
DAMN.
I WASN'T SUPPOSED TO DAMAGE THE PREMISES.
WHEEZE
WHEEZE
WHEEZE
DON'T MAKE ME RUN. I'M VERY OLD.
WHY DON'T YOU JUST GIVE UP THEN?
CHCKL
BECAUSE IT'S YOU...
...WHO MUST GIVE UP.
ZHT
!
AND YOU WHO ARE...
...TRAPPED LIKE A RAT NOW.

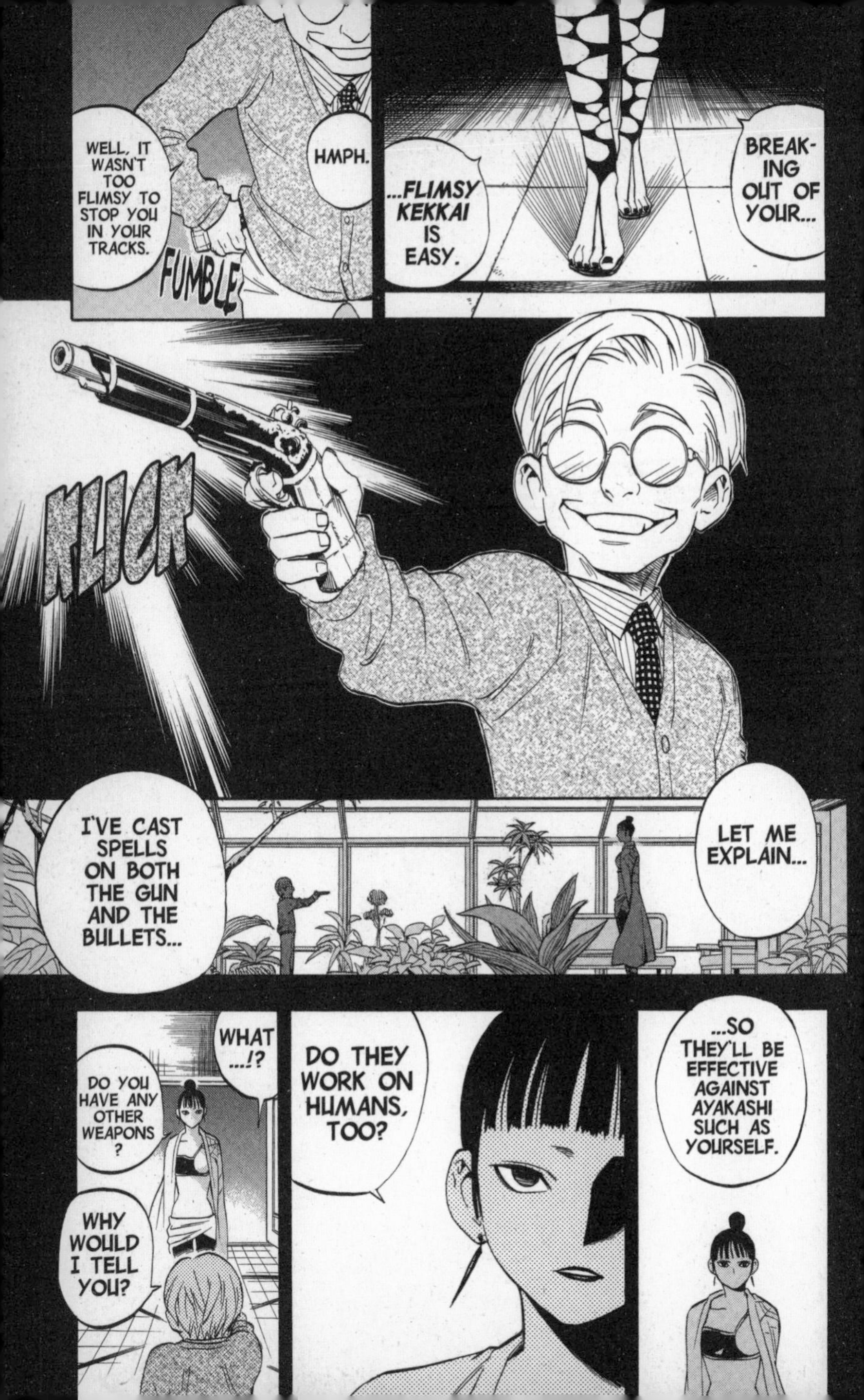
BREAKING OUT OF YOUR...
...FLIMSY KEKKAI IS EASY.
HMPH.
WELL, IT WASN'T TOO FLIMSY TO STOP YOU IN YOUR TRACKS.
FUMBLE
KLICK
LET ME EXPLAIN...
I'VE CAST SPELLS ON BOTH THE GUN AND THE BULLETS...
...SO THEY'LL BE EFFECTIVE AGAINST AYAKASHI SUCH AS YOURSELF.
DO THEY WORK ON HUMANS, TOO?
WHAT...!?
DO YOU HAVE ANY OTHER WEAPONS?
WHY WOULD I TELL YOU?

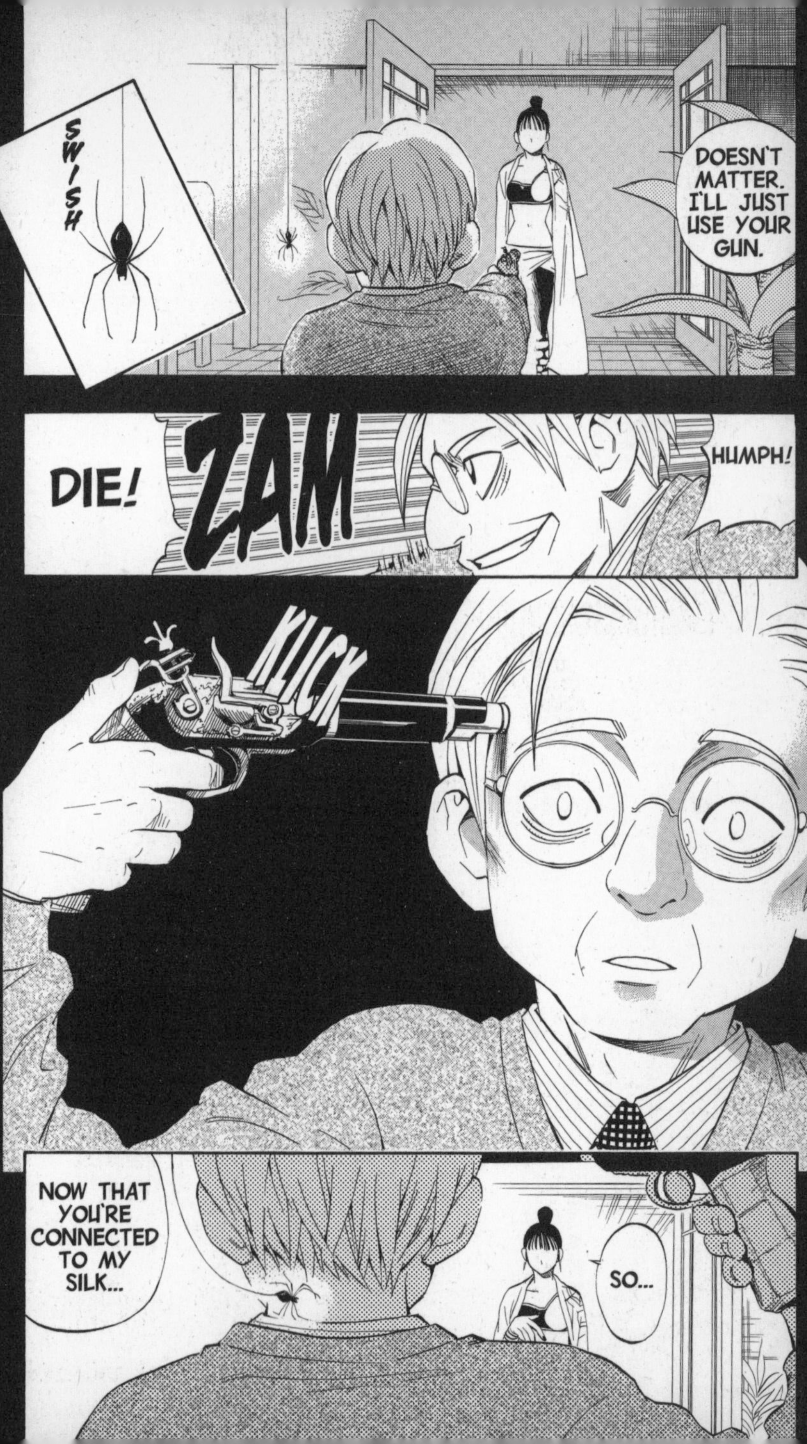
DOESN'T MATTER. I'LL JUST USE YOUR GUN.
SWISH
HUMPH!
ZAM
DIE!
KLICK
SO...
NOW THAT YOU'RE CONNECTED TO MY SILK...

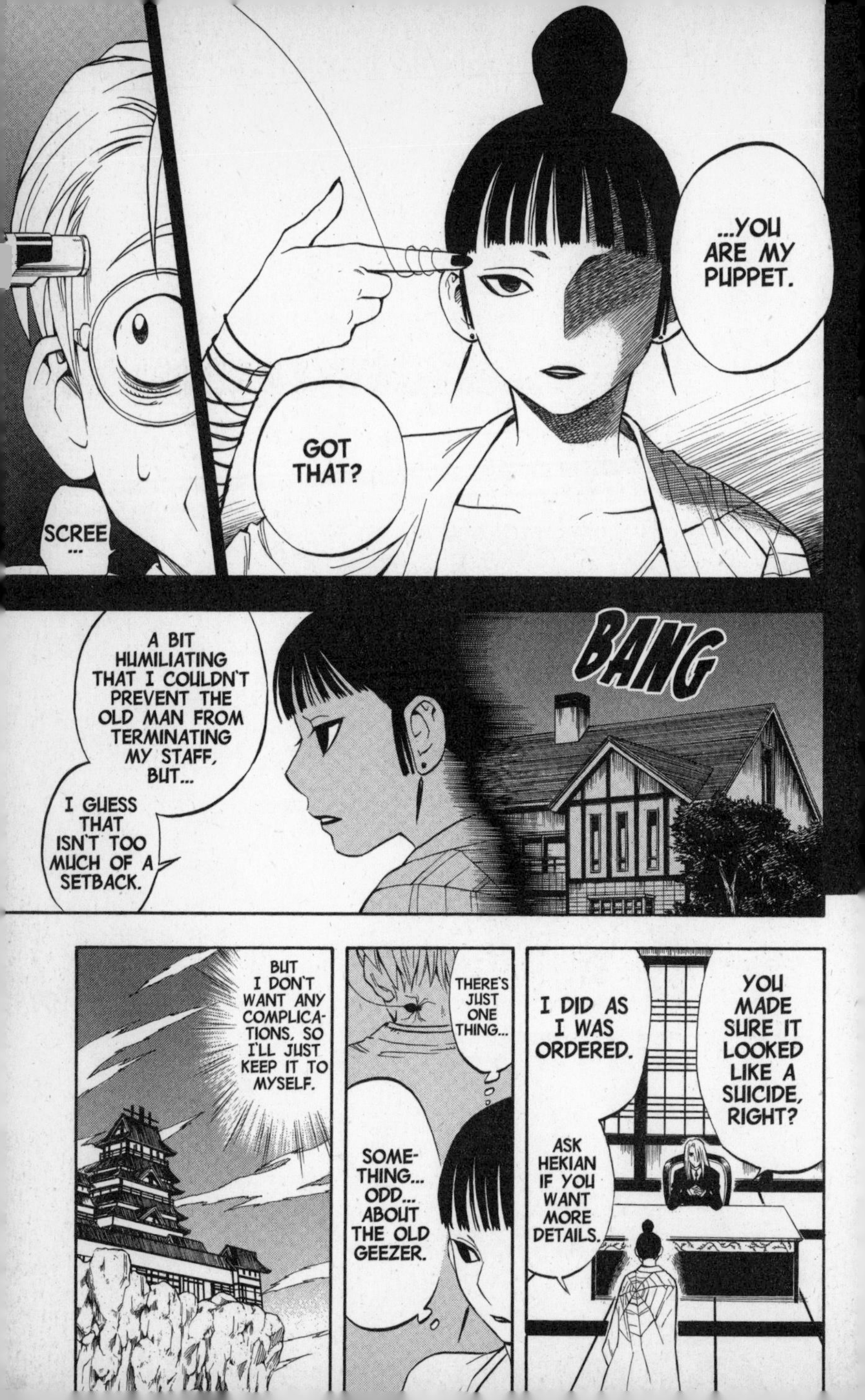
...YOU ARE MY PUPPET.
GOT THAT?
SCREE...
BANG
A BIT HUMILIATING THAT I COULDN'T PREVENT THE OLD MAN FROM TERMINATING MY STAFF, BUT...
I GUESS THAT ISN'T TOO MUCH OF A SETBACK.
YOU MADE SURE IT LOOKED LIKE A SUICIDE, RIGHT?
I DID AS I WAS ORDERED.
ASK HEKIAN IF YOU WANT MORE DETAILS.
THERE'S JUST ONE THING...
SOMETHING... ODD... ABOUT THE OLD GEEZER.
BUT I DON'T WANT ANY COMPLICATIONS, SO I'LL JUST KEEP IT TO MYSELF.

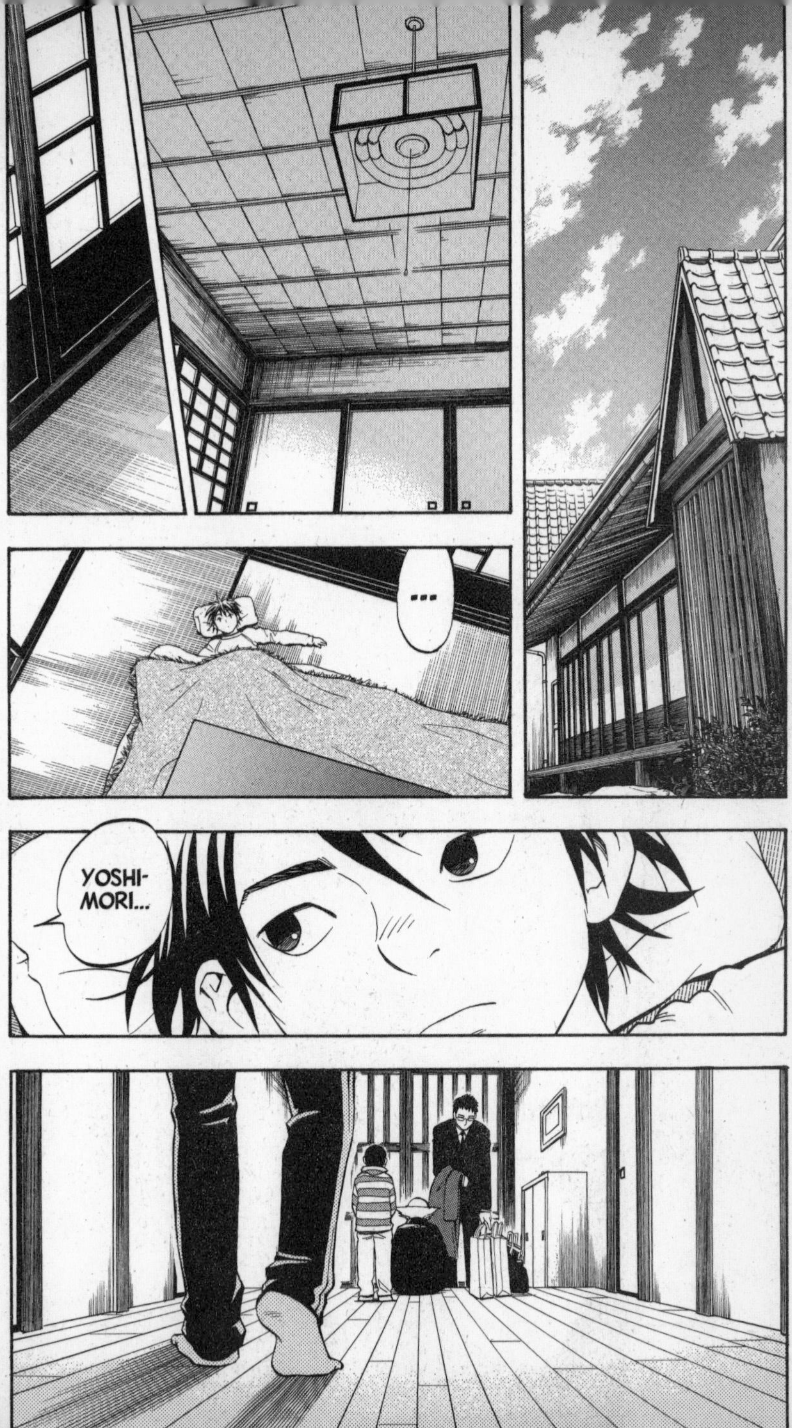
...
YOSHI-MORI...

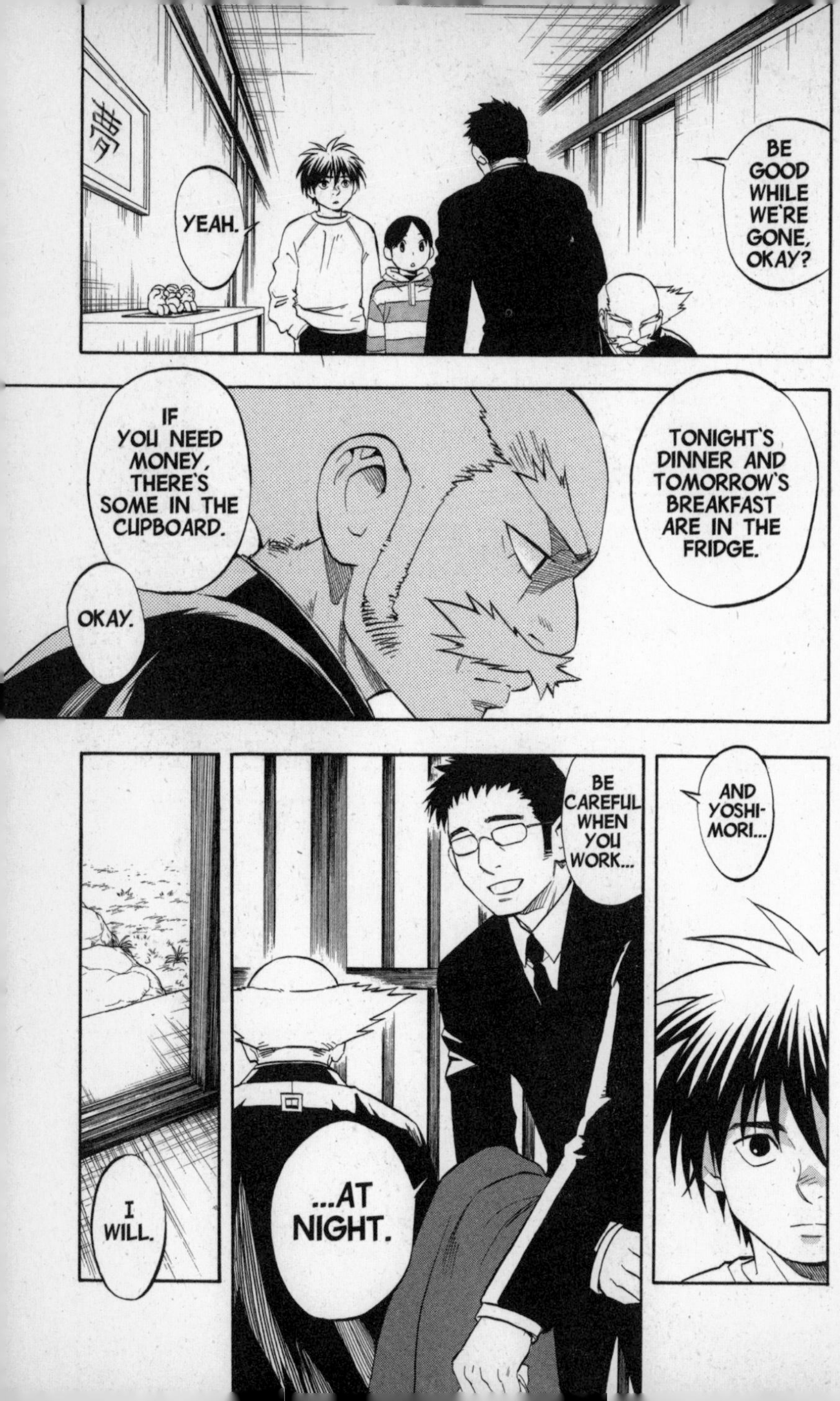
BE GOOD WHILE WE'RE GONE, OKAY?
YEAH.
TONIGHT'S DINNER AND TOMORROW'S BREAKFAST ARE IN THE FRIDGE.
IF YOU NEED MONEY, THERE'S SOME IN THE CUPBOARD.
OKAY.
AND YOSHIMORI...
BE CAREFUL WHEN YOU WORK...
...AT NIGHT.
I WILL.

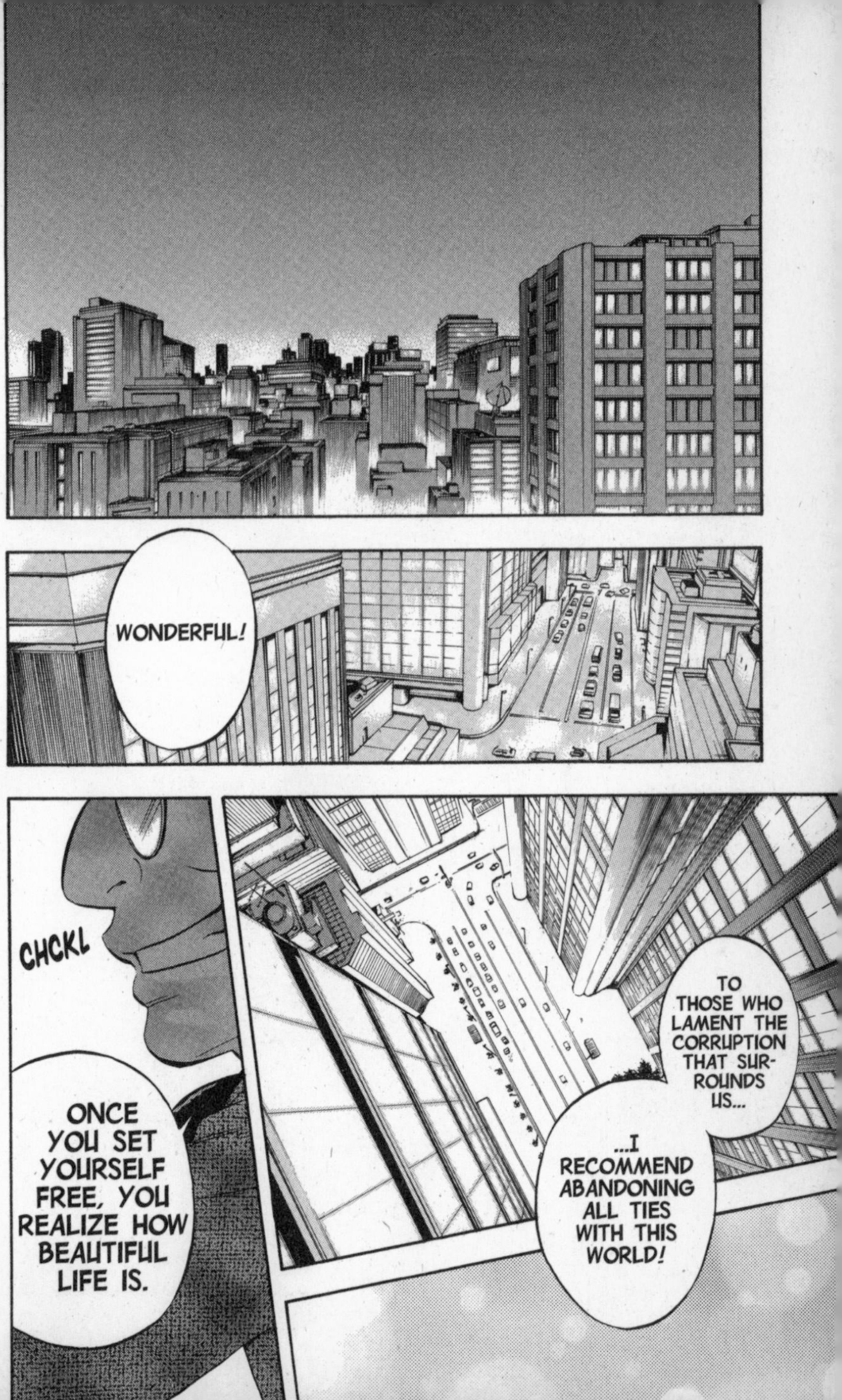
WONDERFUL!
TO THOSE WHO LAMENT THE CORRUPTION THAT SURROUNDS US...
...I RECOMMEND ABANDONING ALL TIES WITH THIS WORLD!
CHCKL
ONCE YOU SET YOURSELF FREE, YOU REALIZE HOW BEAUTIFUL LIFE IS.

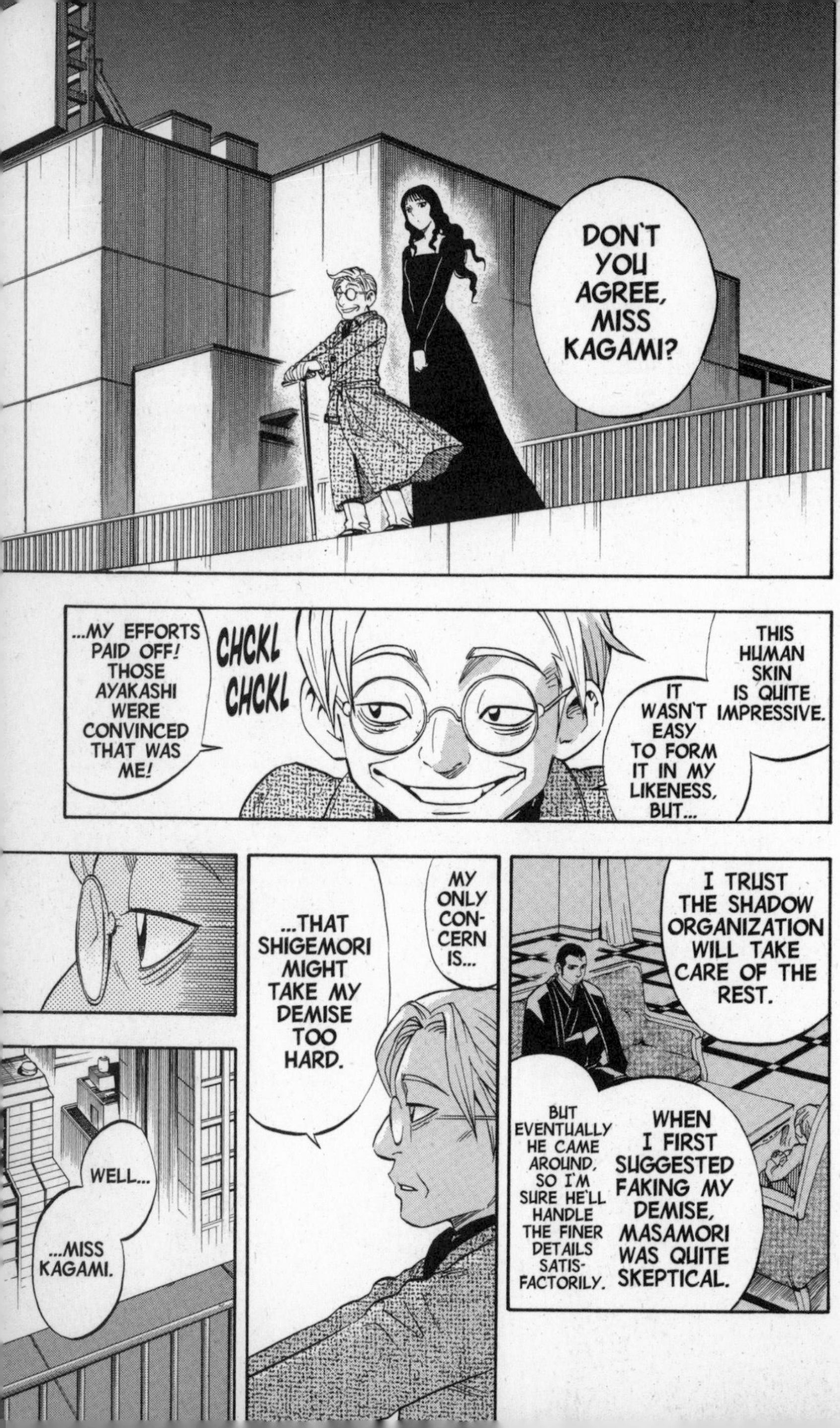
DON'T YOU AGREE, MISS KAGAMI?
THIS HUMAN SKIN IS QUITE IMPRESSIVE.
IT WASN'T EASY TO FORM IT IN MY LIKENESS, BUT...
CHCKL CHCKL
...MY EFFORTS PAID OFF! THOSE AYAKASHI WERE CONVINCED THAT WAS ME!
I TRUST THE SHADOW ORGANIZATION WILL TAKE CARE OF THE REST.
WHEN I FIRST SUGGESTED FAKING MY DEMISE, MASAMORI WAS QUITE SKEPTICAL.
BUT EVENTUALLY HE CAME AROUND, SO I'M SURE HE'LL HANDLE THE FINER DETAILS SATIS-FACTORILY.
MY ONLY CON-CERN IS...
...THAT SHIGEMORI MIGHT TAKE MY DEMISE TOO HARD.
WELL...
...MISS KAGAMI.

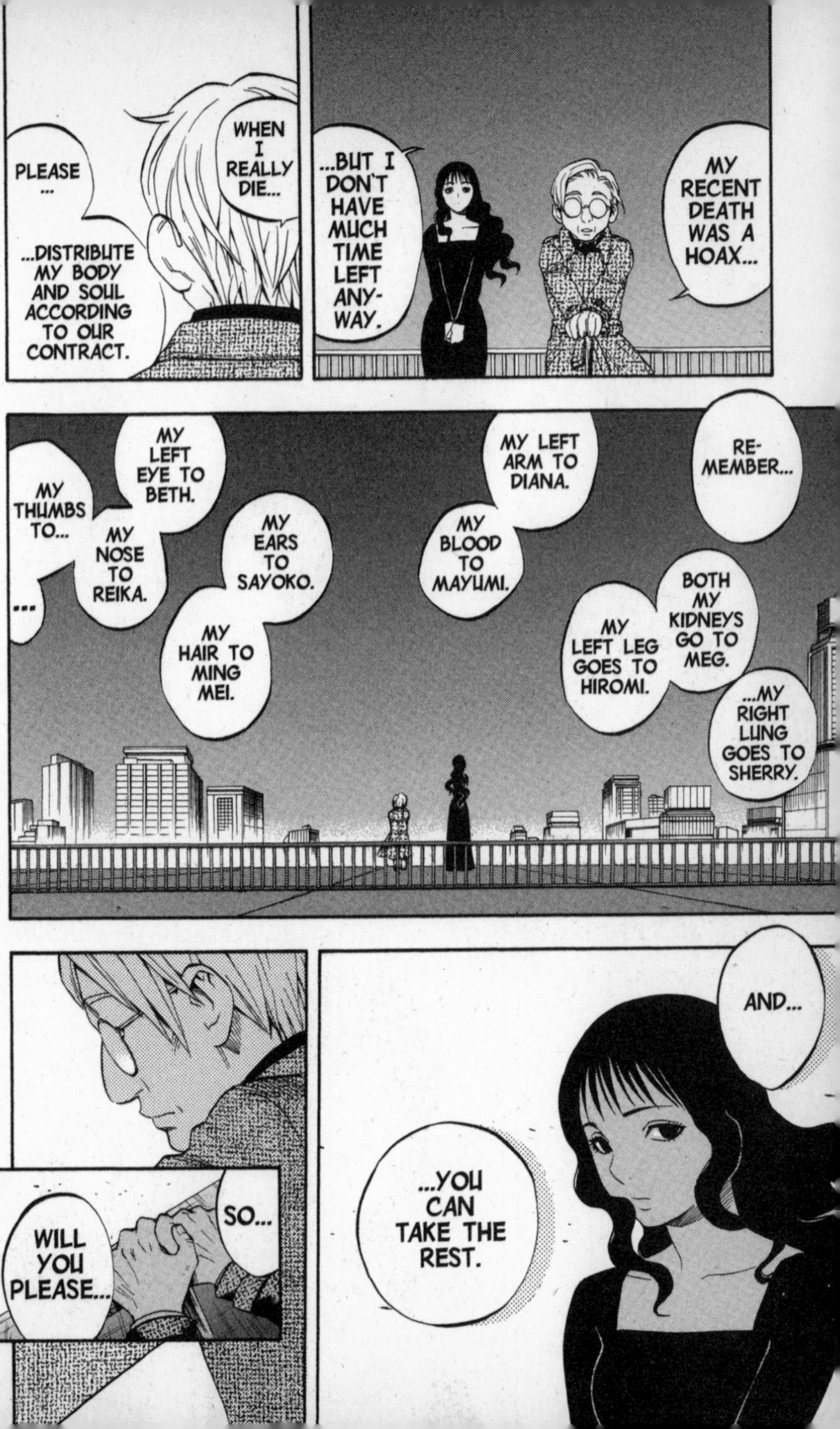
MY RECENT DEATH WAS A HOAX...
...BUT I DON'T HAVE MUCH TIME LEFT ANY-WAY.
WHEN I REALLY DIE...
PLEASE...
...DISTRIBUTE MY BODY AND SOUL ACCORDING TO OUR CONTRACT.
RE-MEMBER...
MY LEFT ARM TO DIANA.
BOTH MY KIDNEYS GO TO MEG.
MY LEFT LEG GOES TO HIROMI.
...MY RIGHT LUNG GOES TO SHERRY.
MY BLOOD TO MAYUMI.
MY EARS TO SAYOKO.
MY HAIR TO MING MEI.
MY LEFT EYE TO BETH.
MY NOSE TO REIKA.
MY THUMBS TO...
...
AND...
...YOU CAN TAKE THE REST.
SO...
WILL YOU PLEASE...

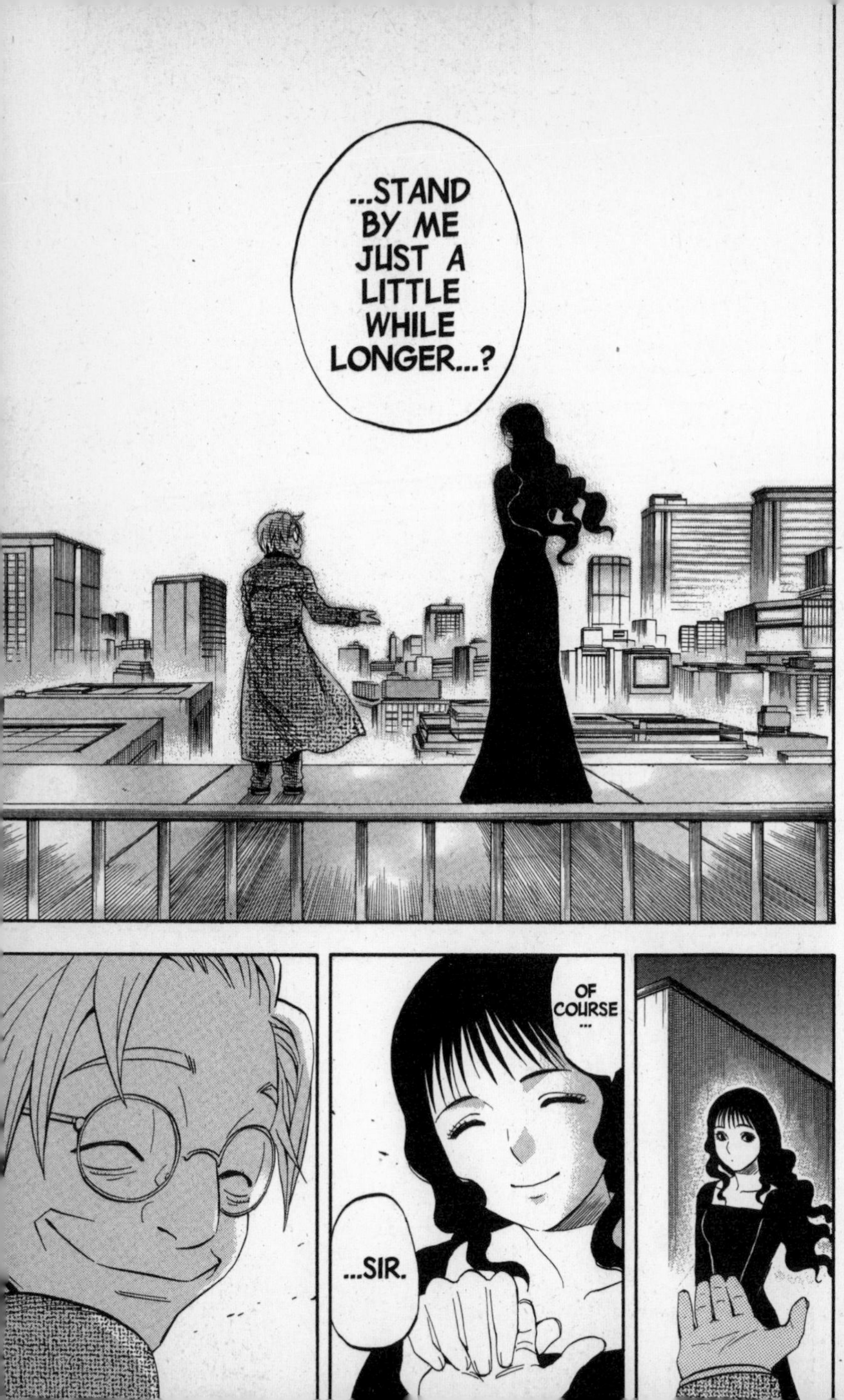
...STAND BY ME JUST A LITTLE WHILE LONGER...?
OF COURSE...
...SIR.

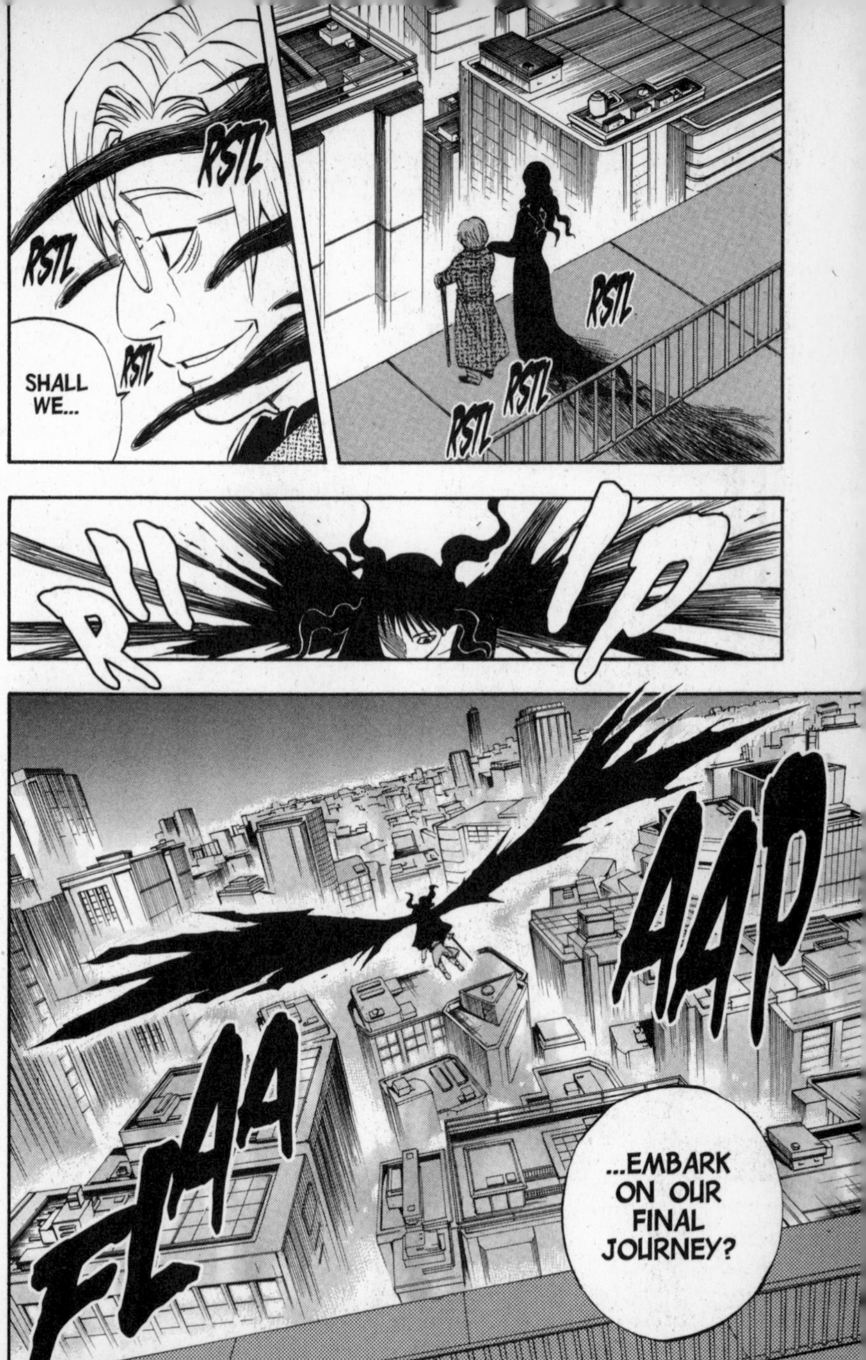
RSTL
RSTL
RSTL
RSTL
RSTL
RSTL
SHALL WE...
RIIP
FLAAAAP
...EMBARK ON OUR FINAL JOURNEY?

Chapter 84: The Master's Throne

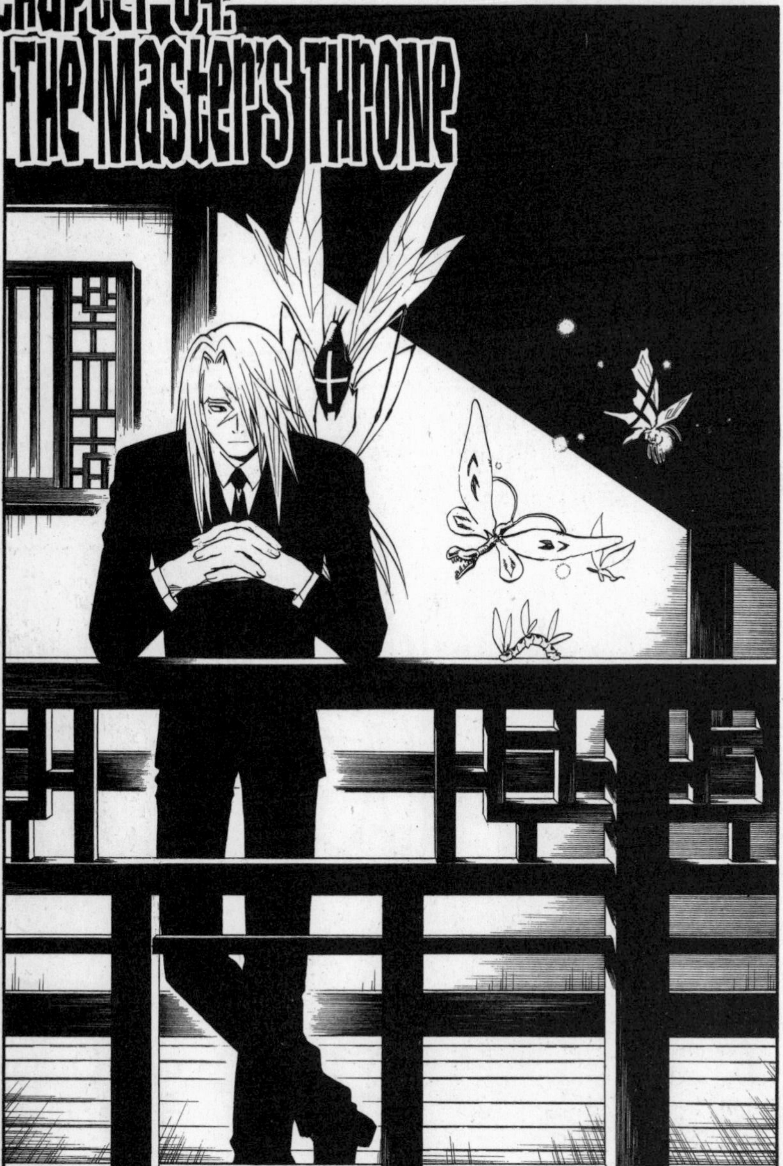

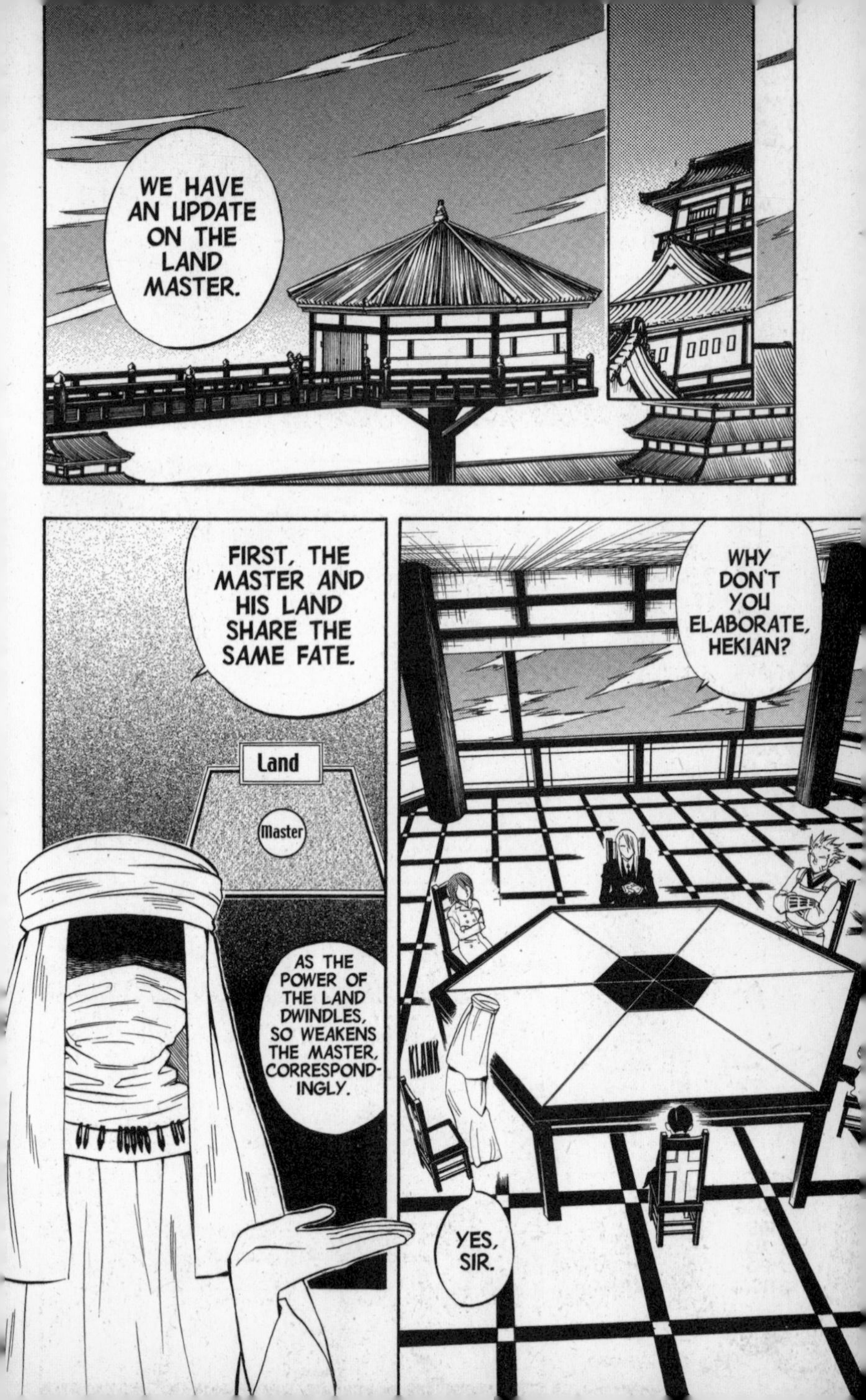
WE HAVE AN UPDATE ON THE LAND MASTER.
WHY DON'T YOU ELABORATE, HEKIAN?
KLANK
YES, SIR.
FIRST, THE MASTER AND HIS LAND SHARE THE SAME FATE.
Land
Master
AS THE POWER OF THE LAND DWINDLES, SO WEAKENS THE MASTER, CORRESPOND-INGLY.

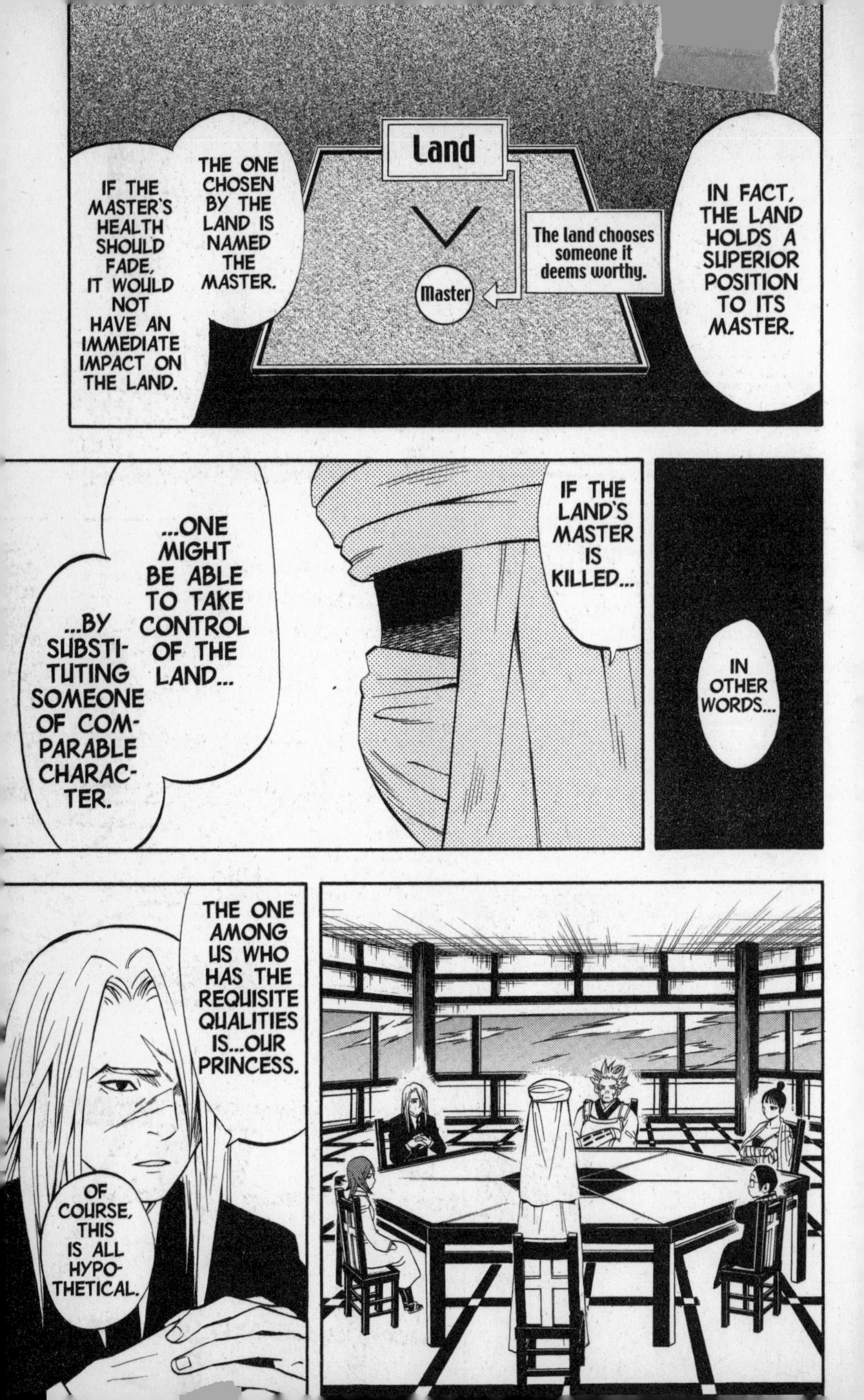
IN FACT, THE LAND HOLDS A SUPERIOR POSITION TO ITS MASTER.
Land
The land chooses someone it deems worthy.
Master
THE ONE CHOSEN BY THE LAND IS NAMED THE MASTER.
IF THE MASTER'S HEALTH SHOULD FADE, IT WOULD NOT HAVE AN IMMEDIATE IMPACT ON THE LAND.
IN OTHER WORDS...
IF THE LAND'S MASTER IS KILLED...
...ONE MIGHT BE ABLE TO TAKE CONTROL OF THE LAND...
...BY SUBSTITUTING SOMEONE OF COMPARABLE CHARACTER.
THE ONE AMONG US WHO HAS THE REQUISITE QUALITIES IS...OUR PRINCESS.
OF COURSE, THIS IS ALL HYPOTHETICAL.

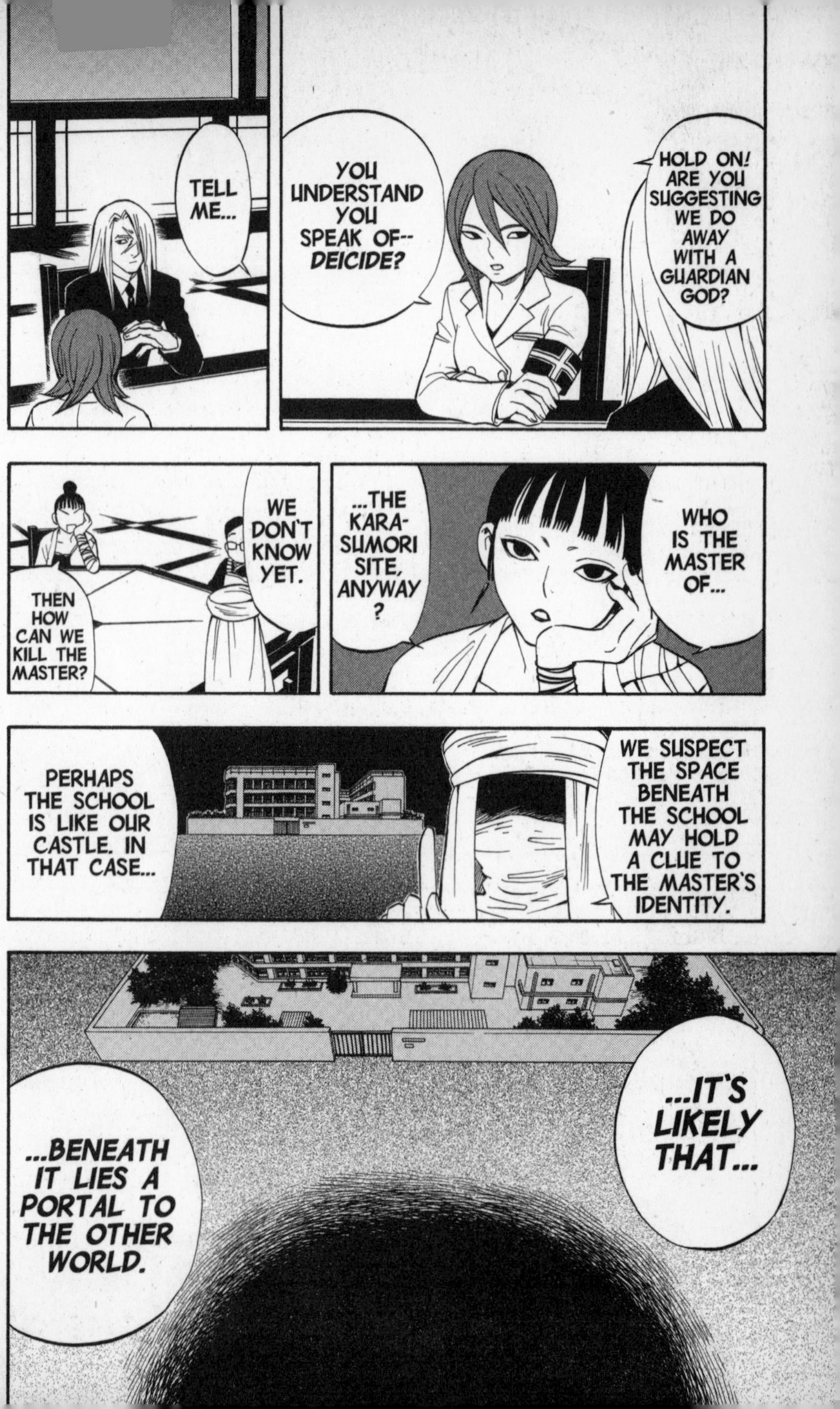
HOLD ON! ARE YOU SUGGESTING WE DO AWAY WITH A GUARDIAN GOD?
YOU UNDERSTAND YOU SPEAK OF-- DEICIDE?
TELL ME...
WHO IS THE MASTER OF...
...THE KARA-SUMORI SITE, ANYWAY?
WE DON'T KNOW YET.
THEN HOW CAN WE KILL THE MASTER?
WE SUSPECT THE SPACE BENEATH THE SCHOOL MAY HOLD A CLUE TO THE MASTER'S IDENTITY.
PERHAPS THE SCHOOL IS LIKE OUR CASTLE. IN THAT CASE...
...IT'S LIKELY THAT...
...BENEATH IT LIES A PORTAL TO THE OTHER WORLD.

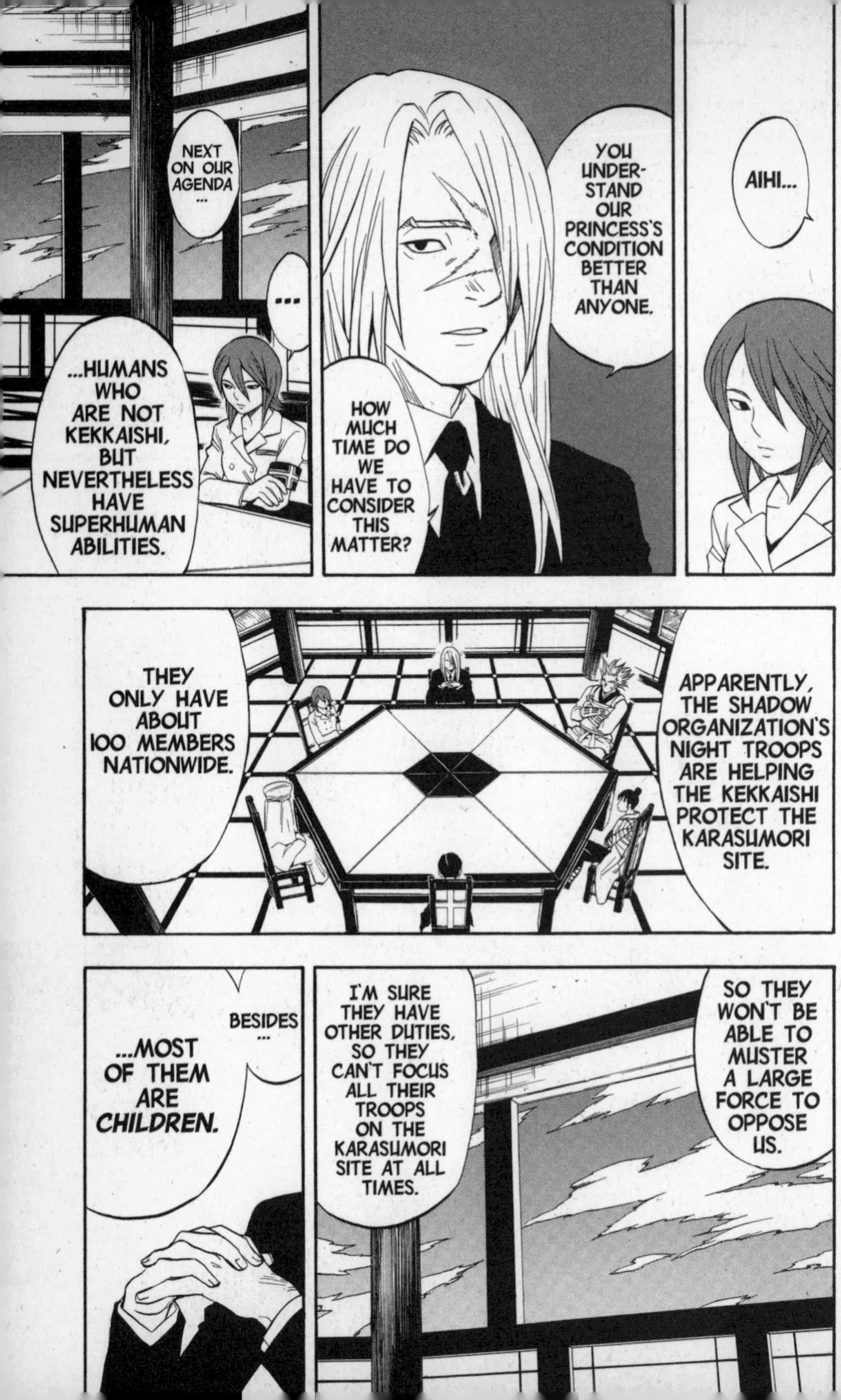
AIHI...
YOU UNDERSTAND OUR PRINCESS'S CONDITION BETTER THAN ANYONE.
HOW MUCH TIME DO WE HAVE TO CONSIDER THIS MATTER?
NEXT ON OUR AGENDA...
...
...HUMANS WHO ARE NOT KEKKAISHI, BUT NEVERTHELESS HAVE SUPERHUMAN ABILITIES.
APPARENTLY, THE SHADOW ORGANIZATION'S NIGHT TROOPS ARE HELPING THE KEKKAISHI PROTECT THE KARASUMORI SITE.
THEY ONLY HAVE ABOUT 100 MEMBERS NATIONWIDE.
SO THEY WON'T BE ABLE TO MUSTER A LARGE FORCE TO OPPOSE US.
I'M SURE THEY HAVE OTHER DUTIES, SO THEY CAN'T FOCUS ALL THEIR TROOPS ON THE KARASUMORI SITE AT ALL TIMES.
BESIDES...
...MOST OF THEM ARE *CHILDREN*.

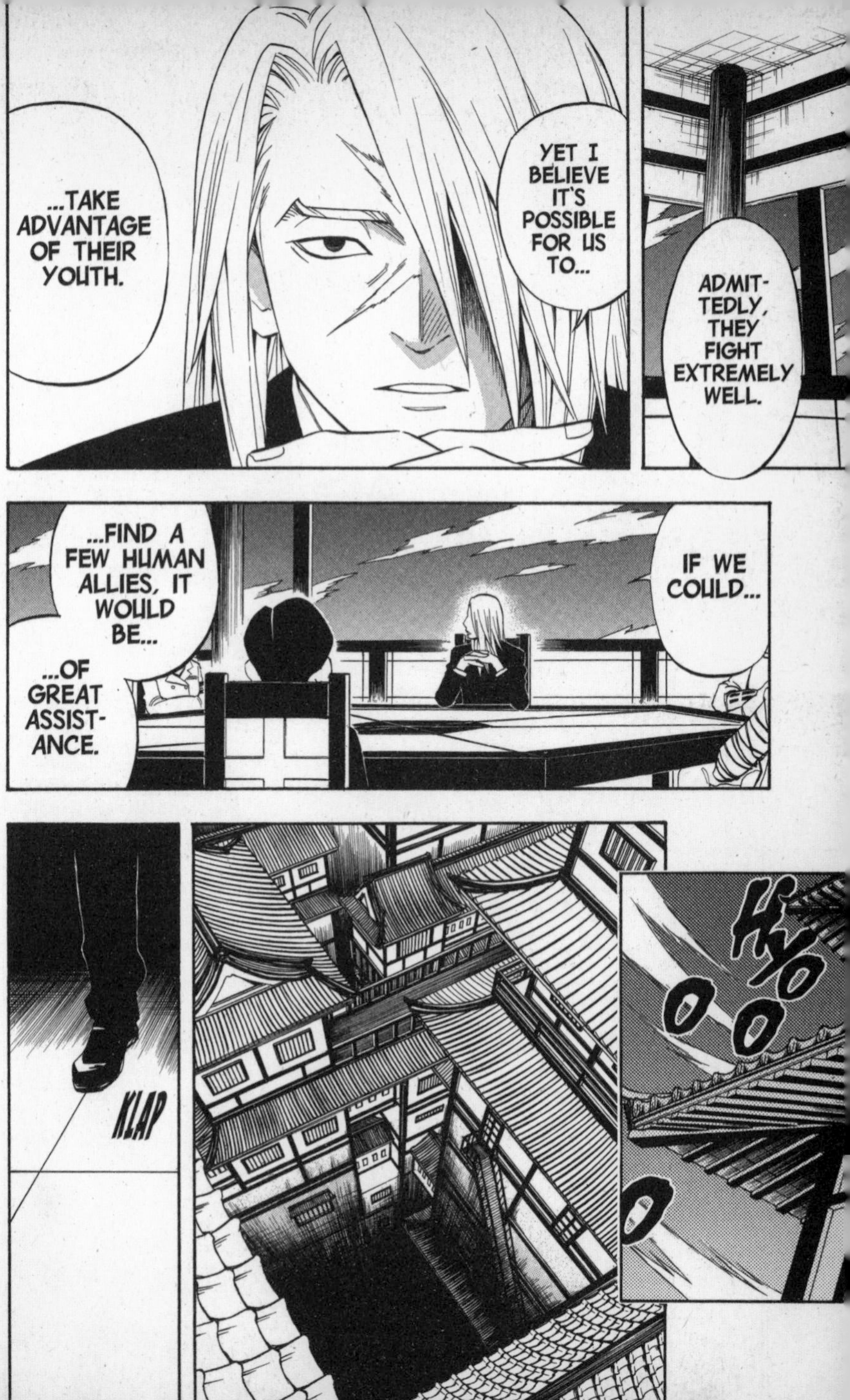
ADMIT-TEDLY, THEY FIGHT EXTREMELY WELL.
YET I BELIEVE IT'S POSSIBLE FOR US TO...
...TAKE ADVANTAGE OF THEIR YOUTH.
IF WE COULD...
...FIND A FEW HUMAN ALLIES, IT WOULD BE...
...OF GREAT ASSIST-ANCE.
KLAP

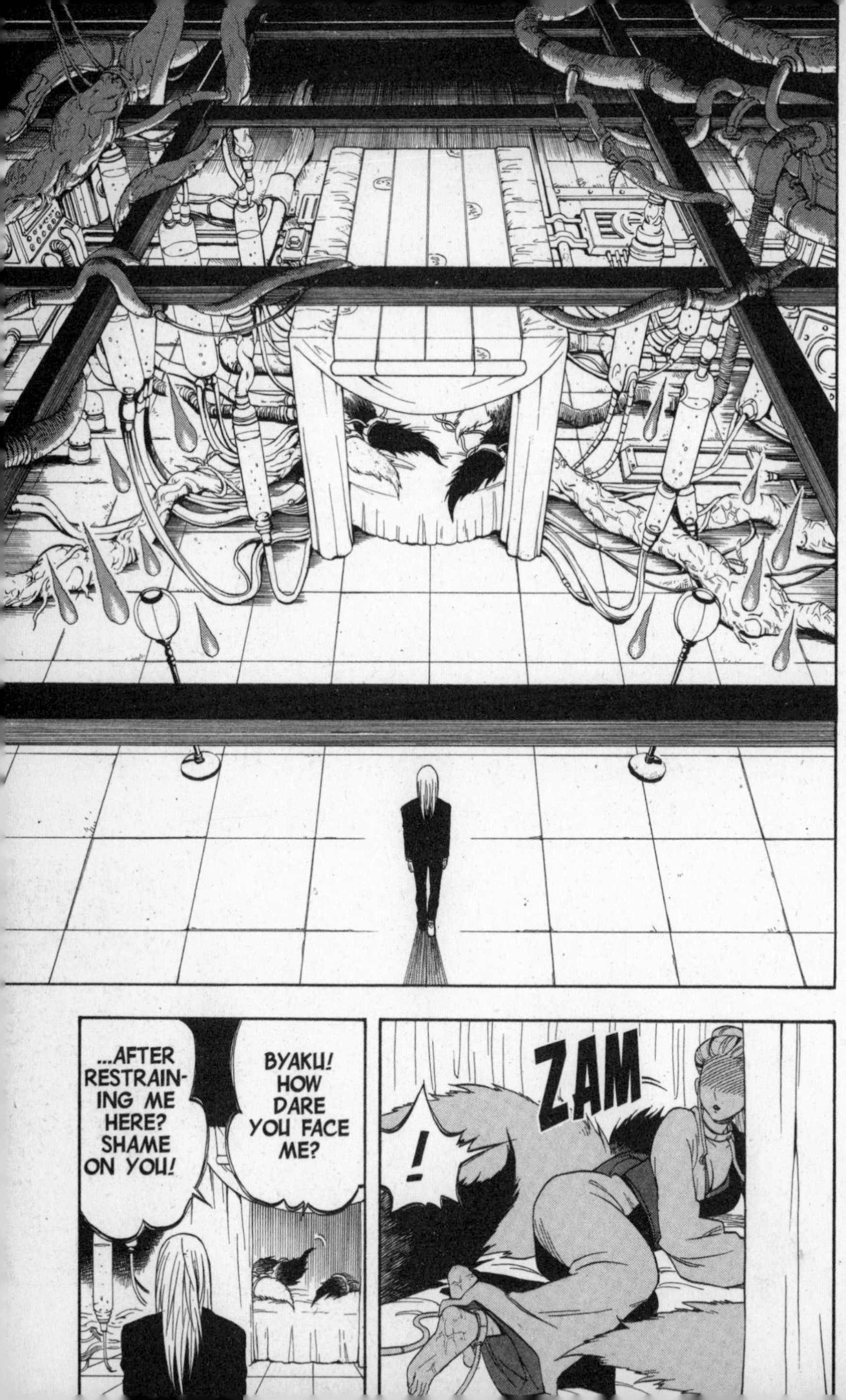
ZAM
!
BYAKU! HOW DARE YOU FACE ME?
...AFTER RESTRAIN-ING ME HERE? SHAME ON YOU!

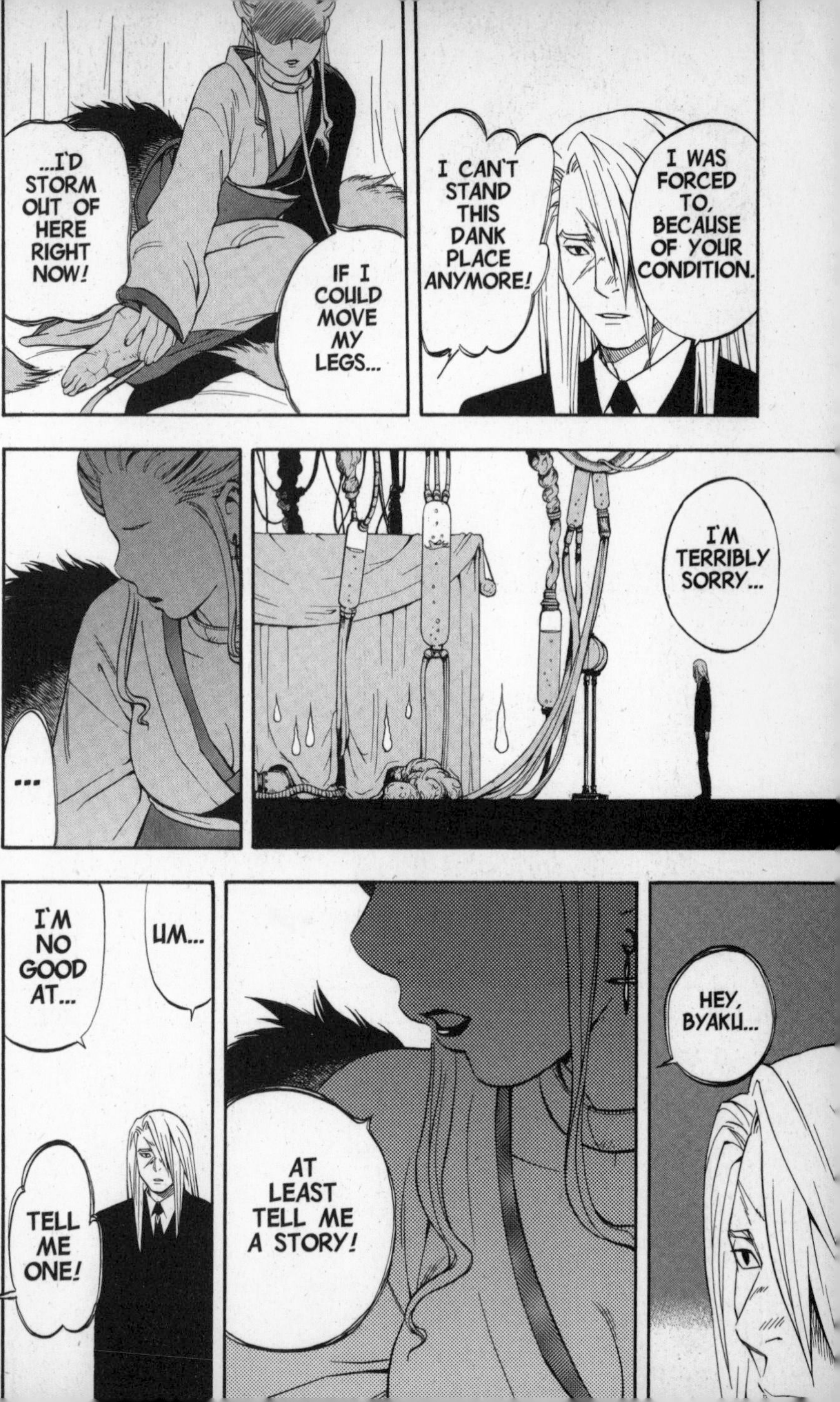
I WAS FORCED TO, BECAUSE OF YOUR CONDITION.
I CAN'T STAND THIS DANK PLACE ANYMORE!
IF I COULD MOVE MY LEGS...
...I'D STORM OUT OF HERE RIGHT NOW!
I'M TERRIBLY SORRY...
...
HEY, BYAKU...
AT LEAST TELL ME A STORY!
UM...
I'M NO GOOD AT...
TELL ME ONE!

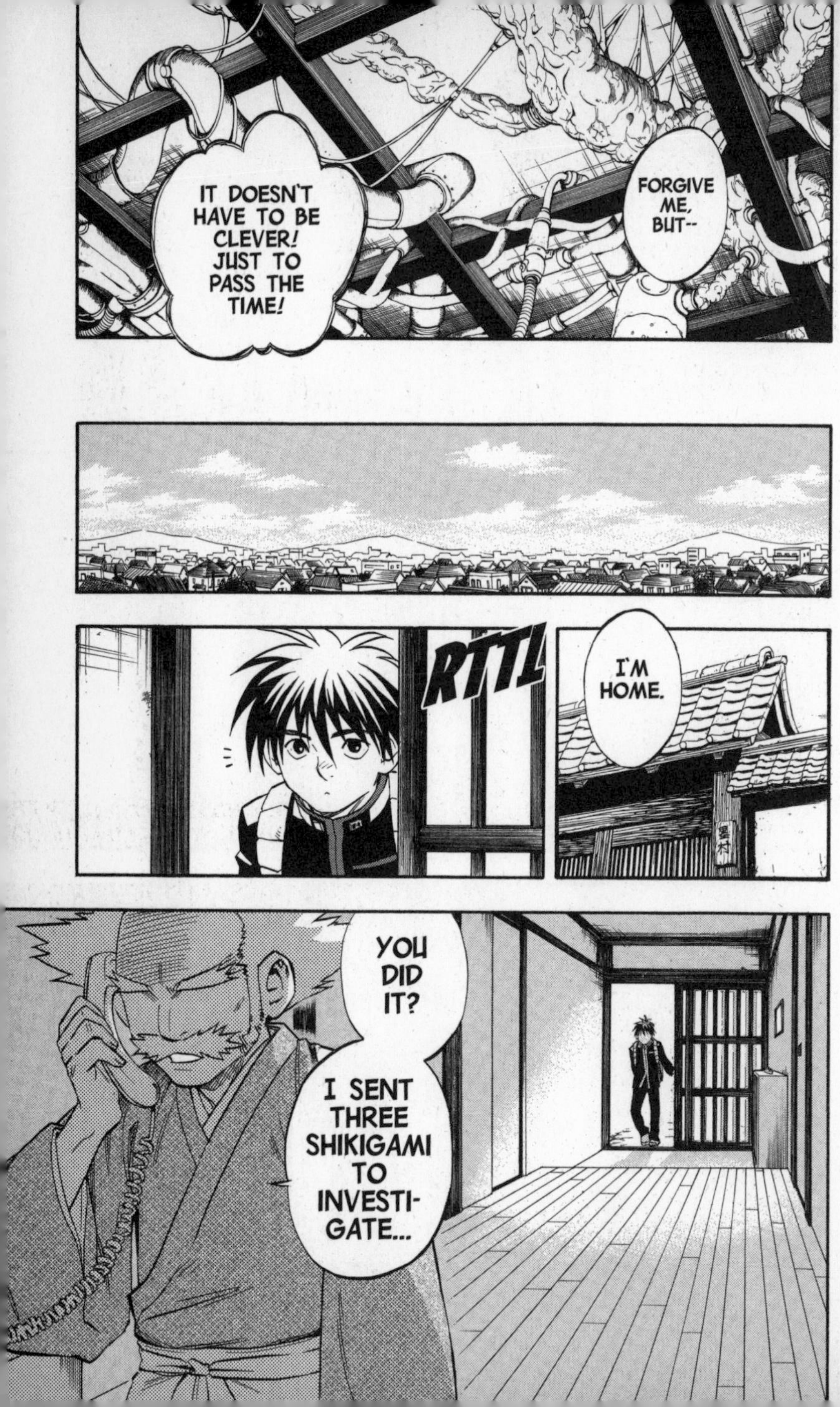
FORGIVE ME, BUT--
IT DOESN'T HAVE TO BE CLEVER! JUST TO PASS THE TIME!
I'M HOME.
墨村
RTTL
YOU DID IT?
I SENT THREE SHIKIGAMI TO INVESTI-GATE...

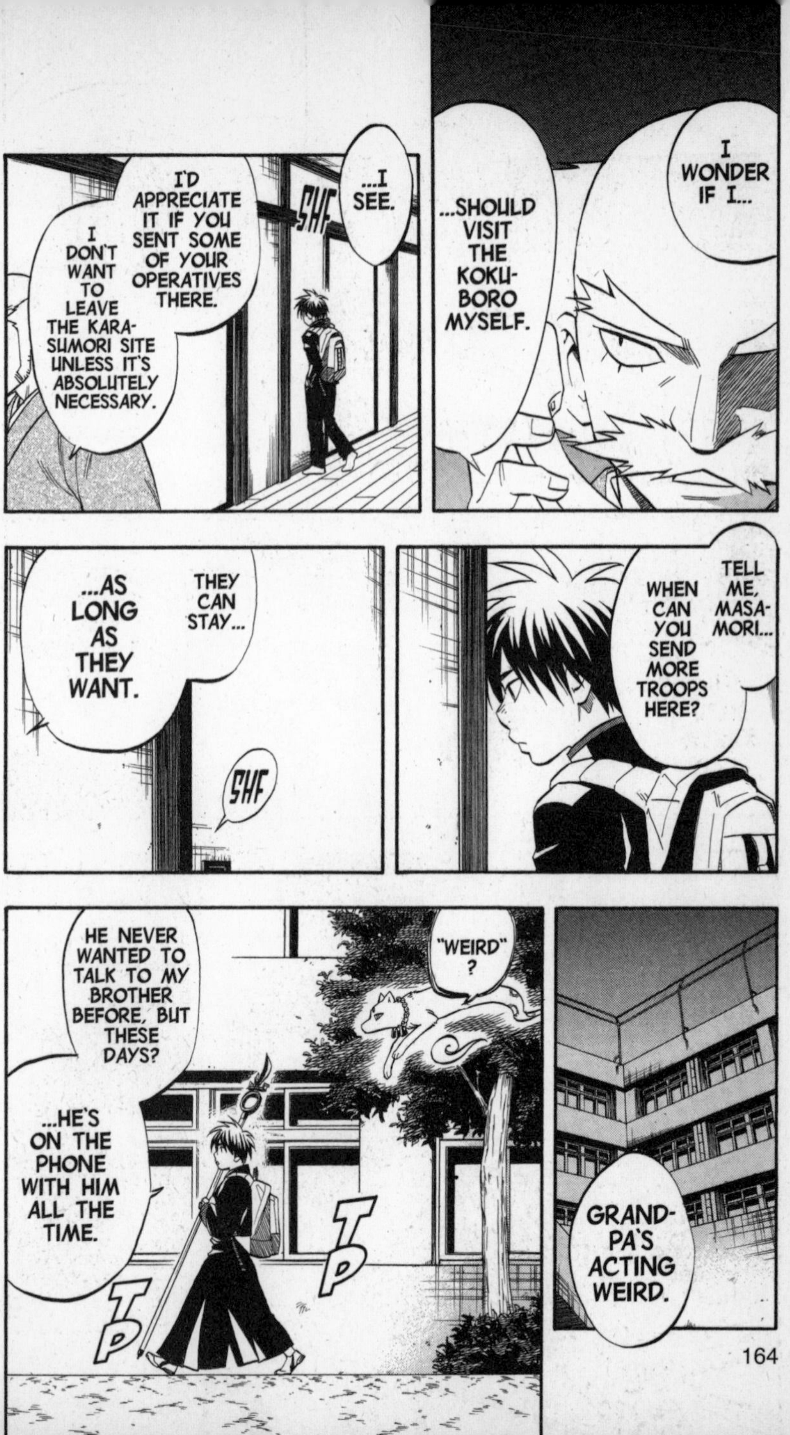
I WONDER IF I...
...SHOULD VISIT THE KOKUBORO MYSELF.
...I SEE.
SHF
I'D APPRECIATE IT IF YOU SENT SOME OF YOUR OPERATIVES THERE.
I DON'T WANT TO LEAVE THE KARASUMORI SITE UNLESS IT'S ABSOLUTELY NECESSARY.
TELL ME, MASAMORI...
WHEN CAN YOU SEND MORE TROOPS HERE?
THEY CAN STAY...
...AS LONG AS THEY WANT.
SHF
GRANDPA'S ACTING WEIRD.
"WEIRD"?
HE NEVER WANTED TO TALK TO MY BROTHER BEFORE, BUT THESE DAYS?
...HE'S ON THE PHONE WITH HIM ALL THE TIME.
TP
TP

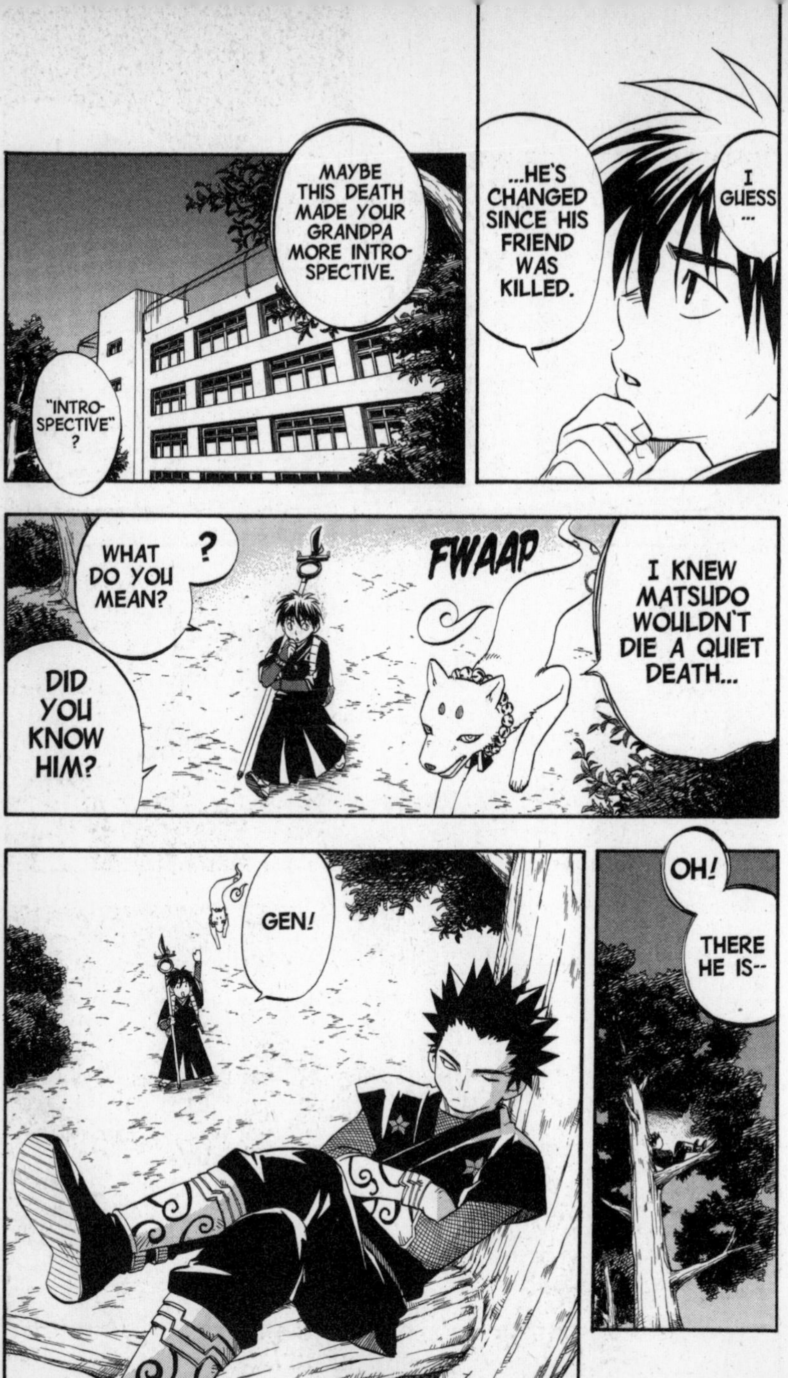
I GUESS...
...HE'S CHANGED SINCE HIS FRIEND WAS KILLED.
MAYBE THIS DEATH MADE YOUR GRANDPA MORE INTRO-SPECTIVE.
"INTRO-SPECTIVE"?
I KNEW MATSUDO WOULDN'T DIE A QUIET DEATH...
FWAAP
?
WHAT DO YOU MEAN?
DID YOU KNOW HIM?
OH!
THERE HE IS--
GEN!

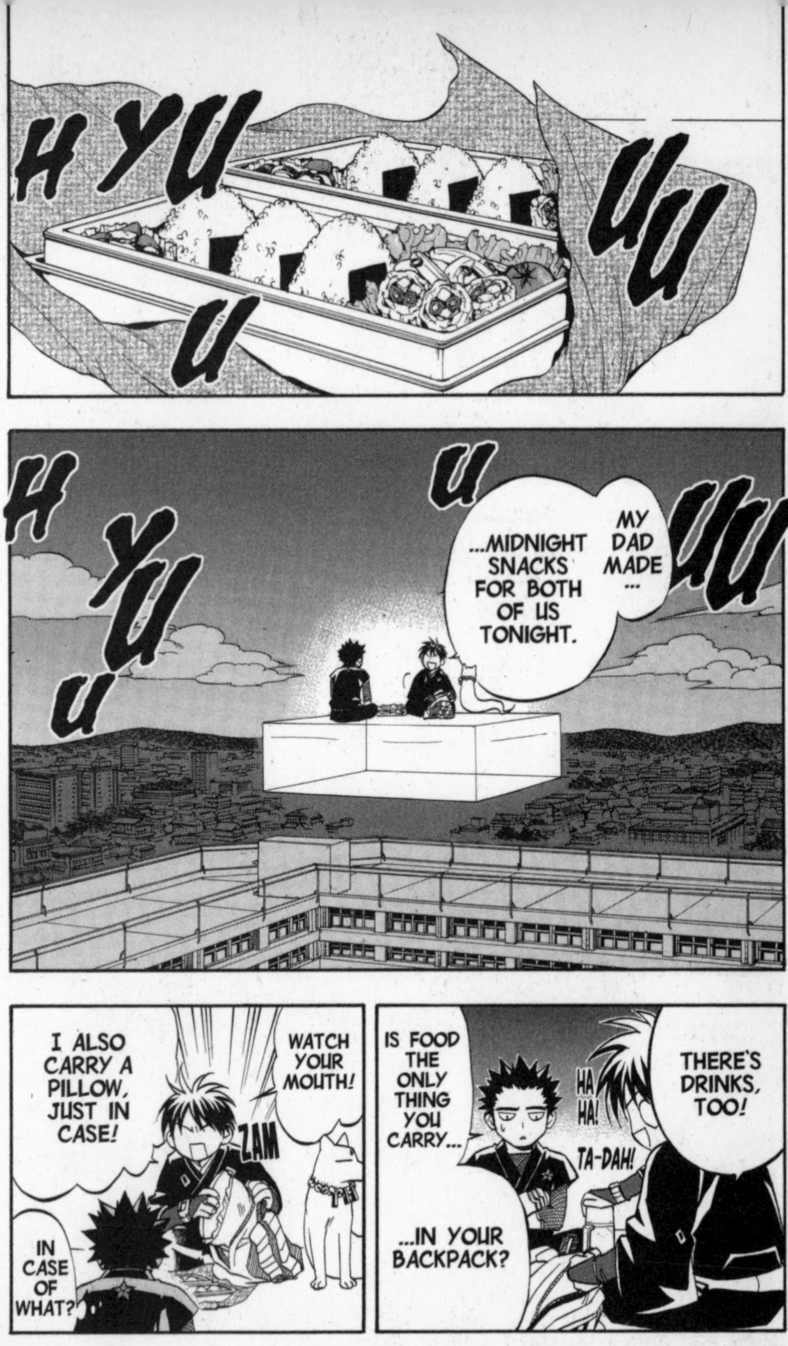
HYU
U
UU
MY DAD MADE...
...MIDNIGHT SNACKS FOR BOTH OF US TONIGHT.
UU
U
H
YUU
U
THERE'S DRINKS, TOO!
HA HA!
TA-DAH!
IS FOOD THE ONLY THING YOU CARRY...
...IN YOUR BACKPACK?
WATCH YOUR MOUTH!
ZAM
I ALSO CARRY A PILLOW, JUST IN CASE!
IN CASE OF WHAT?

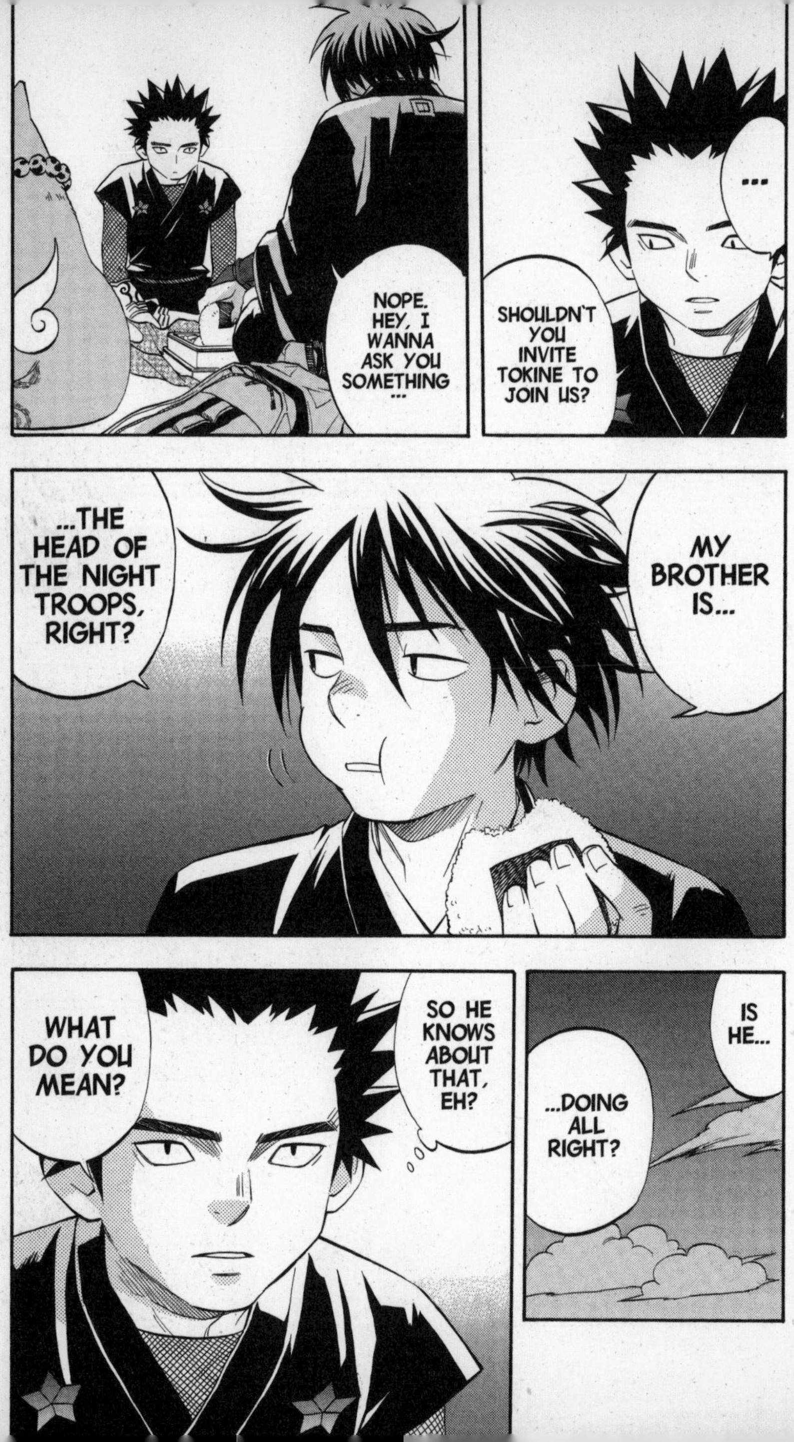
...
SHOULDN'T YOU INVITE TOKINE TO JOIN US?
NOPE. HEY, I WANNA ASK YOU SOMETHING ...
MY BROTHER IS...
...THE HEAD OF THE NIGHT TROOPS, RIGHT?
IS HE...
...DOING ALL RIGHT?
SO HE KNOWS ABOUT THAT, EH?
WHAT DO YOU MEAN?

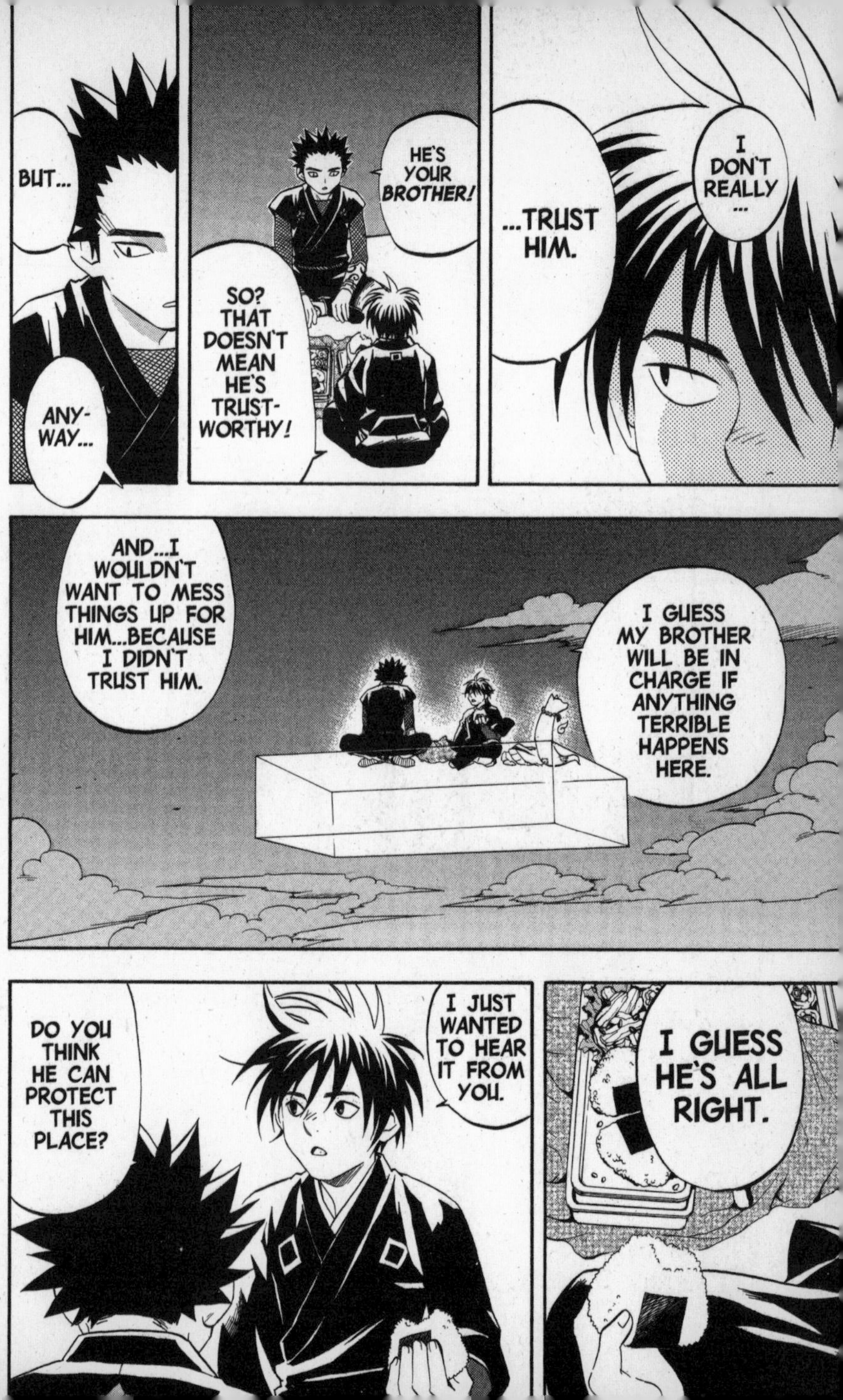

I DON'T REALLY ...
...TRUST HIM.
HE'S YOUR BROTHER!
SO? THAT DOESN'T MEAN HE'S TRUST-WORTHY!
BUT...
ANY-WAY...
I GUESS MY BROTHER WILL BE IN CHARGE IF ANYTHING TERRIBLE HAPPENS HERE.
AND...I WOULDN'T WANT TO MESS THINGS UP FOR HIM...BECAUSE I DIDN'T TRUST HIM.
I GUESS HE'S ALL RIGHT.
I JUST WANTED TO HEAR IT FROM YOU.
DO YOU THINK HE CAN PROTECT THIS PLACE?

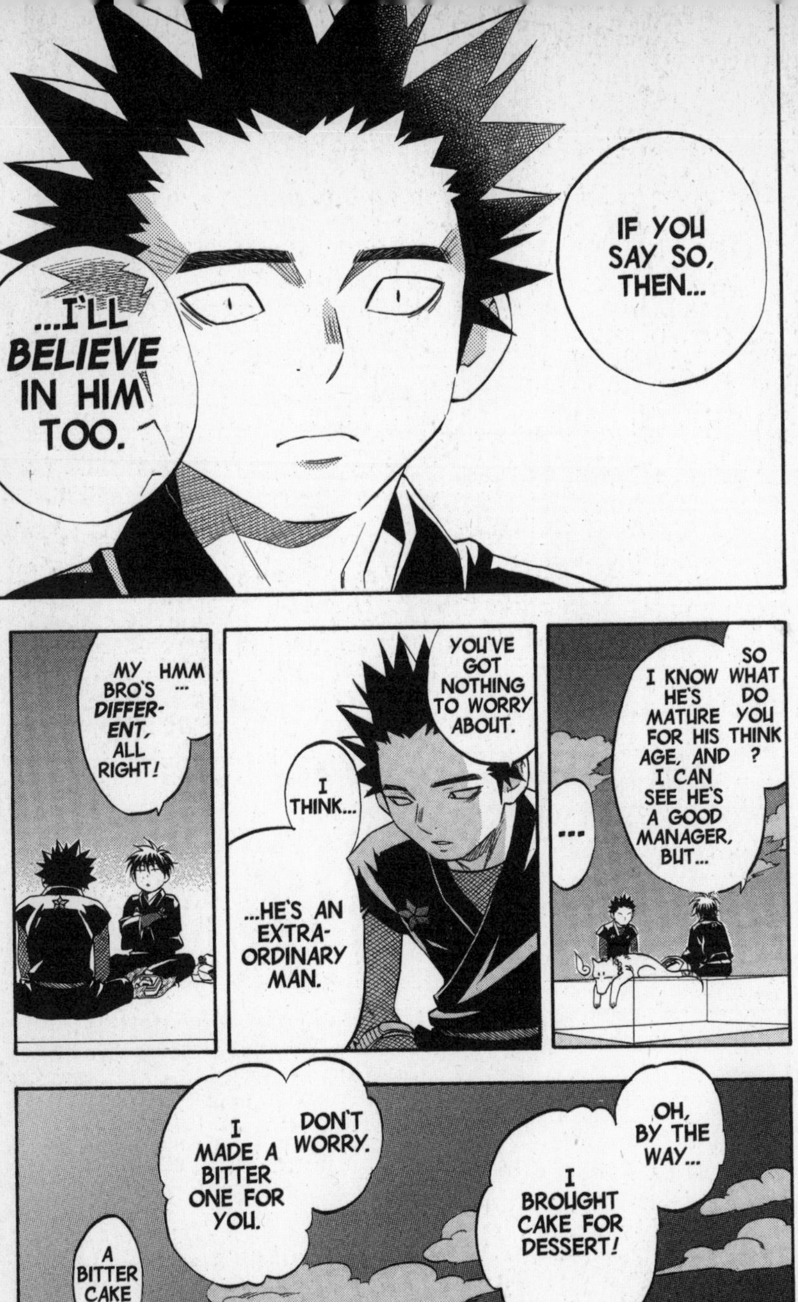
IF YOU SAY SO, THEN...
...I'LL **BELIEVE** IN HIM TOO.
SO WHAT DO YOU THINK ?
I KNOW HE'S MATURE FOR HIS AGE, AND I CAN SEE HE'S A GOOD MANAGER, BUT...
...
YOU'VE GOT NOTHING TO WORRY ABOUT.
I THINK...
...HE'S AN EXTRA-ORDINARY MAN.
HMM ...
MY BRO'S *DIFFERENT,* ALL RIGHT!
OH, BY THE WAY...
I BROUGHT CAKE FOR DESSERT!
DON'T WORRY.
I MADE A BITTER ONE FOR YOU.
A BITTER CAKE !?

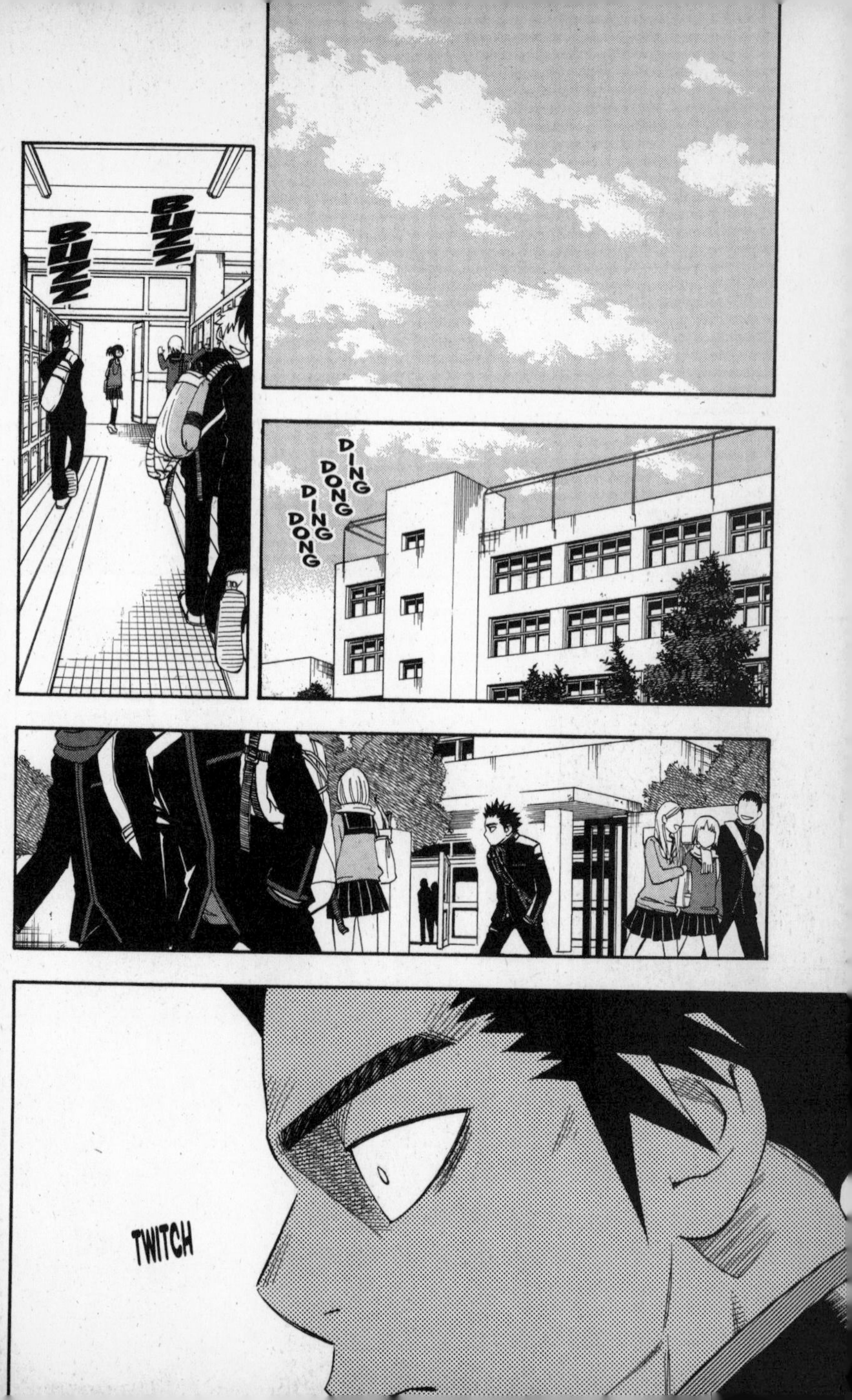
DING DONG DING DONG
BUZZ BUZZ
TWITCH

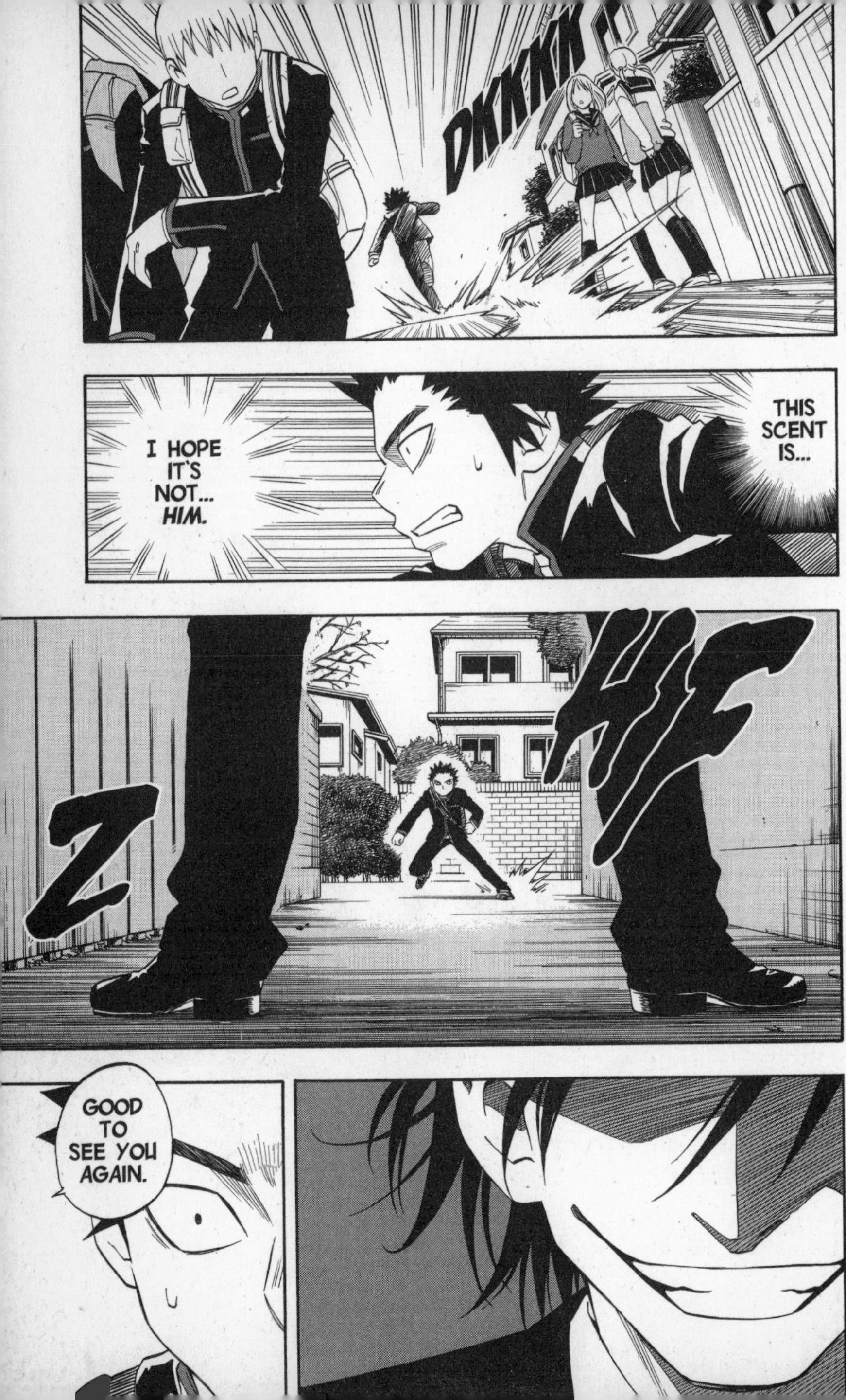
DKKKK
THIS SCENT IS...
I HOPE IT'S NOT... *HIM.*
GOOD TO SEE YOU AGAIN.

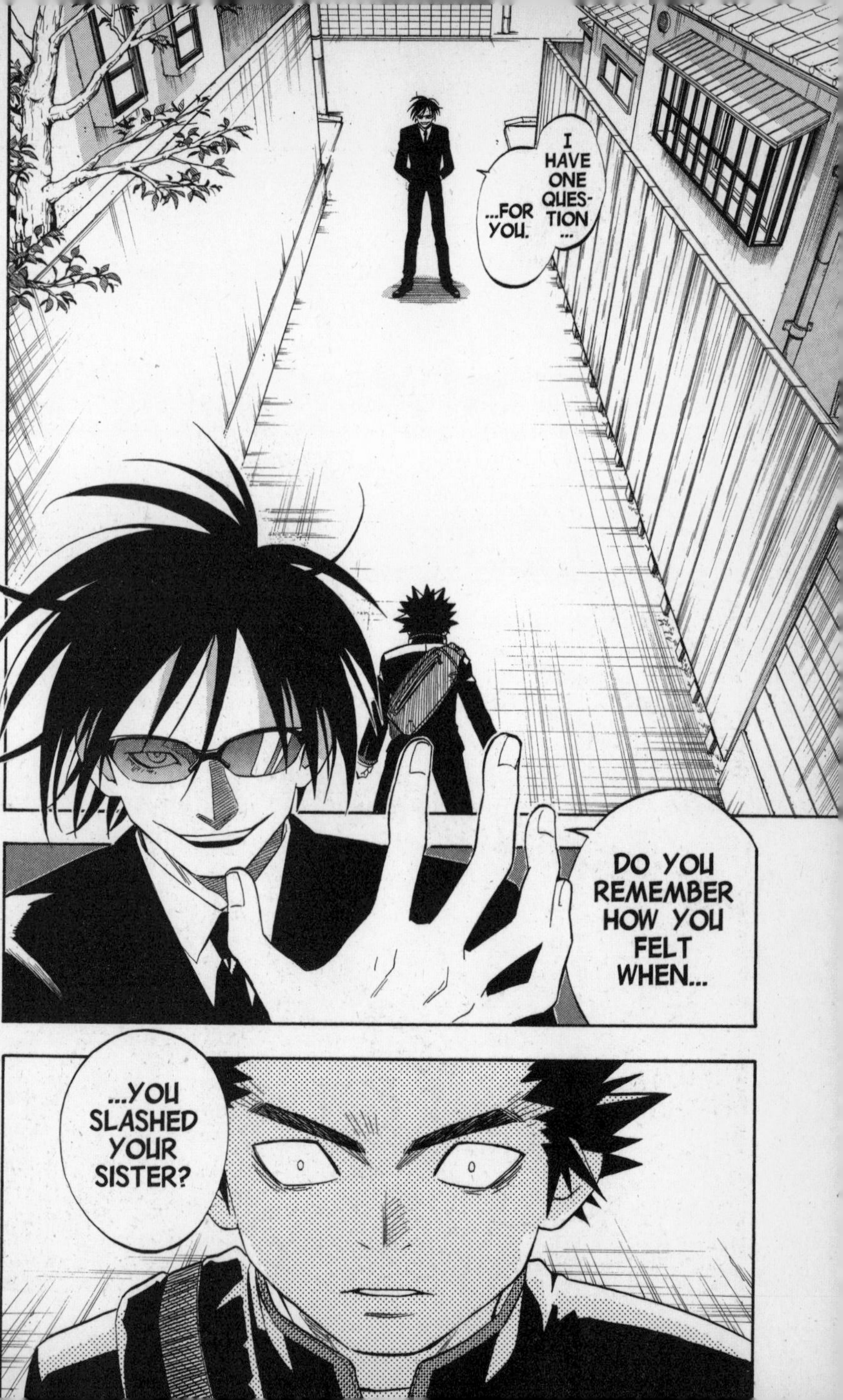
I HAVE ONE QUESTION...
...FOR YOU.
DO YOU REMEMBER HOW YOU FELT WHEN...
...YOU SLASHED YOUR SISTER?

Chapter 85: AGONY

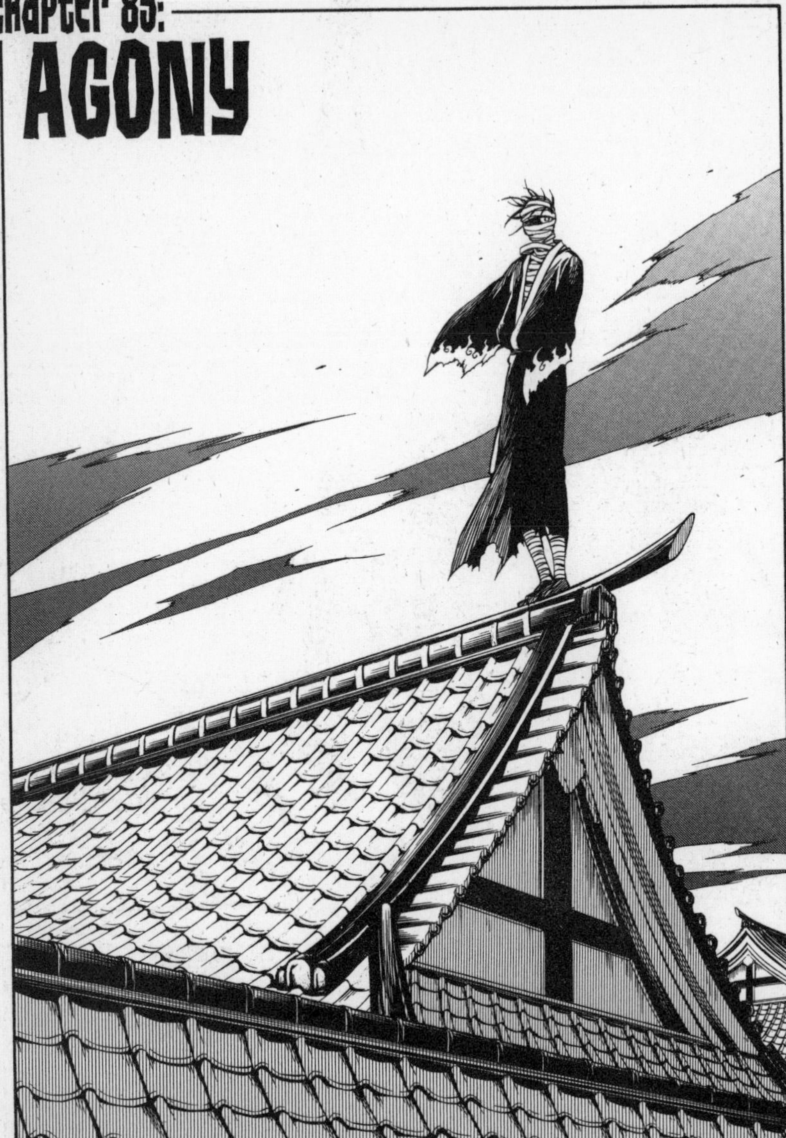

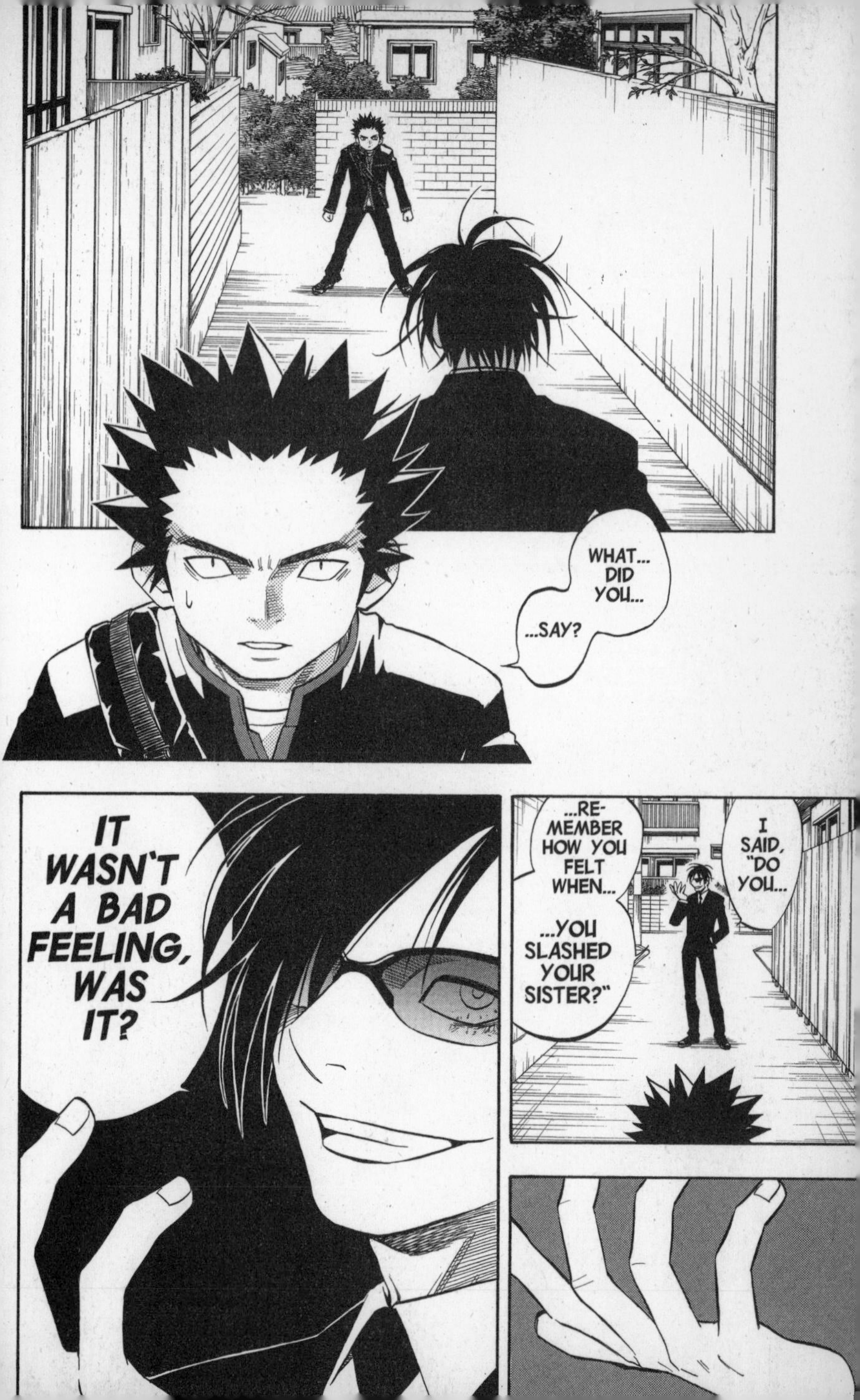
WHAT... DID YOU...
...SAY?
I SAID, "DO YOU...
...RE-MEMBER HOW YOU FELT WHEN...
...YOU SLASHED YOUR SISTER?"
IT WASN'T A BAD FEELING, WAS IT?

KRRRK

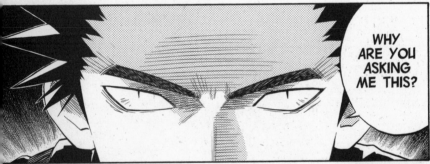

WHY ARE YOU ASKING ME THIS?

...YOU COULD UNLEASH YOUR POWER-- COM-PLETELY ?

DON'T YOU WISH...

I SUSPECT...

SNIKK

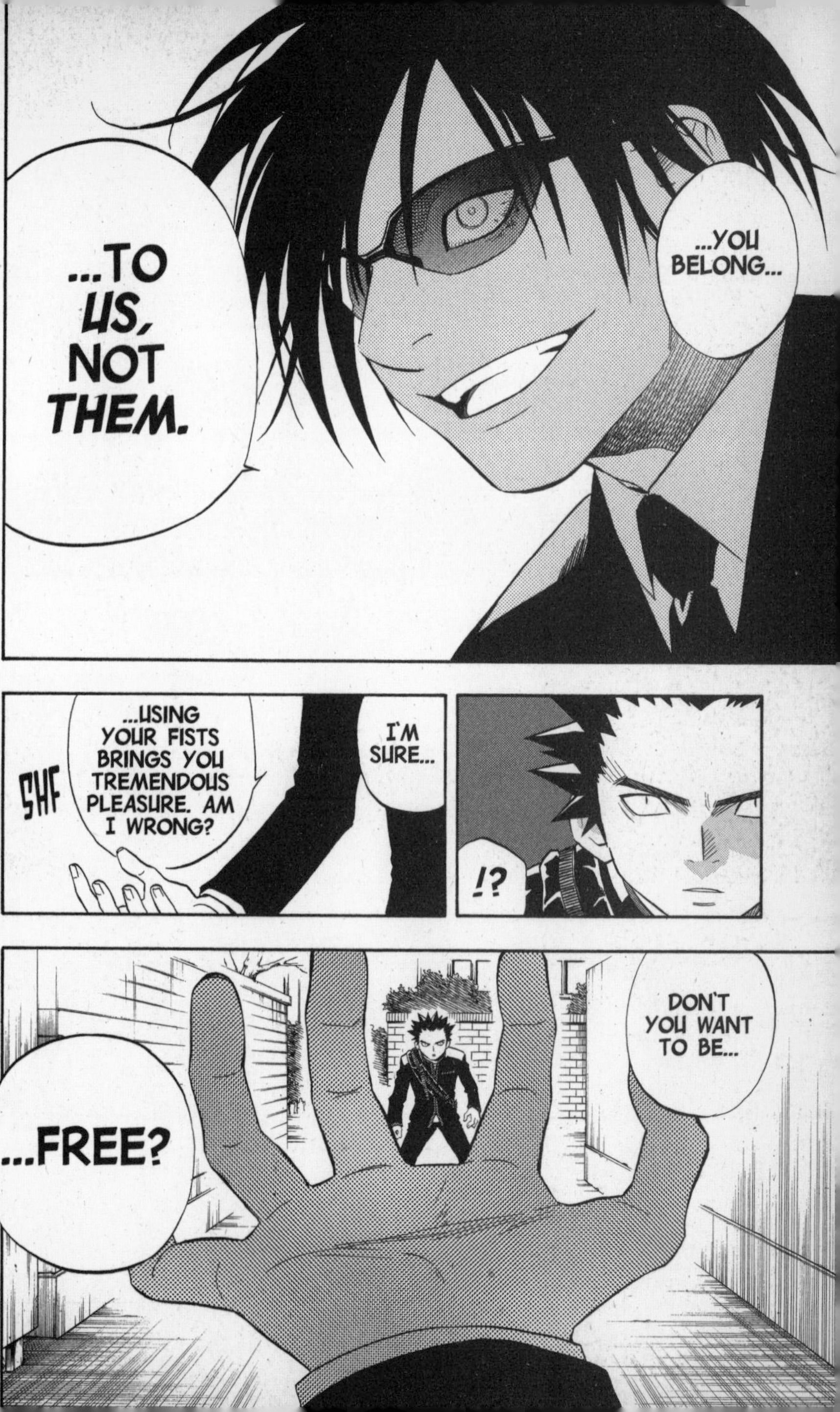
...YOU BELONG...
...TO US, NOT THEM.
!?
I'M SURE...
...USING YOUR FISTS BRINGS YOU TREMENDOUS PLEASURE. AM I WRONG?
SHF
DON'T YOU WANT TO BE...
...FREE?

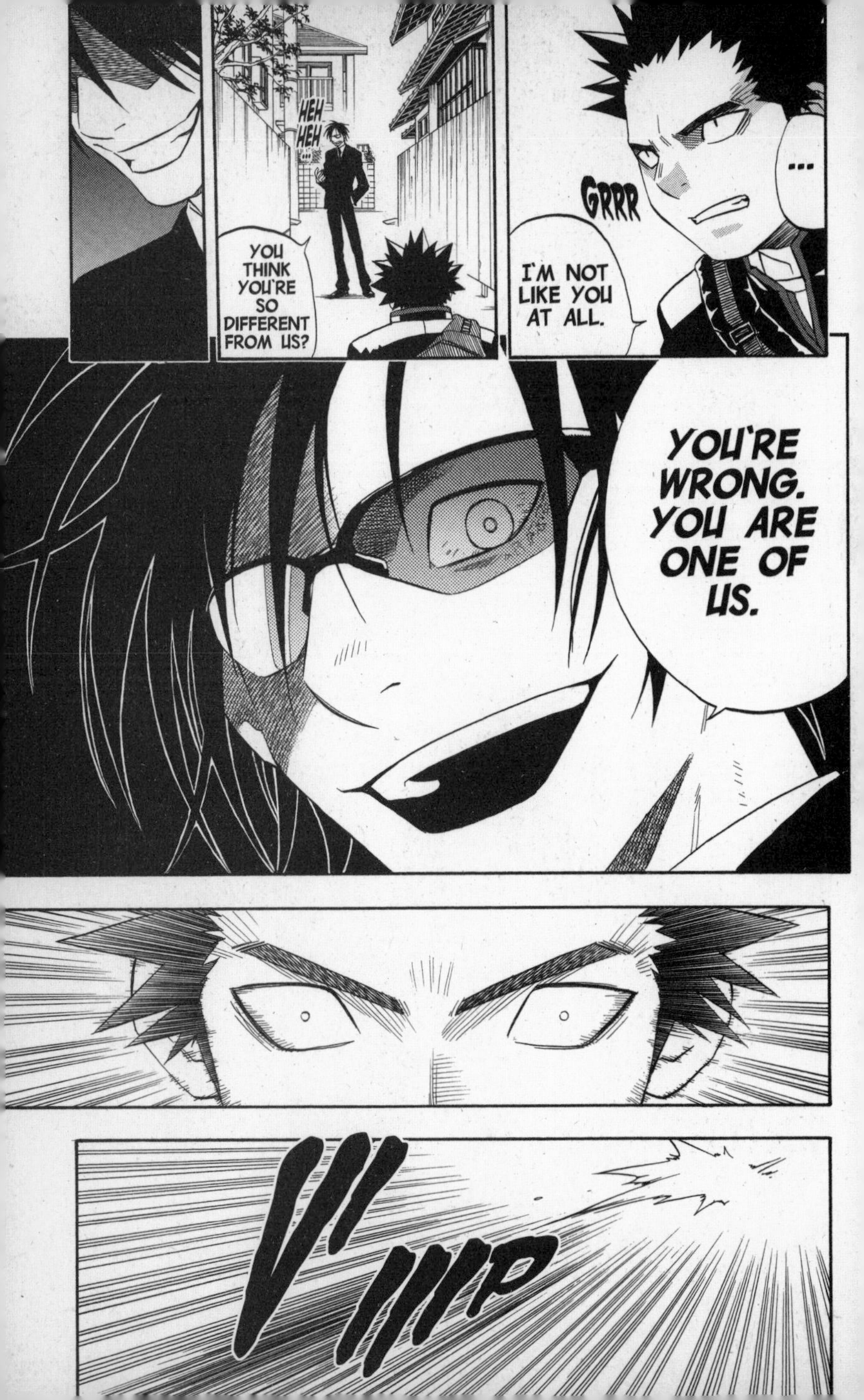
...
GRRR
I'M NOT LIKE YOU AT ALL.
HEH HEH ...
YOU THINK YOU'RE SO DIFFERENT FROM US?
YOU'RE WRONG. YOU ARE ONE OF US.
VIIIP

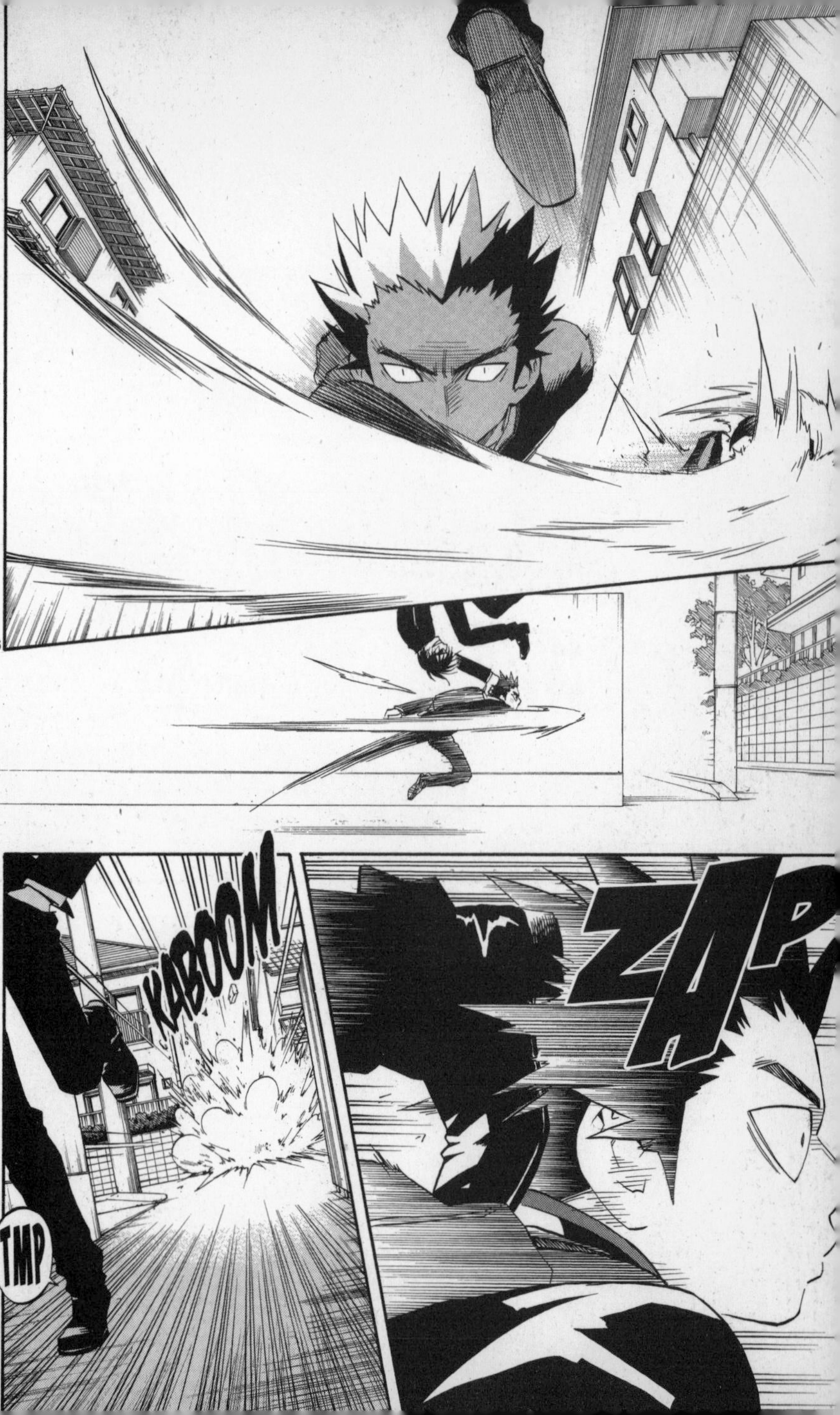
ZAP
KABOOM
TMP

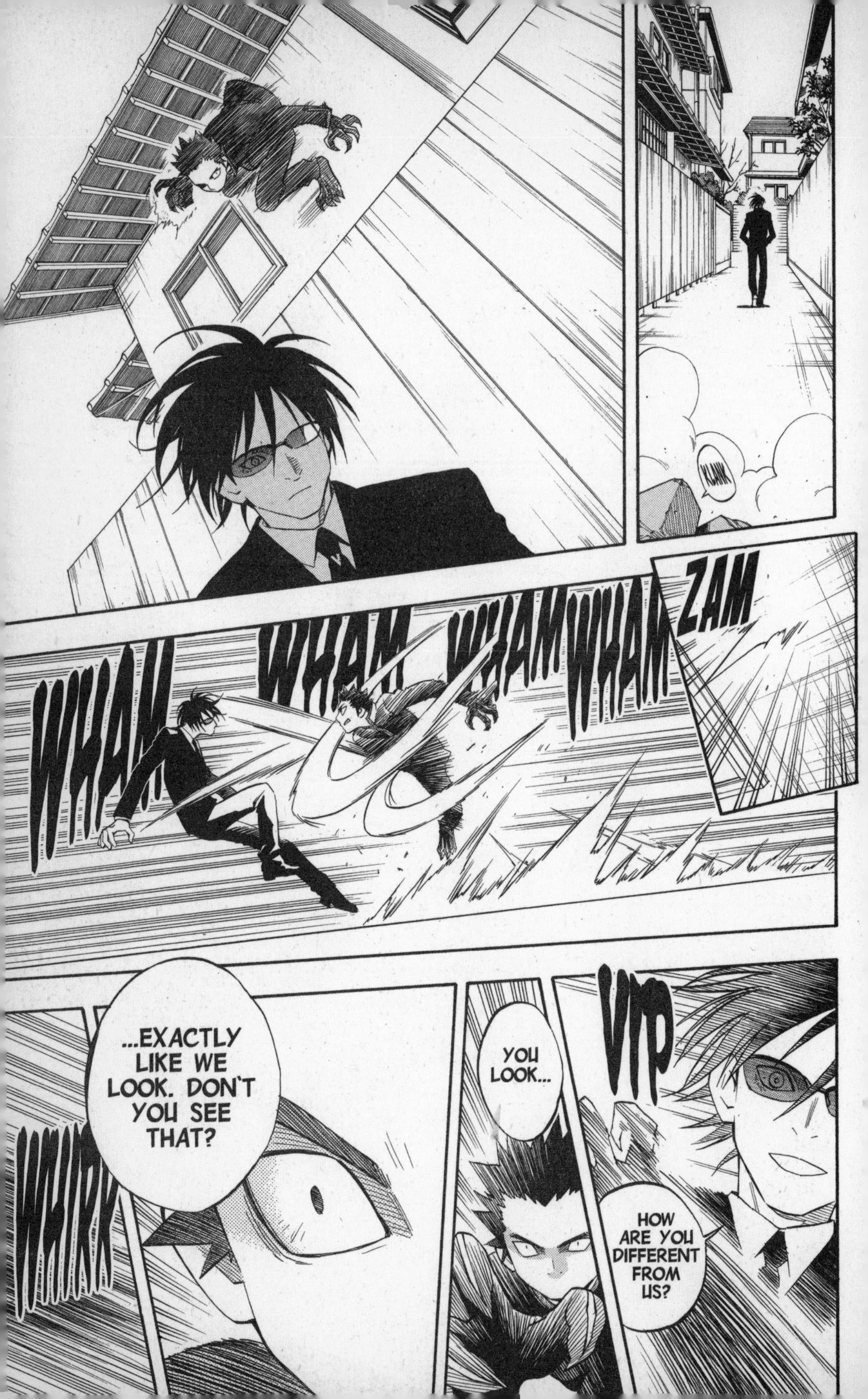
KLANK
ZAM
WHAMWHAM
WHAM
WHAM
VIP
HOW ARE YOU DIFFERENT FROM US?
YOU LOOK...
...EXACTLY LIKE WE LOOK. DON'T YOU SEE THAT?
WHIRK

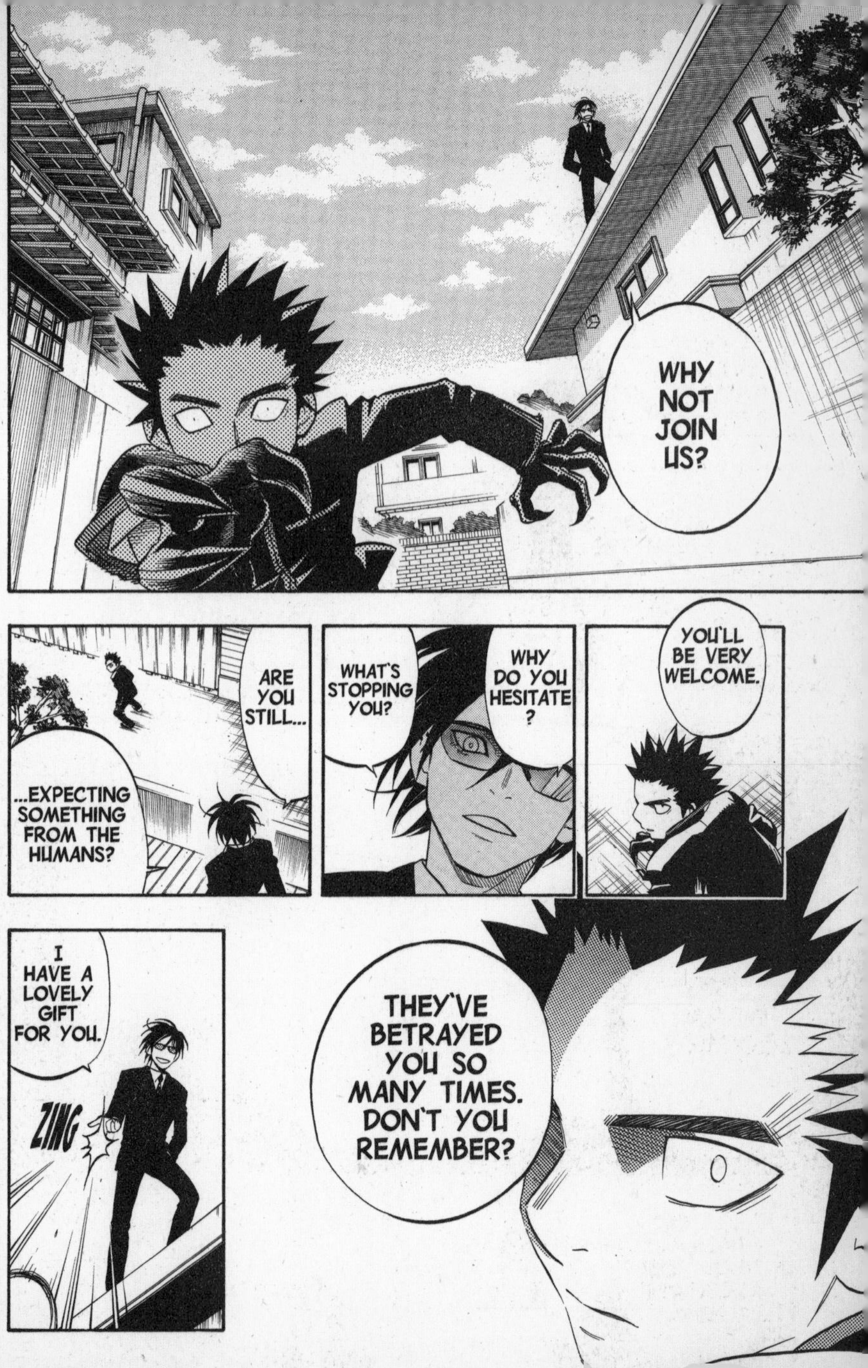
WHY NOT JOIN US?
YOU'LL BE VERY WELCOME.
WHY DO YOU HESITATE?
WHAT'S STOPPING YOU?
ARE YOU STILL...
...EXPECTING SOMETHING FROM THE HUMANS?
THEY'VE BETRAYED YOU SO MANY TIMES. DON'T YOU REMEMBER?
I HAVE A LOVELY GIFT FOR YOU.
ZING

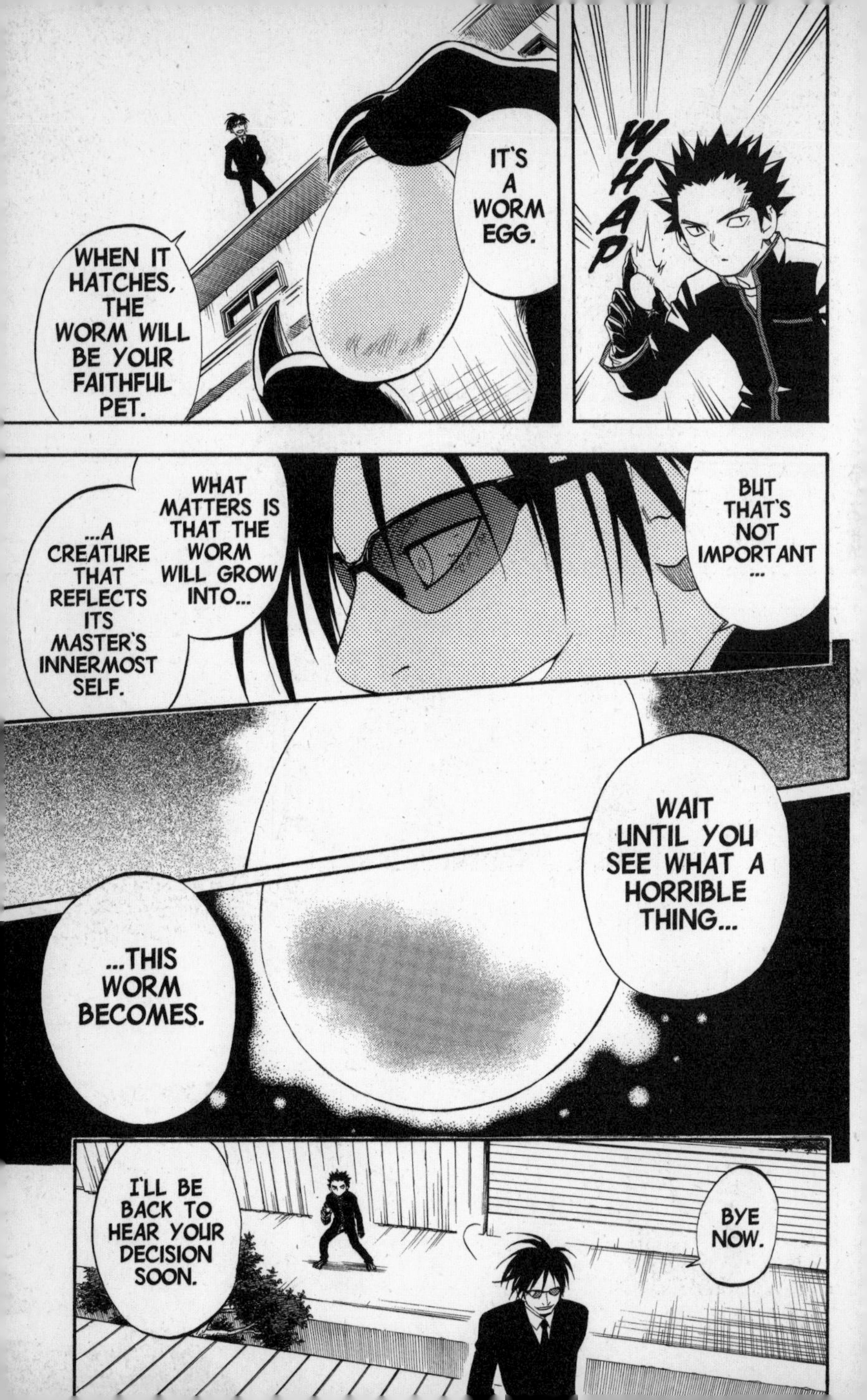
WHAP
IT'S A WORM EGG.
WHEN IT HATCHES, THE WORM WILL BE YOUR FAITHFUL PET.
BUT THAT'S NOT IMPORTANT...
WHAT MATTERS IS THAT THE WORM WILL GROW INTO...
...A CREATURE THAT REFLECTS ITS MASTER'S INNERMOST SELF.
WAIT UNTIL YOU SEE WHAT A HORRIBLE THING...
...THIS WORM BECOMES.
BYE NOW.
I'LL BE BACK TO HEAR YOUR DECISION SOON.

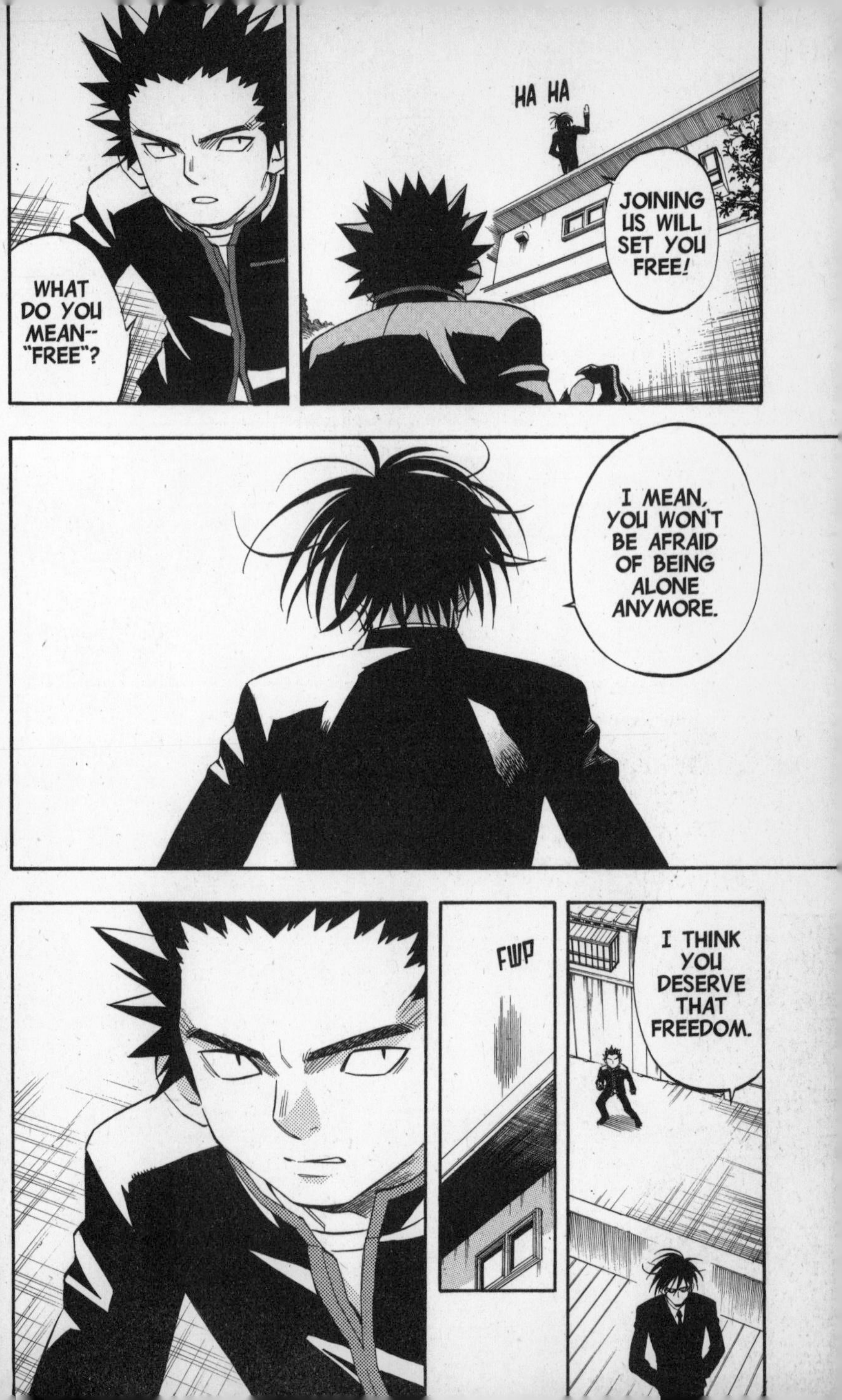
HA HA
JOINING US WILL SET YOU FREE!
WHAT DO YOU MEAN-- "FREE"?
I MEAN, YOU WON'T BE AFRAID OF BEING ALONE ANYMORE.
I THINK YOU DESERVE THAT FREEDOM.
FWP

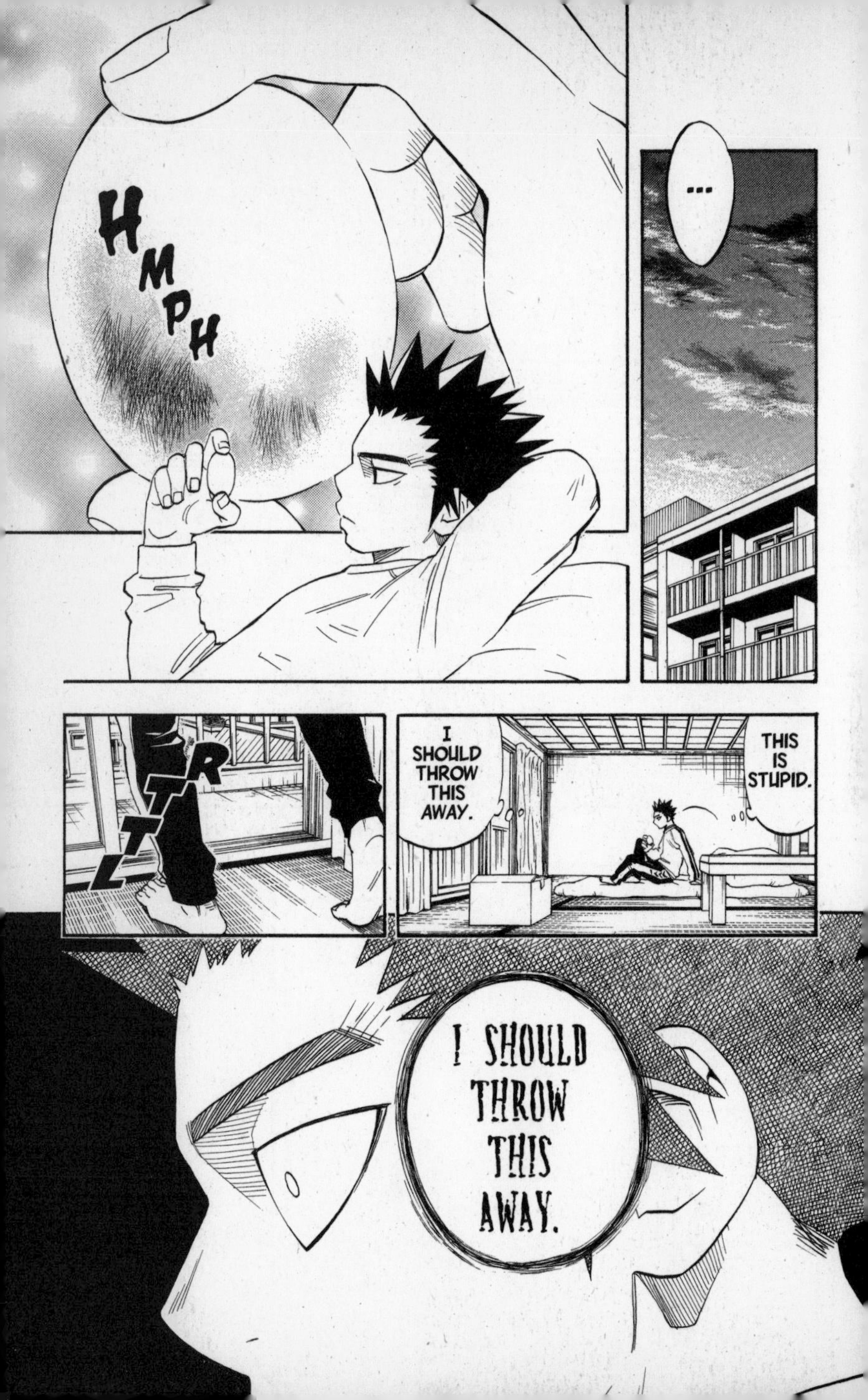
...
HMPH
THIS IS STUPID.
I SHOULD THROW THIS AWAY.
RTTL
I SHOULD THROW THIS AWAY.

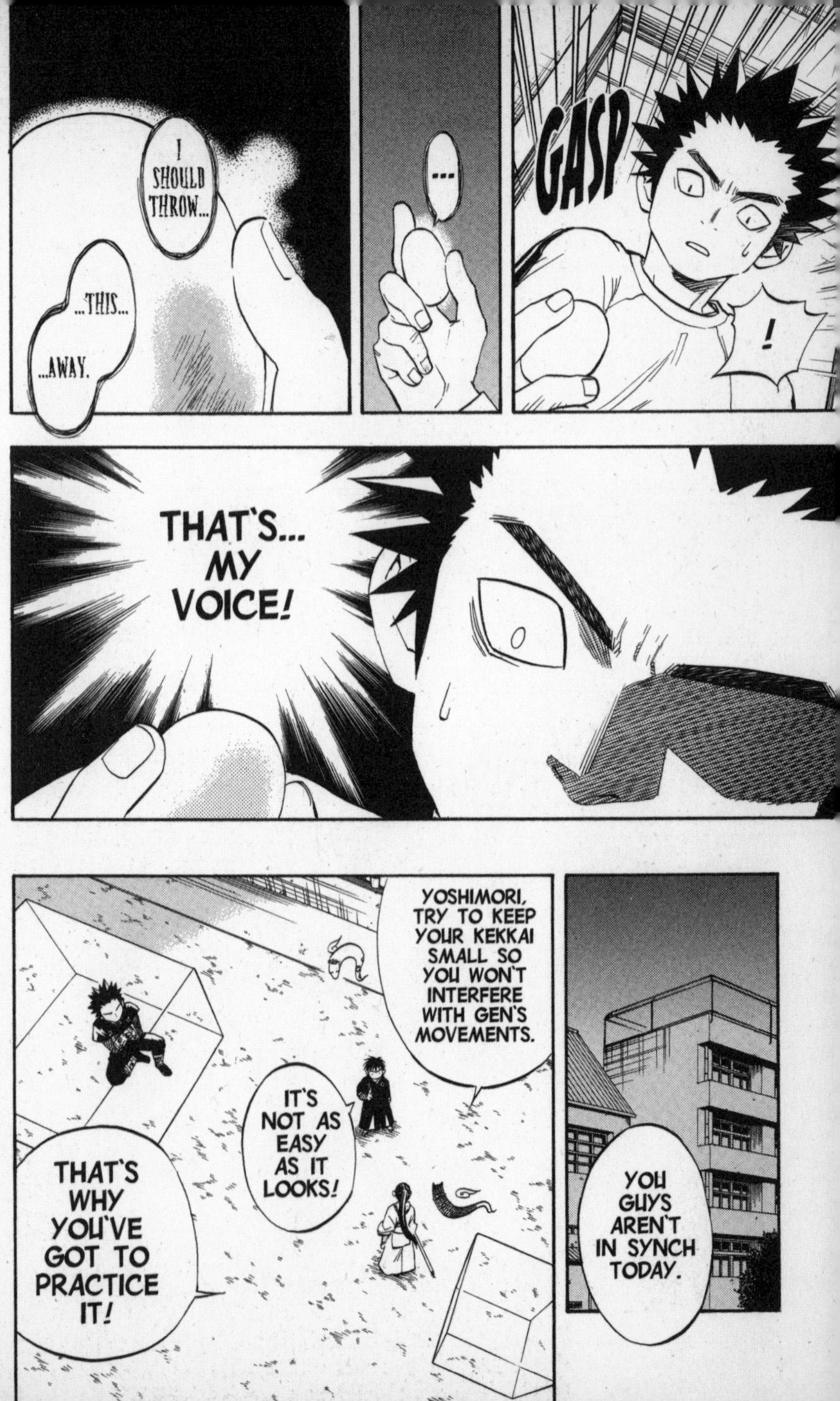
GASP
!
...
I SHOULD THROW...
...THIS...
...AWAY.
THAT'S... MY VOICE!
YOU GUYS AREN'T IN SYNCH TODAY.
YOSHIMORI, TRY TO KEEP YOUR KEKKAI SMALL SO YOU WON'T INTERFERE WITH GEN'S MOVEMENTS.
IT'S NOT AS EASY AS IT LOOKS!
THAT'S WHY YOU'VE GOT TO PRACTICE IT!

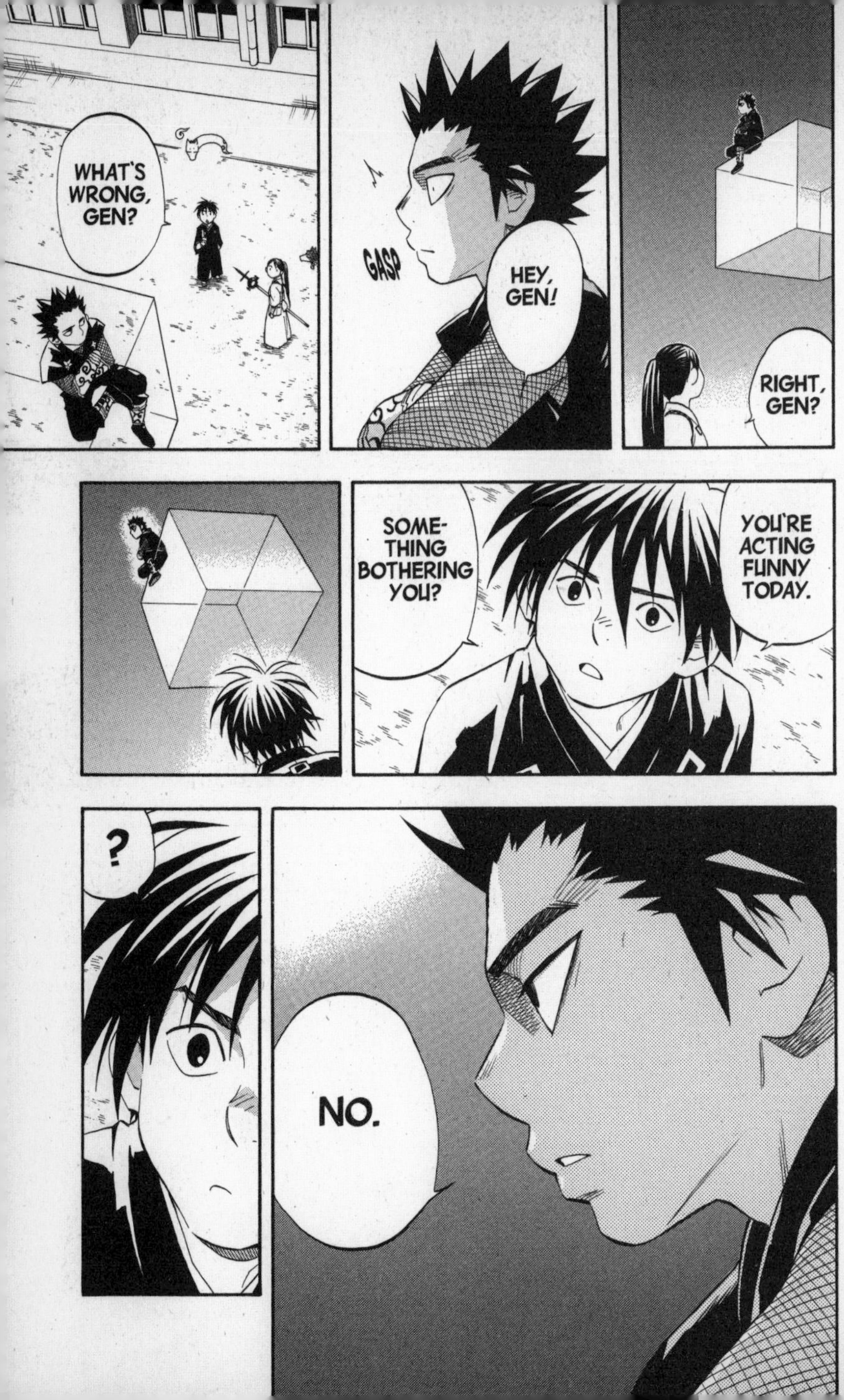
RIGHT, GEN?
HEY, GEN!
GASP
WHAT'S WRONG, GEN?
YOU'RE ACTING FUNNY TODAY.
SOME-THING BOTHERING YOU?
NO.
?

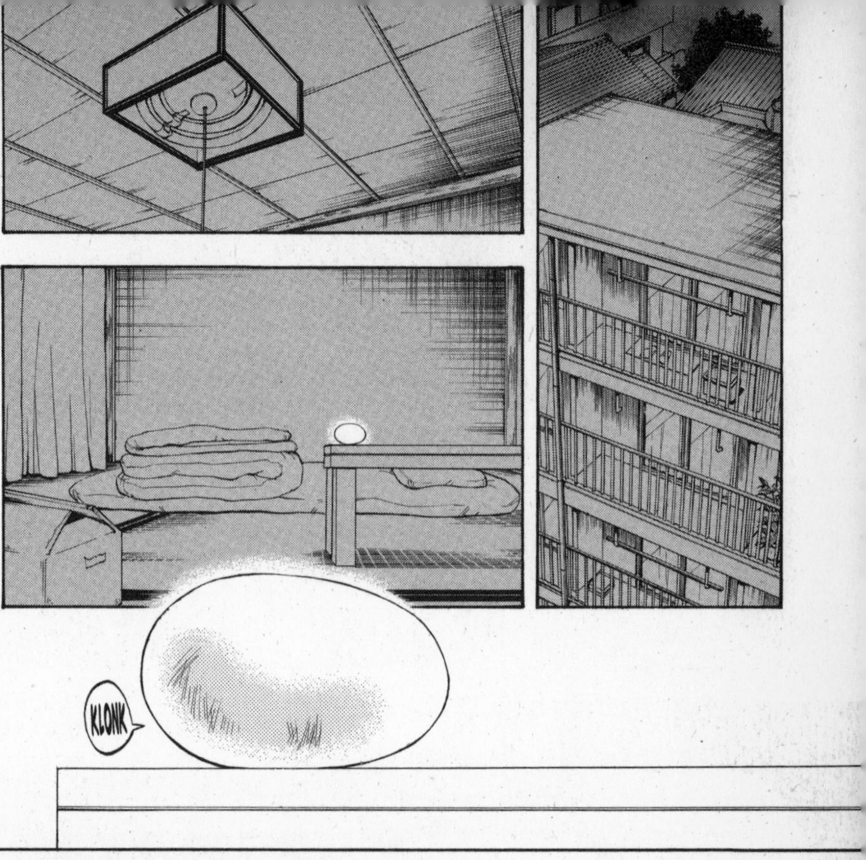
KLONK

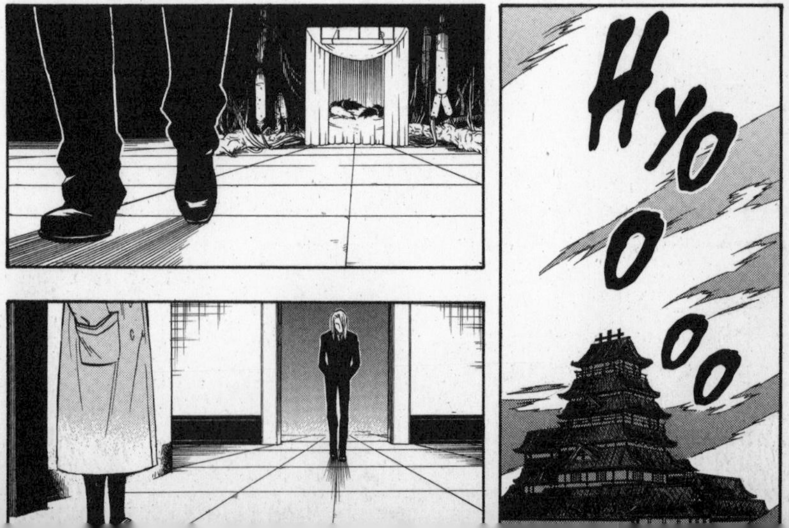
HYOOOO

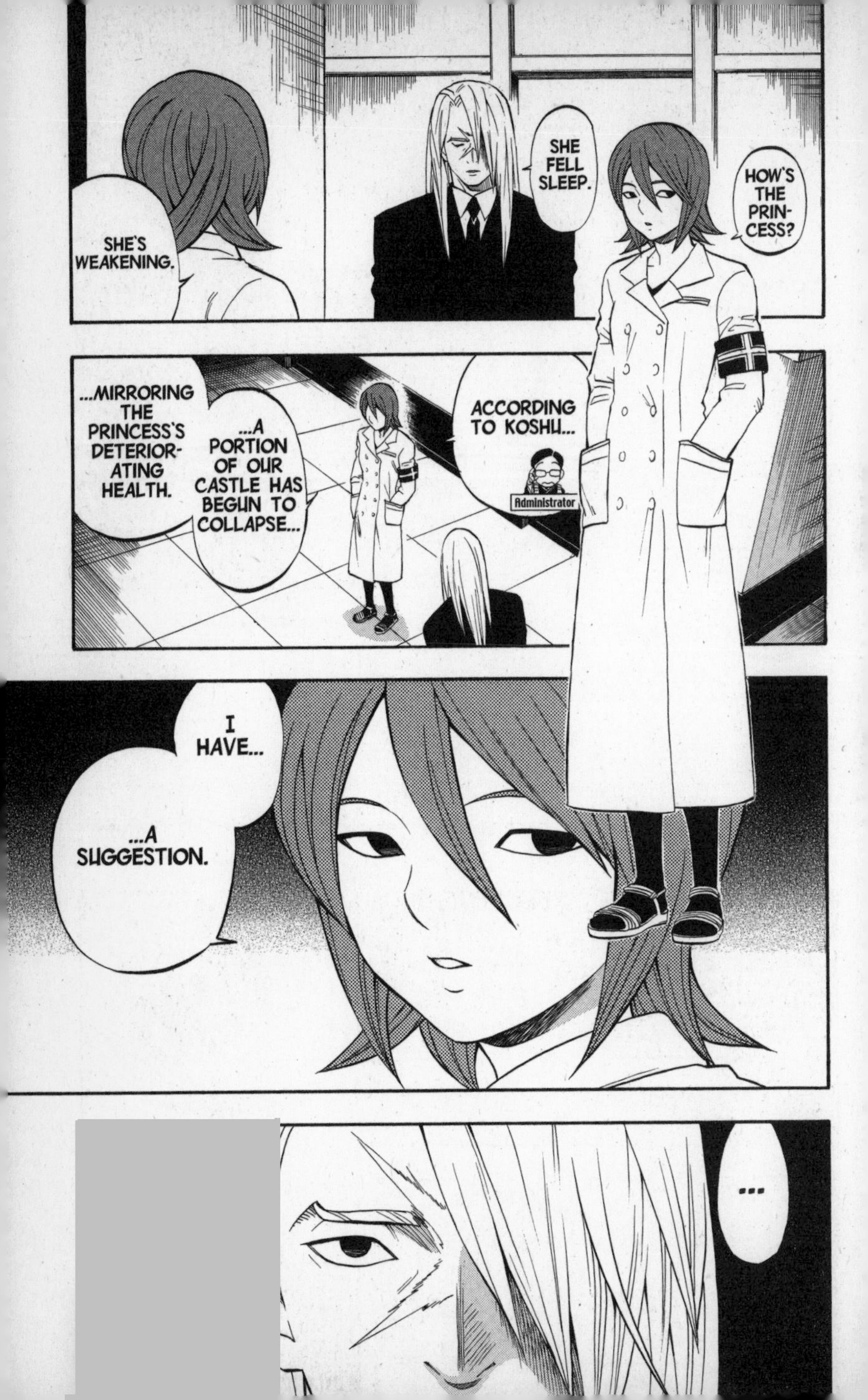
HOW'S THE PRIN-CESS?
SHE FELL SLEEP.
SHE'S WEAKENING.
ACCORDING TO KOSHU...
Administrator
...A PORTION OF OUR CASTLE HAS BEGUN TO COLLAPSE...
...MIRRORING THE PRINCESS'S DETERIOR-ATING HEALTH.
I HAVE...
...A SUGGESTION.
...

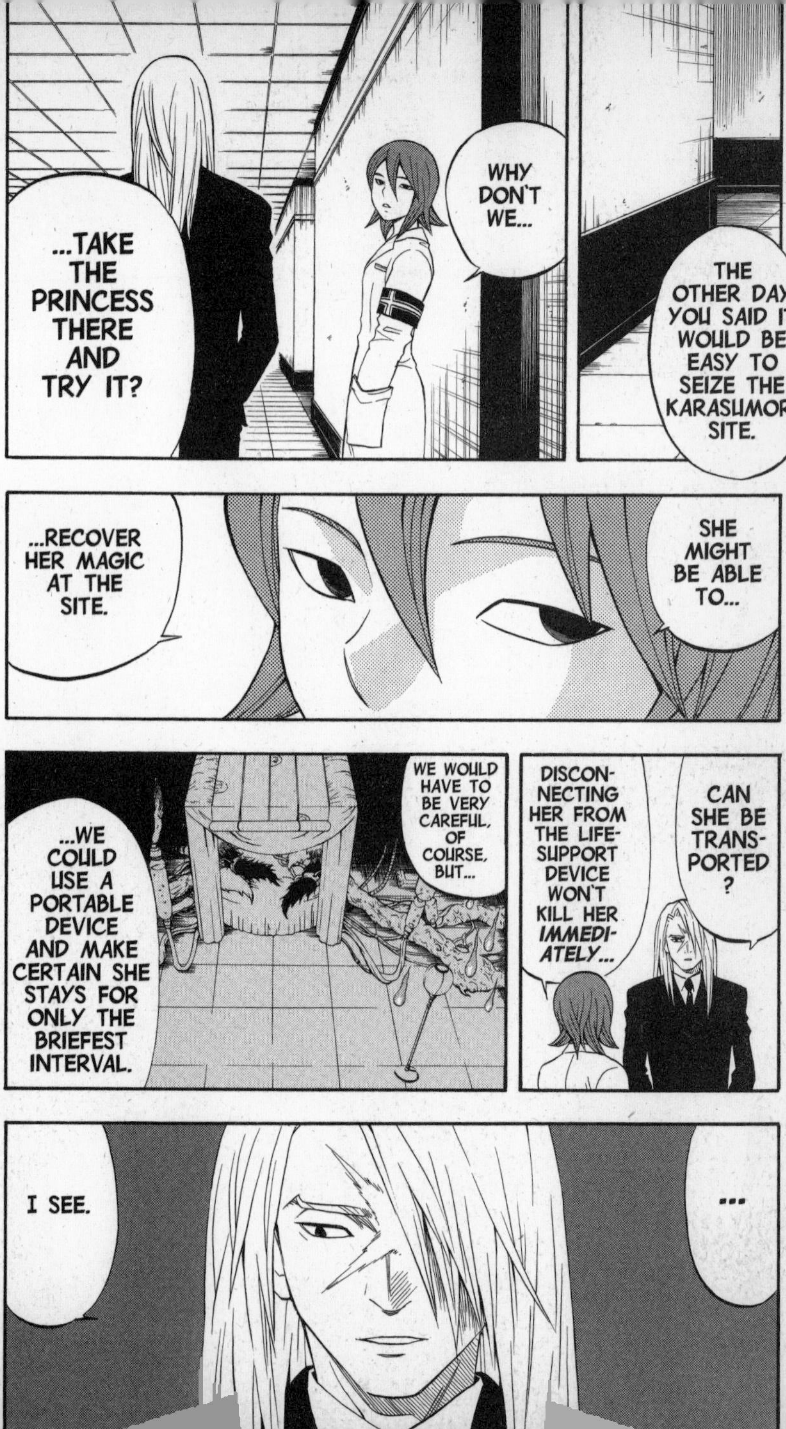
THE OTHER DAY YOU SAID IT WOULD BE EASY TO SEIZE THE KARASUMORI SITE.
WHY DON'T WE...
...TAKE THE PRINCESS THERE AND TRY IT?
SHE MIGHT BE ABLE TO...
...RECOVER HER MAGIC AT THE SITE.
CAN SHE BE TRANSPORTED?
DISCONNECTING HER FROM THE LIFE-SUPPORT DEVICE WON'T KILL HER *IMMEDIATELY*...
WE WOULD HAVE TO BE VERY CAREFUL, OF COURSE, BUT...
...WE COULD USE A PORTABLE DEVICE AND MAKE CERTAIN SHE STAYS FOR ONLY THE BRIEFEST INTERVAL.
...
I SEE.

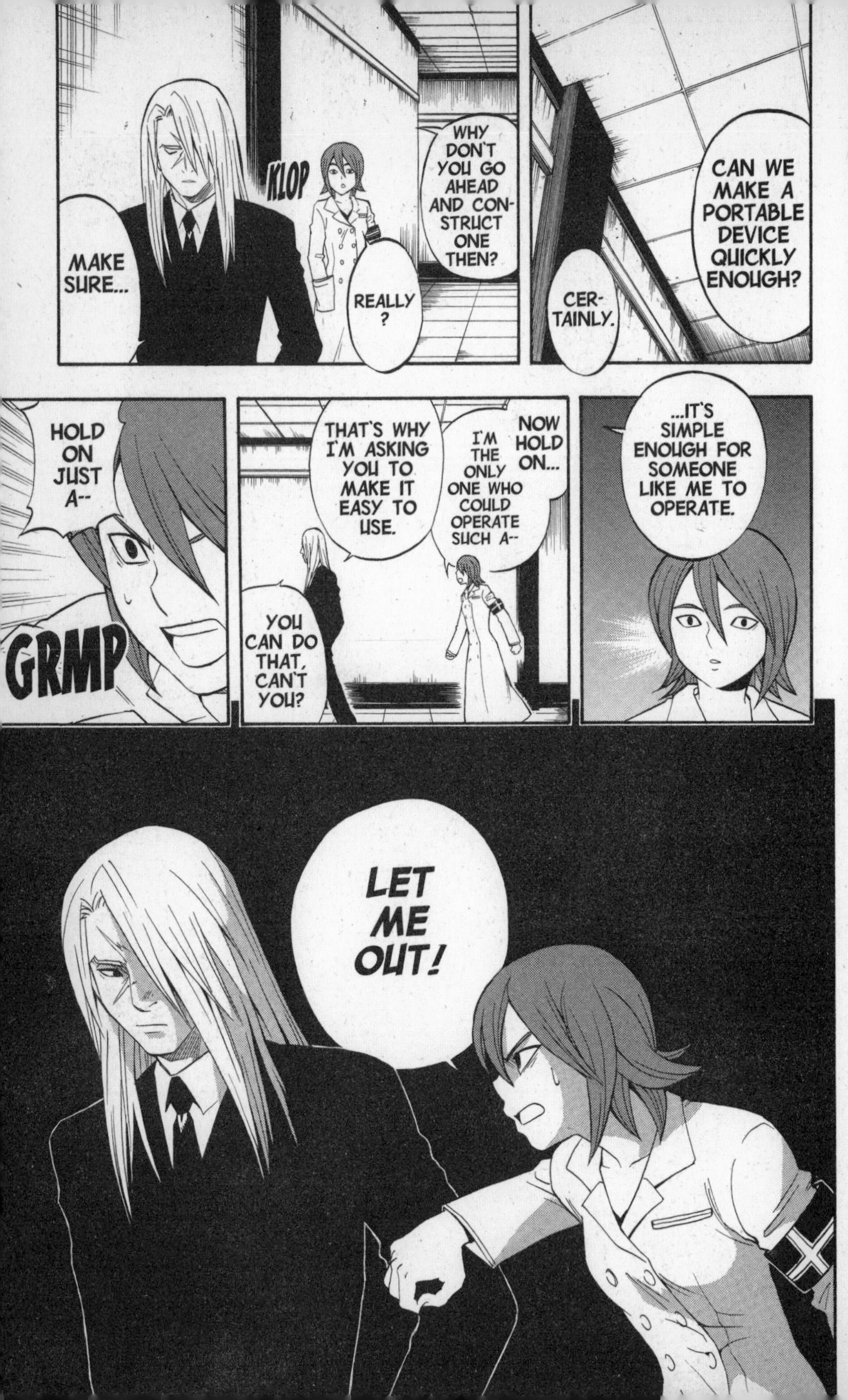
CAN WE MAKE A PORTABLE DEVICE QUICKLY ENOUGH?
CER-TAINLY.
WHY DON'T YOU GO AHEAD AND CON-STRUCT ONE THEN?
REALLY?
KLOP
MAKE SURE...
...IT'S SIMPLE ENOUGH FOR SOMEONE LIKE ME TO OPERATE.
NOW HOLD ON...
I'M THE ONLY ONE WHO COULD OPERATE SUCH A--
THAT'S WHY I'M ASKING YOU TO MAKE IT EASY TO USE.
YOU CAN DO THAT, CAN'T YOU?
HOLD ON JUST A--
GRMP
LET ME OUT!

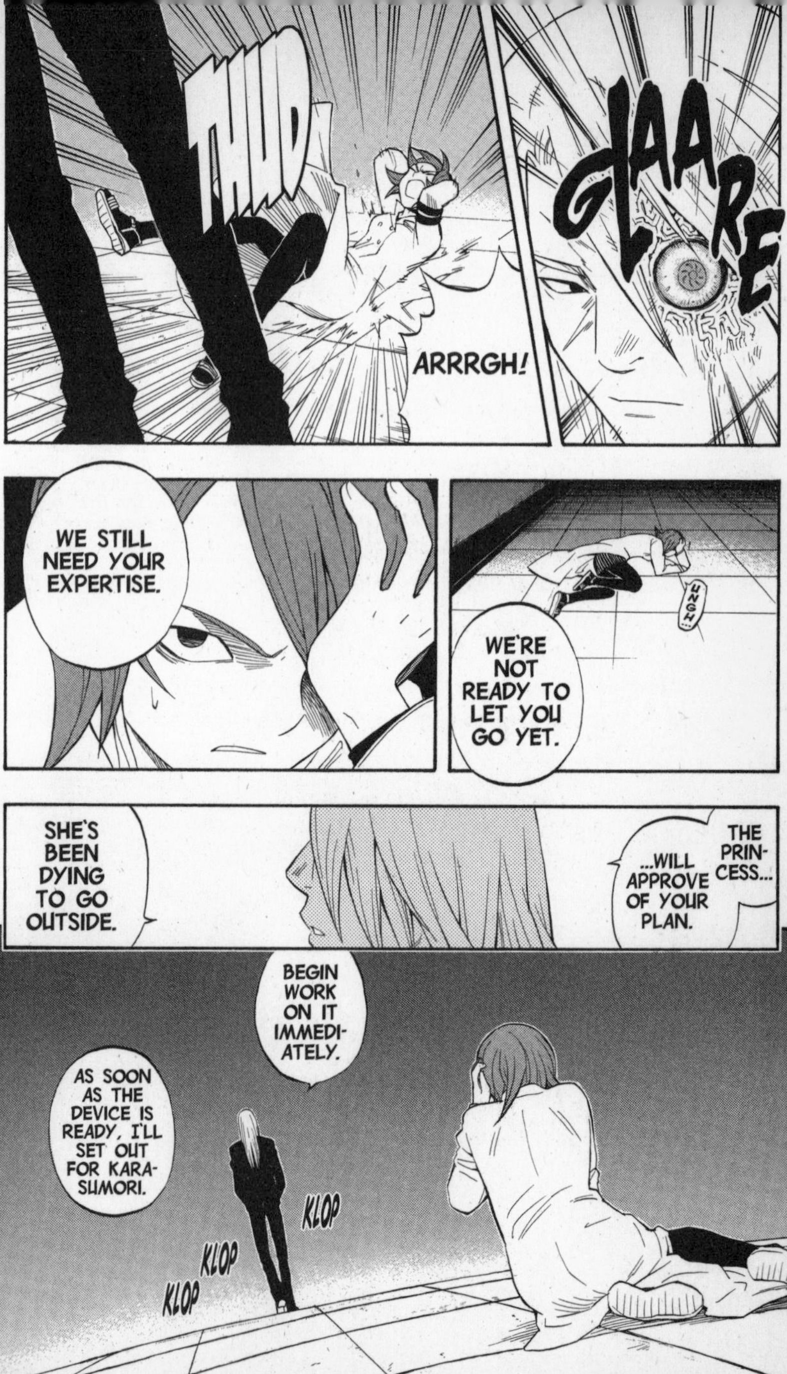
GLAARE
THUD
ARRRGH!
UNGH...
WE'RE NOT READY TO LET YOU GO YET.
WE STILL NEED YOUR EXPERTISE.
THE PRINCESS...
...WILL APPROVE OF YOUR PLAN.
SHE'S BEEN DYING TO GO OUTSIDE.
BEGIN WORK ON IT IMMEDIATELY.
AS SOON AS THE DEVICE IS READY, I'LL SET OUT FOR KARASUMORI.
KLOP
KLOP
KLOP
END OF KEKKAISHI VOL. 9

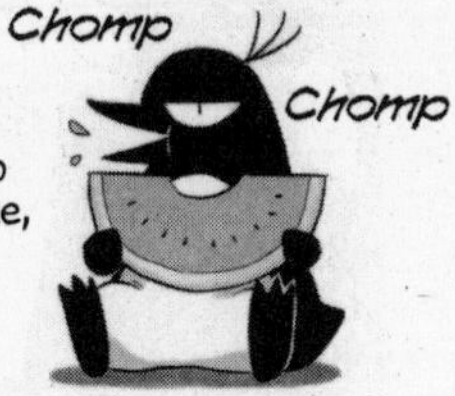
Chomp
Chomp

When I bite into seeds by mistake, the pleasure diminishes for a moment.

MESSAGE FROM YELLOW TANABE

I love watermelon. On hot summer days, I'm filled with joy just knowing there's a cold one in the fridge. What will I do in the fall?

KEKKAISHI

VOLUME 9
VIZ MEDIA EDITION
STORY AND ART BY YELLOW TANABE

Translation/Yuko Sawada
Touch-up Art & Lettering/Stephen Dutro
Cover Design & Graphic Layout/Amy Martin
Editor/Annette Roman

Managing Editor/Annette Roman
Editorial Director/Elizabeth Kawasaki
Editor in Chief, Books/Alvin Lu
Editor in Chief, Magazines/Marc Weidenbaum
Sr. Director of Acquisitions/Rika Inouye
Sr. VP of Marketing/Liza Coppola
Exec. VP of Sales & Marketing/John Easum
Publisher/Hyoe Narita

Printed in the U.S.A.

Published by VIZ Media, LLC
P.O. Box 77010
San Francisco, CA 94107

VIZ Media Edition
10 9 8 7 6 5 4 3 2 1
First printing, May 2007

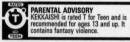

PARENTAL ADVISORY
KEKKAISHI is rated T for Teen and is
recommended for ages 13 and up. It
contains fantasy violence.

store.viz.com

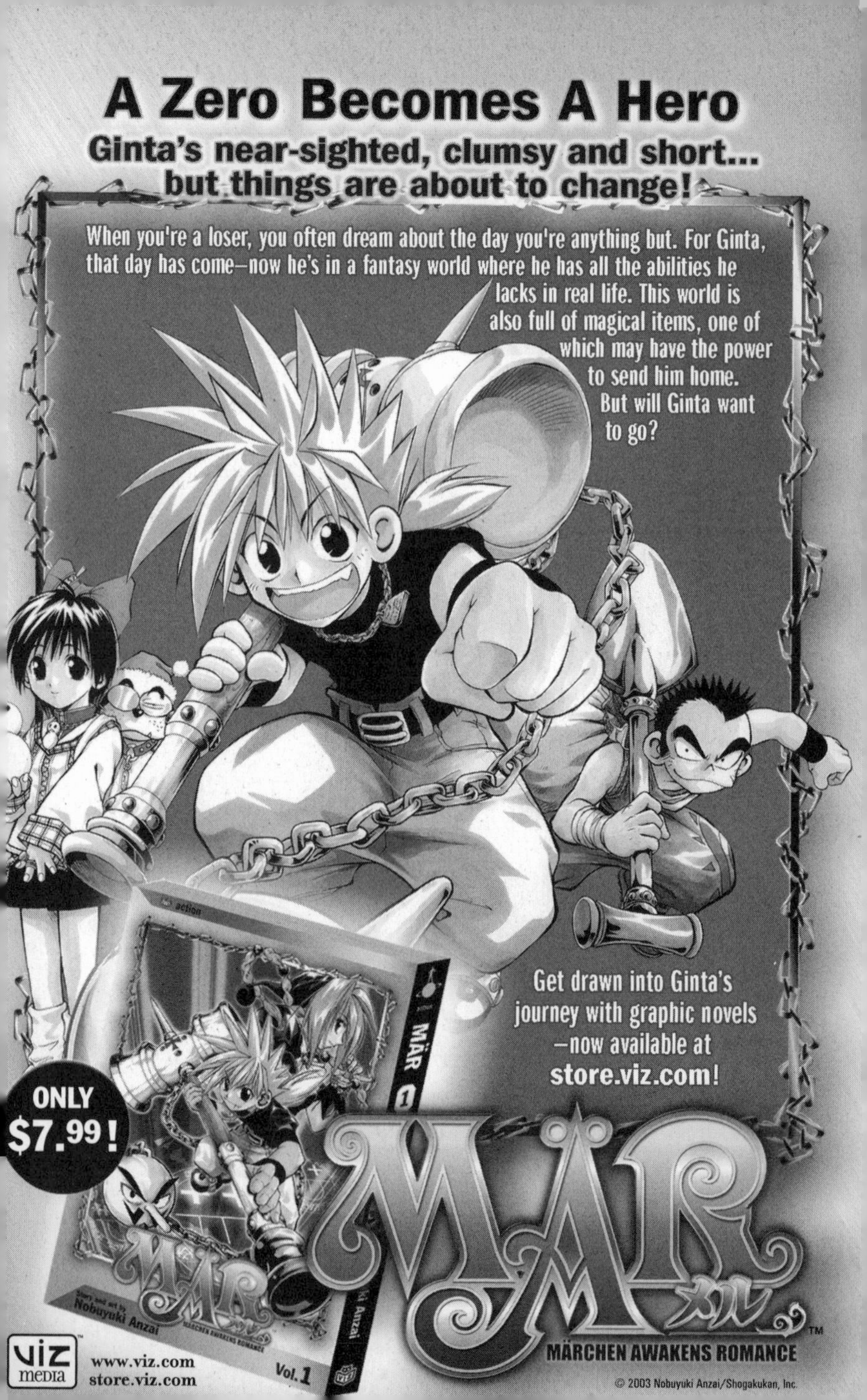
A Zero Becomes A Hero
Ginta's near-sighted, clumsy and short...
but things are about to change!
When you're a loser, you often dream about the day you're anything but. For Ginta, that day has come—now he's in a fantasy world where he has all the abilities he lacks in real life. This world is also full of magical items, one of which may have the power to send him home. But will Ginta want to go?
Get drawn into Ginta's journey with graphic novels —now available at store.viz.com!
ONLY $7.99!
action
MÄR
1
Nobuyuki Anzai
Vol. 1
MÄR
TM
MÄRCHEN AWAKENS ROMANCE
VIZ media
www.viz.com
store.viz.com
© 2003 Nobuyuki Anzai/Shogakukan, Inc.

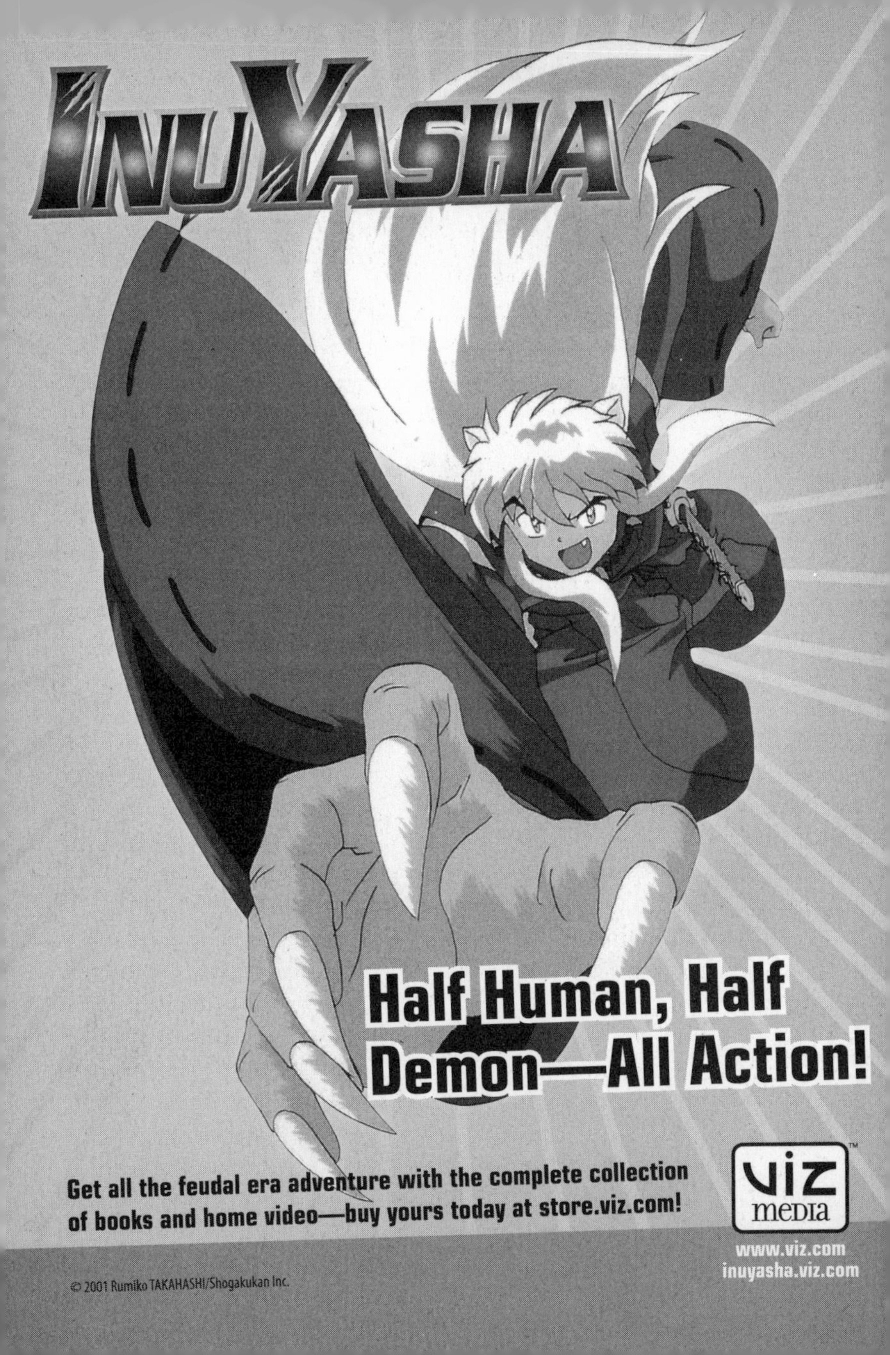

INUYASHA
Half Human, Half Demon—All Action!
Get all the feudal era adventure with the complete collection of books and home video—buy yours today at store.viz.com!
VIZ media
www.viz.com
inuyasha.viz.com
© 2001 Rumiko TAKAHASHI/Shogakukan Inc.

Read the action from the start with the original manga series

Full color adaptation of the popular TV series

Art book with cel art, paintings, character profiles and more

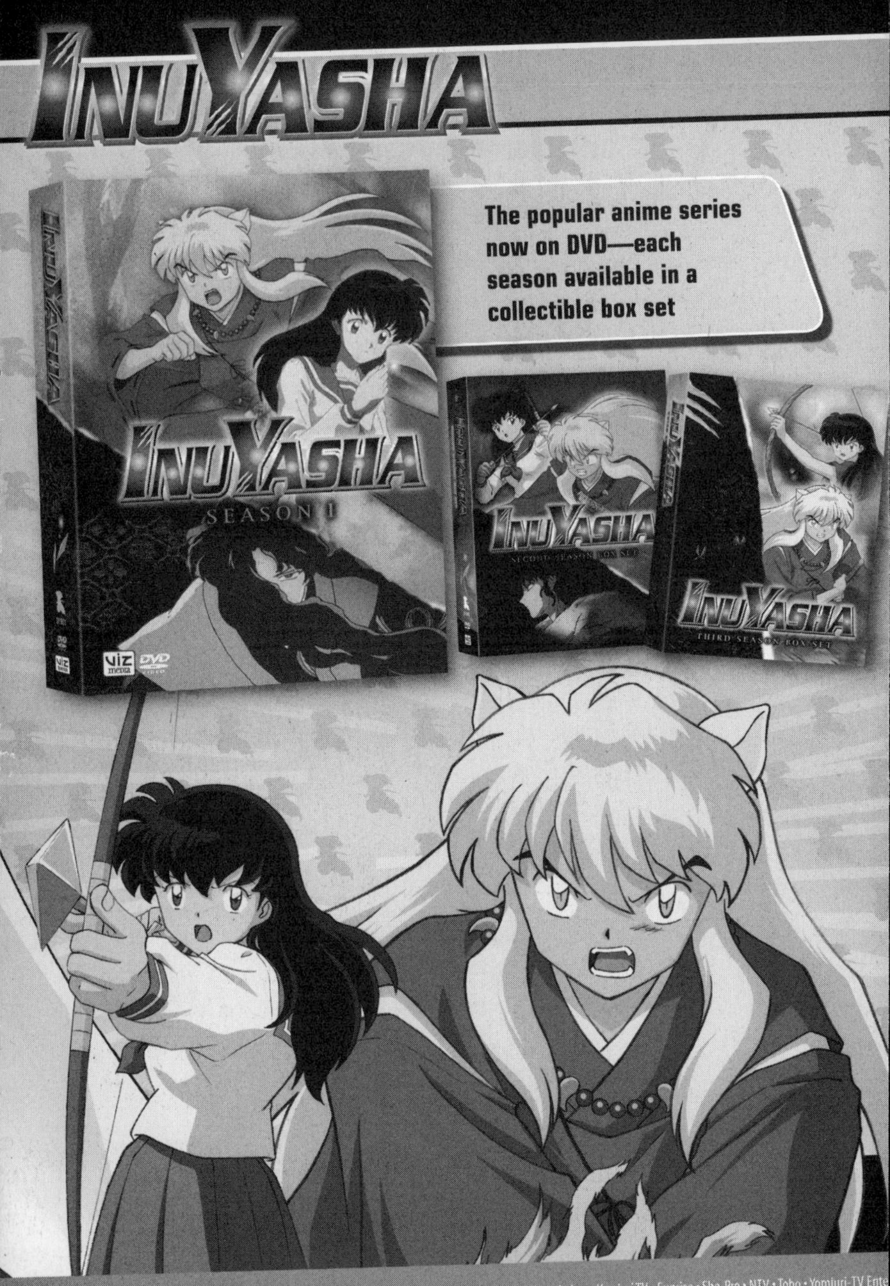
InuYasha
The popular anime series
now on DVD—each
season available in a
collectible box set
InuYasha
Season 1
InuYasha
InuYasha
Third Season Box Set

LOVE MANGA?
LET US KNOW WHAT YOU THINK!

HELP US MAKE THE MANGA
YOU LOVE BETTER!